Censorship and the Limits
of the Literary

Censorship and the Limits of the Literary

A Global View

Edited by
Nicole Moore

Bloomsbury Academic
An imprint of Bloomsbury Publishing Inc

B L O O M S B U R Y
NEW YORK • LONDON • NEW DELHI • SYDNEY

Bloomsbury Academic

An imprint of Bloomsbury Publishing Inc

1385 Broadway	50 Bedford Square
New York	London
NY 10018	WC1B 3DP
USA	UK

www.bloomsbury.com

BLOOMSBURY and the Diana logo are trademarks of Bloomsbury Publishing Plc

First published 2015

© Nicole Moore and Contributors, 2015

Library of Congress Cataloging-in-Publication Data
A catalog record for this book is avaliable from the Library of Congress.

ISBN: HB: 978-1-6289-2009-3
ePub: 978-1-6289-2010-9
ePDF: 978-1-6289-2011-6

Typeset by Fakenham Prepress Solutions, Fakenham, Norfolk NR21 8NN

Contents

List of Illustrations

Introduction

Nicole Moore

Article 19 of the *Universal Declaration of Human Rights*, which famously begins 'Everyone has the right to freedom of opinion and expression', ends by averring that this right extends 'through any media and regardless of frontiers'. In 1948, this was an assertive charge for a polarized world; in 2015, it is a utopic principle, forever unfulfilled. In the early twenty-first century, censorship, especially state-implemented control over material forms of communication, remains a key challenge to any vaunted unitary culture for the globalizing world. In other ways, it is an instrument against differentiated dissent, enforcing hegemonic models of homogenized culture in contexts where local expressions of political or moral identity are found offensive or dangerous. Censorship embodies the tension between the historical legal limits of the nation state and the new planetary reach of the communicative sphere, and contemporary regulation of mediascapes is no longer isomorphic with the borders of a single country or the spread of a single language. Legal theorists such as Scott Beattie yet argue that pervasive regulatory control of electronic communication is now impossible, Edward Snowden's exile in Russia and Julian Assange's current confinement to the Ecuadorian Embassy in London notwithstanding. In 2014 the finale of the fourth season of the HBO series *Game of Thrones* became the most illegally-downloaded media product in history. About contemporary censorship, former British Labour Member of Parliament Denis MacShane advances a paradox: 'Increased freedom and increased censorship coexist. This wasn't meant to happen.'[1]

If 'freedom of opinion and expression' is its doctrine, art and literature have been understood as this liberty's apex – the fora in which the unfettered liberal imagination has manifested its worth. Well before the trial of *Madame Bovary*, the opposition between literature and censorship had a life in Western law: the defence of artistic merit defines the literary against the offensive categories of obscenity, sedition and blasphemy, and also out of the reach of censorship, by definition – 'art for art's sake'. The problematic US 'Brennan doctrine' of the 1950s, moreover, aligned the literary also with 'social merit', claiming protection under the US Constitution by definitively distinguishing it from obscenity, while leaving 'obscenity' as an undifferentiated category without 'redeeming value'.[2] Literature's categorical expression has depended, in courts of law and regimes of regulation, on its ability to differentiate itself from the law's proper object, and the ambiguities at stake have seemed to describe the form as such. In the anxious, crisis-driven consolidations of the early twenty-first-century, humanities scholars seek to define the literary as a localizable phenomenon once more, identifying its 'singularity' and its 'innovation' as features essential to the function.[3] As the 'bourgeois in frock-coat' of the Second Empire's literary establishment proved to Flaubert, however, literature is not untainted by the confining operations of regulation, nor is censorship, as Robert Darnton articulates, 'a thing-in-itself, an isolated phenomenon that is always and everywhere the same, the mere antithesis to freedom of thought'.[4]

This volume seeks to explore the degree to which, rather than removed and antithetical opposites, literature and censorship have been dialectical forms of culture, each actively defining the other in ongoing, agonistic engagement. In so far as regimes of regulation determine the character of print culture, they address, shape and even produce the conditions of literary possibility. And in so far as literature seeks to assert its own limits, in turn it addresses, provokes and determines the instruments of censorship used to measure such. Literature has not consistently stood as censorship's heroic adversary, nor has censorship always refused the prerogatives of the literary. Literature has not been a straightforward instrument in the exercise of free speech, seen as a feature of modelled democracy, even outside the constraints of the expansive, state-implemented regulation typical of what can thus be called totalitarianism. Chris Hilliard can cite A. V. Dicey's *Introduction to the Study of the Law of the Constitution* in 1915 (8th edn) to demonstrate the absence of a strong doctrine of freedom of expression in British law: 'no-one can maintain that the law of England recognises anything like that natural right to the free communication of thoughts and opinions which was proclaimed in France a little over a hundred years ago to be one of the most valuable Rights of Man'.[5] Simon During's complexly contrarian *Against Democracy* makes the case that literature was not on the side of 'political democracy' until 1945 or so, and argues that, in the West, 'twentieth-century literary high culture, in particular, was largely shaped in the rhythms and forms through which it adapted to its translation into and out of mundane experience as ordered in (sometimes merely emergent) democratic state capitalism'.[6] A global perspective on this question, attendant to the determining relations between national jurisdictions and publishing economics, border controls and structures of distribution, regulative regimes and diverse linguistic cultures of the book, expands the orders of experience at stake significantly.

In its address to this dynamic between literature and censorship, the volume reflects a moment of congruence, when new directions in a number of scholarly fields are converging. Five new directions can be identified in particular. After Michel Foucault, through the late 1990s, scholars came to some broad agreement about the productive features of censorship – its ability to produce as well as suppress meaning – drawing on Foucault's repressive hypothesis and further interest in the constitutive relations between discourse and power, such as that articulated (albeit differently) by Pierre Bourdieu and Judith Butler. This manifested in what was then called 'the new censorship' scholarship, dominated by post-structuralist investigation of the foundational relationship between language and repression, speech and silence. In an introduction to a pivotal edited collection, Robert Post asserted that 'censorship is the norm rather than the exception. Censorship materialises everywhere.[7] Similarly, Michael Holquist declared that 'Censorship is. One can only discriminate among its more or less repressive effects.[8] This line has been much quoted in consequent engagements with this scholarship, which draw on the critique offered, by Richard Burt and others, of the 'Manichean vision' of censorship and freedom, and which is now represented in conceptualizations stretching from Tudor-Stuart censorship and Jacobean press constraints to Celia Marshik's 'censorship dialectic' in British modernism.[9] A further set of engagements interrogate, however, the normalization consequent to a position that posits censorship as a constitutive aspect of all communication.[10]

Beate Müller's interrogation, in particular, characterizes what can be seen as a second new direction in the field, coming from Eastern Europe.[11] In the wake of the opening-up of the voluminous archives of censorship records from the former communist bloc, Müller sought to differentiate between the mundane, everyday communicative selectivity analysed by Butler and Bourdieu, and the prescriptive and repressive regimes of control exercised by countries with Soviet-style socialist government. Her critique of the largely US-based new scholarship was not merely about degrees of comparative description, but the definition of censorship itself. Before and after Müller has come a large body of work responding to the hugely-expansive (for some states, comprehensive) records of communist print and theatre censorship, from German, Russian and other European scholars, as well as in English.[12] As I've outlined elsewhere, the capacity of 'censorship' to describe exercised, coercive power was being defended, against what was seen to be a redefinition too expansive and mundane.[13] At the same time, this volume, as others like it, cannot and does not confine its analysis to the state's use of sovereign powers to control the literary – our definition of censorship includes both instances of often untraceable 'self-censorship', evident multifariously in the history of print publication, and of what might be termed 'soft censorship', indirectly produced by the 'chilling effect' of more direct forms.[14] Tyne Daile Sumner's chapter teases out the subtexts at play in mid-century American confessional poetry in the context of the Cold War to instance the latter, for example. Together, the essays in this collection address censorship's ability to form, produce or enact institutional forms of the literary, and in that address foreground the exercise of reticulated coercive power as well as systematic control by regimes whose aims were comprehensive.

The opening-up of the Eastern Bloc's archives was coeval, in a further direction, with developments in book-history approaches to print culture, and these have been led by Darnton's work on the archives of the *ancien régime* and pre-revolutionary France. Book history's material emphasis on trading economics and regulatory frameworks as well as the roles of institutions, bureaucracies, libraries, publishers, distributors, booksellers and readers has shifted literary censorship scholarship markedly away from a focus on the figure of the wronged author, or on the encoded, censored page, to the scope, extent and experience of censorship in specifiable, reconstructed circumstances. And the work of print history scholars in making accessible sufficient records from national censorship regimes to allow quantification has now enabled the use of new digital methods, in the mode of the 'new empiricism' or the 'distant reading' techniques articulated by Franco Moretti and others.[15] Simon Burrow's work in this volume begins where Darnton leaves off in subjecting Bourbon-era publishing records to illuminating quantitative analysis. Above all, these recent methods have fostered a move from the instance to the system. Darnton's newest work reminds us that comparative history is a 'demanding genre, not merely because of the need to command different languages but owing to the problems inherent in making comparisons'.[16] Contemporary censorship scholarship is now able to place into calculable contrast the systematic practices of regimes as different and yet analogous as eighteenth-century France, nineteenth-century India, twentieth-century white Australia, Catholic Ireland, fascist Italy, cold-war East Germany, apartheid South Africa and, to some degree, the UK during the Second World War.[17]

The fourth direction this volume reflects comes also in the wake of Foucault, pursuant on his history of sexuality, and before that feminist and gay and lesbian interest in the cultural suppression of sex and sexual identities. Critics like Jonathan Dollimore and Lee Edelman question whether the dynamic between censorship and literature is driven by nothing that inheres in either the literary or the structures of government, but only in the third, fundamental repression of sex itself. The lifting of the profound censorship of homosexual content of all kinds has been perhaps the most dramatic shift in literary expression, in the English-speaking world at least, of the last 200 years. And, by the late 1990s, some scholars were able to suggest that critical scholarly interest in censorship had been subsumed by the question of obscenity. After illuminating new work on the early modern period, from scholars such as Lynn Hunt, Valerie Traub and Joan DeJean, which put the question of gender tellingly into play, the history of literary censorship in Britain, France, the US and settler colonial states like Australia, New Zealand and Canada has been dominated by a newly-serious attention to obscenity as the most pervasive offence for legal regulation. In the wake of the work of sexuality scholars like Robert Aldrich, Dennis Altman, Anjali Arondekar, Anne McClintock and others, often combining their post-colonial interests with Foucauldian frames, as did Ann Laura Stoler, the censored history of literary sexuality has been examined in many geopolitical contexts. In this expansive field of interest, the imbrication of the political with the moral remains at stake; perhaps more exactly enmeshed as the national and the sexual.

This broadly international purview then informs the last of the five scholarly directions to which this collection contributes, perhaps most significantly. The decentring of metropolitan literary histories has been a long time coming, via comparative literature, commonwealth models, post-colonial theories and methods, cosmopolitanism and its critiques, and since the 2000s a globalized revision of the 'world literature' ambit. In the contemporary moment, a newly-expansive big picture is accessible, with profoundly re-constitutive interest from the US and Europe (catching up with their empires) in resituating the point of view from which that big picture can be seen. This transnational moment is liberating for comparative accounts of censorship, which formerly have been restricted by the borders of nation states, even when tracing forms of censorship unidentical to state-sponsored regimes of regulation.[18] The essays in this volume engage with more than twelve countries or nation states, placing into revealing contiguity a set of case studies examining national regimes, publishing industries, book trades, reading contexts or authorial circumstances, including from some states and colonies that no longer exist. A number of chapters importantly identify connections and parallels between countries, including transferred or inherited legislative frameworks, shared or mirrored institutional structures, as well as identical logics and counterclaims from the censors and the censored, such as in the court room. The definitions of censorship at work are crucially congruent: Peter McDonald's key essay on South African apartheid censorship points to the fact that censors denied theirs was a censorship system, since it examined books after rather than pre-publication, for instance, and so does Burrows in his account of the French regime under the Bourbon kings, and so have I in referencing severe Australian Customs controls elsewhere,[19] while the eighteenth-century shift from pre- to post-publication in England is illuminating for Tuite's chapter. A number of essays apply similar conceptual or theoretical approaches to the work of censorship, particularly its legal frames and discursive staging, enabling productive comparisons, for the volume as a whole, across wide-ranging literary histories and political geographies: both modern time and global space.

In their geo-political diversity, the chapters span the history of the modern relationship between censorship and the literary, with delineated groupings into four, chronologically-ordered parts. Like many accounts of what we can term modern censorship, the volume begins at the posited birth of the Enlightenment, in mid-eighteenth-century France, when the European notion of 'literature' is hardening into familiar form, and the beginnings of a recognizable state apparatus are being deployed by the *ancien régime* to control an increasingly literate population's reading. Burrows' account of French censorship 'on the eve of revolution' contests conventional heralding of the incendiary eruption of a free public sphere by tracking the regime's control over print publication in analysable, quantitative detail. Pervasive censorship meant that the strongest threats to the regime came from the elites rather than the populace – the revolution was not enacted in print, he suggests. Clara Tuite's chapter then takes us across the channel to British Regency law courts, where charges of blasphemous sedition against the satires of autodidact William Hone concentrated the legislative controls of the previous century and a half (or longer in the case of theatre censorship) into a hugely-popular challenge to the equation between church and state. Hone's spectacular victories informed John Keats's conception of 'negative capability', Tuite reveals, and offer an illuminating way to code the negative agency of censorship in reactively producing literature, with implications for treatments in other chapters, including my own. If Tuite's chapter is the joyous street, then Mary Spongberg's is the raucous Royal court. Still in Regency Britain, this chapter's focus is the gendered structures of speaking and silence that delimited the voices around the Queen Caroline affair, despite the forces of relative liberalization pursuant on the repressive law courts, including Hone's trials. Spongberg's focus on neglected writer Mary Hays exposes the double standards at play, in the wake of Wollstonecraft's death, in the treatment of women's public speech, subsequently absented from history. Karen Crawley moves with the nineteenth century from blasphemous sedition to popular obscenity in re-examining the determining legal decisions of mid-nineteenth-century Britain and America, particularly those deliberated under the UK's *Obscene Publications Act* and the US's *Comstock Act*. She shares with Tuite a Butlerian interest in how the law is compelled to speak that which it would prohibit; this chapter examines the dimension of performativity in obscenity law, exposing the rhetorical foundations of legal decisions important for the implementation of modern censorship regimes across the English-speaking world.

The next section takes us outside Europe and the US to examine contexts in which these founding relations between imperialism and censorship, and particularly obscenity and empire, can be laid bare. Paul Tickell gives us a big-picture survey of the punishing controls extended by the Dutch regime in the East Indies through the beginning of the twentieth century, from press controls and the fostered dominance of the central state publisher to the use of exile to West Papua. The profound impacts on contemporary Indonesian literature are there to be traced. Geoffrey Little pursues the volume's materialist interest in the institutions of literature via an examination of librarian training in mid-twentieth-century Quebec, exposing its central role in the (post-)colonial Catholic state's severe restrictions on book access and reading, as an assertion of cultural identity in sharp distinction from Protestant Anglophone Canada. The way in which the literary is not just at stake but is defined and thus produced by such institutions of censorship is then examined directly by my own essay, discussing two very different cases from the records of the Australian Customs' Literature Censorship Board in the 1930s and 1940s: deliberated bans on le comte de Lautréamont's poetic *roman noir The Lay of Maldoror* and James Noble Gifford's exemplary pulp title *Furnished Room*. This central question is eruditely explicated by Peter McDonald's essay on the South African apartheid regime, in which he confronts the 'monstrous' spectre of the 'censor critic'. Tracking the theorized conceptions of literature at play for the many South African censors with parallel careers as literary professionals, he pursues the dynamic relations between censorship and the literary enacted not just in that severe regime, but in so far as a literary field may exist.

Australian and South African book censorship regimes were analogous in many respects, not only because of inherited legislation and legal systems in British colonial environments (shared also with New Zealand and Ireland), but in the ways in which bureaucratic modernity militated for highly-regulated methods and complex infrastructures. The expansive records of these two regimes make them thus, in turn, practicably comparable at once to the *ancien régime*, colonial India and the pre-publication regimes of former Soviet countries, especially the German Democratic Republic, because centralized records of assessment from all of these states are now available. The third section draws together essays examining censorship during the Cold War. In Ilona Urquhart's chapter, Leo Strauss, one of Soviet censorship's old cultural enemies, is used to read one of its high profile victims, providing an acute recasting of Mikhail Bulgakov's extraordinary suppressed modernist novel *The Master and Margarita*. This is one of the chapters close up to the literary's response to censorship, with a highly-engaged rather than 'distant' reading. Christina Spittel's transnational chapter on the treatment of West German fiction in the GDR's centralized book publication system furthers work by German book historians but also comparative work by Darnton and others, including our own collaborative research, and draws on comprehensive records of censors' deliberations. Tyne Daile Sumner's chapter follows this, rereading American confessional poets in tense, cold-war contexts. She tracks the threat of censorship versus the impulse towards confession, showing how pressures of expression swing between those polarities by reading ostensibly private and personal poems within the period's global structures of silencing and surveillance. Last in this section is Loren Glass, also in the US, extending his influential account of the great post-war obscenity cases by elucidating the conse-quent shift not as a movement towards freedom of expression but as an insistence, rather, on freedom to *read*.

The final, contemporary section has much to say about our world right now. Jeremy Fisher tracks the lifting of repressive censorship on gay male literary expression in Australia from the dismantling of comprehensive literary censorship in 1971, reflecting on homosexuality's status as at once the most troubling category of the twentieth-century obscene and that which has been most transformed. Three final essays, one each on contemporary Iran, Egypt and China, conclude the volume, addressing some of the most repressive censorship regimes on earth. All by younger scholars, they offer acute insights on different issues that remain differently at stake. Sanaz Fatouhi examines the recent proliferation of memoirs published by Iranian women living outside Iran, as first an outpouring of expression after repression, but also to indicate the gendered dimensions of that control, particularly evident in the reception of the genre. Jumana Bayeh's chapter exposes powerfully the role of liter-ature, especially diasporic literature, in taking up the role of political dissent denied to the press in contemporary Egypt, both as an historical fact and an ongoing urgency. Countering the reductive model of the 'Facebook revolution', Bayeh analyses the work of writers such as Nawal El Saadawi and Naguib Mafouz, within Egypt, and, outside the country, particularly Ahdaf Soueif, to show its role in enacting acutely subversive political critique. Finally, Lynda Ng offers an account of transgressive literary work in internet-age China, tracking some of the key banned works against their receptions in both China and the West. This last chapter examines concepts crucially at play for the volume as a whole, in the determining social and political relations of literature, readerships, state control and cultural value in a globalizing world.

Acknowledgements

Some of these chapters were developed from papers delivered at a specially-themed conference of the Australasian Association for Literature, and thanks are due to the Association and to the University of New South Wales, Canberra for financial and administrative support. Thanks to Stanford University Press for permission to print revised and expanded material from Loren Glass's *Counter culture Colophon* in Chapter 12. I am grateful, too, for the research assistance and copy-editing skills of Dr Michael Austin.

Notes

1 Denis MacShane, 'You Can't Read this Book: Censorship in an Age of Freedom' *The Observer*, 12 February 2012, available at http://www.theguardian.com/books/2012/feb/12/cant-read-book-cohen-review [accessed 14 April 2014].

2 See Whitney Strub's *Obscenity Rules: Roth v. United States and the Long Struggle over Sexual Expression* (Lawrence, KA: University Press of Kansas, 2013).

3 See Derek Attridge's *The Singularity of Literature* (London and New York: Routledge, 2004), pp. 1–3, and further discussion of this interest in my chapter in the volume.

4 Robert Darnton, 'Censorship, A Comparative View: France 1789, East Germany 1989', in Olwen Hufton (ed.), *Historical Change and Human Rights: The Oxford Amnesty Lectures* (New York: Basic Books, 1995), p. 129.

5 Chris Hilliard, '"Is it a Book That You Would Wish Your Wife or Your Servants to Read?" Obscenity Law and the Politics of Reading in Modern England', *American Historical Review*, June (2013): 657.

6 Simon During, *Against Democracy* (New York: Fordham University Press, 2012), p. 11.

7 Robert Post (ed.), *Censorship and Silencing: Practices of Cultural Regulation*, p. 2.

8 Michael Holquist, 'Corrupt Originals: The Paradox of Censorship', *PMLA*, 109 (1) (1994): 19.

9 Debora Shuger, *Censorship and Cultural Sensibility: The Regulation of Language in Tudor-Stuart England* (Philadelphia: University of Pennsylvania Press, 2006), pp. 2–5; Celia Marshik, *British Modernism and Censorship* (Cambridge: Cambridge University Press, 2006*)*, pp. 14–15.

10 Hafid Gafaiti, 'Between God and the President: Literature and Censorship in North Africa', *Diacritics*, 27 (2) (1997); Beate Müller, 'Censorship and Cultural Regulation: Mapping the Territory', in Beate Müller (ed.), *Censorship and Cultural Regulation in the Modern Age*, (Amsterdam: Rodopi, 2004); Nicole Moore, 'Censorship Is', *Australian Humanities Review*, 54 (2013): 45–65; Robert Darnton, *Censors at Work: How States Shaped Literature* (New York and London: W. W. Norton, 2014), pp. 19–20.

11 Müller, 'Censorship and Cultural Regulation'.

12 English language scholarship includes Herman Ermolaev, *Censorship in Soviet Literature 1917–1991* (Lanham, MD: Rowman and Littlefield, 1997); Olga M. Ushakova on 'Soviet censorship of European modernism', in Catherine O'Leary and Alberto Lázaro (eds), *Censorship Across Borders: The Reception of English Literature in Twentieth-Century Europe* (Newcastle-upon-Tyne: Cambridge Scholars Publishing, 2011) and other essays in the volume, as well as Müller's edited collection *Censorship and Cultural Regulation in the Modern Age*, especially Helen Freshwater's essay 'Towards a Redefinition of Censorship'. The most authoritative accounts of the German Democratic Republic print regime come from Siegfried Lokatis and his collaborators at the Leipziger Buchwissenschaft centre; see also Laura Bradley, *Cooperation and Conflict: GDR Theatre Censorship* (Oxford: Oxford University Press, 2010), and Nicole Moore and Christina Spittel (eds), *Reading through the Iron Curtain: Australian Literature in the German Democratic Republic* (London: Anthem Press, 2015). For broad discussion of literary censorship in the Eastern Bloc, see Marcel Cornis-Pope and John Neubauer (eds), *History of the Literary Cultures of East Central Europe*, vol. 3 (Amsterdam and Philadelphia: John Benjamin, 2007).

13 Moore, 'Censorship Is'.
14 Thanks to Paul Giles for clarifying this idea of 'soft censorship'.
15 Franco Moretti, *Distant Reading* (New York: Verso, 2013) and the Stanford Literary Lab; Katherine Bode and Robert Dixon (eds), *Resourceful Reading: The New Empiricism, eResearch and Australian Literary Culture* (Sydney: Sydney University Press, 2009).
16 Darnton, *Censors at Work*, p. 15.
17 See Deana Heath, *Obscenity and the Politics of Moral Regulation in Britain, India and Australia* (Oxford: Oxford University Press, 2010); Robert Darnton, *Censors at Work*; Peter D. McDonald, *The Literature Police: Apartheid and its Cultural Consequences* (Oxford: Oxford University Press, 2009); Moore, 'Censorship Is'; Marita Bullock and Nicole Moore, *Banned in Australia* (AustLit, 2008); Simon Burrows, Mark Curran, Vincent Hiribarren, Sarah Kattau and Henry Merivale, *The French Book Trade in Enlightenment Europe Project, 1769–1794*, 6 May 2014, available at http://fbtee.uws.edu.au/stn/ [accessed September 2014]; Simon Eliot, Simon Tanner, Alejandro Giacometti, Henry Irving, José Miguel Viera, *MOI Online:A Publishing and Communication History of the Ministry of Information* (Institute of English Studies, Kings College, London). Available at http://www.moidigital.ac.uk/ [accessed November 2014].
18 Other examples of transnational approaches include Francesca Billiani (ed.), *Modes of Censorship and Translation: National Contexts and Diverse Media* (London and New York: Routledge, 2014), and O'Leary and Lázaro (eds), *Censorship Across Borders*.
19 Nicole Moore, 'Censorship', in Michael F. Suarez SJ and H. R. Woudhuysen (eds), *Oxford Companion to the History of the Book* (Oxford: Oxford University Press, 2010), p. 596.

References

Attridge, D., *The Singularity of Literature*, London and New York: Routledge, 2004.
Beattie, S., *Community, Space and Online Censorship: Regulating Pornotopia*, Farnham and Burlington, VT: Ashgate, 2009.
Billiani, F. (ed.), *Modes of Censorship and Translation: National Contexts and Diverse Media*, London and New York: Routledge, 2014.
Bode, K. and R. Dixon (eds), *Resourceful Reading: The New Empiricism, eResearch and Australian Literary Culture*, Sydney: Sydney University Press, 2009.
Bradley, L., *Cooperation and Conflict: GDR Theatre Censorship*, Oxford: Oxford University Press, 2010.
Bullock, M. and N. Moore, *Banned in Australia: Federal Book Censorship 1900–1973*, AustLit, 2008. Available at http://www.austlit.edu.au/specialistDatasets/Banned [accessed October 2014].
Burrows, S., M. Curran, V. Hiribarren, S. Kattau and H. Merivale, *The French Book Trade in Enlightenment Europe Project, 1769–1794*, 6 May 2014. Available at http://fbtee.uws.edu.au/stn/ [accessed September 2014].
Cornis-Pope, M. and J. Neubauer (eds), *History of the Literary Cultures of East Central Europe*, vol. 3, Amsterdam and Philadelphia: John Benjamins, 2007.

Darnton, R., 'Censorship, a Comparative View: France 1789, East Germany 1989', in Olwen Hufton (ed.), *Historical Change and Human Rights: The Oxford Amnesty Lectures*, New York: Basic Books, 1995, pp. 101–30.

Darnton, R., *Censors at Work: How States Shaped Literature*, New York and London: W. W. Norton, 2014.

Dollimore, J., *Sex, Literature and Censorship,* Cambridge and Boston: Polity, 2001.

During, S., *Against Democracy: Literary Experience in the Era of Emancipations*, New York: Fordham University Press, 2012.

Eliot, S. and S. Tanner, A. Giacometti, H. Irving, J. Miguel Viera, *MOI Online: A Publishing and Communication History of the Ministry of Information*, Institute of English Studies, Kings College, London. Available at http://www.moidigital.ac.uk/ [accessed November 2014].

Ermolaev, H., *Censorship in Soviet Literature 1917–1991*, Lanham, MD: Rowman and Littlefield, 1997.

Gafaiti, H., 'Between God and the President: Literature and Censorship in North Africa', *Diacritics*, 27 (2) (1997): 59–84.

Heath, D., *Obscenity and the Politics of Moral Regulation in Britain, India and Australia*, Oxford: Oxford University Press, 2010.

Hilliard, C., '"Is it a Book That You Would Wish Your Wife or Your Servants to Read?" Obscenity Law and the Politics of Reading in Modern England', *American Historical Review*, June (2013): 653–79.

Holquist, M., 'Corrupt Originals: The Paradox of Censorship', *PMLA*, 109 (1) (1994): 14–25.

MacDonald, P. D., *The Literature Police: Apartheid and its Cultural Consequences*, Oxford: Oxford University Press, 2009.

MacShane, D., 'You Can't Read this Book: Censorship in an Age of Freedom', *The Observer*, 12 February 2012. Available at http://www.theguardian.com/books/2012/feb/12/cant-read-book-cohen-review [accessed 14 April, 2014].

Marshik, C., *British Modernism and Censorship*, Cambridge: Cambridge University Press, 2006.

Moore, N., 'Censorship', in M. F. Suarez SJ and H. R. Woudhuysen (eds), *Oxford Companion to the Book*, Oxford: Oxford University Press, 2010, pp. 596–8.

Moore, N., 'Censorship Is', *Australian Humanities Review*, 54 (2013): 45–65. Available at http://www.australianhumanitiesreview.org/archive/Issue-May-2013/AHR54_3_Moore.pdfC [accessed September 2014].

Moore, N. and C. Spittel (eds), *Reading through the Iron Curtain: Australian Literature in the German Democratic Republic,* London: Anthem Press, forthcoming 2015.

Moretti, F., *Distant Reading,* New York: Verso, 2013.

Müller, B., 'Censorship and Cultural Regulation: Mapping the Territory', in B. Müller (ed.), *Censorship and Cultural Regulation in the Modern Age*, Critical Studies Vol. 22, Amsterdam: Rodopi, 2004, pp. 1–32.

O'Leary, C. and A. Lázaro (eds), *Censorship Across Borders: The Reception of English Literature in Twentieth-Century Europe*, Newcastle-upon-Tyne: Cambridge Scholars Publishing, 2011.

Shuger, D., *Censorship and Cultural Sensibility: The Regulation of Language in Tudor-Stuart England*, Philadelphia: University of Pennsylvania Press, 2006.

Strub, W., *Obscenity Rules: Roth v. United States and the Long Struggle over Sexual Expression,* Lawrence, KA: University Press of Kansas, 2013.

Part I

1

French Censorship on the Eve of the Revolution

Simon Burrows

The censorship apparatus of the *ancien régime* has generally been seen as ineffectual, helpless even, when faced with a rising tide of philosophic and scandalous works. Eventually, these flooded the entire kingdom and set the scene for a revolution characterized by the freedom of radically subversive texts to circulate in public space. This conclusion is generally tied to the teleological myth of a heroic enlightenment that swept everything before it and helped 'cause' the French revolution of 1789.[1] With thousands of clandestine, pirated and unlicensed works circulating, no one was quite sure what was and was not permitted. Meanwhile, at the heart of the regime, enlightened administrators such as Guillaume-Chrétien de Lamoignon de Malesherbes, who between 1750 and 1763 served as the *Directeur de la librairie* [Controller of the Book Trade], connived at the circulation of enlightenment classics such as the *Encyclopédie* and protected the *philosophes* who produced them.[2] Moreover, highly subversive works of scandal and political pornography were pumped into the Bourbon realm by entrepreneurial extra-territorial publisher-wholesalers such as the Swiss-based Société typographique de Neuchâtel [hereafter STN].[3] So extensive was this clandestine and pirate commerce that Roger Chartier suggests the illegal sector accounted for half of all books sold in pre-revolutionary France. However, he does not distinguish between the types of illegal work, which ranged from hardcore pornography and scandalous political *libelles* through to pirate copies of innocuous, permitted works.[4]

This chapter suggests that this model is inadequately attuned to developments in the final two decades before 1789, when a resurgent Bourbon government tightened its control over the printed word, both inside and beyond French borders. This campaign crushed the extra-territorial publishing industry and brought howls of protest from domestic publishers.[5] If the French Revolution was a revolution of print, it was a reaction against a tightening and increasingly effective royal publishing and censorship regime, not the ultimate triumph of an autonomous public sphere. At the heart of Bourbon police apparatus was a system of licencing and amnesties put in place in August 1777 and a brutal decree of 12 June 1783 aimed (ostensibly) at foreign-produced political *libelles*. These measures, together with others aimed at the newspaper press, consolidated a century-old practice of bringing printers, publishers and writers into collaboration with the regime.

The inner workings of the Bourbon censorship apparatus are well documented. Theoretically, most new books could circulate legally only if they had been vetted by the regime's censors and granted an official permission. Passing through the censorship process often involved elaborate negotiations and resubmission. Individual censors often commented on the literary merit of manuscripts as well as suggesting amendments to content that might offend religion, order or good morals, the three watchwords of the censorship system. As the *Almanach de la librairie [Book Trade Almanac]* explained, authors and publishers approaching the *Bureau de la librairie* (the branch of the royal administration charged with regulating the book trade), for permission to publish had a range of options. For posters, ephemera and theatrical works they should apply for a *permission de police*, but for new books they must choose between a simple and cost-free publishing permission (*permission de sceau*) or a *privilège*, which cost 36 *livres* 12 *sous* but gave the holder exclusive rights for between two and ten years.[6] However, some works, including perennial religious bestsellers such as the Scriptures and Thomas à Kempis' *Imitation de Christ*, were owned under perpetual *privilège* by the University of Paris.[7] Within the system of permissions, further gradations developed over time. For example, books denied full approval might circulate under '*permissions tacites*'. Originally designed to allow the legal circulation of works produced abroad, these were soon extended to editions published in France, but not avowed as such. Many 'tacitly permitted' works had to appear under a false, foreign imprint, thereby placing subterfuge at the heart of the legal book trade. Such works did not enjoy the same protections as 'privileged' titles.[8] Equally, many foreign-produced works, most famously the third edition of the *Encyclopédie*, gained *permissions* only after lengthy wrangling between foreign publishers and the Bourbon government.[9] The gradations, complexities, politics and unevenness in the workings of this system promoted a reflexive self-censorship by publishers and authors, who usually worked in partnership with their censors. The whole censorship apparatus was, moreover, only advisory to the *Bureau de la librairie*, which enjoyed the power to discipline publishers and printers. Decisions and *privilèges* could be, and were, occasionally revoked by the *Bureau* or higher authority. A case in point is Claude-Adrien Helvétius' materialist classic *De l'Esprit [Of the Mind]*, whose publication provoked outrage and the sacking of its censor, Jean-Pierre Tercier.

Tercier's case highlights that the system depended upon the foibles of individuals. In fact, French censorship depended on the decisions of a handful of censors. The *Directeur de la librarie* had between 122 and 189 censors during the final four decades of the *ancien régime*, but these were divided among several specialist and very unequal categories, *viz* Theology, Jurisprudence, Natural History, Agriculture, Medicine, Surgery, Chemistry, Mathematics and Physics, '*Belles Lettres*, History etc.', Geography, Engraving, Architecture and Genealogy.[10] Even within the larger categories, a handful of men did the bulk of the work. Just five of the 84 censors available examined 40 per cent of the 2,759 works of '*Belles Lettres* and History' submitted between 1750 and 1763.[11] This equates to an average workload of almost one-and-an-half books per month each.

The backgrounds of censors varied considerably, but most were themselves authors. As such, they commented on fellow writers' works as government-sanctioned literary reviewers. Their reports, which were frequently published in the works they approved, offered a seal of literary as well as ideological approbation.[12] The position of censor, though not directly remunerated, was widely sought after and political opinions had little bearing on the success of applicants. There is evidence, too, that censors valued their intellectual independence. For example, Jean-Baptiste-Claude Cadet de Sainville resisted pressure from the physiocrat *controlleur-général des finances* [finance minister] Anne-Robert Turgot to suppress a pamphlet on the grain trade by Turgot's rival and critic Jacques Necker, the Geneva-born financier who would himself become finance minister in 1777. But he also recommended for publication works hostile to Necker's views.[13] Caught in the ministerial crossfire, Sainville used criteria other than ideology or support of the ministry to make his judgements, invoking literary merit alongside considerations of style – authorial restraint, decorous language and, in debate, playing the issue and not one's opponent.[14] However, censors were not neutral arbiters. Enmeshed in the power networks of their academic fields, the temptation to settle literary and professional scores was always present, particularly as the censor's identity was theoretically secret. In practice, secrecy was often breached and writers sometimes requested and were granted a particular censor. Nor did the censor have to come from an official list. The *Directeur de la Librairie* frequently sent controversial or useful works to the appropriate minister for approval.[15] Thus political and personal considerations might enter the formal censorship process at multiple points, particularly as careerist censors might fear offending powerful interest groups or patrons. Nevertheless, the system was flexible enough in practice that, having been suitably amended, the vast majority of works submitted to the censors were finally approved.[16] Moreover, within accepted and state-sanctioned limits, the censorship process could operate as editorial quality control, shaping and even facilitating literary output.

Successful passage through the censorship system did not necessarily ensure a happy ending, since central government's right to censor books was contested by other bodies. The Faculty of Theology at the Sorbonne, the high clergy and the *parlements* all claimed a right of *post facto* censorship. By the later eighteenth century, the claims of the first two bodies were considerably weakened. Nevertheless, the bishops continued to issue encyclicals condemning ungodly works and the Assembly of the Clergy regularly petitioned for the restoration of a formal ecclesiastical censorship apparatus while negotiating its annual '*don gratuit*' – a voluntary financial gift to the Crown paid *in lieu* of taxation. While such pleas were ultimately unsuccessful, the Clergy's requests for the condemnation of works contrary to religion sometimes succeeded. In contrast, the Sorbonne's star was rapidly waning, abetted by its heavy-handed and self-defeating condemnation of Jean-François Marmontel's philosophic novel *Bélisaire [Belisarius]* in 1768. In asserting – in the capital of the enlightenment – that religious intolerance was an essential feature of Catholicism, the Faculty shattered its own credibility.[17] It also helped catapult *Bélisaire* to the top of the best-seller tables for a decade and more afterwards.[18]

Issuing from the highest sovereign law courts in France, the claims of the *parlements* were a more direct challenge to monarchical censorship authority, especially as the *parlements* also had to register royal edicts and new taxes before they could be applied to the territories under their jurisdiction and could thus obstruct royal governance. Of course, many works condemned by the *parlements* were clandestine titles containing precisely the types of attack on religion, good order and morality that the monarchy and clergy also wished to suppress. Among them, in the period 1765–74 alone, were Voltaire's *Dictionnaire philosophique* [*Philosophical Dictionary*] and *Dieu et les hommes* [*God and Men*]; Helvétius' *De l'Esprit*; and the arch-materialist Baron d'Holbach's *Contagion sacrée* [*The Holy Disease*], *Bon Sens* [*Common Sense*] and *Christianisme dévoilé* [*Christianity Unmasked*]. The Paris *Parlement* also condemned works that touched on its prerogatives or defended its enemies, however, including the rather improbably-titled *Histoire impartiale des Jesuits* [*Impartial History of the Jesuits*] in 1768; the *Lettres provinciales* [*Provincial Letters*] in 1772; *La Voeu de la noblesse* [*The Nobility's Wish*] in 1773; and Pierre-Augustin Caron de Beaumarchais' judicial *Mémoires* in 1774. Conversely, many *remonstrances*, edicts and pronouncements of the *parlements* were suppressed by *arrêts* [decrees] of the Royal Council.[19]

From the late 1740s and 1750s the *parlements* began using *arrêts*, remonstrances and pamphlets to assert constitutional claims to be the guardians of the kingdom's fundamental laws, thus setting themselves up as the legitimate forum of opposition to Royal policy. The *parlements* also declared themselves immune from censorship on several key issues, while insisting on their rights to condemn their opponents' views. Such debates were played out particularly over religious controversies and the *parlements*' claims to jurisdiction in certain matters of religious practice. As confrontation with the Crown heated up, the Paris *Parlement* moved in 1756 from condemning the pamphlets of its episcopal enemies, many of which were immune to censorship, to condemning works officially approved by royal censors, notably the abbé du Marsy's *La Christiade ou le Paradis reconquis* [*The Christiade or Paradise Regained*] and Isaac-Joseph Berruyer's *Histoire du peuple de Dieu* [*History of God's People*]. Goaded by the *parlements*, the government acted. On 16 April 1757, amidst hysteria generated by Robert-François Damiens's assassination attempt on Louis XV, the Royal Council reasserted its supremacy by decreeing that:

> All those convicted of having composed, having had composed, and having had printed writings that attack religion, disrupt minds, undermine our authority, and disturb the order and tranquillity of our territories, will be punished by death.[20]

This draconian policy was never enforced. Nor, even in all its theoretical horror, did it quite match the obscenity of previous centuries, when printers were sometimes burned. Still, as we shall see, the Bourbon regime could be ruthless against those who offended it.

The government's preference, however, was to work with the producers of printed products, to try to cement their co-operation. This had been effected above all by a system of licensing for printers and booksellers, first introduced in 1667. From 1704 the number of printers in each town was limited by law. In some cases the government formally reduced printer numbers, and this nationwide exercise was repeated again in 1777.[21] This system allowed the government close control. It also enriched those printers and booksellers lucky enough to hold a licence, further encouraging them to toe the line. Effectively the government was attempting to 'licence loyalty', as Jane McLeod has put it, and to a large degree this worked. As wealthy local notables, most printers and booksellers were satisfied with the *status quo*. Although many profited from the Revolution and several became prominent in national affairs, before 1789, few, if any, favoured a free press.[22] That said, after 1777, many expressed concerns about the tightening of the system.

The primary aims of the six decrees promulgated on 30 August 1777 were to tighten the regulation of the book trade, to consolidate the trade in French hands and to curb copyright piracy. To these ends the government declared an amnesty on all pirated books already in France, provided booksellers and printers declared them to inspectors and had them stamped. It also introduced a new *permission simple*, whereby printers and publishers could pay a small fee to reprint any work no longer protected by *privilège*. The revenue raised would finance the appointment of a centrally-paid inspector for each of the country's 20 *Chambres Syndicales* (guilds). Meanwhile, existing *privilèges* were reviewed, and those reserving many classic works in the hands of Parisian printers were annulled.[23] This greatly increased the range of marketable works available to provincial publishers, who hitherto had often relied on job-printing. The registers of *permissions simples* survive, recording print runs for almost 3,000,000 copies of 1,785 editions between 1777 and 1789.[24] Yet the vast majority of the books given *permissions simples* were religious in nature.[25] So were most of those stamped under the amnesty of 1777: the pirate sector of the book trade was generally composed of innocuous books, many of which underpinned the altar and French confessional state.[26]

Some books, however, were beyond all possibility of toleration. These included scandalous works against Marie-Antoinette, notably the *Vie privée de Marie-Antoinette d'Autriche, Reine de France* [*The Private Life of Marie-Antoinette of Austria, Queen of France*], the *Amours de Charlot et de Toinette* [*The Love Life of Charlie and Toinette*] and the *Portefeuille d'un talon rouge* [*Briefcase of a Dandy*].[27] These works, which have spawned a large secondary literature, allegedly dragged the reputation of the Queen through the dirt, desacralized the monarchy and helped to provoke the French revolution.[28] It has generally been assumed that such sensational works circulated widely before the revolution, as did a handful of scandalous pamphlets about Louis XV's final two mistresses, Madame de Pompadour and Madame du Barry.[29] Yet is this credible? After all, Marie-Antoinette was no *haute bourgeoise* parvenu like Pompadour, nor a plebeian courtesan like Du Barry. She belonged to the oldest, most powerful royal dynasty in Europe. She was the daughter of an Empress, sister of an Emperor, wife of the King of France, mother of the heir to the Bourbon throne and the incarnation of the Bourbon-Habsburg alliance. Slurs against her marital chastity were crimes of near unthinkable *lèse-majesté*. This truth has long been overlooked due to the diamond necklace affair, a criminal scandal in which Cardinal Louis de Rohan had the temerity to base his defence on claims that he had been duped into participating in a spectacular swindle by a prostitute impersonating the queen, in a fleeting midnight *rendez-vous* in the Versailles palace gardens. Rohan, a prince of the Church and distant cousin of the Queen, was perhaps the only man in France who could with impunity have concocted such a tale, let alone persuaded the *Parlement* of Paris to accept his defence. Rohan's actions and the *parlement*'s nakedly political verdict provoked the Queen's implacable hatred, since they implied that Marie-Antoinette was the kind of wanton woman who might indeed arrange such an assignation.[30]

Rohan might dare venture such allegations, but lesser mortals who dabbled in *libelles* against the monarchy or highly placed courtiers lived in terror. The regime had a record of silencing such dissidents before their works got to market. Between 1659 and 1789, some 300 writers, including Voltaire, were imprisoned arbitrarily in the Bastille, usually for relatively short periods.[31] *Libellistes* were usually treated rather severely when captured, but the priority was to silence them by any means possible. In 1744, the journalist Dubourg was seized from the Rhineland, carried to Mont Saint-Michel, and suspended bent in a cramped cage. Wracked in agony, he was released by death 18 months later. The Marquis de Fratteaux was seized on the streets of London in 1753 and whisked off to the Bastille, where he spent more than two decades. His fate was widely publicized. From 1763 to 1764, the renegade diplomat Charles d'Eon de Beaumont used the British press to allege that similar attempts were being prepared against him, while between 1770 and 1772 his fellow Burgundian exile, Charles Théveneau de Morande, survived several kidnap and assassination attempts whilst working on a scandalous life of Du Barry.

In the end Morande and d'Eon were both bought off by the monarchy, which used the playwright Beaumarchais as an agent, and in 1778 and 1781 the French government paid to suppress two further *libelles*, and the *Amours de Charlot et de Toinette* and *Le Guerlichon femelle* [*The Fancywoman*].[32] Knowledge of such pay-offs spawned a minor industry in blackmail pamphlets in London and the Low Countries, always with the aim of negotiating a suppression fee, but this remained a dangerous business. In 1784, Anne-Gédeon de Lafite, Marquis de Pelleport, was lured to Calais, seized and imprisoned in the Bastille for composing such *libelles*. His friend, the future revolutionary Girondin leader Jacques-Pierre Brissot, though probably innocent of any involvement, was arrested, held for three months, and then sent into internal exile. Finally, in 1791, the Countess de La Motte, the mastermind behind the diamond necklace scam, hurled herself from the third floor window of a London apartment block to escape British bailiffs, believing they were working with French kidnappers intent on preventing publication of her mendacious memoirs against the Queen. She died a few weeks later of internal wounds.[33]

These tales of scandal and skullduggery suggest that, when the French government targeted its efforts carefully and pragmatically, its control apparatus could prove terribly effective. Although a number of titles were printed and suppressed, there is no credible evidence that anti-Marie-Antoinette *libelles* circulated among the public prior to 1789. Whenever rumours of their existence seeped out, secret policemen, as well as the authors of underground newsletters, booksellers and journalists found them as elusive as the scarlet pimpernel. Surviving copies seem to have emerged from the Bastille in the Revolution – hastily reprinted, some were marketed with the tagline: 'This work was found in the Bastille.'[34] And once government stopped paying the blackmailers in 1783, the production line for *libelles* ceased operating overnight.[35] But by then another decree, on 12 June 1783, had had profound effects on the wider trade.

The full effects of the decrees of 30 August 1777 and 12 June 1783 on the trade of a major foreign publisher, the STN, can now be quantified, using a database that breaks down and renders analysable details of their trade, recording the supply origins and sales destinations for around 450,000 books.[36] Drawn from the extensive surviving archival records, the data has been enriched with key markers of the illegality of works to enable specific manipulation within the dataset, noting, for example, all 720 works belonging to Darnton's *Corpus of Clandestine Literature*.[37] Previous studies of the illegal trade, including those by Darnton and by the current author, have suggested that the decree of 12 June 1783 for a while seriously disrupted the illegal trade in these works – but was this correct?[38]

The 12 June 1783 decree was ostensibly targeted at preventing scandalous pamphlets against Marie-Antoinette reaching France. This was probably only a pretext. Requiring the redirection to Paris for inspection of all book imports into France, the decree marked the culmination of a century-long reduction in points of entry and significantly increased the cost of importing books for the provinces. It particularly harmed the Swiss booksellers, as they were located further from Paris than their Dutch or Rhenish rivals. But how effective was this measure against the clandestine trade? Mapped data of evidence derived from the STN database (see Fig. 1.1) suggests that the decree severely damaged the Swiss book-dealers' trade in pornographic works – defined by the STN database as books containing explicit descriptions of the genitals or sexual acts for the purpose of sexual arousal. And it also damaged their regular trade. Yet despite protests from Swiss publishers and French book dealers alike, the Bourbon government did not relent.[39]

Static maps can deceive however and further research suggests that 12 June 1783 was not the turning point. Instead, the decrees of 30 August 1777 (although targeted at a different kind of illegal work) had already driven clandestine pornographic works from the French market. These decrees stamped out much cross-border commerce: the sector hit hardest appears to have been the hardcore clandestine trade. A measure designed to curb book trade copyright piracy had the collateral effect of inhibiting the trade in pornography. Figure 1.2 overleaf shows that, prior to 1777, the French were the STN's best clients for such material, taking almost every book sold. This compares to France's average market share across all books of about 36 per cent. But after 1777 the French took very little of this literature.

How did this compare to the decrees' impact on the wider market? For the totality of Darnton's 720 work *Corpus*, which includes materialist philosophy, anti-clerical ribaldry and politically-scandalous works alongside pornography, there is a similar fall – though not as significant as for pornography (see Fig. 1.3). Some clandestine works were still slipping through.

Despairing of off-loading their illegal stock, in April 1779 the STN dumped much of it on a dealer named Malherbe, who in turn used it to supply a band of roving *colporteurs* (travelling booksellers) across western France. This dumping of books – unique in the STN's history – has been excluded from Figs 1.2 and 1.3 (along with

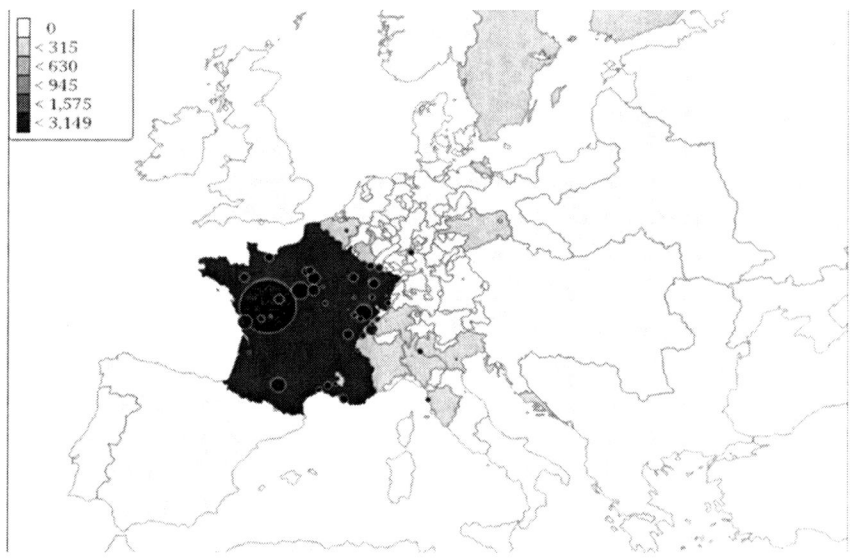

Fig. 1.1: STN sales of illegal pornographic works to France, broken down by
    state and town, January 1769–June 1783 (above) and July 1783–December
    1787 (below). (NB. Size of dots gives relative sales by town, but scale is not
    proportionate between the two maps. Similar sized dots represent almost ten
    times as many sales on first map as on second map).

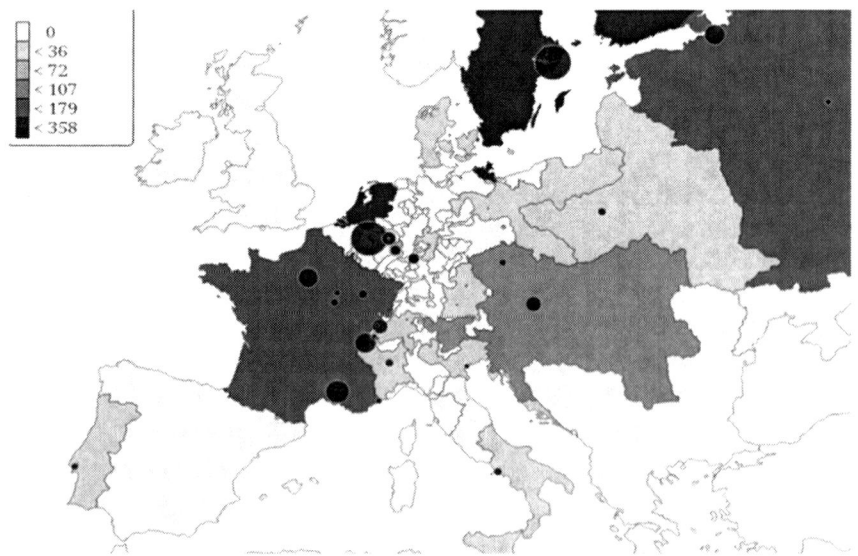

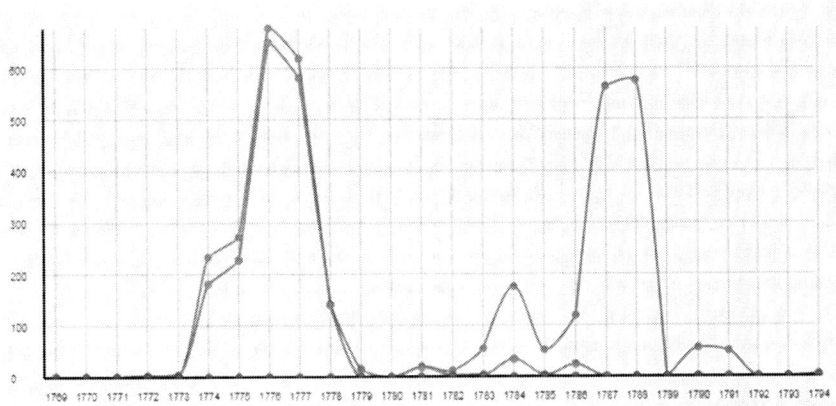

Fig. 1.2: STN global and French sales of pornographic works compared (upper line = global sales; lower line = sales to France). [N.B. Commissioned works and foreign wholesalers excluded].

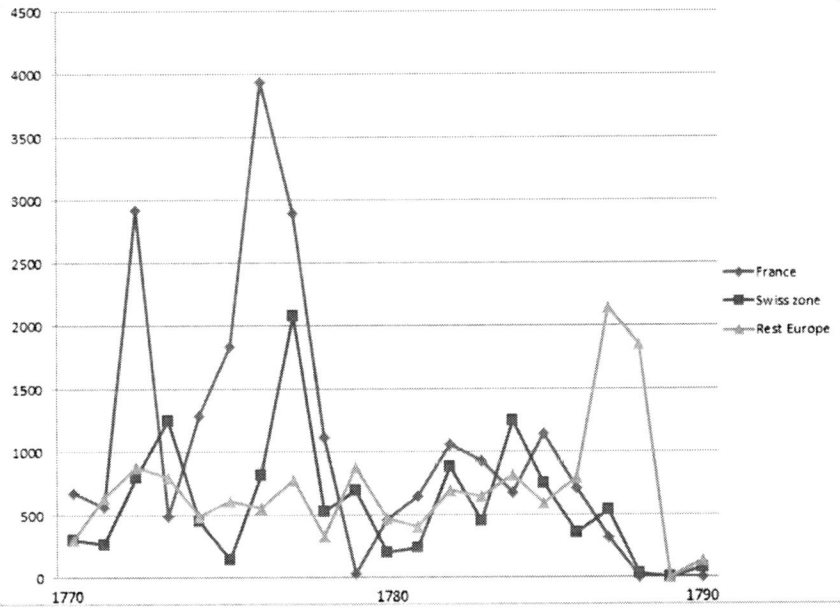

Fig. 1.3: Annualized STN sales of the 720 works in Darnton's libertine corpus by area, 1770–90 (excluding commissions and foreign wholesale clients).

insignificant sales to other non-Swiss wholesalers) because it causes major data distortions, as evidenced below. A slump also hit STN book sales to France generally, but the dip was less than for clandestine literature and lasted less time. The STN trade in legal books recovered quite quickly from mid-1778, driven by the activities of a travelling

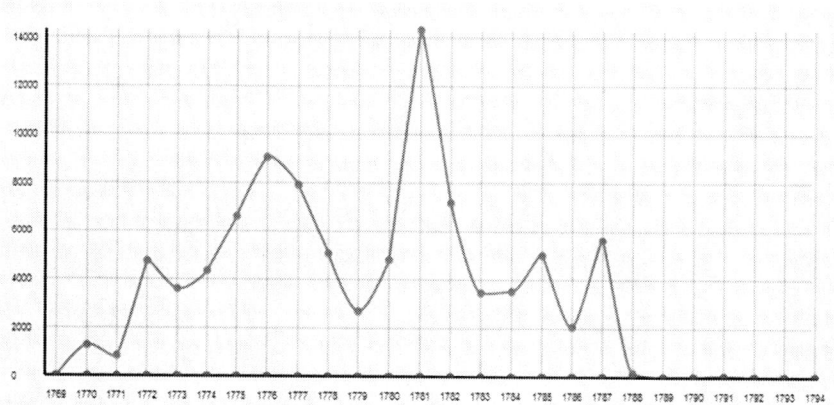

Fig. 1.4: Total STN sales to France, 1769–94.

salesman called Favager, reaching a new peak in 1781.[40] The new trade was short-lived, however: after the decree of 12 June 1783 the STN's French sales never again reached the more modest levels they had enjoyed in the mid-1770s.

The digital evidence suggests that the French decrees did squeeze pornography out of that market and were fairly effective against other clandestine books. However, they did so largely in 1777 not 1783. Contrary to its original intent, a measure designed to stop piracy actually killed the clandestine and pornographic trades, while the 1783 decree against radical pornography delivered a body blow to Swiss export publishing in general.

Could the French also control the wider public sphere in France or across Europe? Increasing evidence suggests that they were becoming more effective at this, too, by the 1770s. One key target was the cosmopolitan international press, produced primarily in the Netherlands, the Rhineland, London and the Papal enclave of Avignon. French-language international gazettes had been produced in the Netherlands since the Huguenot diaspora and served as Europe's elite press throughout the eighteenth century.[41] By 1781, one in three newspapers distributed by the French mail service was an international gazette, and these also circulated widely throughout Europe. Containing a diet limited primarily to political news information, with little editorial colour, these gazettes nevertheless offered ideological and practical challenges to the French government. Faced with a growing need for financial credit and hence to inspire public confidence, it needed the gazettes to promote its own news agenda and supplement information from its governmental and diplomatic networks.[42] But the French government feared to intervene too publicly, since it was important that news appeared independent, so it indulged in a cat-and-mouse style game with journalists within and beyond its borders, seeking to influence their copy but not too obviously. For this purpose they used techniques ranging from diplomatic threats and outright bans to bribery and news management.[43] Such policies could have striking impact. In the first three months of 1771 the Dutch gazettes were full of stories and documents relating to chancellor René-Nicolas de Maupeou's attempts to radically remodel the French *parlements*. Most such documents were propagandist proclamations emanating from the *parlements*, but a series of threats to ban Dutch gazettes from France had their desired result. By mid-March pro-*parlement* propaganda materials had disappeared from the gazettes and they remained excluded for the duration of the Maupeou crisis. More effective still was a 1781 round-up of the *nouvellistes* (newsmongers) who supplied the gazettes with Parisian copy: *embastilled* for ten days, on their release they were either banned from corresponding with foreign editors or placed under surveillance and licensed.[44]

Yet, despite the success of its seduction of printers and its campaigns to control illegal works, literary piracy, foreign imports and newspaper journalism, mounting evidence suggests that the French government's censorship apparatus faced the wrong direction. Censorship was predicated on the assumption that the printed word had the potential to disrupt order and even to threaten the regime. But it was also assumed that this threat came primarily from low-born malcontents and disreputable foreign elements.[45] Historians, too, have tended to assume that a rising tide of 'public opinion' from an increasingly democratic public became a growing challenge, and that printers, authors and other cultural intermediaries became increasingly frustrated with the censorship regime. Eventually, in the revolution of 1789, this alliance of public and cultural intermediaries swept all before it.[46]

In reality, the threat came from within the elite, and the most significant oppositional genre was not books or newspapers, but political pamphlets. They remained the most effective printed genre for political comment up to the revolution.[47] This was certainly the retrospective view of the Parisian police chief Jean-Charles-Pierre Lenoir, whose office worked closely with the *Direction de la Librairie*. Writing in post-revolutionary exile in his (unpublished) memoirs, Lenoir painstakingly explored the links between printing and politics during his watch in the 1770s and 1780s.[48] He was adamant that the main danger to the government came not from a rising of the public sphere or any accompanying process of ideological erosion, but rather unbridled factionalism and rampant pamphleteering in the heart of the political elite itself. In the controlled and censored press system of the *ancien régime*, only the elite and those they protected could safely fund and produce political pamphlets with immunity and in secrecy.[49] Such pamphlets were usually produced for immediate clandestine circulation and were often distributed outside formal commercial channels and for a limited audience. Despite the influence attributed to public opinion by contemporaries and historians, many pamphlets were not aimed at the general populace nor even a bourgeois readership. Instead, they aimed at a narrower elite audience, suggesting that their authors believed that real power and influence continued to be vested in the court rather than public opinion.

Many pamphlets emanating from this aristocratic and parliamentary elite were able to evade the censorship. As we have seen, the *parlements* asserted immunity for publications defending their own prerogatives, and the bishops pumped out polemical tracts with the same *de facto* freedom. High profile litigants were also free to publish legal trial briefs in which they argued their cases before the public, and many leading lawyers used this freedom to publish anthologies of their best and most prominent speeches. Over the century, as Sarah Maza has shown, a politicized bar increasingly (ab)used this freedom to publish polemical trial briefs depicting their clients as victims of arbitrary government and despotic ministers. Such pamphlets did seek to address a wider public and were often distributed or sold in their thousands.[50] In this way radical reformers, zealous *parlementaires* and political opportunists were able to turn incidents such as the Kornmann affair, a seemingly innocuous adultery and divorce case, into an opportunity to attack the ministry, just as Rohan and his allies used his appearance before the Paris *Parlement* over the diamond necklace scandal to settle scores with the Crown.[51]

The extent of elite complicity in pamphleteering was laid bare by the Le Maître affair of 1785–6. In December 1785, a wealthy lawyer, Pierre-Jacques Le Maître, was apprehended at the gates of Paris carrying the page proofs for a clandestine pamphlet. The new police minister, Louis Thiroux de Crosne, considered releasing him, no doubt figuring he had powerful allies, but against the minister's better judgement was persuaded to interrogate him with a view to a public trial. In the weeks that followed, Le Maître drip-fed his interrogators enough information to implicate numerous present and former allies in the pamphleteering campaigns of the past two decades, and the trail led straight to the top.[52] Le Maître's involvement with clandestine pamphleteering dated back to the early 1770s and the *parlements'* campaigns against the Maupeou ministry. Lenoir's memoirs tell how leading activists in the *parlementary* network, notably the abbé Jabineau and Le Maître himself, revealed ties to prominent figures, including Malesherbes and Armand-Thomas Hue de Miromesnil, who in 1774 was appointed Keeper of the Seals (*Garde des Sceaux*). Lenoir reports that his own friend and patron, Jean-Frédéric Phélypeaux, comte de Maurepas, the elder statesman who served as political mentor to Louis XVI, was also involved.[53] According to Lenoir, these men were central to the clandestine pamphleteering of the Maupeou years (1771–4), but operated within established political parameters, respecting the person of the reigning monarch. Only after Louis XV's death in 1775 and the consequent disgrace of Du Barry did scandalous printed pamphlets against monarch and mistress begin to circulate.[54] For Lenoir, the pamphleteering of the Maupeou era, seen by some historians as a dress rehearsal for revolution, was the ephemeral output of a political faction brought together by circumstances.[55]

Such factional alliances were temporary and mutated over time. In the political world of the *ancien régime*, where political advancement depended on the king's favour and ministries were but collections of individuals, talented 'outs' often moved rapidly from opposition to government. Moreover, opposition was articulated against a particular minister or cabal, not royal government in general. A wise ruler tried to keep a lid on interpersonal politics, but also rewarded and advanced talented and powerful critics, as long as they played within the rules. Thus by 1783 the factions lined up rather differently. Though Le Maître had begun his pamphleteering career in the service of Miromesnil, at that time first *Président* of the *Parlement* of Rouen, a decade later he was attempting to oust him from government, while working for a new patron, Chrétien-François de Lamoignon, a kinsman of Malesherbes. That particular campaign foundered when Lenoir persuaded the king to declare that Miromesnil enjoyed his full confidence. However, by the time of his arrest, Le Maître was involved in a new virulent campaign against Miromesnil and the *controlleur-général* Charles-Alexandre de Calonne. Against the background of the diamond necklace affair, which was beginning to create bitter divides between the allies of the Queen and members and clients of the Rohan clan, Le Maître's arrest threatened to expose raw nerves at the heart of government. When Le Maître shrewdly named one of the queen's favourites as one of his major collaborators, he ensured that the eventual result would be a cover-up. With so many powerful figures in both *parlements* and successive ministries implicated, the Paris *Parlement* quietly quashed all proceedings.[56]

Lenoir's evidence also suggests that much of the apparently radical, pre-revolutionary output of prominent revolutionary writers and politicians, including Honoré-Gabriel Riqueti, comte de Mirabeau, Brissot, Jean-Louis Carra and Antoine-Joseph Gorsas, should be tied to wealthy patrons. He claimed that Mirabeau's celebrated attacks on *agiotage* (speculating on artificially inflated share values) were commissioned by 'the government', which was also directing the efforts of Mirabeau's patron, the future revolutionary finance minister Etienne Clavière, and apparently Brissot, too.[57] On a more personal level, he was convinced that retrospective attacks on his record as Lieutenant-Général of Police of Paris were orchestrated by other ministers, including the reactionary Baron de Breteuil and Lomenie de Brienne, the conniving archbishop of Toulouse. Lenoir bitterly resented these attacks, believing they took place with the connivance of his successor de Crosne.[58] Tellingly, Lenoir was also convinced that most pornographic *libelles* against the queen drew their materials from court, where verbal and manuscript slanders had been circulated by anti-Austrian elements from early in the reign. Courtiers, in his view, also printed and protected many of the scandalous pamphlets that appeared in France itself.[59]

Whether Lenoir's suspicions and testimony were correct in every detail is less significant than his more general description of how factional politics operated. He relates that his attempts to smash the *Parlementaire* and Jansenist networks had been frustrated by the classic cellular organizational structures through which pamphlets were produced and disseminated. Hence, under interrogation, the abbé Jabineau informed Lenoir that the Jansenist-*parlementaire* network printed its *Maupeouana* on around 20 clandestine presses. This was a substantial number: in May 1769 the licenced printers of Paris had 317 presses between them, but only 160 were in use (*roulantes*).[60] Unlike the Parisian printers' equipment, which was under near constant surveillance by the *inspecteurs de la librairie*, the Jansenist-*parlementaire* presses were frequently transported from place to place to minimize the risk of detection, and their operators were unaware of one another's identities. Likewise, the pedlars and *colporteurs* did not know which printers supplied them. The whole operation was funded from a secret war chest operated by princes of the blood, peers of France and other leaders in the legal and financial worlds. These people were all but untouchable. Although many of their presses were mothballed after the Maupeou crisis, Jabineau warned that the whole machinery would be ready at the first sign of political crisis – which, according to Lenoir, is precisely what happened in 1789.[61]

The Bourbon government's attempts to control the printed word were thus surprisingly effective, particularly in the final years before the revolution. The censorship apparatus shaped the bulk of literary output in ways that were far from uniformly negative, while the publishing industry had been, to a considerable degree, seduced by government, though it retained links to other powerful patrons, especially in the *parlements*. The circulation of the most obnoxious forms of political pamphlet had been seriously disrupted or completely curtailed. Piracy had been largely eliminated; foreign publishing scotched. But these objectives and the assumptions that lay behind them were largely misdirected. In so far as the printed word represented a threat to the regime, the danger from abroad or below had been largely neutralized. Instead, the most politically destabilizing material came from within the elite itself, as a consequence of rampant factionalism and unbridled infighting. Thus, when the pre-revolutionary crisis broke, France's ruptured and fratricidal elite quickly splintered and turned on itself. Such a rupture is generally a pre-condition for successful revolution. The pamphleteering of the pre-revolution was thus both symptom and aggravating factor of the rift that made possible the greatest of all revolutions.

Notes

1 Jane McLeod, *Licencing Loyalty. Printers, Patrons and the State in Early Modern France* (University Park, PA: Penn State University Press, 2011), pp. 6–7, asserts that this position is universal among previous historians of censorship and 'great historians' of the French revolution.

2 Robert Darnton, *The Business of Enlightenment: A Publishing History of the Encyclopédie, 1775–1800* (Cambridge, MA, and London: Harvard University Press, 1979), pp. 10–11, 12–13.

3 See especially Robert Darnton, *Forbidden Best-Sellers of Pre-Revolutionary France* (New York and London: Norton, 1996). For reassessments of the STN's illegal trade see my articles 'French Banned Books in International Perspective' in David Andress (ed.), *Experiencing the French Revolution* (Oxford: SVEC, 2013), pp. 19–38 and 'Charmet and the Book Police: Clandestinity, Illegality and Popular Reading in Late Ancien Régime France' (forthcoming).

4 Roger Chartier, 'Book Markets and Reading in France at the End of the Old Regime' in Carol Armbruster (ed.), *Publishing and Readership in Revolutionary France and America* (Westport, CT: Greenwood Press, 1993), pp. 117–37 (esp. 123–6). Raymond Birn, *Royal Censorship of Books in 18th-Century France* (Stanford: Stanford University Press, 2012) is more cautious, estimating that half the books circulating in France between 1750 and 1789 were 'tacitly permitted', 'produced abroad' or 'clandestine', p. 4.

5 Bibliothèque nationale de France [BNF], MS Fr 21, 833ff. 68–150, *passim*, contains a series of memoirs from Bassompierre in Geneva and French provincial booksellers in Lille and Lyon protesting the decree of 12 June 1783; the STN archives in the Bibliothèque publique et universitaire de Neuchâtel [BPUN] contain many letters

explaining the effects of the 1777 decrees. For example, BPUN, MS 1134ff. 140–1, Charmet to STN, 20 February 1778, explains that Charmet dare not assist the STN's illegal trade and is abandoning his own following the appointment of the local inspector. This document has been published in Robert Darnton, 'A Literary Tour of France', at www.robertdarnton.org.

6 *Almanach de la librairie* (Paris: Moutard, 1781), pp. 11–14.

7 Nicole Hermann-Mascard, *La censure des livres à Paris à la fin de l'ancien régime (1750–1789)* (Paris: Presses universitaires de France, 1968), pp. 67–8.

8 Birn, *Royal Censorship*, p. 3.

9 See for example, Darnton, *The Business of Enlightenment*; Louise Seaward, 'Censorship through co-operation: the *Société typographique de Neuchâtel* (STN) and the French Government, 1769–1789', *French History* 28 (1), (2014): 23–42.

10 *Almanach de la librairie* (1781): 2–7.

11 Birn, *Royal Censorship*, pp. 58–9.

12 See Robert Darnton, *Censors at Work: How States Shaped Literature* (New York: Norton, 2014), esp. p. 9.

13 Birn, *Royal Censorship*, pp. 101–2.

14 Ibid., p. 102.

15 Hermann-Mascard, *La Censure des livres*, p. 43.

16 Darnton, *Censors at Work*, p. 25.

17 Hermann-Mascard, *La Censure des livres*, pp. 54–5.

18 *Bélisaire* is among the most frequently encountered works in stock sale records for Parisian booksellers from the 1770s and 1780s. It will rank among bestselling novels in the FBTEE-2.0 database. On this database see below note 36.

19 The examples here are taken from a manuscript list of about 1,500 condemned works in BNF, MS Fr 21,814, ff. 83–202.

20 For an account of these events and translation of the decree: Birn, *Royal Censorship*, pp. 26–7.

21 BNF, MS Fr 21,832 ff. 1–22, 'Etat général des imprimeurs du royaume fait en 1777'.

22 See McLeod, *Licencing Loyalty*.

23 The decrees are reproduced in the *Almanach de la librairie* (1781), pp. 151–87.

24 The registers are at BNF, MS Fr. 22,018–22,019. The records they contain have been collated and published in Robert L. Dawson, *The French Book Trade and the Permission Simple of 1777: Copyright and the Public Domain*, SVEC 301 (Oxford: Voltaire foundation, 1992), pp. 353–609. They are currently being edited and enriched for incorporation into the FBTEE-2.0 database.

25 See Dawson, *French Book Trade*.

26 This statement is based primarily on my case study of the 'estampillage' records for Besançon in Burrows, 'Charmet and the Book Police'. The surviving records of the *estampillage* visitations at BNF, MS Fr. 21,831–21,834 are currently being added to the FBTEE-2.0 database.

27 A 'talon rouge', meaning literally 'red heel' was a fashionable man about town. I have translated it as 'dandy' as the nearest English contemporary equivalent: 'fop' and 'macaroni' might also have served.

28 Much of this work was inspired by Robert Darnton, beginning with his seminal article: 'The High Enlightenment and the Low-life of Literature in Prerevolutionary France', *Past and Present*, 51 (1971): 81–115. For an introduction to and debunking

of this literature, see Simon Burrows, *Blackmail, Scandal and Revolution: London's French Libellistes, 1758–1792* (Manchester: Manchester University Press, 2006).

29 On the circulation of Louis XV, Pompadour and du Barry *libelles*, see Burrows, *Blackmail, Scandal and Revolution*, p. 76. The FBTEE-1 database confirms the popularity of Mairobert's *Anecdotes sur Madame la Comtesse du Barry* (1775).

30 The diamond necklace affair has spawned a large literature. On its effects on public opinion see Sarah Maza, 'The Diamond Necklace Affair Revisited: The Case of the Missing Queen' in Lynn Hunt (ed.), *Eroticism and the Body Politic* (Baltimore, MD and London: Johns Hopkins University Press, 1991), pp. 63–89; Burrows, *Blackmail, Scandal and Revolution*, pp. 131–65.

31 Robert Darnton, 'Censorship, a Comparative View: France 1789, East Germany, 1989', *Representations*, 49.1 (1995): 47.

32 The translation of the title here is that of Marion Ward in her biography of Nathaniel Parker Forth, and (since the word 'Guerlichon' is not documented elsewhere) presumably derived from the eighteenth-century 'greluchon', meaning the favoured lover of a prostitute. However, it should be noted that several nineteenth-century sources record a cult of (an otherwise unknown) Saint Guerlichon built around veneration of a priapic Roman statue: the saint was said to be able to cure female infertility. The cult was based around the abbey of Bourg-Dieu in Berry.

33 Burrows, *Blackmail, Scandal and Revolution*, pp. 88–136. On these incidents see also Robert Darnton, *The Devil in the Holy Water, or the Art of Slander from Louis XV to Napoleon* (Philadelphia: University of Pennsylvania Press, 2010). On Brissot's involvement: Simon Burrows, 'The Innocence of Jacques-Pierre Brissot', *Historical Journal* 46 (2003): 843–71.

34 See the 1789 edition(s) of the *Essai historique sur la vie de Marie-Antoinette d'Autriche*.

35 See Médiathèque d'Orléans [MO], MS 1422 p. 56. This is part of the police minister Jean-Charles-Pierre Lenoir's unpublished manuscript memoirs (MO, MS 1421–1423), now available online at http://bibnumerique.bm-orleans.fr/_app_php_mysql/fonds_lenoir/recherche_alpha_cles.php.

36 The FBTEE-1 database, consultable at http://fbtee.uws.edu.au/main/, was developed at the University of Leeds with funding from the British Arts and Humanities Research Council (AHRC). It was published online on 25 June 2012. In its current form it records the entire trade of the STN as recorded by accounting records in the BPUN. The project is now housed at the University of Western Sydney where further data from other sources is being added, prior to the release of a new version of the database (FBTEE-2.0).

37 Robert Darnton, *The Corpus of Clandestine Literature in France, 1769–1789* (New York and London: W. W. Norton, 1995).

38 Burrows, *Blackmail, Scandal and Revolution*, p. 125; Robert Darnton, 'Trade in the Taboo: the Life of a Clandestine Book Dealer in Prerevolutionary France', in Paul J. Korshin (ed.), *The Widening Circle: Essays on the Circulation of Literature in Eighteenth-Century Europe* (Philadelphia: The University of Pennsylvania Press, 1976), p. 19.

39 On these protests see note 5 above.

40 For Favarger's journal of his trip see: Robert Darnton (ed.), 'A Literary Tour of France' at www.robertdarnton.org.

41 For a synthesis of literature on the international gazettes: Simon Burrows, 'The

Cosmopolitan Press', in Hannah Barker and Simon Burrows (eds), *Press Politics and the Public Sphere in Europe and North America, 1760-1820* (Cambridge: Cambridge University Press, 2002), pp. 23–47.

42 Burrows, 'Cosmopolitan Press'; Gilles Feyel, 'La Diffusion des gazettes étrangères en France et la révolution postale des années 1750' in Henri Duranton, Claude Labrosse and Pierre Rétat (eds), *Les Gazettes européennes de langue française sous l'ancien régime* (Saint-Etienne: Presses Universitaires de Saint-Etienne, 1988), p. 69.

43 For a synthesis of government news management techniques see Burrows, 'Cosmopolitan Press', pp. 30–4.

44 Jeremy D. Popkin, *News and Politics in the Age of Revolution: Jean Luzac's Gazette de Leyde* (Ithaca and London: Cornell University Press, 1989), pp. 72–3; Burrows, 'Cosmopolitan Press', p. 33.

45 McLeod, *Licencing Loyalty*, pp. 192–241.

46 The literature on the rise of the public sphere and cultural origins of the Revolution is too vast to discuss here. Useful starting points include Roger Chartier, *The Cultural Origins of the French Revolution*, transl. Lydia D. Cochrane (Durham, NC and London: Duke University Press, 1991) and James van Horn Melton, *The Rise of the Public in Enlightenment Europe* (Cambridge: Cambridge University Press, 2002). According to Darnton, *Forbidden Best-Sellers*, p. 246, by 1787-8, 'The regime stood condemned. It had lost the final round of the long struggle to control public opinion. It had lost its legitimacy.'

47 On the primacy of pamphlets until 1789: Vivien R. Gruder, 'Political News as Coded Messages: the Parisian and Provincial Press in the Pre-revolution, 1787–1788', *French History* 12 (1998): 1–24.

48 On Lenoir's memoirs, see above note 35.

49 See MO, MS 1423/3ff. 191, 263–6; Popkin, 'Pamphlet Journalism at the End of the Old Regime', *Eighteenth-Century Studies* 22 (1989): 351–67 supports Lenoir's view.

50 Sarah Maza, *Private Lives and Public Affairs: The Causes Célèbres of Prerevolutionary France* (Berkeley: University of California Press, 1993).

51 On the Kornmann affair see Maza, *Private Lives*, pp. 295–311.

52 On the Le Maître affair see Popkin, 'Pamphlet journalism'; Simon Burrows, 'Police and Political Pamphleteering' in David Adams and Adrian Armstrong (eds), *Print and Power in France and England, 1500-1800* (Aldershot: Ashgate, 2006), pp. 99–112.

53 MO, MS 1423/3, pp. 191, 263, 265.

54 MO, MS 1423/3, p. 309. This appears to be accurate: the classic anti-Du Barry *libelles* and private lives of Louis XV started appearing from 1775.

55 The classic study is Durand Echeverria, *The Maupeou Revolution: A Study in the History of Libertarianism* (Baton Rouge and London: Louisiana State University Press, 1985).

56 MO, MS 1423/3, pp. 191–2.

57 MO, MS 1422, p. 460.

58 MO, MS 1421, pp. 44–7.

59 MO, MS 1422, pp. 306–7, 309–10.

60 MO 1423/3 p. 264; BNF, MS 22,081 ff. 349–54, 'Visites des inspecteurs de la librairie, Mai 1771', f. 354.

61 MO, MS 1422, p. 268; MS 1423/3, p. 264.

References

Adams, D. and A. Armstrong (eds), *Print and Power in France and England, 1500–1800*, Aldershot: Ashgate, 2006.

Almanach de la librairie, Paris: Moutard, 1781.

Andress, D. (ed), *Experiencing the French Revolution*, Oxford: SVEC, 2013.

Anon., *Essai historique sur la vie de Marie-Antoinette d'Autriche*.

Armbruster, C. (ed.), *Publishing and Readership in Revolutionary France and America*, Westport CT: Greenwood Press, 1993.

Barker, H. and S. Burrows (eds), *Press Politics and the Public Sphere in Europe and North America, 1760–1820*, Cambridge: Cambridge University Press, 2002.

Birn, R., *Royal Censorship of Books in 18th-Century France*, Stanford: Stanford University Press, 2012.

Burrows, S., 'The Cosmopolitan Press', in H. Barker and S. Burrows (eds), *Press Politics and the Public Sphere in Europe and North America, 1760–1820*, Cambridge: Cambridge University Press, 2002.

Burrows, S., 'The Innocence of Jacques-Pierre Brissot', *Historical Journal* 46 (2003): 843–71.

Burrows, S., *Blackmail, Scandal and Revolution: London's French Libellistes 1758–1792*, Manchester: Manchester University Press, 2006.

Burrows, S., 'Police and Political Pamphleteering', in D. Adams and A. Armstrong (eds), *Print and Power in France and England, 1500–1800*, Aldershot: Ashgate, 2006.

Burrows, S., 'French Banned Books in International Perspective', in D. Andress (ed.), *Experiencing the French Revolution*, Oxford: SVEC, 2013.

Burrows, S., 'Charmet and the Book Police: Clandestinity, Illegality and Popular Reading in Late Ancien Régime France', (forthcoming).

Burrows, S. and M. Curran, *The French Book Trade in Enlightenment Europe* [FBTEE-1], available at http://fbtee.uws.edu.au/main/ [accessed 5 November 2014].

Chartier, R., *The Cultural Origins of the French Revolution* (trans. Lydia D. Cochrane), Durham, NC and London: Duke University Press, 1991.

Chartier, R., 'Book Markets and Reading in France at the End of the Old Regime', in C. Armbruster (ed.), *Publishing and Readership in Revolutionary France and America*, Westport: CT, 1993.

Darnton, R., 'The High Enlightenment and the Low-Life of Literature in Prerevolutionary France', *Past and Present*, 51 (1971): 81–115.

Darnton, R., 'Trade in the Taboo: The Life of a Clandestine Book Dealer in Prerevolutionary France', in P. J. Korshin (ed.), *The Widening Circle: Essays on the Circulation of Literature in Eighteenth-Century Europe*, Philadelphia: University of Pennsylvania Press, 1976.

Darnton, R., *The Business of Enlightenment: A Publishing History of the Encyclopédie, 1775–1800* Cambridge, MA and London: Harvard University Press, 1979.

Darnton, R., 'Censorship, a Comparative View: France 1789, East Germany, 1989', *Representations* 49 (1) (1995): 40–60.

Darnton, R., *The Corpus of Clandestine Literature in France, 1769–1789*, New York and London: Norton, 1995.

Darnton, R., *Forbidden Best-Sellers of Pre-Revolutionary France*, New York and London: Norton, 1996.

Darnton, R., *The Devil in the Holy Water, or the Art of Slander from Louis XV to Napoleon*, Philadelphia: University of Pennsylvania Press, 2010.

Darnton, R., *Censors at Work: How States Shaped Literature*, New York: Norton, 2014.

Darnton, R., 'A Literary Tour of France', available at www.robertdarnton.org [accessed 5 November 2014].

Dawson, R. L., *The French Book Trade and the Permission Simple of 1777: Copyright and the Public Domain*, SVEC 301, Oxford: Voltaire Foundation, 1992.

Duranton, H., C. Labrosse and P. Rétat (eds), *Les Gazettes européennes de langue française sous l'ancien regime*, Saint-Etienne: Presses Universitaires de Saint-Etienne, 1988.

Echeverria, D., *The Maupeou Revolution: A Study in the History of Libertarianism*, Baton Rouge and London: Louisiana State University Press, 1985.

Feyel, G., 'La Diffusion des gazettes étrangères en France et la révolution postale des années 1750', in H. Duranton, C. Labrosse and P. Rétat (eds), *Les Gazettes européennes de langue française sous l'ancien regime, Saint-Etienne*: Presses Universitaires de Saint-Etienne, 1988.

Gruder, V. R., 'Political news as coded messages: the Parisian and provincial press in the pre-revolution, 1787–1788', *French History* 12 (1998): 1–24.

Hermann-Mascard, N., *La censure des livres à Paris à la fin de l'ancien régime* (1750–1789), Paris: Presses universitaires de France, 1968.

Hunt, L. (ed.), *Eroticism and the Body Politic*, Baltimore, MD and London: Johns Hopkins University Press, 1991.

Korshin, P. J. (ed.), *The Widening Circle: Essays on the Circulation of Literature in Eighteenth-Century Europe*, Philadelphia, The University of Pennsylvania Press, 1976.

Maza, S., 'The Diamond Necklace Affair Revisited: The Case of the Missing Queen', in Lynn Hunt (ed.), *Eroticism and the Body Politic*, Baltimore, MD and London: Johns Hopkins University Press, 1991.

Maza, S., *Private Lives and Public Affairs: The Causes Célèbres of Prerevolutionary France*, Berkeley: University of California Press, 1993.

McLeod, J., *Licencing Loyalty. Printers, Patrons and the State in Early Modern France*, University Park, PA: Penn State University Press, 2011.

Melton, J. van Horn, *The Rise of the Public in Enlightenment Europe*, Cambridge: Cambridge University Press, 2002.

Popkin, J. D., *News and Politics in the Age of Revolution: Jean Luzac's Gazette de Leyde*, Ithaca and London: Cornell University Press, 1989.

Popkin, J. D., 'Pamphlet Journalism at the End of the Old Regime', *Eighteenth-Century Studies* 22 (1989): 351–67.

Seaward, L., 'Censorship through Co-operation: The Société Typographique de Neuchâtel (STN) and the French Government, 1769–1789', *French History* 28 (1) (2014): 23–42.

2

Not Guilty: Negative Capability and the Trials of William Hone

Clara Tuite

His Not Guilty is a thing, which not to have been, would have dulled still more Liberty's Emblazoning.

John Keats

I.

In May 1817, the radical English writer, printer, publisher and multimedia pressman, William Hone, was charged with blasphemous and seditious libel. He had written and published three liturgical parodies that used well-known passages from the Anglican *Book of Common Prayer* to attack the Tory government of Lord Liverpool. In the UK, govenment is carried out in the name of the monarch. By the early 19th century British monarchs had very few powers. *The Late John Wilkes's Catechism of a Ministerial Member, The Political Litany, Diligently Revised* and *The Sinecurist's Creed, or Belief.* Hone was charged on *ex officio* information and imprisoned under a newly-minted *Suspension of Habeas Corpus Act* (1817), the latest, together with the *Seditious Meetings Act*, of the so-called 'Gagging Acts', which were a series of increasingly repressive legislative instruments, enacted from 1795 to 1819, designed to regulate popular radical activity.[1]

After five months' imprisonment without trial, Hone was released to find that he would have to face court after all. The trials took place over three successive days, on 18–20 December, before a jury of the King's Bench at the Guildhall in London, presided over by Lord Chief Justice Ellenborough. In the first two trials, Hone was charged with blasphemous and seditious libel, and in the third exclusively with blasphemous libel. Hone undertook his own defence and won. The trials were a widely-reported sensation, and Hone's triumphant acquittal brought him instant national celebrity, making him a legend of popular radicalism. This popular celebrity encouraged Hone to publish *The Three Trials of William Hone* in January 1818, and the trials quickly became recognized as landmark cases in the establishment of a British free press and the fight against censorship.

In this essay, I engage the Hone trials as an initiatory instance of the nineteenth-century literary censorship trial, and I explore censorship as a feature of the literary field by analysing the trials as together a complex literary, social and political performance event. For the extraordinary theatricality of Hone's trials resisted and defeated government censorship by turning the institutional machinery of censorship into a parody of itself. Hone defeated government censorship by forcing censorship's regulatory regime into a self-parodic role, within Hone's own parodic performance. By focusing on this mode of parodic performance – the interpellation of government censorship within a performance that defeats it – I seek to demonstrate the productivity of censorship. A larger question of the essay, then, is to what extent does the genre of the courtroom trial spectacularize the productivity of censorship? How can censorship be understood to function as a productive phenomenon? Here, I mean productive not in the sense that censorship is benign, but in the sense that it facilitates textual and performative agency as well as the productive reception and performance of the literary text. I wish to emphasize the way in which censorship – through the machinery of the libel trial – acknowledges the force and significance of the relationship between the literary text and the world in which it acts and, more importantly, it acts upon.

II.

Prohibitions on libel and slander were the earliest forms of legal control exercised by the British state upon writing and speech, respectively. From the seventeenth century, when heresy was distinguished from blasphemy, blasphemy changed from being a purely ecclesiastical offence to a civil one.[2] Blasphemous libel and seditious libel were both notoriously difficult to define. Modern censorship is based on a shift from pre-publication to post-publication censorship. In England, pre-publication censorship of published works ended in 1695 with the lapsing of the Licensing Act (although it continued for theatrical performances). After 1695, censorship occurred indirectly through regulatory measures in copyright and libel laws, whereby all kinds of printed materials could be tried at the King's Bench for obscene, seditious or blasphemous libel. Central here was the 1710 Statute of Anne, which sought to regulate the press through economic controls. Before then, the Long Parliament's decree of 1641–2 was 'an instrument for establishing criminal responsibility for books deemed libellous, seditious, or blasphemous'.[3] During the period of Queen Anne (1702–14), the law of seditious libel became a way of controlling the freedom of the press and suppressing its oppositional tendencies.

This strategy was consolidated in the 1790s, when the British government met the emergence of a radical press in the wake of the French Revolution with the *Treasonable and Seditious Practices Act* (1795). These measures intensified during the post-Waterloo climate of repression, when the government exploited the long-standing instability between blasphemy and sedition. The great Marxist cultural historian, E. P. Thompson, referred to this post-Waterloo period of 1815–19 as 'the heroic age of popular Radicalism'.[4] As the high period of state repression, it was also therefore the heroic age of libel trials, when a number of key radicals such as William Cobbett,

Daniel Isaac Eaton and Richard Carlile were charged with seditious libel. Eighteen seventeen, the year that Hone was tried, saw over 20 prosecutions of radical pressmen for seditious libel, and many more were imprisoned without trial.

While the system of post-publication control had traditionally been celebrated as a sign of the freedom of the English press, it also entailed for writers an uncertainty and an impending threat of intervention. As Cobbett argued, after being convicted of libel in 1810 and sentenced to two years' prison in Newgate: 'I would rather give the preference to a Licenser of the press, than I would leave the definition and the punishment of libel to the dictum of any judge. ... [W]hile there is no boundary; while all is left to the opinions and tastes of others, can any man be said to be *free* to write?'[5] This supposed freedom to write, then, was rather a freedom on the part of the government to fit the deed to the crime. Nevertheless, it also demonstrated, however perversely, the productivity of censorship. For the very ambiguity of the prohibitions themselves shaped the texts and informed their tactics and strategy. In view of this productivity, I suggest, the link between heroic radicalism and libel trials is not coincidental, but structural.

The trials of William Hone illuminate changing censorship laws at this vitally important moment; they are exemplary in demonstrating the complex imbrication of seditious and blasphemous libel, and how this imbrication worked on the part of the Liverpool Tory government (1812–27) as a strategy of repression. The fact that censorship measures failed to distinguish between blasphemy and sedition made the system open to abuse by the government, as demonstrated by Lord Ellenborough's alteration of the original charge in Hone's third trial from sedition to blasphemy because he thought the charge of sedition would not result in a successful prosecution.

As well as its significance for the radical cause of political reform, the courtroom trial is an exemplary instantiation of the literary institution. As Pierre Bourdieu demonstrates in his analysis of the censorship trials of Baudelaire and Flaubert, the mid-nineteenth-century French courtroom trial is a vital form of symbolic practice in the so-called 'conquest of autonomy' of the literary sphere.[6] So too, I contend, is the post-Waterloo Regency period in England a vital and indeed initiatory period in the conquest of literary autonomy, and the assertion of this autonomy against the institutions of politics, law and religion. The Regency period (which dates constitutionally from 1811 until 1820, when the Prince Regent became George IV, but extends forward to George IV's death in 1830 and back to the first years of the nineteenth century) is marked by a rise in the number of publishers being targeted and taken to court by the state and a proliferation of sensational courtroom trials. This form of post-publication censorship facilitates the conquest of literary autonomy by providing a forum for the contestation of seditious, blasphemous and obscene libel laws through appeals to the multiplicity of meaning that later comes to be recognized as a prerogative of literature.

Of course, there is no pure aesthetic space: such an idea is invention.[7] Autonomy is provisional, and literature is always politically entailed, as Hone's writings amply demonstrate. However, this invention is productive, and the belief that the aesthetic *should* comprise an autonomous sphere and be able to constitute its own rules and interests, as distinct from those of law, politics and religion, was a transformative development in nineteenth-century culture. This autonomization of literature finds its origins in the Romantic cult of the author, and the Regency period is the high moment of canonical Romanticism when Byron, Shelley and Austen, for example, were all working. The pervasiveness of courtroom trials for seditious, blasphemous, and obscene libel during this period reminds us that the flourishing of Romanticism coincides with what Andrew Franta calls 'the rise of the law of libel'.[8]

III.

Hone's trials are instrumental for the emergence of the literary field in a period marked by courtroom trials that stage a face-off between the Tory government, in its defence of what William St Clair refers to as 'old-canon literature' (a kind of conduct literature directed at the 'reinforcement of what were regarded as the larger truths of natural religion'[9]), and radical or progressive publishers and labouring-class cultural producers and practitioners, who celebrate free-thinking, Enlightenment values and the democratization of cultural production. Hone was a pivotal figure not only for disseminating free-thinking culture to the masses, but also for doing so precisely through the forms of old-canon culture: recycled, parodied and resignified. Hone's writing is highly literary, extraordinarily intertextual and dense with allusion. It crafts its compelling political satires, by recycling popular genres such as nursery rhyme, almanacs, advertisements and songs, and circulating these in an intertextual loop with the Bible, and with ancient, medieval and modern works of politics, philosophy and literature, particularly the seventeenth-century classics of religious literature such as *Paradise Lost* and *Pilgrim's Progress* in which Hone's labouring-class Methodist upbringing had been steeped.

Hone's literariness and literary rhetoric are predicated on a highly developed conceptualization and practice of parody and allegory. Allegory is central both to religion and literature – to their complex interrelations and to the evolving distinction between them – and the Hone trials are so intriguing partly for how they spectacularized these interrelations. Hone was fascinated by allegory and saw it as a form of parody. 'Allegory is of the Nature of Parody', he wrote in the manuscript of the major work on parody that he planned, now held in the British Library.[10] This conjunction of allegory with parody speaks to the profoundly historical and literary quality of Hone's political parodies, and demonstrates how they were conceived not as opportunistic attacks but as complex and multilayered works of intertextuality.

Each of the three liturgical parodies that were prosecuted used a sacred genre (catechism, litany, creed) to mount a political critique. *The Late John Wilkes's Catechism*, the target of the first trial, took the catechism, a manual of questions and answers that were memorized by believers, to attack the repression of freedom of speech under the Liverpool cabinet. *The Political Litany*, subject of the second trial, took the litany, a series of petitions – invocations or supplications – recited by the clergy and responded to by the congregation, to attack the Prince Regent and the House of Lords: 'Son of

George, we beseech thee to hear us. ... O House of Lords, that takest away so many thousands of pounds in pensions, have mercy upon us'.[11] *The Sinecurist's Creed*, subject of the third and final trial, took the Athanasian Creed, which affirms a belief in the Holy Trinity (Father, Son and Holy Ghost), to attack the authority of the three most prominent ministers in the cabinet: George Canning, the moderate Tory cabinet minister, attacked both for political hypocrisy and for corruption and ransacking the public purse; Lord Castlereagh, the foreign minister, a supporter of violence in Ireland during the rebellion of the 1790s; and Henry Addington (Lord Sidmouth), Home Secretary: 'O blessed and glorious Trinity, three persons and one Minister, have mercy on us miserable subjects'.[12] The parody refers to these three, respectively, as 'Old Bags', 'Derry Down Triangle' (after the wooden frames on which Irish rebels were tortured) and 'The Doctor' (Canning's mocking term for his old rival Sidmouth).

The Late John Wilkes's Catechism was named after the patron saint of Regency radicalism, John Wilkes, who in 1776 introduced the first formal motion for parliamentary reform. This was after having himself been prosecuted for seditious and treasonable libel in 1763, for his criticism in the famous Number 45 of his radical journal the *North Briton* of the King's speech at the opening of Parliament. He too, like Hone, was charged with blasphemy as well as sedition, and had also used the government's own forums of power to mock the government. Hone's writings formed a primary medium for the dissemination of Wilkite radicalism.[13] A powerful re-animation of Wilkite traditions also occurred in the protests and alehouse festivities of the Spenceans – agricultural reformers in favour of land redistribution, named after Thomas Spence, the bookseller and agrarian reformer, who supported the redistribution of land and the anti-enclosure movement. The Spenceans met in pubs and taverns, sharing debates and satirical political toasts, and were singled out in the *Seditious Meetings Act* of 1817, after which they were eventually penetrated by spies. Hone's liturgical parodies were sung by the Spenceans as part of the counter-theatre of tavern entertainments, and were enormously popular throughout the country in 1817 even before the trials of December.[14]

Hone's *John Wilkes's Catechism* channels the rhetorical power of Wilkes's radical legacy to parody the catechism in its strict form as, according to the OED, 'a summary of the principle of a religion in the form of questions and answers':

> A Catechism, that is to say, An Instruction, to be learned of every Person before he be brought to be confirmed a Placeman or Pensioner by the Minister.
> Question.
> WHAT is your Name?
> Answer. Lick Spittle.
> Q. Who gave you this Name?
> A. My Sureties to the Ministry, in my Political Change, wherein I was made a member of the Majority, the Child of Corruption, and a Locust to devour the good Things of this Kingdom.
> Q. What did your Sureties then for you?

A. They did promise and vow three things in my Name. First, that I should renounce the Reformists and all their Works, the pomps and vanity of Popular Favour, and all the sinful lusts of Independence. Secondly, that I should believe all the Articles of the Court Faith. And thirdly, that I should keep the Minister's sole Will and Commandments, and walk in the same, all the days of my life.

Q. Dost thou not think that thou art bound to believe and to do as they have promised for thee?

A. Yes verily, and for my own sake, so I will; and I heartily thank our heaven-born Ministry, that they have called me to this state of elevation, through my own flattery, cringing, and bribery: and I shall pray to their successors to give me their assistance, that I may continue the same unto my life's end.

Q. Rehearse the Articles of thy Belief.

A. I believe in GEORGE, the Regent Almighty, maker of New Streets and Knights of the Bath.[15]

In Hone's parodic inversion of the catechism, the cause of reform is associated with the devil ('I renounce the Reformists and all their Works'), and popular favour and independence are cast as sins. The Minister replaces God as his 'sole Will and Commandments' replaces God's. Hone thereby attacks the government's identification of itself with divine law. And he is promptly prosecuted for this parody through the power of the (parodied) law that arrogates this divine authority.

Hone's parody of the Ten Commandments extends this critique by casting infractions against the people as rules of that same divine law:

VI. Thou shalt not call starving to death murder.
VII. Thou shalt not call Royal gallivanting adultery.
VIII. Thou shalt not say, that to rob the Public is to steal.
IX. Thou shalt bear false witness against the people.[16]

Each day, the Attorney General, Sir Samuel Shepherd, commenced proceedings by asserting that Hone's parodies, though political in content, worked to ridicule the liturgy they used. In his defence, Hone claimed he did not ridicule the scriptures but merely the politicians who abused scripture in their abuse of power. And Hone was breathtakingly emphatic in his declaration of intention in the *Political Litany*'s parodic supplication of Britain's 'rulers', writing here in the third person: 'He *intended* to laugh at them. They were his vindictive prosecutors, and his hypocritical persecutors; and laugh at them he would, till they ceased to be the objects of his laughter by ceasing to be Ministers'.[17]

Insisting on the purely political intentions of his parodies, which used Christian forms of public worship to satirize the government and assert the separation of religion and politics, Hone's tactic was to exploit the legal principle of precedent, launching spirited recitals of and providing commentary on celebrated historical parodies by figures such as Martin Luther, Bishop Latimer and even the serving government minister himself, George Canning: 'yes … Mr Canning, who ought, at that moment, to be standing in his place, but who had been raised to the rank of a Cabinet Minister, and was one of those very men who were now persecuting him. ... Mr Hone hoped that the Attorney-General would bring Mr. Canning to justice – (*Cheering*).[18]

In laying out its charges in the first trial, the government expressly denied that the parody was political, as though pre-empting Hone's defence: 'It has nothing of a political tendency about it, but it is avowedly, set off against the religion and worship of the Church of England, as established by Act of Parliament'.[19] Denying the charge of blasphemy, Hone testified to his own Christian principles, here again writing in the *Trials* in the third person:

> They were not to enquire whether he was a member of the Established Church or a Dissenter; it was enough that he professed himself to be a Christian. ... He had, however, been held up as a man unfit to live, as a blasphemer, a monster, a wretch; he had been called a wretch who had kept body and soul together by the sale of blasphemous publications.[20]

Hone was emphatic that the parody was not blasphemous. However, even if Hone's intentions were not blasphemous, as Hone himself insisted, the textual effects *were* – if by blasphemy we mean challenging the authority of the Church as identified with the State. For, by this construction, any challenge to the state was a challenge to God, and it was the effects rather than intentions that the state sought to suppress with its libel law. Treason, on the other hand, was concerned with intention.[21]

The Hone trials contributed to the emergence of literature as an autonomous sphere – somewhat counter-intuitively, it was the radical publisher who *limited* the text's meaning (to authorial intention), while the reactionary government *extended* it (to encompass textual effects). The trials provided a rhetorical and intellectual space for refining the distinction between form and content, and this distinction was critical to Hone's defence: the creed, the catechism and the Lord's Prayer were not the targets of satire, but its vehicles.[22] As Hone narrates of himself in *Three Trials*, '[h]e never intended by these parodies to excite ridicule against the Christian religion. ... His intention was merely political. It was done to excite a laugh. Was a laugh treason? Surely not'.[23] The distinction between form and content was crucial then both to the definition of literature and its function of aesthetic mediation, and to the political intention of the parodies: to separate precisely those spheres of religion and politics that were conflated in the government's misuse of the legislation.

IV.

Paradoxically, the decision to defend himself conferred certain privileges upon Hone: the right to call witnesses, to cross-examine and to review the case for the jury in a final speech. It was, in effect, to command a particular kind of audience. One of the great ironies of the trial is the fact that, while Hone was charged under legislation that was part of a heavily repressive policing of public meetings, the trial itself created its own public meetings and its own kind of subversive performance.

All three trials drew enthusiastic crowds, whose effusive audience-participation in the form of 'involuntary burst[s] of laughter' and 'loud huzzaing' perplexed the crown officials, who could only respond with some very feebly improvised and unwittingly self-parodic forms of crowd control. When the Attorney General read out Hone's lines: 'O House of Lords, that takest away so many thousands of pounds in pensions, have mercy upon us', there was, Hone tells us, 'an involuntary burst of laughter' from the crowd, to which the Attorney General responded with a lame rhetorical question: 'Will any one now say that the dangerous, the impious and profane publication before you, has not been the means of raising scoffing among the scoffers?'[24] Significantly, the audience was not confined to such popular scoffers and huzzaers, as Hone proudly recorded in the proceedings of the public meeting held to raise financial support after his acquittal: 'The Meeting was one of the most numerous and respectable we have for a long time witnessed. The great room was completely filled, at an early hour, by an anxious auditory, amongst whom we observed several elegantly dressed females.'[25] Indeed, the case galvanized support for the reform movement across gender, religion and class, from aristocratic Whigs, such as Francis Burdett, to literati such as Byron and Shelley (also aristocratic Whigs), and William Hazlitt and John Keats. The list of subscribers to raise funds for Hone included 'A Musselman, who thinks it would not be an impious Libel to Parody the Koran'.[26]

The crowds at Hone's trials were particularly delighted by the Attorney-General's required rendition of the *Late John Wilkes's Catechism of a Ministerial Member*, in which the member is enjoined 'to believe the words of Lord Castlereagh alone; to have remembrance of nothing but what is in the *Courier*'. The *Courier* was the Tory-aligned paper in which the Poet Laureate Robert Southey (referred to in another Hone parody as 'Slobber'd Mouthey') vilified Byron. As much as he might try to make the distinction between the genre and its parody stick – 'We say, "I believe in God," &c. &c.; here he says, "I believe in George, the Regent Almighty, Maker of New Streets, and Knight of the Bath"'[27] – the Attorney-General had no choice but to speak these libellous words. Moreover, he was compelled to perform them in such a way as to convince the jury of their libellous power (surely a contradictory enterprise if the intention was to secure a guilty verdict), unwillingly participating in the parodic celebration (denunciation) of 'George, the Regent Almighty' as the supreme creator of new streets and bogus titles, even as he sought to denounce it. The absurd, hilarious figure of 'George, the Regent Almighty' exposes the fact that the government's identification of the Regent with the Almighty underpinned its criminalization of freedom of speech.

The Political Litany relies on similar genre play, replacing 'Son of God, we beseech thee to hear us!' with 'Son of George, we beseech thee to hear us'. When read out in court by the Attorney General, declared Hone, 'these parts of the parody produced an involuntary burst of laughter from the auditory, which evidently proceeded, not from a wish to disturb the Court, but was really the irresistible impulse arising from the matter of the parody'.[28] The son of George was the scandalous Prince of Wales, who became Regent in 1811 after his father, 'mad' King George III, became too ill to reign, and who would reign in his own right as George IV from 1820. A dissolute womanizer, the Regent was also reviled across the political spectrum for putting his own wife on trial for adultery.[29]

In his turn, Hone was an able performer of his own written texts. His self-defence became a virtuosic, embodied performance of the printed parodies, fully realizing Hone's conception of the printed text as a performance event and enlisting the public's support through their 'involuntary' laughter and applause. In his conception, printed letters form a kind of collectivity, as words on the page, with a radical potential to disturb the peace. Hone's *Political Showman* of 1821 exclaims joyfully:

> [T]hese SEDITIOUS MEETINGS OF LETTERS! …
> O PRINTING! How hast thou *"disturbed the peace"*!

This text avenged his prosecution by representing the Liverpool government and its European allies in the popular entertainment forms of freak-show and cabinet of curiosities – 'walk up, walk up!' Here, in the illustration by Hone's collaborator, George Cruikshank, the printing press is presented as a nimble circus performer, much like Hone himself was in his trials (Fig. 2.1).

The vulnerability of the government's case against Hone was amply demonstrated by its perverse insistence on how vulnerable the Christian litany was (and even more so, 'pious minds') to forms of blasphemous parody. These enter Trojan-horse like:

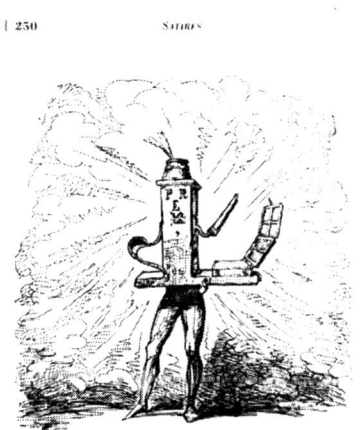

Fig. 2.1: 'The Showman,' from William Hone, *The Political Showman at Home!* (London: Printed for William Hone, 45, Ludgate Hill, 1821). [Source: https://archive.org/stream/politicalshowman00honeiala#page/n1/mode/2up]

> It was not necessary to remind the Jury that the Litany was a most solemn prayer
> to the Almighty, to the Redeemer of the World, and to the Holy Ghost, and had
> justly been considered the most sublime part of the public service of the Church;
> and it was impossible to make the most distant approach to its style and form in a
> parody, without exciting in the most pious mind ideas that would never otherwise
> have entered it; and the taint of profaneness and ridicule, even of the most sacred
> subjects, was rapidly disseminated.[30]

Here, the government relies on the historical imbrication of religion and law that
derived from the state's responsibility to protect the Church as a primary social institution. This sacred responsibility endowed the state, in turn, with the prerogative to
prosecute in the name of God, thereby endowing political power with divine power.

Hence, the prosecution invokes the authority of tradition as it quotes Matthew
Hale, the seventeenth-century judge and Chief Justice of the King's Bench (1671–5), to
the effect that 'the Christian religion is parcel of the Common Law of England'.[31] How
then to distinguish one from the other? This was where the state's power derived from
obscurity. It was the very incoherence and amorphousness of the 'blasphemous libel',
as distinct from 'seditious libel', much more narrowly defined, that made it particularly
useful for government prosecutions, and therefore open to government abuse. 'I take
this to be a proposition of law', said the Attorney-General, Sir Samuel Shepherd, 'that
he who attempts to parody these three sacred parts of Christian belief, and presents
them to the mind in a ridiculous shape, does that which is calculated to bring them
into contempt, and is, therefore, by the law of the land, guilty of a libel.'[32] But did
the divine almighty really need human protection from looking 'ridiculous' to mere
mortals? Maybe it was that idea that was ridiculous.

Thomas Starkie's *Treatise on the Law of Slander and Libel* (1812) acknowledged
precisely this: that it was 'absurd' to 'attempt to redress or avenge insults to a supreme
and omnipotent Creator'.[33] To remove such absurdity, Starkie reclassified blasphemy as a
threat to 'the very foundation of all human laws', thereby enabling it to come within the
purview of 'municipal laws'.[34] This echoed William Blackstone's *Commentaries* (1765–9),
which claimed that 'the sole consideration of the law [was] the tendency which all libels
have to create animosities, and to disturb the public peace'.[35] In this, the government had
a pretext for suppressing freedom of speech in the name of protecting social order.[36]

Hone's exuberant and mercurial flights of witty self-defence seized upon the
contradictions in this argument and exploited their full performative potential for the
assembled crowd. As he records in the *Three Trials*:

> Mr Justice Abbott thought it better that the defendant should not read any more
> of this parody: it could only shock the ears of well-disposed and religious persons;
> and he must again repeat that the law did not allow one offence to be vindicated
> by another. He wished the defendant would not read such things.[37]

To which Hone replied: 'I must go on with these parodies [...] or I cannot go on
with my defence'.[38] Hone eloquently underscored the incoherence of the law in its
incapacity to clearly delineate what constituted a libel:

The Attorney-General, and every man with whom laws originated, would do well to render them so clear, that they could be easily understood by all; that no person could be mistaken. Was it to be supposed that he, with a wife and a family of seven children, would, if his mind were ever so depraved, have sat down and written a libel, if he were aware it was one. None but a *maniac* would act so indiscreetly. There were, however, very few men who understood the law of libel. It was, in fact, a shadow – it was undefinable.[39]

In summing up in the first trial, the Attorney General directed the jury by emphasizing the legal principle that libel was concerned not with intentions but effects:

The intention of the party was to be gathered only from his acts; and even though the jury should be of opinion that the primary object of the defendant was not to ridicule and bring into contempt any part of the established forms of Divine worship, if that had been done incidentally, if it had been a secondary purpose and consequence, it would still be their duty to find him guilty.[40]

The judge, Lord Ellenborough, at times echoed the Attorney-General's views. In the third trial, Hone invoked the legal principle of Fox's 1792 Libel Bill that restored a system whereby juries, not judges, determined criminality, by questioning the propriety of the judge giving his opinion, and pointing out that 'the judge was not bound to give an opinion', and, more importantly, that 'the jury ... were not bound to follow his lordship's opinion'.[41]

The jury retired and returned to find the defendant not guilty:

NOT GUILTY.
 The loudest acclamations were instantly heard in all parts of the Court; *Long live the honest Jury*, and *an honest Jury for ever*, were exclaimed by many voices: the waving of hats, handkerchiefs, and applauses continued for several minutes. When order had been somewhat restored, My Justice ABBOTT interposed, and desired that those who felt inclined to rejoice at the decision, would reserve the expressions of their satisfaction for a fitter place and opportunity. The people accordingly left the Court, and as they proceeded along the streets, the language of joy was most loudly and unequivocally expressed; everyone with whom they met, and to whom they communicated the event, being forward to swell the peal.[42]

And so it was with the next two trials: not guilty. Hone's marvellous win – for the common people and the freedom of the press – and the instantaneity of Hone's celebrity in his account engender a new form of public worship, the *celebratio* (worshipful crowd), who celebrate not God and the Tory ministers, but the brilliant wit and showmanship of their contemporary radical hero.

So, in this way, the Crown's prosecution of Hone backfired by enabling a forum for the production of a blasphemous form of public worship: the attempt to suppress the blasphemous parodies produced instead a blasphemous public performance that erupted in joyful ridicule and re-animated forms of Wilkite popular protest, carrying the torch for Wilkes and his cause of parliamentary reform. If, as the crown argued, Hone's parodic print publications were seditious because blasphemous, the trials themselves re-mediated and amplified this seditious parodic ridicule by eliciting popular protest against the repressive prosecuting Christian state. While the audience's laughter was, as Hone's printed versions of the trials claimed, to some extent 'involuntary' and the effect of an 'irresistible impulse', the audience's performance can also be understood in relation to the logic of Wilkite popular protest in the defence of the freedom of the press and parliamentary reform. As Joseph M. Butwin notes, 'Hone and his judges see the laughter of the audience as a political response, sought by one, forbidden by the other'.[43] The capacity of Hone's self-defence to turn the courtroom into a space of what Butwin refers to as 'seditious laughter' demonstrates the vulnerability of the government and of a regime that used libel laws to censor public speech. And that capacity to enjoin laughter was vindicated by the jury's judgement: 'Was a laugh treason?' Hone asked, to which the answer was a resounding 'No'.[44] This judgement was seen as a triumph also for the democratic principle of Fox's 1792 Libel Act in empowering juries to determine criminality.

What also backfired was the government's attempt to conscript Hone in the production of a distinction between polite literature and its vulgar other. For, while the government sought to present Hone as that vulgar other, he was in fact the embodiment of literature's wit and transformative power, just as he so forcefully embodied and articulated the radical case of reform.

V.

Hone's religious parodies and the trials constitute a vital event in an evolving distinction between literature and blasphemy. Literature is both an emergent social institution and a liminal category of analysis at this particular historical moment and in the social space of Regency Britain. Hone's trials, I contend, are so significant in the history of the relationship between literature and censorship because they illuminate powerfully how the developing institution of literature was produced, partly through the contested meanings that emerged in these courtroom trials. These worked to strengthen and refine the distinction between the literal and the figurative upon which the institution of literature was predicated as the domain of the figurative.

Censorship trials were vitally important to the emergence of the modern literary institution and literature as a category. For it is precisely in arguing why a text is not blasphemous, seditious or obscene that a conception of literature starts to develop. Literature develops as a form of writing that is something other than scripture, and not simply other to scripture but richly distinct and multifaceted: ludic, imaginative, experimental, parodic, satirical and explorative. By forcing the development of such argument and the distinction between the offensive and the literary, the institution of censorship can be said to function productively, however perversely.

Hone's trials illuminate a vital, if liminal, moment in the history of censorship by exposing how the identification of blasphemy with sedition enabled government repression in post-Waterloo Regency Britain.[45] They demonstrate the Tory government's sleight of hand by which attacks on the government were cast as attacks on God, and Hone's acquittal by jury in a court of law gave this critique powerful institutional legitimation. Through his embodied performance and re-reading of the parodies Hone also demonstrated the extraordinary productivity of censorship as a mode of cultural and specifically literary production: *not* by acknowledging the power of the state but by resisting it and turning its forms on itself. Even more delightful was the fact that Hone's prosecutors became accomplices in this performance of seditious and blasphemous mirth.

As John Keats wrote of Hone's acquittal, 'Lord Ellenborough has been paid in his own coin'.[46] Such triumphs under a brutally repressive and violent government regime (one that would shortly turn its own cavalry upon its peacefully demonstrating citizens in the Peterloo massacre of 1819) were rare, precious and duly honoured. Hone's acquittal was celebrated by Keats, in a letter to his brothers, George and Tom Keats, of 22 December, just after the acquittal, as a triumph of English liberty: 'Hone the publisher's trial, you must find very amusing; & as Englishmen very encouraging – his *Not Guilty* is a thing, which not to have been, would have dulled still more Liberty's Emblazoning'.[47] Recounting a dinner conversation with a group of 'fashionables', Keats recounts how:

> several things dovetailed in my mind, & at once it struck me, what quality went to form a Man of Achievement especially in Literature & which Shakespeare possessed so enormously – I mean *Negative Capability*, that is when man is capable of being in uncertainties, Mysteries, doubts, without any irritable reaching after fact & reason – Coleridge, for instance.[48]

Keats refers directly here to Shakespeare as he produces his famous coinage 'negative capability', and the term has ever since almost always been understood as referring exclusively to Shakespeare. However, to do this is to ignore the compelling digressive, associative and metonymic logic at work in Keats' letter, where Shakespeare, Coleridge and Edmund Kean performing *Richard III* are all invoked associatively in the conversational orbit of the figure, and which in fact brings it back to Hone. This logic works its way to the powerful dialectical figure of the 'Not Guilty' as a form of 'Liberty's Emblazoning', and to Hone's particular kind of oppositional energy and digressive, allegorical power, as the most fully embodied form of negative capability. It is Hone's triumphant 'Not Guilty' verdict that offers the most exemplary form of negative capability, and that can therefore be seen as a key contextual event in Keats' formulation of the term. Not just Hone's verdict, but the powerful rhetorical work of Hone's parodies as written texts and embodied performances, all represent a profoundly important 'Achievement … in Literature' and a powerful act and articulation of the principles of radical opposition.

Such negative capability also describes the spirit of blasphemous joy that attended the trials and spilled out into the street after the acquittal. It is the dialectical energy of the exultant crowd of 25,000 that greeted Hone outside the Guildhall, which 'proceeded along the streets [where] the language of joy was most loudly

and unequivocally expressed [and where] everyone with whom they met, and to
whom they communicated the event, being forward [*sic*] to swell the peal' (*Three
Trials* 70). The crowd went to the City of London Tavern, where, on Monday 29
December, a Meeting of the Friends of the Liberty of the Press raised a subscription
for Hone.

Amidst the toasts and cheers, the government actors in this courtroom drama
would also have been given their due for playing their part in this popular counter-
ritual and radical triumph – not least for delivering Hone's lines. For negative
capability marks, too, the perverse productivity of a censorship that seeks to silence
but instead magnifies radical eloquence, blasphemous joy and seditious celebration.

Notes

1 A. Aspinall and E. Anthony Smith (eds), *English Historical Documents*, Vol XI
   1783–1832 (London: Eyre & Spottiswoode, 1959), pp. 319–22, 330, 335–9.

2 Joss Marsh, *Word Crimes: Blasphemy, Culture, and Literature in Nineteenth-Century
   England* (Chicago: University of Chicago Press, 1998), p. 18.

3 Mark Rose, 'The Author in Court: *Pope v. Curll* (1741)', in Martha Woodmansee and
   Peter Jaszi (eds), *The Construction of Authorship: Textual Appropriation in Law and
   Literature* (Durham, NC: Duke University Press, 1994), p. 214.

4 E. P. Thompson, *The Making of the English Working Class* (London: Penguin, 1977),
   p. 660.

5 William Cobbett, *Cobbett's Political Register* (London, 1814), pp. 196–8.

6 Pierre Bourdieu, *The Rules of Art: Genesis and Structure of the Literary Field* (trans.
   S. Emmanuel) (Stanford, CA: Stanford University Press, 1995), p. 47.

7 Ibid., p. 105ff.

8 Andrew Franta, *Romanticism and the Rise of the Mass Public* (Cambridge: Cambridge
   University Press, 2007), p. 143.

9 William St Clair, *The Reading Nation in the Romantic Period* (Cambridge: Cambridge
   University Press, 2004), pp. 133–4.

10 William Hone, 'History of Parody', BL Add. MS 40108. William Hone Papers (British
   Library, London), F.317r.

11 William Hone, *The Three Trials of William Hone, for Publishing Three Parodies; viz.
   The Late John Wilkes's Catechism, The Political Litany, and the Sinecurist's Creed;
   on Three Ex-Officio Informations, at Guildhall, London, on Three Successive Days*
   (London: Printed by and for William Hone, 67, Old Bailey, 1818), p. 74.

12 Ibid., p. 173.

13 Marcus Wood, *Radical Satire and Print Culture, 1790–1822* (Oxford: Clarendon Press,
   1994), pp. 115–21.

14 See Ian McCalman, *Radical Underworld: Prophets, Revolutionaries, and Pornographers
   in London, 1795–1840* (Oxford: Clarendon Press, 1998), pp. 18ff., 122–3.

15 Hone, *Three Trials*, p. 8.

16 Ibid.

17 Ibid., p. 126.

18 Ibid., p. 45, 59.

19 Ibid., p. 4.
20 Ibid., p. 14.
21 See Franta, *Romanticism and the Rise of the Mass Public*, p. 145.
22 Marsh, *Word Crimes*, p. 35.
23 Hone, *Three Trials*, p. 126.
24 Ibid., p. 74.
25 William Hone, *Trial by Jury and Liberty of the Press*, 2nd edn (London: Printed by and for William Hone, 67 Old Bailey, 1818), p. 3.
26 Ibid., p. 22.
27 Hone, *Three Trials*, p. 5.
28 Ibid., p. 74.
29 See Mary Spongberg's essay on the Queen Caroline affair in this volume.
30 Hone, *Three Trials*, p. 102.
31 Ibid., p. 2.
32 Ibid., p. 4
33 Qtd in Marsh, *Word Crimes*, p. 19.
34 Ibid.
35 William Blackstone's *Commentaries on the Laws of England*, 4 vols (Oxford: Clarendon Press, 1765–9), IV, p. 150.
36 In December 1819, the government went one step further with the *Blasphemous and Seditious Libels Act,* which linked blasphemy and sedition, and tightened the screws on the popular press by giving magistrates the power to search private as well as public houses and by adding a 4d. tax on periodical publications. It also provided for transportation for publishers convicted twice of seditious libel.
37 Hone, *Three Trials*, p. 20.
38 Ibid.
39 Ibid., p. 38.
40 Ibid., p. 66.
41 Ibid., p. 148, p. 186.
42 Ibid., p. 70.
43 Joseph M. Butwin, 'Seditious Laughter', *Radical History Review*, 18 (1978): 19.
44 Hone, *Three Trials*, p. 126.
45 In January 1817, the parodic homily *The Black Dwarf,* by Hone's friend Thomas Wooler, had also attacked the government's exploitation of religion's imbrication with law, in a parody of the King James Bible: 'The LORD giveth, and the LORDS taketh away. Blessed be the way of the LORDS' (Wooler, p. 3).
46 John Keats, 'Letter to George and Tom Keats, 21, 27 (?) December 1817', in Robert Gittings and Jon Mee (eds), *Selected Letters* (Oxford: Oxford University Press, 2002), p. 41.
47 Ibid.
48 Ibid., p. 42.

References

Aspinall, A. and E. Anthony Smith (eds), *English Historical Documents*, Vol XI 1783–1832, London: Eyre & Spottiswoode, 1959.

Blackstone, W., *Commentaries on the Laws of England*, 4 vols. Oxford: Clarendon Press, 1765–69.

Bourdieu, P., *The Rules of Art: Genesis and Structure of the Literary Field* (trans. S. Emmanuel), Stanford: Stanford University Press, 1995.

Butwin, J., 'Seditious Laughter', *Radical History Review*, 18 (1978): 17–34.

Cobbett, W., *Cobbett's Political Register*, London, 1814.

Franta, A., *Romanticism and the Rise of the Mass Public*, Cambridge: Cambridge University Press, 2007.

Hone, W., 'History of Parody', BL Add. MS 40108. William Hone Papers. British Library, London.

Hone, W., *The Three Trials of William Hone, for publishing Three Parodies; viz. The Late John Wilkes's Catechism, The Political Litany, and the Sinecurist's Creed; on Three Ex-Officio Informations, at Guildhall, London, on Three Successive Days*, London: Printed by and for William Hone, 67, Old Bailey, 1818.

Hone, W., *Trial by Jury and Liberty of the Press*, London: Printed by and for William Hone, 67 Old Bailey, 1818. 2nd edn.

Hone, W., *The Political Showman – At Home! Exhibiting his Cabinet of Curiosities and Creatures – All Alive!* London, Printed for William Hone, 1821.

Keats, J., 'Letter to George and Tom Keats, 21, 27 (?) December 1817', in *Selected Letters*, R. Gittings and J. Mee (eds), Oxford: Oxford University Press, 2002.

Marsh, J., *Word Crimes: Blasphemy, Culture, and Literature in Nineteenth-Century England*, Chicago: University of Chicago Press, 1998.

McCalman, I., *Radical Underworld: Prophets, Revolutionaries, and Pornographers in London, 1795–1840*, Oxford: Clarendon, 1998.

Rose, Mark. 'The Author in Court: *Pope v. Curll* (1741)', in Martha Woodmansee and Peter Jaszi (eds), *The Construction of Authorship: Textual Appropriation in Law and Literature*, Durham, NC: Duke University Press, 1994, pp. 211–29.

St Clair, W., *The Reading Nation in the Romantic Period*, Cambridge: Cambridge University Press, 2004.

Thompson, E. P., *The Making of the English Working Class*, London: Penguin, 1977.

Wood, M., *Radical Satire and Print Culture, 1790–1822*, Oxford: Clarendon, 1994.

Wooler, T., *Black Dwarf*, 1 (1817).

3

The Gender of Censorship: John Wilson Croker, Mary Hays and the Aftermath of the Queen Caroline Affair

Mary Spongberg

Even before the 'Queen Caroline Affair' in 1820, the marriage of England's George IV to Caroline of Brunswick had provided ample opportunities for the production of the sort of political pornography that many Britons had come to associate with the *ancien régime* in France.[1] Histories of British censorship during this period tend to focus on the state's failure to curb the growth of such literature, suggesting that a more liberal and tolerant attitude to such materials prevailed. Certainly attempts to censor materials savaging the royal marriage appear to have been half-hearted and haphazard. It was rumoured that the Prince of Wales paid the famed caricaturist George Cruikshank £100 not to draw his 'His Majesty in any immoral situation'.[2] The palace also bought up many 'secret histories' and other porno-political tracts to avoid the hint of scandal that they inevitably caused. Fox's 1792 Libel Act had restored the right of juries to decide what constituted libel and whether a defendant was guilty. The Act had fostered a free press in Britain and generated the belief that an Englishman 'might publish anything which twelve of his countrymen think is not blameable'.[3] Given the low esteem in which the Prince of Wales was generally held following his 'secret' marriage to the Catholic widow Maria Fitzherbert, and his much publicized affairs with actresses and the wives of peers, attempts to censor such materials brought them to greater public notice, further damaging his already tawdry reputation.[4]

By the end of the Napoleonic wars, the Prince of Wales, now Prince Regent, had become so unpopular that the British government intervened to curtail the freedom of the press and adopted other measures to inhibit political protest. A variety of Acts were passed to gag the kind of political protest expressed in cheap press outlets such as William Cobbett's *Weekly Political Register* and T. J. Wooler's *Black Dwarf*, as discussed in Clara Tuite's essay preceding (Chapter 2). In 1817, habeas corpus was suspended and the Home Secretary Henry Addington, Lord Sidmouth, abrogated to magistrates the power to issue warrants for the arrest of anyone suspected of seditious or blasphemous libel. Such action, as Joss Marsh has observed, marked 'a startling, not to say unconstitutional extension of power to an untrained body of state officials'.[5] Many radical writers and publishers were arrested. Yet even the passing of the newly repressive 'Six Acts' in 1819, which included a *Criminal Libel Act*, proved largely ineffective in preventing the lampooning of the sexual politics of the period, and failed to stop the avalanche of scandalous materials pertaining to the royal marriage that appeared when Caroline returned from exile on the Continent to be crowned alongside her erstwhile husband.

Caroline's appearance in England in June 1820, and George IV's tyrannical attempts to divorce her, fuelled public appetite for such seditious materials. Earlier works that had been produced in the wake of the 'Delicate Investigation' resurfaced and, as the trial of Queen Caroline for adultery commenced, these works were expanded upon with new material garnered from the evidence.[6] Scandalous histories of George's mistresses were also drawn from earlier works and incorporated into the 'pro-Caroline canon'.[7] Caroline's trial provided confirmation of much sexual misconduct, and neither the King nor the Queen were spared in the wealth of satirical prints and pamphlets that appeared at this time. Working-class radicals and middle-class reformers alike used this opportunity to publicize the King's unfitness for the throne, his drunkenness, his bigamous marriage to Mrs Fitzherbert and his frequent adulteries.[8] Men such as William Hone, who had been brought to trial for blasphemous sedition in 1817, as Tuite's essay in this volume elaborates, were at liberty three years later to produce mountains of smutty literature satirizing the sexual politics of the royal marriage. The palace again sought to suppress such works, by offering hefty payments to their publishers, but such action led to the further production of pirate editions and imitations, often more scandalous than the originals.[9]

The history of censorship during the Queen Caroline Affair is thus told as the story of its failure. For Thomas Laqueur, censorship failed in 1820 because England lacked the elaborate system of court patronage and extensive network of censors that had ensured those who subjected the French king to such ribald derision risked serious punishment.[10] Iain McCalman, however, suggests rather that the sheer volume of smut produced in the period overwhelmed the government, making censorship unfeasible.[11] These histories of censorship are ostensibly masculinist histories, the stories of ultra-radical male writers and publishers who used the sexual politics of the Regency to damage the monarchy and threaten the establishment. The idea that censorship failed in this period has rarely been interrogated. Yet the existence of volumes of quasi-pornographic political pamphlets does not in itself indicate the complete failure of censorship. This chapter will argue that the focus on radical men and their particular critique of the royal marriage has obscured an alternative history of censorship, a gendered history, that might account for the silence of women in these debates.

The very idea that the state needed to intervene to silence or suppress political opinion is, in itself, something that pertains largely to the activities of men in this period, and indeed perhaps throughout history. The right of women to a political voice, or to address ideas or opinions publicly, or even to express them privately, was frequently contested. It has rarely required the instruments of state to gag women's voices, given their subordination to their male kin. Yet, and perhaps because of this subordination, English women identified with the Queen and rallied on her behalf. Women's participation in the popular protests around the Queen's trial is often regarded as contributing to the rise of domestic ideology that blossomed during the Victorian period and came to characterize the English middle classes.[12] There is, however, little evidence of female-authored moral commentary on the royal marriage and there are very few female-authored texts specifically dealing with the 'Queen Caroline Affair'. Unlike in the 1790s, when women were remarkably prolific in their production of political critique in the form of novels and plays, political tracts and poetry, few individual female voices can be discerned either in defence or condemnation of Queen Caroline.

The female radicalism of the 1790s was, of course, short-lived, and in the early years of the nineteenth century few women wrote explicitly political novels or plays. The scandal that followed the publication of William Godwin's revealing *Memoirs of the Author of a Vindication of the Rights of Woman* (1797) damaged the reputation of his dead wife, Mary Wollstonecraft, and produced a rabid anti-Jacobin offensive against the women writers of her circle. In the years between the death of Mary Wollstonecraft and the return of Queen Caroline to England, those women who chose to write on political subjects were the subject of vitriolic critiques from male reviewers from all sides of the spectrum. The 'war of ideas' that characterized the 1790s was reanimated during the Queen Caroline Affair, as was the misogyny that characterized the anti-Jacobin response to Godwin.[13] Edmund Burke's idea that the Queen was owed generous loyalty due to her rank and sex was again debated, but in 1820 the context was very different. The ill-fated Queen was not set upon by ruffians in her boudoir, but rather maltreated by her husband, the King of England.

Early histories of Victorian feminism argued that women's political protest was critical to Caroline's acquittal, positioning the Affair as an important landmark in the formation of the middle class and the consequent rise of interest in the 'woman's cause'. Such a trajectory has been contested, however. 'Public opinion' during this period was, as Dror Wahrman has observed, emphatically male.[14] While male radicals wrote on behalf of women during the Queen Caroline Affair, for the most part women themselves engaged in collective acts of protest, particularly the signing of petitions.[15] These petitions celebrated the virtues of the Queen and condemned George IV's attempt to divorce his wife. Such petitions were written in a tone of submission and deference, using 'the language of "separate spheres" to justify or legitimize' women's participation in politics, rather than to challenge the sexual double standard.[16] Such acquiescent language did not necessarily protect women petitioners, whose very engagement in the political process saw them represented as 'shameless females' who 'insulted the King'.[17] While Caroline's cause became the 'woman's cause', women's political voices were very much constrained, both by defenders of the Queen and by those who would assail her.[18]

This chapter interrogates the strangely muted quality of female protest during the affair, suggesting not that women's political voices were suppressed by censorship, but rather that female support for the Queen was subdued by the lewd nature of political protest, both for and against the Queen. While it is impossible to write a history of censorship around what has not been written, analysing the ways in which men silence women or render it impossible for them to voice political dissent can provide an important counter-narrative in this period. While Dror Wahrman has written about the ways in which women were excluded from the more radical protests against the King, in this chapter I wish to focus on the vicious rearguard action against the Queen led by the King's chief supporter, John Wilson Croker (1780–1857), and the sole female respondent to his campaign, Mary Hays (1759–1843).[19] This campaign generated an atmosphere that made it impossible for respectable women to write or, indeed, appear in support of the Queen, and turned the tide against her in the months before her death. Croker believed that the press was one of the main vectors for revolution and asserted that the 'most ambitious agitators would rapidly tailor their principles to any mass movement regardless of its "humbug"'.[20] Yet during the Queen Caroline Affair he manipulated the press to his own ends, damaging the reputation of the Queen irreparably, while defending the sexual double standard that had long characterized aristocratic sexual mores.

Only one woman, the writer Mary Hays, steeled in the scandal that followed Mary Wollstonecraft's supporters after her death, risked her reputation to speak out against this campaign and the double standard that Croker enshrined in his defence of the King. Following the trial of Queen Caroline, he used the press to damage the reputation of any woman who appeared to support her. That Hays came out of retirement to write a defence of Queen Caroline, titled *Memoirs of Queens, Illustrious and Celebrated,* in 1821, has never been examined by historians of the Queen Caroline Affair, nor has her inauguration of the genre of collective royal lives received much attention from literary critics.[21] Yet *Memoirs of Queens* provides an important example of how censorious social conditions can produce distinctive forms of expression, revealing much in this instance about the gendering of history and of censorship.[22]

John Wilson Croker and the anti-Caroline campaign

John Wilson Croker, Irish politician and Secretary to the Admiralty, was a founding editor of the *Quarterly Review,* and in this capacity he had already done much to stifle the works of writers whose politics he reviled. Croker was kin to Edmund Burke, both through marriage and through shared political temperament. He despised the French Revolution and those who admired its principles. In the pages of the *Quarterly Review,* he initiated a second 'war of ideas' that reanimated the debate between Mary Wollstonecraft and Edmund Burke, and revived negative attitudes to women writers from male critics on all sides of the political spectrum.[23] Croker's early reviewing for the *Quarterly* was marked by a misogynist approach towards women who dared to write on politics in England or the war with France. He viewed the works of Anna Laetitia Barbauld and Fanny Burney as extending the 'war of ideas' promoted by Jacobin writers such as Wollstonecraft and was scathing in his commentaries. His reviews of Barbauld's epic poem 'Eighteen-Hundred and Eleven' in 1812 and Burney's novel *The Wanderer* in 1814 effectively ended their careers.[24] In the wake of his criticism, Barbauld never published poetry again, nor did Burney write another novel. Many critics have pondered the extreme misogyny of his response to Burney, who was no Jacobin.[25] Croker savaged Burney's prose and condemned the novel 'with astonishingly gendered ferocity, as an antiquated form emanating from a fatally female author', as Jocelyn Harris has observed.[26] Croker's review undoubtedly damaged the reception of *The Wanderer*, but also appeared designed to specifically attack the genre preferred by most women writers of the period.

Croker was a master political propagandist and, from the moment Caroline sought to return to England, he became the King's chief damage controller. It was he who had insisted that the Queen's name be struck from the liturgy, as he argued that such inclusion would be 'a final settlement of all questions in her favour'.[27] Croker understood the symbolic power of this gesture; indeed, he described it later as a 'vitally holy act' and argued that the King had no option but to take such an action, as he had been presented 'with the existence of a prima facie case, of gross and long continued adultery, alleged to be committed by the Princess of Wales, now de jure the Queen'.[28]

The Queen's 'acquittal' allowed forces loyal to the King to mount a rearguard action against her, using evidence presented at the trial to smear her reputation and vindicate the King.[29] Croker kept a stable of willing writers in his service to defame Caroline and damage the reputation of women who supported the Queen.[30] One such writer, Theodore Hook, assisted Croker in this task, establishing the *John Bull* in 1820, a scurrilous weekly periodical produced to combat Caroline's popularity.[31] While early biographers claimed that Croker had no connection with the *John Bull*, it now seems certain he was intimately involved with its editor and its production.[32]

Hook had been a minor government official, but by 1820 he sustained himself as a writer.[33] In the *John Bull*, Hook, a skilled comic, consciously adopted the 'very weapons' used by radicals against the King to instill loyalty and traduce the Queen and her female supporters.[34] Croker was an avid archivist and had established an extensive collection of testimonies from those who survived the French Revolution. He collected scandalous gossip about the Queen in the same way and these salacious tales filled *John Bull*.[35] Always committed to the 'facts', Croker had no qualms about revealing whatever was known of the Queen's sexual activities. The editorial of the first issue bears the stamp of Croker's style and his obsession with the damaging power of the press to sway public opinion and morality. The journal announced it was on the side of right and intended 'to speak "the plain truth" about the Queen and her supporters.[36] In this first edition, too, the paper publicly named the wives of Whig grandees who had visited the Queen, while also besmirching their reputation. Using the pretext that such women had come forward to 'vouch for the Queen's purity', *John Bull* reported that it would 'enquire into the value of their evidence, and the motives which have induced them to distinguish themselves in this marked and indelicate manner from all other women of England'.[37]

Such an excuse gave the editors licence to publish various secrets about such women, including the scandalous claim that the wife of the Queen's Whig lawyer Henry Brougham had given birth to a baby less than nine months after her marriage. In the second edition more women were targeted. In her letters of the period Harriet, Countess Granville wrote:

> There is a new paper, which causes great sensation. Its object seems to be to frighten women from visiting the Queen. Its name is 'John Bull'. The first victim is

the Duchess of Bedford giving an account of her attachment to the first Duke, her marriage with this. Lady Jersey next, very abusive. Mrs Brougham's seven months' child … It is an odious publication both as to its motive and its execution.[38]

Threatened with such scrutiny, few women continued to visit the Queen and this further diminished Caroline's position.

Such outrageous material ensured *John Bull's* instant success.[39] The first edition sold out within hours and by its fifth week circulation reached around 10,000 copies.[40] In its wake, an 'explosion' of loyalist tracts and newspapers appeared, using similar tactics to counter pro-Caroline propaganda.[41] Radical support for the Queen evaporated as this relentless wave of anti-Caroline materials emerged.

Croker also sought to win the hearts and minds of those less likely to be won over by such coarse means. With the permission of George IV, he produced a *Letter from the King to His People*, a splendid piece of political propaganda that ran through 28 editions in the period between the Queen's trial and her death in August 1821. This was not an apologia for errant behaviour as might be expected in such a circumstance. Croker instead penned a revisionary history of England, in which the French Revolution and the rise of radicalism in Britain are cited as the true causes of the Brunswick-Hanover marriage. George IV is painted as the hapless victim of the situation, a Prince pressed into service of a country in crisis and forced into an expedient but loveless marriage. While aimed at a more discerning audience than *John Bull*, the *Letter* contained equally volatile material, including the unchivalrous claim that Caroline was not a virgin when she married. The 'generous loyalty to rank and sex' so cherished by Burke was violently cast aside by Croker as he refuted point by point every assertion of her innocence made by the Queen's supporters. Croker's revelations negated claims that the King had abandoned Caroline, exposing her to the difficulties and temptations she had faced since their separation, thus rendering invalid her chief line of defence.[42] Croker's assertion that the 'virtual dissolution' of royal marriage occurred with its consummation effectively absolved the King of all his subsequent adulteries, while also demolishing Caroline's reputation.[43]

Croker systematically deconstructed every tale of Caroline's victimization that had circulated since the first days of her marriage, always offering 'proof' of her wrongdoing: in his version of the Regency, the Princess alone is to blame for the decadence of the period. Challenging Caroline's regal status, Croker asked rhetorically:

> If therefore I am to define the office or duty of a Queen consort, I might sum it up in a few words, 'To give a tone to the morals of the country'. Does not the late reign furnish an indisputable proof of the truth of this axiom? [44]

Casting George IV not as King but as victimized husband, Croker appealed to the men of Britain to uphold the double standard of morality, plaintively pleading: 'Would any husband in England take back such a wife?'[45]

Edmund Burke had represented the invasion of Marie Antoinette's boudoir as emblematic of the worst excesses of the French revolution and eloquently mourned the veil of modesty this had torn away from the monarchy. He had steadfastly refused to acknowledge any fault on the part of the French Queen, ignoring evidence of her political intrigues and casting her instead as a timid gothic heroine. Burke's system of *antient chivalry* required such an image of the Queen, and he had been generally despised for such 'foppery'.[46] No such system informed Croker and his cronies, who left no shred of this veil intact, exposing the monarchy to further disrepute by revealing sensational details of the Queen's private life. The right of men to a different standard of sexual morality was taken for granted by the King's defenders and asserted vigourously in the pamphlet war that erupted again after the Queen's 'acquittal'. This time it was supporters of the King who produced mountains of smut to blacken the Queen's reputation. While such men celebrated 'gallantry', this gallantry did not extend to preserving the reputation of their Queen. In the face of these revelations, the homage Burke insisted was owed all women, but especially Queens, proved false, as Wollstonecraft had contended long before. In her last months the Queen, her reputation permanently sullied, was left friendless and unprotected until her timely death in August 1821.

Memoirs of Queens

By focusing on the one female-authored text from the period that responded to Croker's campaign, Hays' *Memoirs of Queens, Illustrious and Celebrated* (1821), it is possible to write a different history of women's participation in this affair. Mary Hays, rational dissenter and friend of Mary Wollstonecraft, was perhaps best known for the scandal that erupted upon the publication of her *Memoirs of Emma Courtney* in 1796. In this semi-autobiographical 'novel', Hays tracked the consequences of her experiment with Godwinian philosophy, as a warning to other women. Through her correspondence with Godwin, Hays had come to believe that women were endangered by his insistence upon sincerity. She wrote to him in 1795 complaining 'I repent of the confidence I have reposed in you – I repent of the ingenuousness of every part of my past conduct. Sincerity is a fine theory – I have tried it, but find it impracticable – *I am its victim*'.[47] Contemporary readers, however, ignored the 'warning' Hays issued in her Preface, and instead focused on the unconventional love story that framed the novel. The autobiographical elements of the text, drawn from Hays unhappy affair with Cambridge mathematician William Friend, and her explicit valorization of women's eroticism, ensured that critics conflated her life and work, representing both as 'an erotic soap-opera, Rousseau's Julie in burlesque'.[48]

Hays' disillusionment with Godwinian philosophy was reinforced by the furore that greeted the appearance of his *Memoirs of the Author of A Vindication of the Rights of Woman*, in the months following Wollstonecraft's death. Godwin's painful recollections of his all too brief life with Wollstonecraft became the object through which women writers on all sides of the political spectrum were vilified in the private writings of conservative men and in the anti-Jacobin press. Even men such as Robert Southey and William Roscoe who knew and admired Wollstonecraft, felt stymied by the *Memoirs*. Southey observed that Godwin stripped 'his dead wife naked', while

Roscoe in a less reverent tone complained that Godwin had mourned Wollstonecraft 'with a heart of stone'.[49] Wollstonecraft and her circle were represented in the anti-Jacobin press as unsexed, and their literary endeavours depicted as morally dangerous and politically treacherous. Such hostile commentary effectively silenced radical women during this period, threatening with disgrace those who claimed friendship with Wollstonecraft.

Hays was the only woman who publicly defended Wollstonecraft at this moment. She produced the first memorial of Wollstonecraft in the *Monthly Magazine* in September 1797. Hays' name was not published with that memoir, but in the next edition of the journal, she appended a note apologizing for this oversight. In 1800 she produced a more detailed obituary: 'Memoirs of Mary Wollstonecraft' in the *Annual Necrology*. Although Hays had been subject to much abuse in the intervening years, she resisted being cowed by her reactionary critics and celebrated the flawed life of her dear friend. She did not shy away from discussing Wollstonecraft's breach with accepted mores, particularly her tragic affair with the American adventurer Gilbert Imlay. Unlike Godwin, who defined Wollstonecraft as a Rousseauvian heroine, Hays presented Wollstonecraft's life choices as constrained by 'sexual distinction' – her straitened circumstances as a woman, her relative seclusion, her poverty and lack of education. Hays believed that the 'sexual distinction' respecting chastity was the most 'fruitful source of the greater part of the infelicity and corruption of society'.[50] In 'Memoirs of Wollstonecraft', she rejected the double standard of sexual morality that had damaged Wollstonecraft's posthumous reputation, instead rendering her experiments in eroticism as the very stuff from which Wollstonecraft's feminist philosophy evolved.[51] Wollstonecraft's reputation was not salvaged by Hays, however, and Hays' own reputation was further sullied. Although she published the very successful *Female Biography* in 1803, she retreated from public life, a retreat that has been frequently attributed to a conservative shift in her politics.

In 1821, Hays came out of retirement to defend Queen Caroline. In *Memoirs of Queens*, she again risked opprobrium by attacking the King and challenging the double standard of morality that saw Queen Caroline vilified and condemned in the brief period between her trial and death. That Hays chose to produce this work in the period when radical support of the Queen had disappeared challenges the idea that her commitment to Wollstonecraftian feminism had declined, but it also suggests an important counter-narrative to the history of censorship in this period. While Hays' work was not censored, her contribution to the Queen Caroline Affair and the failure of modern critics to engage with this extraordinary political protest extend the parameters we must consider when we examine the suppression of women's political voices.

Although we cannot know for certain when Hays began to write her biography of Queen Caroline, textual evidence suggests that it was completed in the dark days that followed Caroline's acquittal but before her death in August 1821. Like many radicals of the time, Hays was troubled by the tyrannous behaviour of George IV and his supporters in the House of Lords. She did not, however, join the ranks of female petitioners who represented Caroline as an aggrieved wife and a grieving mother; rather, she penned a political biography of the Queen that critiqued the sexual double standard and vehemently denounced George IV and his supporters.

Gary Kelly has observed that Hays used her *Memoirs of Queens* to write a 'history of the wrongs of woman in the highest ranks of society', continuing the theme established by Wollstonecraft in her last novel, *The Wrongs of Woman, or Maria*. Hays, however, also drew upon tropes she had established in her own life of Wollstonecraft two decades before. Hays had presented the circumstances of Wollstonecraft's relationship with Imlay as a particular effect of the female condition. In so doing, she subverted the very idea that chastity could be the pre-eminent virtue for woman, arguing that such virtue could never be achieved while the prejudices generated by the distinction of sex shaped relations between men and women. The template Hays had established for her life of Wollstonecraft was used again in the *Memoirs*, to generate sympathetic histories of *queens* whose lives and reputations had been marred by that same double standard.

In her first experiment with collective lives, *Female Biography* in 1803, Hays used the lives of queens to demonstrate the importance of educating women in the same manner as men. In *Memoirs of Queens*, however, it was not intellectual equality that compelled Hays back to the realm of political debate. Indeed, Hays rejected the need to make such arguments, suggesting they were long settled. Instead, she argued that the purpose of this work was to establish that 'there can be, *but one moral standard of excellence for mankind*, whether male or female'. Hays' life of Caroline formed an emphatic counter to the smear campaign launched by Croker against the Queen and her female supporters. Hays presented Queen Caroline as a sexually wronged woman, much as she had with Wollstonecraft, linking the sexual double standard more generally with political repression. She explicitly connected such observations to Croker's campaign, asserting that 'the licentious distinctions made by the domineering party, in the spirit of tyranny, selfishness, and sensuality, are at the foundation of the heaviest evils that have afflicted, degraded, and corrupted society'.[52] Perhaps more eloquently than the Queen's Whig lawyers, Hays argued that the laws used to condemn Caroline were specious and evidence of any crime was flimsy. Underpinning her arguments was a rejection of the questionable moralizing that Croker had used in his *Letter from the King* and Hays explicitly refuted his suggestion that the Queen was responsible for the nation's moral state:

> Incontinence whether in a man or in a woman, is a moral offence and a violation of the most important branch of temperance, but it carries with it no civil disen-franchisement, and its punishment is left to public opinion, to the usages and customs established in social intercourse – and heavy enough upon *woman* does this chastisement fall. If higher virtues are to be expected from *queens*, on account of the eminence of their station, and the greater importance of their example, the same reasoning, the same rule, surely applies to *kings*.[53]

The idea that political tyranny and sexual tyranny are intricately bound together informed Hays' life of Caroline, but also those of Anne Boleyn, Marie Antoinette, Mary Stuart, Agrippina and the other embattled queens whose lives she records.

Whereas queens in *Female Biography* excited in female readers 'a worthier emulation', in the *Memoirs* they served a rather different purpose, to suggest instead that the 'throne itself', did not prevent queens from suffering 'the peculiar disadvantages that have hitherto attended her sex'.[54] In these *Memoirs* Hays recalled Edmund Burke, but challenged any sense that chivalry ensured the honour of women or offered them protection, casting Queen Caroline as the most emphatic victim of such hypocrisy. By using the Queen Caroline case to highlight the wrongs of all women as they related to the policing of the double standard, Hays continued the arguments put forward by Wollstonecraft in *Maria,* while vindicating once again the life of her dear friend. This was not a retreat from feminism, as others have suggested, but demonstrates that Hays continued to believe in the revolutionary change she and Wollstonecraft imagined in the 1790s, and to fight against tyranny in 1821, when all others had fallen silent.

The gender of censorship

Most critics have read *Female Biography* and *Memoirs of Queens* as proto-Victorian texts: early examples of the collections of female prosopography that became popular in the mid-nineteenth century.[55] They have assumed that both works shared the generic quality of Victorian collective biographies of women, and have ignored their more radical and original features.[56] In this context, *Memoirs of Queens* has been treated as an abridged version of *Female Biography* and as an early attempt to codify acceptable feminine behaviour through biography.[57] In *Memoirs of Queens,* however, Hays initiated a new genre – the collective royal biography – and used the text to rail against the scandalous treatment of Queen Caroline at the hands of her husband. The *Memoirs* provided Hays with another vehicle to explore the relation between the sexual double standard, female suffering and the denial of women's sexual subjectivity. Wollstonecraft only touched upon such themes in her later works, but this was what characterized Hays' feminism. With the *Memoirs of Queens,* Hays not only reignited the sexual aspect of the 'war of ideas', but courageously refuted the belief that there must be a different standard of morality for men and women, and she did this in the face of extreme repression. While *Memoirs of Queens* was not censored in 1821, the failure of modern critics to acknowledge Hays' refusal to be silenced during this time of gendered political repression suggests various forms of literary censorship still at work, and a need to consider how the history of censorship continues to exclude women's voices.

Notes

1 According to Iain McCalman, Britain had been a locus of porno-political material since the reign of Louis XV. See 'Mad Lord George and Madame La Motte: Riot and Sexuality in the Genesis of Burke's Reflections on the Revolution in France', *Journal of British Studies,* 35, 3 (1996), p. 362.

2 Tamara Hunt, *Defining John Bull: Political Caricature and National Identity in Late Georgian England* (Aldershot: Ashgate, 2003), p. 323 fn.125 FL.

3 Lord Kenyon, cited in Joss Marsh, *Word Crimes: Blasphemy, Culture and Literature in Nineteenth-Century England* (Chicago: University of Chicago Press, 1998), p. 22.

4 Iain McCalman, *Radical Underworld: Prophets, Revolutionaries and Pornographers in London, 1795–1840* (Oxford: Clarendon, 2002 [1998]), p. 169.

5 Joss Marsh, *Word Crimes*, p. 22.

6 The 'Delicate Investigation' refers to the secret investigation held between 1806 and 1807, into claims that Caroline had given birth to an illegitimate child. See Flora Fraser, *Unruly Queen: The Life of Queen Caroline* (New York: Anchor Books, 2009 [1996]), pp. 166–192 and pp. 213–235, 164.

7 Iain McCalman, *Radical Underworld*, p. 165.

8 Lisa Z Sigel, *Governing Pleasures: Pornography and Social Change in England 1815–1914* (Philadelphia, PA: Temple University Press, 2002), p. 17.

9 Iain McCalman, *Radical Underworld*, p. 164.

10 Thomas Laqueur, 'The Queen Caroline Affair: Politics as Art in the Reign of George IV', *Journal of Modern History* 54 (4) (1982): 442.

11 Iain McCalman, *Radical Underworld*, p. 166.

12 See for instance Catherine Hall, 'The Early Formation of Victorian Domestic Ideology', in S. Burman (ed.), *Fit Work for Women* (London: Croom Helm, 1979), pp. 15–32; Leonore Davidoff and Catherine Hall, *Family Fortunes: Men and Women of the English Middle Class 1780–1850* (London: Hutchinson, 1987); Anna Clark, 'Queen Caroline and the Sexual Politics of Popular Culture in London, 1820', *Representations*, 31 (1990), pp. 47–68; Dror Wahrman, '"Middle Class" Domesticity Goes Public: Gender, Class and Politics from Queen Caroline to Queen Victoria', *Journal of British Studies* 32 (1993): 396–432.

13 Mary Spongberg, '"All histories are against you?" Family History, Domestic History and the Feminine Past in *Northanger Abbey* and *Persuasion*', in Kate Mitchell and Nicola Parsons (eds), *Reading Historical Fiction: The Revenant and Remember Past* (Basingstoke: Palgrave, 2013), pp. 50–66.

14 Dror Wahrman, '"Middle Class" Domesticity Goes Public', p. 404.

15 Thomas Laqueur, 'The Queen Caroline Affair', p. 444. Anna Clark identifies one female author of a Carolinite ballad, Eliza Treager. See 'Queen Caroline and the Sexual Politics of Popular Culture', p. 59.

16 James N McCord, 'Taming the Female Politician in Early-Nineteenth Century England', *Journal of Women's History*, 13 (4) (2002): 33.

17 Anna Clark, 'Queen Caroline and the Sexual Politics of Popular Culture', p. 60.

18 Thomas Laqueur, 'The Queen Caroline Affair', p. 444, Tamara L Hunt, "Morality and Monarchy in the Queen Caroline Affair", *Albion: A Quarterly Journal concerned with British Studies*, 23 (4) (1991): 716. Hunt, however, focuses largely on the number of women involved in writing petitions and in the popular protests around the Queen's trial.

19 Dror Wahrman, '"Middle Class" Domesticity Goes Public', pp. 396–432. See also Louise Carter, 'British Masculinities and the Queen Caroline Affair of 1820' *Gender & History*, 20 (2) (2008): 248–69.

20 Robert Portsmouth, *John Wilson Croker and the Invention of Modern Conservatism* (Dublin: Irish Academic Press, 2010), p. 43.

21 Mary Spongberg, 'The Ghost of Marie Antoinette: A Prehistory of Victorian Royal Lives' in Lynette Felber (ed.), *Clio's Daughters: British Women Making History 1790–1899* (Newark: University of Delaware Press, 2007), pp. 71–96.

22 The only extended discussion of Hays' *Memoirs of Queens* appears in Gina Luria Walker's critical biography *Mary Hays 1759–1843: The Growth of a Woman's Mind*

(Hampshire: Ashgate, 2006). Gary Kelly also briefly mentions this text in his *Women, Writing and Revolution* (Oxford: Clarendon Press, 1993), pp. 259–60.

23 Ina Ferris, *The Achievement of Literary Authority: Gender, History and the Waverley Novels* (Ithaca, NY: Cornell University Press, 1991).

24 On Barbauld see James Chandler, *England in 1819: The Politics of Literary Culture and the Rise of Romantic Historicism* (Chicago: University of Chicago, 1998), pp. 114–20; William McCarthy, *Anna Laetitia Barbauld: Voice of the Enlightenment* (Baltimore: Johns Hopkins Press, 2008), pp. 477–88.

25 See Margaret Anne Doody, *Frances Burney: A Life in Works* (New Brunswick, NJ: Rutgers University Press, 1988); Janice Thaddeus, *Frances Burney: A Literary Life* (New York: St Martins, 2000), pp. 169–70.

26 Jocelyn Harris, *A Revolution Almost Beyond Expression: Jane Austen's Persuasion* (Newark: University of Delaware Press, 2007), p. 25.

27 Flora Fraser, *The Unruly Queen: The Life of Queen Caroline* (London: John Murray, 1996), p. 348.

28 [John Wilson Croker] *A Letter from the King to His People* (London: William Turner, 1820), p. 21.

29 The Queen was not really acquitted, but found guilty by a majority of nine. Given this slim majority Lord Liverpool suspended proceedings against her. See Jonathan Fulcher, 'The Loyalist Response to the Queen Caroline Agitations', *Journal of British Studies*, 34 (4) (1995): 492–3.

30 Robert Portsmouth, *John Wilson Croker*, p. 44.

31 Anna Clark, *Scandal: The Sexual Politics of the British Constitution* (Princeton, NJ: Princeton University Press, 2004), p. 189.

32 Myron F. Brightfield, Croker's first biographer claimed that Croker had no connection with the *John Bull*, see *John Wilson Croker* (London: George Allen & Unwin, 1940), pp. 172–7. Robert Portsmouth's recent study, however, demonstrates that Croker and Hook were well acquainted and that Croker fed Hook much of the gossip that found its way into the *John Bull*. See Portsmouth, *John Wilson Croker*, pp. 44–53.

33 William F. Newton Dunn, *The Man who was John Bull: Biography of Theodore Edward Hook 1778–1841* (London: Allendale Publishing, 1996), p. 130.

34 Jonathan Fulcher, 'The Loyalist Response', p. 493.

35 Robert Portsmouth, *John Wilson Croker*, p. 47.

36 Robert Portsmouth, *John Wilson Croker*, p. 47.

37 William F. Newton Dunn, *The Man Who Was John Bull*, p. 124.

38 Harriet, Countess Granville, *Letters of Harriet, Countess of Granville, Edited by her Son, the Hon. F Leveson Gower*, Vol. 1 (London: Longmans, 1894), p. 201.

39 William F. Newton Dunn, *The Man who was John Bull*, p. 129.

40 Myron F. Brightfield, *Theodore Hook and his Novels*, p. 127.

41 Jonathan Fulcher, 'The Loyalist Response' p. 494.

42 Many respectable sources used such arguments against the King's right to divorce his wife. See Louise Carter, "British Masculinities", p. 255.

43 [John Wilson Croker] *A Letter from the King to his People*, p. 6.

44 [John Wilson Croker] *A Letter from the King to his People*, p. 28.

45 [John Wilson Croker] *A Letter from the King to his People*, p. 29.

46 Burke was advised by his good friend Sir Philip Francis that what he wrote of Marie Antoinette was 'pure foppery'. See Claudia L Johnson, *Equivocal Beings: Politics,*

Gender and Sentimentality in the 1790s (Chicago: University of Chicago Press, 1995), p. 4.

47 Marilyn L Brooks (ed.), *The Correspondence (1779-1843) of Mary Hays, British Novelist,* (Lewiston: Edwin Mellen Press, 2004), p. 436.

48 The phrase in Barbara Taylor's. See *Mary Wollstonecraft and the Feminist Imagination,* (Cambridge, 2003), p. 188.

49 Pamela Clemit and Gina Luria Walker (eds), *Memoirs of the Author of A Vindication of the Rights of Woman* (Peterborough: Broadview, 2001), p. 11; Claire Tomalin, *The Life and Death of Mary Wollstonecraft* (London: Penguin, 1974), p. 233.

50 Brooks, *The Correspondence,* Letter to Godwin dated 1 October 1795 and article in the *Monthly Magazine,* 1797. p. 399.

51 Mary Spongberg, 'Remembering Wollstonecraft', in Daniel Cook and Amy Culley (eds), *Women's Life Writing 1700-1850: Gender, Genre and Authorship* (London: Palgrave, 2012), pp. 165–80.

52 Mary Hays, *Memoirs of Queens, Illustrious and Celebrated* (London: T. J. Allman, 1821), p. vi.

53 Mary Hays, *Memoirs of Queens,* p. 129.

54 Mary Hays, *Memoirs of Queens,* p. iv.

55 Rohan A Maitzen includes Hays among 'Victorian' writers of collective biography, but she only cites Hays' later collection, *Memoirs of Queens.* See 'This Feminine Preserve: Historical Biographies by Victorian Women', *Victorian Studies,* 38 (1995): 371–93. Alison Booth also situates Hays as anticipating Victorian female prosopographies. See *How to Make it as a Woman: Collective Biographical History from Victoria to the Present* (Chicago: University of Chicago Press, 2004), p. 19.

56 Miriam Elizabeth Burstein, 'From Good Looks to Good Thoughts: Popular Women's History and the Invention of Modernity, ca 1830-1870', *Modern Philology,* 97 (1) (1997): 48.

57 Jeanne Wood argues that Hays evokes exemplary biography when she states her desire 'to excite a worthier emulation' and appears to concede the expectation of biography's proper reputation when she excludes Mary Wollstonecraft. 'Alphabetically Arranged', pp. 127–8.

References

Brightfield, M. F., *John Wilson Croker,* London: George Allen & Unwin, 1940.

Brooks, M. L. (ed.), *The Correspondence (1779-1843) of Mary Hays, British Novelist,* Lewiston: Edwin Mellen Press, 2004.

Booth, A., *How to Make it as a Woman: Collective Biographical History from Victoria to the Present,* Chicago: University of Chicago Press, 2004.

Burstein, M. E., 'From Good Looks to Good Thoughts: Popular Women's History and the Invention of Modernity, ca 1830-1870', *Modern Philology,* 97 (1) (1997): 46–75.

Carter, L., 'British Masculinities and the Queen Caroline Affair of 1820', *Gender & History,* 20 (2) (2008): 248–69.

Chandler, J., *England in 1819: The Politics of Literary Culture and the Rise of Romantic Historicism,* Chicago: University of Chicago, 1998.

Clark, A., 'Queen Caroline and the Sexual Politics of Popular Culture in London, 1820', *Representations*, 31 (1990): 47–68.

Clark, A., *Scandal: The Sexual Politics of the British Constitution,* Princeton, NJ: Princeton University Press, 2004.

Clemit, P. and G. L. Walker (eds), *Memoirs of the Author of A Vindication of the Rights of Woman,* by William Godwin, Peterborough: Broadview, 2001.

[Croker, J. W.] *A Letter from the King to His People,* London: William Turner, 1820.

Davidoff, L. and C. Hall, *Family Fortunes: Men and Women of the English Middle Class 1780-1850,* London: Hutchinson, 1987.

Doody, M. A., *Frances Burney: A Life in Works,* New Brunswick, NJ: Rutgers University Press, 1988.

Dunn, W. F., *The Man Who Was John Bull: Biography of Theodore Edward Hook 1778-1841,* London: Allendale Publishing, 1996.

Ferris, I., *The Achievement of Literary Authority: Gender, History and the Waverley Novels,* Ithaca, NY: Cornell University Press, 1991.

Fraser, F., *Unruly Queen: The Life of Queen Caroline,* New York: Anchor Books, [1996] 2009.

Fulcher, J., 'The Loyalist Response to the Queen Caroline Agitations', *Journal of British Studies*, 34 (4) (1995): 492–3.

Granville, Countess H., *Letters of Harriet, Countess of Granville, edited by her son, the Hon. F. Leveson Gower,* Vol. 1. London: Longmans, 1894.

Hall, C., 'The Early Formation of Victorian Domestic Ideology', in S. Burman (ed.), *Fit Work for Women,* London: Croom Helm, 1979, pp. 15–32.

Harris, J., *A Revolution Almost Beyond Expression: Jane Austen's Persuasion,* Newark: University of Delaware Press, 2007.

Hays, M., *Memoirs of Queens, Illustrious and Celebrated,* London: T. J. Allman, 1821.

Hunt, T., *Defining John Bull: Political Caricature and National Identity in Late Georgian England,* Aldershot: Ashgate, 2003.

Hunt, T., 'Morality and Monarchy in the Queen Caroline Affair', *Albion: A Quarterly Journal concerned with British Studies* 23(4) (1991): 697–722.

Johnson, C. L., *Equivocal Beings: Politics, Gender and Sentimentality in the 1790s,* Chicago: University of Chicago Press, 1995.

Kelly, G., *Women, Writing and Revolution,* Oxford: Clarendon Press, 1993.

Laqueur, T., 'The Queen Caroline Affair: Politics as Art in the Reign of George IV', *Journal of Modern History*, 54 (4) (1982): 417–66.

McCalman, I., 'Mad Lord George and Madame La Motte: Riot and Sexuality in the Genesis of Burke's *Reflections on the Revolution in France*', *Journal of British Studies*, 35 (3) (1996): 343–67.

McCalman, I., *Radical Underworld: Prophets, Revolutionaries and Pornographers in London, 1795-1840,* Oxford: Clarendon, 2002 [1998].

McCarthy, W., *Anna Laetitia Barbauld: Voice of the Enlightenment,* Baltimore: Johns Hopkins Press, 2008.

McCord, J. N., 'Taming the Female Politician in Early-Nineteenth-Century England', *Journal of Women's History*, 13 (4) (2002): 31–53.

Maitzen, R. A. 'This Feminine Preserve: Historical Biographies by Victorian Women', *Victorian Studies*, 38 (1995): 371–93.

Marsh, J., *Word Crimes: Blasphemy, Culture and Literature in Nineteenth-Century England,* Chicago: University of Chicago Press, 1998.

Portsmouth, R., *John Wilson Croker and the Invention of Modern Conservatism,* Dublin: Irish Academic Press, 2010.

Sigel, L. Z., *Governing Pleasures: Pornography and Social Change in England 1815–1914,* Philadelphia, PA: Temple University Press, 2002.

Spongberg, M., 'The Ghost of Marie Antoinette: A Prehistory of Victorian Royal Lives', in Lynette Felber (ed.), *Clio's Daughters: British Women Making History 1790–1899,* Newark: University of Delaware Press, 2007, pp. 71–96.

Spongberg, M., 'Remembering Wollstonecraft', in Daniel Cook and Amy Culley (eds), *Women's Life Writing 1700–1850: Gender, Genre and Authorship,* London: Palgrave, 2012, pp. 165–180.

Spongberg, M., '"All histories are against you?" Family History, Domestic History and the Feminine Past in *Northanger Abbey* and *Persuasion*', in Kate Mitchell and Nicola Parsons (eds), *Reading Historical Fiction: The Revenant and Remembered Past,* Basingstoke: Palgrave, 2013, pp. 50–66.

Taylor, B., *Mary Wollstonecraft and the Feminist Imagination,* Cambridge: Cambridge University Press, 2003.

Thaddeus, J., *Frances Burney: A Literary Life,* New York: St Martins, 2000.

Tomalin, C., *The Life and Death of Mary Wollstonecraft,* London: Penguin, 1974.

Wahrman, D., '"Middle Class" Domesticity Goes Public: Gender, Class and Politics from Queen Caroline to Queen Victoria', *Journal of British Studies,* 32 (1993): 396–432.

Walker, G. L., *Mary Hays 1759–1843: The Growth of a Woman's Mind,* Hampshire: Ashgate, 2006.

Wood, J., 'Alphabetically Arranged: Mary Hays, Female Biography and the Biographical Dictionary', *Genre,* 31 (2) (1998): 117–42.

4

'The Chastity of our Records': Reading and Judging Obscenity in Nineteenth-Century Courts

Karen Crawley

Judging a work as obscene has always been a matter not of the content of that work, but rather of *who* is reading or viewing it. It is axiomatic that modern obscenity law, in its statutory and judicial forms, emerged in the nineteenth century, when dramatically increased literacy rates, cheaper printing methods and greater population concentration created an 'anonymous, amorphous public, in which distinctions of sex and class could no longer be relied upon to determine who could read what'.[1] One of the century's most comprehensive legislative attempts to control the unruly circulation of pamphlets, newspapers, cheap literature and photographs, the United Kingdom's *Obscene Publications Act 1857* (also known as Lord Campbell's Act), was crafted by a political elite that feared the subversive impulses of a newly literate working class, or in blunt terms, 'the uncontrolled mass of women and the mob'.[2] The *Act* authorized the police to search suspect premises, to seize material they believed to be obscene and to get permission for the destruction of these materials from magistrates. Lord Campbell introduced and justified the Bill in Parliament as a necessary response to the increased circulation of pornographic materials at affordable prices: 'It was not alone indecent books of a high price, which was a sort of check, that were sold, but periodical papers of the most licentious and disgusting description were coming out week by week, and sold to any person who asked for them, and in any numbers'.[3] He reassured the Parliament that the Bill was directed neither towards a gentleman's private erotica collection nor 'the masterpieces of Correggio',[4] stating that 'the keeping, or the reading, or the delighting in such things, must be left to taste, and was not a subject for legal interference'.[5] Rather the *Act* was directed to 'people who designedly and industriously manufactured books and prints with the intention of corrupting the public morals'.[6] The *Act* reflected concern with the health of the unruly public body, targeting those purveyors of texts and displayers of images who created a new, excited sensibility among young working-class men and women, creating 'dangerously motivated and suggestible audiences'[7] and threatening to compromise the codes of respectable behaviour advocated for women on the streets of the city.[8]

The legal definition of obscenity that appeared a decade later in *R v. Hicklin* (1868), and would eventually be adopted throughout Anglo-American common law, confirmed that the focus of these new obscenity laws was to protect a vulnerable new public. The *Hicklin* case concerned a notorious anti-Catholic pamphlet, *The Confessional Unmasked; shewing the depravity of the Roman priesthood, the iniquity of the Confessional, and the questions put to females in confession*, produced in the tradition of Protestant critique directed at the Catholic confessional's purported tendency to fill the minds of its listeners with filth, and distributed by the Protestant Evangelical and Electoral Union.[9] Observing that the pamphlet contained 'the most filthy and disgusting and unnatural description[s] it is possible to imagine',[10] Lord Chancellor Alexander Cockburn famously defined obscene works as those having 'the tendency to deprave and corrupt those whose minds are open to such immoral influences and into whose hands a publication of this sort might fall'.[11] While the phrase 'deprave and corrupt' seems to presuppose 'a straightforwardly causal, if not crudely mechanistic, model of receptivity',[12] the word 'tendency' invited judicial consideration not just about the impact a work might have on the 'minds' of its potential readership but about the 'hands' into which 'a publication of this sort may fall'. Obscene texts were only a problem insofar as they might fall into the hands of women, children and working-class men who would be unable to resist the corrosive influence of sexual materials. If such material was expensive, access would be restricted to those with sufficient powers of judgement to read such books without being corrupted in the process. It was of critical importance to Justice Cockburn's judgement that the *Confessional Unmasked* had been sold as a shilling pamphlet and 'sold at the corners of streets … and of course it falls into the hands of persons of all classes, young and old, and the minds of those hitherto pure are exposed to the danger of contamination and pollution from the impurity it contains'.[13] The legal definition of obscenity thus turned on questions of access, as many censorship historians have established: a work has the potential to corrupt to the extent that it was available to a large number of potentially corruptible people.

The *Hicklin* test's emphasis on the *effects* of representation has dominated obscenity law ever since, although courts have moved from asking what harm obscenity might present to those most vulnerable (women, children and the working class), to a measure related to the impact of the work on the average person.[14] This protective argument has ostensibly become more democratic (all of society now shares in this vulnerability to obscenity), reflecting the emergence of the modern subject of moral regulation – the subject who must be protected from him or herself. To this account of obscenity law as essentially a repressive, state-sponsored mechanism – an ideological smokescreen for class interests and patriarchy – we must add a consideration of obscenity law as also productive, part of the discursive process that creates legal subjects as self-governing individuals.[15] Scholars have shown how nineteenth-century obscenity law inaugurated new ways of thinking about sex: as private, secret and shameful, as well as exciting and dangerous. It was part of a project of regulating and also constituting sexual bodies, and female bodies in particular: the criminal regulation of obscenity in the English-speaking world coincided with an extension of laws against prostitution, the criminalization of abortion and the emergence of a cult of domesticity. Obscenity judgements formed a key part of the mid-nineteenth-century discourse around female sexuality, which had to be contained within the boundaries of marriage and family. In this sense, obscenity law not only targeted sexual behaviour, but also helped constitute it.

In this Foucauldian (but now conventional) emphasis on law's instrumental power – whether repressive or productive – what has largely remained unexplored is how the law constituted *itself* through judgements about obscenity. Scholars working at the intersection of law and the humanities have long insisted that law is not simply a set of rules and regulations, but is 'a kind of rhetorical and literary activity'.[16] Law's authority, grounded in the sanctioned violence it has the power to enact,[17] is constituted through embodied performances by those speaking for law or exercising its force (judges, police, legislators), who determine law's limits, claim for it an interiority and a rational logic, animate its purposes and distinguish between legitimate judgement and arbitrary violence. Judicial rhetoric is a key site for the discursive production of law. Judicial opinions comprise not only rhetorical examples of legal discourse, but a literal or material corpus of text, an archive or repository of authoritative statements, revered and sacred.[18]

Since the eighteenth century, the legal judgement of obscenity in the law of England has depended not upon sexual content, but 'upon the imagined presence or absence of sexual arousal in any given viewing public'.[19] Michael Gamer has argued that eighteenth-century obscene libel was not identified by its subject matter but by reference to readerly effects; it was 'not so much a kind of writing as a category of reader response – a legal interpretation of the social effects of a certain kind of reading'.[20] Lynda Nead has likewise insisted that the distinction between art and obscenity has never been exclusive, but 'the product of acts of judgement performed by those who have particular knowledge and power'.[21] This act of judgement is not democratic, but a privilege bestowed upon the connoisseur, defined as he who can resist the affective address of the work or artefact. The arbiter must be one for whom the sexual impulses arising from the obscene work can be disavowed.

The predicament of a court arbitrating on obscenity is bound up in the irony of censorship, which is so often doomed to make present what it seeks to make absent. Judith Butler has observed that, in order for the law to regulate a phenomenon, it must transform it into legal discourse, and thus inadvertently 'establish it as a site of contestation, that is, as the scene of public utterance that it sought to pre-empt'.[22] She writes that 'the censor is compelled to repeat the speech that the censor would prohibit',[23] and 'language that is compelled to repeat what it seeks to constrain invariably reproduces and restages the very speech that it seeks to shut down'.[24] This phenomenon is particularly visible in nineteenth-century judgements of obscenity, which occurred when the modern judicial institution was constituting itself as a kind of *public* writing, a literal corpus or archive of decisions that could be accessed and read by a newly literate public – the very public to which obscenity laws were responding. In these cases, such as the William Hone trials discussed by Clara Tuite in a previous chapter, the judges were explicitly faced with the question of whether the text of the court judgement could reproduce obscene words without being held hostage to their obscene effects, and by implication, whether it is possible to intervene in the traffic of representations without the form of that intervention itself becoming compromised. The court is thereby obliged to both address and elide its own materiality as a textual archive.

The targets of these obscenity prosecutions often defied easy categorization; by definition, they were not self-evidently pornographic texts, or hermetic obscene 'objects' with a single and easily identified author, but rather layered texts, compiled from various sources and reflecting a variety of different purposes. The text at issue in *Hicklin*, *The Confessional Unmasked,* was particularly ambiguous. Anonymously authored, it consisted of extracts taken from the writings of several Catholic theologians on the practice of confession, containing descriptions of sexual concerns women confessed to priests. These were reproduced in Latin on one side of the page and translated into English on the opposite page. A chapter on 'The Sin of Onan', for example, debated whether 'if the husband withdraws after spending, but before the wife has spent, can she immediately, by touching, excite herself to spend?'[25] Another chapter, 'On the Carnal Sins which Man and Wife Commit with Each Other', not only prohibited 'connection in the hinder vessel', but explained that it was a 'mortal sin for a man to rub his ____ against the hinder vessel of his wife' or to 'commence operations' in that area, only to complete congress 'in the vessel ordained by nature'.[26] The relative sinfulness of 'the various possible postures' of sexual intercourse was also outlined, with those 'postures' described in detail. The extracts were interspersed with editorial comments such as: 'In the latter part of the pamphlet I have given a few extracts without abridgement, to shew into what minute and disgusting details these *holy men* have entered. This alone has been my object, and not the filling of the work with obscenity'.[27] *The Confessional Unmasked,* then, appears precisely the sort of publication that *The Times*, in 1857, had suggested would be 'absurd' to suppose subject to Campbell's bill, because of its lack of intention to corrupt.[28] Yet, as Katherine Mullin points out, the pamphlet's striking popularity – with several editions appearing in 1867 and 1868 claiming that 50,000 copies were sold – strongly suggests that it was being marketed and consumed as pornography.[29]

The pamphlet was distributed at meetings led by evangelical speaker William Murphy and, after a particularly violent bout of 'Murphy riots' in the West Midlands British city of Wolverhampton in 1867, the city's Watch Committee obtained a warrant to search the premises of Henry Scott, a member of the Protestant Electoral Union, and seized a quantity of pamphlets. The pamphlets were brought before two justices of the borough of Wolverhampton (one of whom was Benjamin Hicklin), who ordered they be destroyed. Scott appealed against the order at the borough Quarter Sessions on the basis that his intention was innocent: he had purchased and distributed the pamphlet in order to expose 'what he deems to be errors of the Church of Rome, and particularly the immorality of the Confessional'.[30] The Recorder quashed the order of the justices, and ordered that the pamphlets be returned to Scott. This order was then successfully appealed, in the Court of the Queen's Bench, the highest appeal court in England. While conceding that the defendant's 'motive ... was an honest one',[31] Chief Justice Cockburn nonetheless found *The Confessional Unmasked* obscene under the *Obscene Publications Act*. By emphasising the 'tendency' of the text, Cockburn effectively declared that intention was irrelevant to the question of obscenity:

I think that if there be an infraction of the law the intention to break the law must be inferred, and the criminal character of the publication is not affected or qualified by there being some ulterior motive in view (which is the immediate and primary object of the parties) of a different and of an honest character.[32]

His fellow judges agreed. As Colin Blackburn noted, Scott 'must be taken to have intended that which is the natural consequence of the act'.[33] In language that clearly demonstrated that obscenity was an issue of public health, the situation was seen to be comparable to a case 'in which a person carried a child which was suffering from a contagious disease, along the public road to the danger of the health of all those who happened to be in that road', which was held 'a misdemeanor, without its being alleged that the defendant intended that anybody should catch the disease'.[34]

The pamphlet's critique of the confessional was based on 'the tendency of questions, involving practices and propensities of a certain description, to do mischief to the minds of those to whom such questions are addressed, by suggesting thoughts and desires which otherwise would not have occurred to their minds'.[35] But, as Cockburn points out:

If that be the case as between the priest and the person confessing, it manifestly must equally be so when the whole is put into the shape of a series of paragraphs, one following upon another, each involving some impure practices, some of them of the most filthy and disgusting and unnatural description it is possible to imagine. I take it therefore, that, apart from the ulterior object which the publisher of this work had in view, the work itself is, in every sense of the term, an obscene publication ...[36]

Cockburn here points out that the compiler of the pamphlet cannot redeem obscenity by framing it as critique, just as the confession to the priest cannot redeem obscenity by framing it as penitence. The judge thus applied Scott's arguments about the corrupting nature of the confessional to the corrupting nature of his pamphlet, which could not avoid provoking the same effect in its readers. Like the 'girl' in the confessional, subject to the questions of the 'depraved' priest, the reader's 'mind' is 'open to immoral influences'. Florence Done calls attention to the gendered trope of feminine readers as sexually corrupted by reading, where that obscenity is figured as an outside 'influence', an intrusion of 'immorality' into an 'open mind', thus conjuring 'an idea of vulnerable bodily openness'.[37] The scene of reading or textual encounter is constituted by a gendered vulnerability. And alongside these layered scenes of textual corruption – between the priest and confessant, and the pamphlet and the reader – lurks the suggestion of further corrupting encounters, between the texts of the law and its legal subjects, which were soon to materialize.

The Protestant Electoral Union, unwilling to let go of such an effective piece of anti-Catholic criticism, promptly issued a new edition of *The Confessional Unmasked*, 'with certain alterations, certain omissions, and certain additions',[38] calculated to ensure that it would not fall foul of *Hicklin*. George Mackey was tried in 1870 for selling this new edition, but the jury was unable to reach a verdict. The Protestant Union then published copies of the *Report of the Trial of George Mackey,* which reproduced within it the entire text of *The Confessional Unmasked,* although it had not been read aloud in open court. This was sold for 1 shilling, sometimes in a cover naming it as a trial transcript, and sometimes in a cover simply stating *The Confessional Unmasked.* When the *Report* was seized by police and ordered destroyed by a magistrate, the bookseller appealed on the basis that the *Report,* being a fair report of proceedings in a court, was privileged, and therefore could not be seized or destroyed.

The court was thus again faced with the problem of citation – the idea that in order to critique or judge something, one must, to some extent, reproduce it. Justice Mellor had already observed in *Hicklin* that 'the nature of the subject itself ... is such that it cannot be discussed without to a certain extent producing authorities for the assertion that the confessional would be a mischevious thing ...' and therefore that obscenity is then 'a question of degree'.[39] Likewise, the appellant's lawyer in *Steele v Brennan* asked the court: 'What effective remedy is there in the hands of persons wishing to suppress a system which they conceive to be pernicious, except to expose the tendency of such a system by reference to the writings in which it is expounded?'[40] Chief Justice Bovill decided that even the newly-expurgated edition of *The Confessional Unmasked,* which after all 'only professes to omit some of the most filthy and abominable passages in the first edition,'[41] still contravened the decision in *Hicklin.* He noted the dissembling function of the book cover: 'The book now before us publishes in offensive detail passages which were not read aloud at the trial. The outer cover of some of the copies does not even allude to the trial, while it does call attention to the offensive matters contained within.'[42] Notably, he decided the issue precisely by recourse to intention:

> It appears to me pretty clear that the book, as a whole, was not intended to be merely a fair report of a trial, but a means of reproducing the offensive publication under the guise of a report of the prosecution of Mackey for such publication.[43]

Justice Keating rejected the idea that it is impossible to discuss the pernicious effects of writing without recourse to extracts of that writing:

> It would be strange indeed that in order to prevent the pollution of the public morals that law should allow pollution to be circulated ... the law would be self-contradictory if it made the publication of an indecent work an indictable offence and yet sanctioned the republication of such a work under cover of its being part of the proceedings in a court of justice.[44]

The law cannot be brought into self-contradiction or made an agent of the public dissemination of obscenity.

> [T]he result would be that the person publishing an obscene work would only have to be brought before a court of justice for such publication, in order to entitle him to republish the same matter with perfect impunity. His trial would frustrate the very purpose which it had in view, viz. the putting a stop to the publication of such matter. This consideration appears to me to reduce the appellant's contention to an absurdity.[45]

Justice Keating's anxiety over the court's own function as an agent of repetition – his fear that, like the book cover, the court records may be used as a dissembling, legitimating cloak for promulgating obscenity to a reading public – is combated by appealing to the court as a private enterprise. He opines that the appellant's Protestant complaints about having no other remedy to impugn such 'obscene' Catholic works are invalid because, while they may not have a political remedy of republishing publicly, they have a 'simple' private legal remedy of *preventing publication*. This remedy keeps matters contained and enclosed in the safe confines of a hierarchical legal regime: 'the question whether the publication of such works is admissible may be made the subject of a prosecution ... upon [which] the matter would be discussed only before the Court and the jury'.[46]

Neither *Hicklin* nor *Steele* dealt with obscene texts 'directly', but rather with obscene texts that had already been resignified – reproduced or extracted – within a framework of opprobrium (the anti-confessional pamphlet in *Hicklin*, the trial transcript in *Steele*). In these legal judgements, the law writes condemning writing. Its own textual status means that it cannot escape or remain outside these layered scenes of reading. After all, the formulation of the 'tendency to deprave and corrupt' test invests the obscenity at the centre of these layers with a power – a 'tendency' – that always threatens to transcend context and survive disavowal or framing as critique. And having just asserted the transcendent power of the obscene, there is no basis for excluding the court or legal record from its corrosive operations. The very notion of a transcendent obscenity described by the courts equally applies to the written records of the court. As obscenity came to be understood in legal discourse as an effect of reading, the *scene of reading* – private, furtive, contagious, corrupting – became a site of moral regulation. And so, in turn, the law became vulnerable to its legal subjects through its status as legible text, open and accessible to the very public whom obscenity law was generated to both protect and defend.

In nineteenth-century United States courts, the problem of citation was confronted even more directly. The very first common law judgement on obscenity in 1815 dealt directly with the vexing practical problem presented by the formal requirements of criminal proceedings, which obliged the particulars of the crime to be alleged in the indictment. The indictment simply stated that the defendants had exhibited 'a certain lewd, wicked, scandalous, infamous and obscene painting, representing a man in an obscene, impudent, and indecent posture with a woman'.[47] The defendant protested that the indictment had failed to describe the painting (the creator and title of which is unknown) with sufficient detail to enable the court to determine whether or not its content was obscene. Both judges disagreed. Justice Tilghman wrote that the jury could judge the question of indecency from evidence or from inspection, and merely designating the matter as obscene would be sufficient: 'I am for paying some respect to the chastity of our records. These are circumstances which may be well omitted.'[48] The indictment refers to the 'obscene painting' as a matter of fact rather than a site of contestation. Indeed, the court never actually saw the painting in question. As Bruce Burgett has noted,

The fact that Sharpless's painting never appears in court reveals the institutional power behind this act of interpellation. Because the painting is neither displayed nor fully described, the court's role in positing a common sensibility that it then defends remains unchallenged. Unlike the 'public eye' whose unity emerges only in and through debate, the eye of the law asserts its coherence by eliminating the occasion of that debate.[49]

The concern with the 'chastity of the records' came up again six years later in Massachusetts, at the 1821 trial of Peter Holmes for publishing the first American edition of John Cleland's *Memoirs of a Woman of Pleasure*. The book contained a 'lewd and obscene print', so both text and print were under indictment, and neither was deemed fit to be shown to the court. The lawyer for Holmes claimed that the jury was called upon to deliver a verdict without having inspected the evidence, to which Chief Judge Parker replied:

> It can never be required that an obscene book and picture should be displayed upon the records of the court: which must be done, if the description in these charges is insufficient. This would be to require that the public itself should give permanency and notoriety to indecency, in order to punish it.[50]

In contrast to English judicial discourse, then, the judges in the United States appear less concerned with the formalities of an indictment and more anxious about the public nature of the court proceedings, as well as acutely conscious of the textual traces left behind by their acts of judgement. The problem of citation is thus bound up in the court's uneasiness with the ideology of law as a public, democratic and accountable institution. Later that century, defendants prosecuted under the *Act for the Suppression of Trade in and Circulation of Obscene Literature and Articles of Immoral Use 1873*,[51] (also known as the Comstock Act) began exploiting the court's reluctance to describe or denote the obscene material that was the subject of the charge. In *United States v Harman* (1891),[52] the obscene material was an issue of an anarchist journal called *Lucifer the Lightbearer,* published by Moses Harman, containing an article headed 'A Physician's Testimony' which, according to the court,

> sets out with much particularity various instances falling within his professional experience and practice of abuses of women by their husbands in coercive cohabitation; of family habits of men, boys, and girls, gratifying an unnamable propensity of the father, and the unnatural intercourse between a man and beasts. These acts are described in blunt, coarse terms, too indecent and filthy to be here given *in haec verba*. The pleader, however, has set the whole article out in exact words in the indictment.[53]

The court retreats to the Latin phrase *in haec verba* – 'in these words' – to further distance itself from having to designate the obscene words used in these stories of incestuous relationships. The court went on to ask about the probable effect of the article upon 'society in general', employing many words of 'repetition' (italicized in the quotation here):

How would such language and matter impress a public assembly of decent men and women? How would it be received in and affect the average family circle of 1,500 subscribers to whom the evidence shows this garbage was sent? The subjects discussed and the language employed are too coarse and indecent for the man of average education and refinement to *recapitulate*. They are so filthy in thought and impure in terms as not to admit of *recitation* without a shock to the common sense of decency and modesty; and it does seem to me that it is not too much to say that no ordinary mind can subject itself to the *repeated* reading and contemplation of such subjects and language without the risk of becoming indurated to all sense of modesty in speech and chastity in thought. The appetite for such literature increases with the feeding. The more it is pandered to, the more insatiable its craving for something yet more vicious in taste.[54]

The court's repeated rejection heightens the sense of power and affective appeal attached to the impugned text – after all, why not simply say it is not appropriate to discuss in detail and move on? The court is drawn to it, and must circle round it, repeating its own refusal to repeat. The court's observation that *Lucifer* will be subject to 'recapitulation', 'recitation' and 'repeated reading' within social and domestic settings sets up a scene of corruption identified by an ongoing and intensifying process of engagement with the texts. For the danger identified to those of upright disposition does not lie in mere exposure to the material, but *repeated* exposure. The court here not only recognizes that obscene or pornographic texts can be pored over, fantasized about, used again and again, but acknowledges a particular theory of repetition being consolidated in regulatory discourse about obscenity at this time, and that is echoed in contemporary claims about pornography's addictive and escalating properties: the repeated exposure to obscene material corrupts and erodes. Of course this repeated exposure is exactly what a judge may face in prosecutions for obscenity. As the *Harman* court moves from conjuring a 'public assembly of decent men and women' to 'the average family circle' to 'the man of average education and refinement', it comes ever closer to characterizing itself. When the *Harman* court speaks of the dangers of repeated reading, it suggests fear of its own judgement being impinged upon, compromised or tainted – its own body under threat.

The unstable position of the court vis-à-vis these obscene materials was rather ingeniously leveraged by the defendant's counsel in *Harman*, who invoked the court's own potential complicity in the obscenity:

The [defendant's] argument is that if the offense in question is completed by the mere overt act of knowingly placing in the post-office an obscene print, publication, etc., it would subject to indictment and punishment *the judge circuit for sending the indictment herein containing the forbidden publication, sent him through the mail by mistake, back to the clerk of the court through the mails…*[55]

The defendant's argument is another attempt to re-open the question of intention deemed irrelevant in *Hicklin*, by maintaining that since refusing to consider intention would leave the judge or clerk mailing the material open to an obscenity charge, and seeing as the law must apply equally to everyone, then the matter of intention always has to be an open question. The *Harman* court dispensed with this argument by suggesting that the defendant had radically misconceived the postal laws, which authorized – not mandated – the government to maintain the postal office and roads, so the government could limit their use as it saw fit; furthermore, that a public officer or judge mailing the material in the manner described by the defendant 'was employing the mails within the purview of the object of the constitution'.[56] The court's argument appears to be that, even though legal officials are sending the forbidden publication via the mail (in the indictment), thus breaching the law, in effect they are *not* breaching the law because their actions are somehow contemplated by it. In an echo of Justice Keating in *Steele*, the court's rejoinder appeals for its logic to nothing more than the impossibility of the law's self-contradiction. In short, if the court is doing it, it must be legal, because what a court does is legal. It cannot be obscene because it is law. Here, the precariousness of the law's self-instantiation, its deliberate fashioning of formal completeness and cohesion, and the illogical basis of its claim to authority, are exposed, and we see the epistemic violence that grounds law. In its encounter with obscene texts, the law's own 'fantasy of sovereign action'[57] is starkly revealed.

Notes

1   Walter Kendrick, *The Secret Museum: Pornography in Modern Culture* (Berkeley: University of California Press, 1996), p. 177; see also Lynn Hunt, 'Introduction: Obscenity and The Origins of Modernity, 1500–1800', in Lynn Hunt (ed.), *The Invention of Pornography: Obscenity and the Origins of Modernity, 1500–1800* (New York: Zone Books, 1993), and Sonya Sceats, 'The Legal Concept of Obscenity: A Genealogy', *Australian Feminist Law Journal*, 16 (2002): 133–45.
2   Lynda Nead, '"Bodies of Judgment", Art, Obscenity, and the Connoisseur', in Costas Douzinas and Lynda Nead (eds), *Law and Image: The Authority of Art and the Aesthetics of Law* (Chicago: University of Chicago Press, 1999), p. 206.
3   *Hansard's Parliamentary Papers*, 144–8 (1857), 145.103 cited in Colligan, *The Traffic in Obscenity from Byron to Beardsley: Sexuality and Exoticism in Nineteenth-Century Print Culture* (Palgrave Macmillan, Basingstoke, Hampshire, 2006) p. 11.
4   Hansard Parliamentary Debates, 3rd series, vol. 146 (25 June 1857), col. 329 quoted in Lynda Nead, *The Female Nude: Art, Obscenity and Sexuality* (London: Routledge, 1992) p. 89.
5   Ibid.
6   Ibid.
7   Lynda Nead, *Victorian Babylon: People, Streets and Images in Nineteenth-Century London* (New Haven, CT: Yale University Press, 2000), p. 149.
8   Ibid.
9   *Regina v. Hicklin*, (1868) 3 L.R.Q. B. 360 [*Hicklin*] p. 362.
10 Ibid.
11 Ibid., p. 371.

12 Peter McDonald, 'Old Phrases and Great Obscenities: The Afterlife of Two Victorian Anxieties', *Journal of Victorian Culture*, 13 (2) (2010): 299.

13 *Hicklin,* p. 372.

14 Judge John Woolsey, in his famous ruling freeing James Joyce's *Ulysses* in the US in 1933, did not change the *Hicklin* test's essential emphasis on effects, defining obscenity as 'tending to stir the sex impulses or to lead to sexually impure and lustful thoughts', but he did stipulate that this was to be judged not by reference to a vulnerable class, but according to a 'person of average sex instincts' (*United States v. One Book Called "Ulysses"*, (1933) 5 F. Supp. 182 (Dist. Court, S.D.N.Y.) p. 184). By the mid-twentieth century, the United States Supreme Court was asking 'whether to the average person, applying contemporary community standards, the dominant theme of the material taken as a whole appeals to a prurient interest' (Justice William Brennan, *Roth v. United States*, (1957) 354 U.S. 476). Likewise, in Australia and elsewhere in the English-speaking world, the *Hicklin* test was adopted and transformed into the community standards test, which evaluates the offensiveness of the material in relation to its likely audience – 'the persons, classes of persons, and age groups to whom or amongst whom the matter was published' (*Crowe v. Graham,* (1967) 121 C.L.R. 375 p. 396) – and by reference to how the material 'would affect the average man, considering his proper modesty in sexual matters', p. 380.

15 Christopher Hilliard, '"Is It a Book That You Would Even Wish Your Wife or Your Servants To Read?" Obscenity Law and the Politics of Reading in Modern England,' *American Historical Review I*, 653 (2013): 655–6.

16 James Boyd White, *Heracles' Bow* (Madison: University of Wisconsin Press, 1985), p. 2. See further Austin Sarat, Matthew Anderson and Catherine O. Frank (eds), *Law and the Humanities* (Cambridge: Cambridge University Press, 2010).

17 Shoshana Felman, *The Juridical Unconscious: Trials and Traumas in the Twentieth Century* (Cambridge: Harvard University Press, 2002) p. 107. See Robert Cover, 'Violence and the Word', in Martha Minow, Michael Ryan and Austin Sarat, *Narrative, Violence and the Law: The Essays of Robert Cover* (Ann Arbor: University of Michigan Press, 1995), p. 203.

18 Cornelia Vissman defined law as 'a repository of forms of authoritarian and administrative acts that assume concrete shape in files.' Cornelia Vismann, *Files: Law and Media Technology* (trans. Geoffrey Winthrop-Young) (Stanford, CA: Stanford University Press, 2008), p. 1.

19 Nead, 'Bodies of Judgment', p. 205.

20 Michael Gamer, 'Genres for the Prosecution: Pornography and the Gothic', 114 *PMLA* (October 1999): 1046.

21 Nead, 'Bodies of Judgment', p. 205.

22 Judith Butler, *Excitable Speech: A Politics of the Performative* (London: Routledge, 1997), p. 130.

23 Ibid., p. 37.

24 Ibid., p. 129.

25 *The Confessional Unmasked* (London: The Protestant Electoral Union, 1867), p. 52. She could, incidentally, because it would aid conception.

26 Ibid., pp. 58, 62, 54. This redaction was included in the edition at issue for the court.

27 *The Confessional Unmasked* cited in *Hicklin.* p. 362.

28 *The Times*, 29 June 1857, p. 8 cited in M. J. D. Roberts, 'Morals, Art and the Law: The Passing of the Obscene Publications Act, 1857', *Victorian Studies*, 28 (4) (1985): 628.

29 Katherine Mullin, 'Poison more Deadly than Prussic Acid: Defining Obscenity after the 1857 Obscene Publications Act (1850–1885)', in David Bradshaw and Rachel Potter (eds), *Prudes on the Prowl: Fiction and Obscenity in England, 1850 to the Present Day* (Oxford: Oxford University Press, 2013), p. 18.
30 *Hicklin*, p. 363.
31 Ibid.
32 Ibid., p. 370.
33 Ibid., p. 375.
34 Ibid., p. 376.
35 Ibid., p. 371.
36 Ibid., p. 371, emphasis mine.
37 Florence Dore, *The Novel and the Obscene: Sexual Subjects in American Modernism* (Stanford, CA: Stanford University Press, 2005), p. 25.
38 *Steele v Brannan* (1871–2) L.R. 7 C.P. 261 at 263 [*Steele*].
39 *Hicklin*, p. 378.
40 *Steele,* p. 265, per Kydd, for the appellant.
41 Ibid., p. 267 per C. J. Bovill.
42 Ibid., p. 269 per C. J. Bovill.
43 Ibid.
44 Ibid., p. 270 per J. Keating.
45 Ibid., p. 271 per J. Keating.
46 Ibid., pp. 271–272 per J. Keating.
47 *Commonwealth v. Sharpless,* (1815) 2 Serg. & R., p. 92, italics in original.
48 Ibid., p. 102.
49 Bruce Burgett, *Sentimental Bodies: Sex, Gender and Citizenship in the Early Republic* (Princeton, NJ: Princeton University Press, 1998), p. 145.
50 *Commonwealth v. Holmes,* (1821) 17 Mass 336, p. 337.
51 *Act for the Suppression of Trade in and Circulation of Obscene Literature and Articles of Immoral Use 1873,* 17 Stat. 598 which amended the *Post Office Act* (1872) 17 Stat. 283.
52 *United States v. Harman* (1891) 45 F. 414. (D.Kan.) [*Harman*].
53 Ibid., p. 414.
54 *Harman*, p. 418, emphasis added.
55 Ibid., p. 419–20.
56 Ibid., p. 420.
57 Butler, *Excitable Speech,* p. 12.

References

Act for the Suppression of Trade in and Circulation of Obscene Literature and Articles of Immoral Use 1873, 17 Stat. 598 which amended the *Post Office Act* (1872) 17 Stat. 283.
Burgett, B., *Sentimental Bodies: Sex, Gender and Citizenship in the Early Republic,* Princeton, NJ: Princeton University Press, 1998.
Butler, J., *Excitable Speech: A Politics of the Performative,* London: Routledge, 1997.
Colligan, C., *The Traffic in Obscenity from Byron to Beardsley: Sexuality and Exoticism in Nineteenth-Century Print Culture,* Basingstoke: Palgrave Macmillan, 2006.
Commonwealth v. Holmes, (1821) 17 Mass 336.

Commonwealth v. Sharpless, (1815) 2 Serg. and R. 91.

The Confessional Unmasked, London: The Protestant Electoral Union, 1867.

Cover, R., 'Violence and the Word', in M. Minow, M. Ryan and A. Sarat (eds), *Narrative, Violence and the Law: The Essays of Robert Cover,* Ann Arbor: University of Michigan Press, 1995.

Crowe v. Graham, (1967) 121 C.L.R. 375.

Dore, F., *The Novel and the Obscene: Sexual Subjects in American Modernism,* Stanford, CA: Stanford University Press, 2005.

Felman, S., *The Juridical Unconscious: Trials and Traumas in the Twentieth Century,* Cambridge, MA: Harvard University Press, 2002.

Gamer, M., 'Genres for the Prosecution: Pornography and the Gothic', *PMLA,* 114 (1999): 1043–54.

Hilliard, C., '"Is It a Book That You Would Even Wish Your Wife or Your Servants To Read?" Obscenity Law and the Politics of Reading in Modern England', *American Historical Review* (2013): 653–78.

Hunt, L., 'Introduction: Obscenity and The Origins of Modernity, 1500–1800', in L. Hunt (ed.), *The Invention of Pornography: Obscenity and the Origins of Modernity, 1500–1800,* New York: Zone Books, 1993.

Kendrick, W., *The Secret Museum: Pornography in Modern Culture,* Berkeley: University of California Press, 1996.

McDonald, P., 'Old Phrases and Great Obscenities: The Afterlife of Two Victorian Anxieties', *Journal of Victorian Culture,* 13 (2) (2010): 294–302.

Mullin, K., 'Poison More Deadly than Prussic Acid: Defining Obscenity after the 1857 Obscene Publications Act (1850–1885)', in D. Bradshaw and R. Potter (eds), *Prudes on the Prowl: Fiction and Obscenity in England, 1850 to the Present Day,* Oxford: Oxford University Press, 2013.

Nead, L., *The Female Nude: Art, Obscenity and Sexuality,* London: Routledge, 1992.

Nead, L., '"Bodies of Judgment", Art, Obscenity, and the Connoisseur' in C. Douzinas and L. Nead (eds), *Law and Image: The Authority of Art and the Aesthetics of Law,* Chicago: University of Chicago Press, 1999.

Nead, L., *Victorian Babylon: People, Streets and Images in Nineteenth-Century London,* New Haven, CT: Yale University Press, 2000.

Obscene Publications Act 1857, 20 and 21 Vict., c.83.

Regina v. Hicklin, (1868) 3 L.R.Q. B. 360.

Roberts, M. J. D., 'Morals, Art and the Law: The Passing of the Obscene Publications Act, 1857', *Victorian Studies,* 28 (4) (1985): 609–29.

Roth v. United States, (1957) 354 U.S. 476.

Sarat, A., Anderson, M. and Frank, C. (eds), *Law and the Humanities,* Cambridge: Cambridge University Press, 2010.

Sceats, S., 'The Legal Concept of Obscenity: A Genealogy', *Australian Feminist Law Journal,* 16 (2002): 133–45.

Steele v. Brannan, (1871–2) L.R. 7 C.P. 261.

United States v. Harman, (1891) 45 F. 414. (D.Kan.).

United States v. One Book Called "Ulysses", (1933) 5 F. Supp. 182 (Dist. Court, S.D.N.Y.).

United States v. Smith, (1891) 45 F. 476.

Vismann, C., *Files: Law and Media Technology* (trans. G. Winthrop-Young), Stanford, CA: Stanford University Press, 2008.

White, J. B., *Heracles' Bow,* Wisconsin: University of Wisconsin Press, 1985.

Part II

5

Controlling Ideas and Controlling People: Libel, Surveillance, Banishment and Indigenous Literary Expression in the Dutch East Indies

Paul Tickell

The Dutch East Indies has frequently been described as a 'police state'.[1] It certainly was a 'surveillance state', where a network of spies and police informants as well as surveillance of the local press kept the colonial state informed of activities that were deemed to be a threat to *Rust en Orde* (peace and order).[2] Yet this characterization of the colonial state also presents us with a number of real paradoxes. On the one hand we are faced with a process of political domination, through control and at times repression, and on the other hand the need to justify colonial possession by benevolent, enlightened rule. As the colonial state became more powerful, the potential for both coercive control and benevolent intervention into people's daily lives increased. This chapter traces the playing-out of this central paradox in the administration of colonial censorship in the East Indies, conceived as a complex of measures at once pervasive and constitutive.

As the Netherlands itself moved to a more permissive stance on censorship, its East Indian colony also followed suit, though with the local European colonial administration warning of calamity or actively stymying much of this liberalization. At the beginning of the twentieth century formal mechanisms of censorship and information control in the Dutch East Indies changed: preventative and pre-publication censorship of printed materials, previously the norm, gave way to post-publication censorship, in which books, newspapers and journals had to be presented to local authorities within 24 hours of their publication. This was a pragmatic control response to the growing amount of print material being produced, and not merely an embrace of liberal principles.[3] It was also a response to the growing European and literate non-European populations of the Indies. Both groups in different ways saw themselves as citizen-subjects of the Netherlands, with claims on the political and civic rights that had become the norm in the Netherlands itself – freedom of the press, freedom of association, full male and later female suffrage.

Print technology came to the Dutch East Indies rather slowly and until the end of the eighteenth century remained a virtual monopoly of the Dutch East India Company. There was virtually no autonomous indigenous involvement in producing the printed word, however, until the mid-nineteenth century. It was only then that newspapers also begin to be published in Malay, the regional *lingua franca*, and Javanese, the language of the largest single ethnic group of the East Indies. And it was only in the first decades of the twentieth century that indigenous Indonesians themselves begin to play significant, autonomous and controlling roles in the world of the press and literature.

Faced with a new and growing audience for print material, a burgeoning of newspapers (containing both reportage and serialized fiction), a taste for realism and the contemporary in imaginative literature, and what in other contexts has been labelled 'the invention of politics' in the Indonesian world,[4] colonial administrations were pressed by two countervailing pressures. There was the need to control a literate population, linked over time and space by modern print culture into what Indonesia specialist Benedict Anderson has famously called 'an imagined community'.[5] There were also pressures on colonial policy and its overtly-stated *mission civilisatrice* that saw the development of literacy, new audiences and new consciousness as an affirmation of 'enlightened' colonial policy. As a consequence of these permissive pressures, I can think of no examples of the Dutch colonial government in the Netherlands East Indies choosing to ban a work of literature published in the Indies itself.[6] Indonesian authors and publishers, however, were never given unrestricted freedom to publish whatever they wanted and colonial authorities had a hefty arsenal of legal tools with which they could control writers.

The most commonly-used laws to control the press and written word in the Dutch East Indies were Articles 63a, 63b, 66a and 66b of the Indies Criminal Code (*Strafwet*).[7] These were used as broad libel (*persdelict* – print offences) and slander (*spreekdelict* – speaking offences) laws. Complaints were also largely lodged by individuals, but as complainants were frequently European civil servants this also represented a kind of *de facto* state repression. These laws do not appear to have been particularly 'anti-indigenous' in a black-letter law sense, and the European/Dutch language press was also frequently subject to complaints, but where there was a racialized difference it was in the respective punishments meted out to Europeans and non-Europeans in the colony.[8] For Europeans, courts were more likely to impose a fine; for non-Europeans (and indigenous Indonesians in particular), a custodial sentence, often with hard labour, was the norm. Imprisonment did have unintended consequences in that it provided activist-authors with time to write. At least two early Indonesian novels were written from prison – Semaun's *Hikajat Kadiroen* (*The Story of Kadirun*) and Soemantri's *Rasa Merdeka* (*The Experience of Freedom*) – both of which describe the new consciousness and activism of young men and women in the Indonesian nationalist and communist movement.[9]

The slander laws associated with these articles were used by the colonial government in the 1920s to control the course of political meetings. As political organizations matured and transformed into truly mass organizations after the First World War, indigenous political and industrial activism increased. Speakers at political and trade union meetings were sometimes prosecuted; their meetings attended by police, local civil administration or by spies. As activism increased and more resources of the colonial state were dedicated to surveillance and monitoring of organized labour and dissident politics, the colonial state's intervention into what was 'sayable' and 'unsayable', often through direct interference in the meetings themselves, can appear more and more comic from a contemporary perspective. For instance, the newspaper *Sinar Hindia* (*The Light of the Indies*) under a rubric entitled *Pergerakan* ('The Movement') reported on local meetings of the Indonesian Communist Party and its associated organizations. It would report on the location, the speakers, the topics covered and almost always, with wry humour, the number of colonial officials attending. More significant meetings, such as Party Congresses, were reported at length in substantial accounts that appear to have delighted in reporting what the movement labelled '*stop-stopan*'. Based on the Dutch (and English) word 'stop' (which is what the observing colonial officials would apparently call out to halt a meeting), this neologism makes fun of these efforts. And newspaper reports would frequently be in dialogue form, recording a discussion between an activist and a colonial official, with the activist asking the colonial official whether an issue was acceptable or not. A list of issues is canvassed and deemed unacceptable by the colonial official, but in the process all of the unacceptable issues have been given a hearing. What the colonial regime appears to have intended was a form of intimidation and control, yet in the clash between Indonesian verbal dexterity and colonial rules and regulations, it appears that frequently the Indonesian side won. At the same time, what this direct 'verbal' intervention indicates is that colonial power on the ground was often not a matter of formal legal process, but was subject to the opinion of perhaps a single local official.

It may be argued that Articles 63a, 63b, 66a and 66b of the Indies Criminal Code, in essence libel and slander laws, were not intended as censorship mechanisms *per se*, in that they were not primarily concerned with banning ideas but protecting individual and corporate reputations. This, however, could not be said for what were the 'big guns' of censorship in the colonial legal arsenal: the *Haatzaaiartikelen* (The Sowing of Hatred Articles) of the Indies Criminal Code. The Sowing of Hatred Articles were a series of broadly-worded laws (Articles 154–7) relating to sedition and *lèse majesté*, used to prosecute those who were judged to have sown racial and communal discord in Indies society or who had brought the Netherlands Indies Government (and its functionaries) into disrepute. Like much colonial law of the Netherlands Indies and the press offences mentioned above, the application of these laws was racially-inflected, in that indigenous and Sino-Indonesian published material was far more frequently judged in violation, while the often toxic racism of the Indies Dutch language press went largely unprosecuted.

Overwhelmingly, the target of these Dutch colonial laws was politically-engaged reportage in politicized and partisan Indonesian and Sino-Indonesian newspapers in the period after the First World War. The emergence of non-traditional literary forms, as well as the partial renovation of some traditional literary forms in the Dutch East Indies, is intimately associated with the emergence of the press, print capitalism and its new audience.[10] Not only were works of creative literature published in these new newspapers, it was not unusual for their authors to be journalists or correspondents for these newspapers as well.

Dutch reaction to this literary activity and activism was mixed. For Dutch liberals the emergence of a modern (or more-or-less Western style) literature in confirmed the success of their education policies, but also a pragmatic cultural bulwark between a limited, but also served as somewhat ascendant, Pan-Islamic 'modernist' movement and the colonial state. The universal value of European culture and its notions of progress were taken for granted, not just by colonial officials, but by this new, educated, indigenous elite, in a more restricted way. While many colonial liberals appear to have displayed both affection and respect for their indigenous 'pupils', there was always an element of patronising condescension involved in this relationship.

For the most part, creative literature escaped the colonial censor's eye. An index of this material's perceived insignificance can be seen in the fact that in the Press Summaries of the Native and Chinese Press serial fiction published in the indigenous press rarely rates a mention. There were, however, a small number of cases in which the colonial regime took exception to works of literature and their authors were punished. Some of these are somewhat celebrated works and are regarded as significant texts within an Indonesian national(ist) literary tradition. Others, along with their authors, are barely known in contemporary Indonesia.

In 1913, the Dutch colonial government in Indonesia proposed to celebrate the centenary of the liberation of the Netherlands from French Napoleonic domination. For many 'East Indian' nationalists this was a step too far.[11] A committee was established to lobby against it and one of the leaders of the Indische Partij (The Indies/ Indian Party), Soewardi Soerjaningrat (later more commonly known as Ki Hajar Dewantoro) authored a brief pamphlet in Dutch, entitled 'Als ik eens Nederlander was' ('If I ever was a Netherlander').[12] The pamphlet was published initially in the Dutch-language newspaper of the party (*De Expres* — *The Express*) and later in pamphlet form in Malay. The pamphlet is clearly political in its intent but, unlike more straight-forward reportage, it has an imaginative bent, as its title suggests.

The negative, even draconian reaction from the Dutch colonial government is a matter of its translation into Malay. Dutch was a language of obvious power and the language of the upper echelons of the colonial administration, but it was Malay (or what we now call Indonesian) that was the effective language of indigenous administration. While no single language provided universal understanding across the multilingual archipelago of the Netherlands East Indies, Malay came closest. It was this capacity to popularize an anti-Dutch message across indigenous ethnic divisions that most probably caused the Dutch to act. The colonial administration saw the pamphlet as an attempt to incite anti-Dutch sentiment and promptly took action against the three leaders of the *Indische Partij*. Soewardi, Tjipto Mangoenkoesoemo and Dr E. F. E. Douwes Dekker (who later adopted the Indonesian name Dr Setiabudi Danuredjo) were arrested and sent into exile in the Netherlands for several years. The punitive response meted out to the author and other proponents of this pamphlet was too late from the point of view of censoring ideas, however. The pamphlet had been published and widely-discussed, and 'banning' its author by sending him into exile in the Netherlands did little but enhance his reputation. As Ahmat Adam notes, the controversy surrounding 'Als ik eens Nederlander was' 'opened the eyes of the government to the danger of press "freedom" provided for by the amendment made in 1906 to the Press Act of 1856,[13] though it would be another 18 years before the Press Act would be substantially modified and tightened.

In 1908, the colonial government established the *Commissie voor de Volkslectuur* (The Commission for Popular Reading Material, which was later and more widely known by its Indonesian-Malay name, *Balai Pustaka* or House of Literature). It took as its task the provision of reading material suitable for the native population. Initially, this involved the production of works of traditional literatures in the major languages of the Indies – Javanese, Sundanese, Malay and other 'smaller' languages. From the early 1920s onwards it began to publish new and original literary works in Malay, which have subsequently come to form the core of an Indonesian canon.

Balai Pustaka represented a direct government intervention by the Dutch into the relatively new world of literary publishing in the East Indies. In part the aim was to exercise a degree of control over what was published, not by banning what was unacceptable, but by commercial production and promotion. Through subsidies, superior distribution networks and the colonial school system, the colonial publisher had an edge over private publishers. *Balai Pustaka*'s books also had a certain amount of prestige and for authors there was also payment for their work. From this position of commercial power, *Balai Pustaka* and the colonial government were able to exercise a degree of subtle control over the development of modern Indonesian literature and popular tastes, resulting in the creation of a tame, largely apolitical fictional literature as the new norm in modern Indonesian literature.

In this mode, the colonial publisher did reject works or request editorial amendments. One case in particular stands out and, while the editorial amendments demanded and ultimately accepted by the author can be seen as part of normal editorial negotiations between authors and publishers, the sensitive and ultimately political nature of these amendments in the colonial context suggests a form of censorship. In 1927, high-profile journalist, author and political activist Abdul Muis submitted the manuscript of a novel to *Balai Pustaka*. With significant amendments, this manuscript would subsequently be published as the novel, *Salah Asuhan*.[14] For almost twenty years before this, Muis had been a leading figure in the world of Malay language journalism, indigenous politics and had also published a number of novels, both through private publishers and in newspapers in serial form, under his own name and under a pseudonym. At various times, his political activities had attracted the attention and negative sanction of the colonial government, though his position on the more moderate end of nationalist politics made him one of the more acceptable indigenous nationalist figures to the Dutch. His acceptability was such that he served as member of the colonial parliament (*Volksraad*) and was the editor of a Malay language newspaper, *Neratja* (Balance), which was directly subsidized by the colonial government.[15]

Muis' original manuscript is lost, but what remains is a suggestive body of correspondence between the author and various editorial staff as to how the novel was to be amended for publication.[16] Both the novel as ultimately published and the original manuscript deal with sensitive issues of interracial marriage, ethnic and cultural authenticity, and Westernization. In his pitch to the publisher, Muis describes the main aim of his novel as:

> to ensure that Western educated young people of my race remain true to their Oriental character, because the Westernised behaviour of some of them often upsets the more conservative members of their families, especially in Western Sumatra, and becomes an obstacle for them to get an education and important lessons for their children. Apart from that most mixed marriages are a disaster for the Oriental and also drag the Western woman into this chaos.[17]

In many ways, Muis' pitch echoed colonial ideology. While supporting ideas of cultural association, especially through education, Muis also supported ideas of separation and distinction between the races of the Indies, like much colonial policy. The negative aspects of interracial marriage lie at the heart of *Salah Asuhan* – both in the version originally submitted to *Balai Pustaka* and in its final published version. Although the plot of Muis' novel is to a considerable degree in harmony with conservative colonial race ideology, in its original form some details were clearly objectionable to the European management of *Balai Pustaka*. Dutch objections were primarily to his negative and at times salacious depiction of the main character, Hanafi's European/ Eurasian wife, Corrie, and are revealed in correspondence between the Dutch management of *Balai Pustaka*, its Malay editors and Muis himself.[18] In the original version, Corrie is depicted as selfish, sexually promiscuous, unfaithful and the cause of the marriage's breakdown. She begins an affair with a popular singer – a figure with popular appeal in inverse proportion to his low social cachet. Ultimately, because of her lavish life style, Corrie becomes indebted to an Arab money lender (a figure rarely liked or respected by either European or indigenous Indies society) and is forced into prostitution to repay her debts. Hanafi attempts a reconciliation with his estranged wife, who is in hospital after being shot by one of her lovers, but she dies before this can happen. Bereft, Hanafi returns to his village, puts his affairs in order and commits suicide by drinking poison.

While this version of the novel is melodramatic, it was not this that the Dutch functionaries of *Balai Pustaka* found objectionable; much of the critique asserted that the novel had little 'educational value'.[19] With considerable revision the novel was finally published. Most of the melodrama remained, but the negative depiction and more risqué aspects of the main European character disappeared. In the published version fault for the marriage breakdown and negative consequences for his indigenous family are put squarely at Hanafi's feet. It is his character flaws and pretensions in assuming the legal status of a European that cause the problems; European society in the Indies, personified by Corrie, becomes victim to an 'uppity natives'' pretensions.

It could be argued that the amendments forced on the author, Abdul Muis, fit into the category of 'editorial suggestions', rather than direct censorship. Muis could have taken his manuscript to a private publisher, as Drewes, the Dutch director of *Balai Pustaka*, suggested.[20] What appears to have allowed Muis to compromise was the considerable publisher's advance. The politically-sensitive issues of race relations were toned down and the colonial ideals not just of 'peace and order' but of European racial dignity were maintained.

Colonialism is a system of domination replete with contradictions. It is easy to see it as completely hegemonic and all-dominating, with the will of the Western colonizer all determining, and to judge it 'bad', 'evil', 'exploitative', 'racist' and so on. In many ways, these sorts of arguments suit the hubris of both the colonizer and anti-colonial liberation movements. 'Little Holland' viewed its domination of the 'garland of emeralds' that straddled the equator as a source of pride (and perhaps in more honest moments a source of moderate surprise).[21] Equally, Indonesian independence from the technologically-superior and militarily-powerful Netherlands is now viewed with similar pride. Of course, these judgements all have an element of truth in them, but they simplify what was always a complex set of relationships that varied over time. This process of simplification is equally true with regard to colonial regimes of censorship. Forces for and against censorship and for and against liberalization varied over time in the Netherlands East Indies. It can be convincingly argued that the ultimate aim of colonialism is the maintenance of colonial power and that therefore its regimes of censorship are but one element in that system. While this rationale probably did not change in any meaningful way in the first half of the twentieth century in colonial Indonesia, the face and methods of colonialism did – and with it the aims and methods of censorship.

Freedom of expression, and social, political and economic development were all part and parcel of this process – or at least until the indigenous population began to take seriously many of the liberating ideologies they took and adapted from the West. The question of freedom versus control and ultimately repression that had always been part of colonial discourse continued to be the subject of colonial debate well into the 1920s, until a series of communist rebellions in 1926 and 1927 decisively shifted that debate towards the control and repression end of the scale. Almost immediately after the first rebellions on Java, in November 1926, the colonial regime began a wave of arrests and newspaper bans, culminating in the exile of leading communist figures to a concentration camp on the upper reaches of the Digul River in West Papua.[22] All of this was publicly announced in Dutch and Indonesian-language newspapers, which forced the raw, coercive power of the colonial state to front and centre in the minds of the Indonesian reading public. Using the repertoire of repressive techniques at its disposal – arrest, banishment, exile, banning publications, closing down newspapers and the (fairly restricted) use of capital punishment – the colonial regime effectively eliminated the communist party, and cast a shadow over other elements of the indigenous Indonesian political movement, forcing it to moderate its public pronouncements to a considerable degree.

Most historians agree that the liberal experiment in Ethical Colonialism – a notion of colonialism that saw the Dutch as having a particular responsibility for the spiritual and material welfare of their colonial subjects – died in the years immediately before the 1926–7 rebellions, with the colonial state moving towards much more activist and draconian forms of control. Following the rebellions, control of the printed word and the legal structures that facilitated this control were also changed. In 1931 press laws were substantially tightened and Indonesian political parties and newspapers were closed down in quick succession. Anti-colonial political activity did not, of course, disappear, but it was undoubtedly more tightly-controlled than at any other point, and the nationalist press became much more circumspect in its criticism of the colonial regime. Colonial repression, both in the sense of what was actually meted out to Indonesian activists as well as what could be threatened, became the norm in a way that had not always been the case before.

With the elimination of the Communist Party, virtually all the authors of a nascent, radical Indonesian literature were either exiled from the Indies or sent into internal exile, usually to one of the most isolated parts of the Indonesian archipelago. Some of these authors died in exile and others, those allowed to return to their previous places of residence, were clearly broken by the experience. In such a controlled environment, literary censorship was barely necessary. Political authors still wrote, and the nationalist movement continued in some cases to be the subject of creative literature, but it was an overwhelmingly 'polite' literature that no longer confronted issues of race or colonial power, let alone economic exploitation, and so much so that the Dutch and Europeans in general disappear from mainstream Indonesian literature.[23] This stands in marked contrast to the 'wild reading matter' (*bacaan liar*) published by independent, non-government publishers prior to the communist rebellions that the colonial publisher actively sought to displace. *Balai Pustaka*, the colonial publishing house, had become a dominant presence in the world of Indonesian literature by the 1930s and had already begun to determine what would or could be incorporated into an emerging Indonesian literary canon.

By the last decade of colonial rule, the permissive and liberal colonial policy of the first decades of the twentieth century was dead. I can think of no declaration that expresses the changes in colonial attitudes more than the often-quoted, 1935 example from the Dutch Governor General, B. C. de Jonge (Governor General from 1931–6): 'We have ruled here for 300 years with whip and club and will be doing it for another 300.'[24] The statement represents a combination of myth, violence, bluster and delusion. The Dutch had not uniformly ruled the Indonesian archipelago for 300 years and, in sweet irony, barely seven years after this statement they were unceremoniously defeated by Japanese invaders. Yet in the 1930s, and in the face of paranoid repression, the Indonesian nationalist movement was tightly controlled, its press muted and a new, repressive Press Law was in place. The Dutch, of course, did not remain for another 300 years, but their 'whips and clubs', in the form of a legacy of censorship and repression, were to be a longer-lasting legacy, with which independent Indonesia has long struggled and only in the twenty-first century begun effectively to dismantle.

Notes

1   Harry A. Poeze, 'Political Intelligence in the Netherlands Indies', in R. Cribb (ed.), *The Late Colonial State in Indonesia: Political and Economic Foundations of the Netherlands Indies, 1880–1942* (KITLV: Leiden, 1994), pp. 229–44.

2   From 1917 onwards, *Balai Pustaka,* the colonial government's publishing house, published monthly summaries of the Indonesian and Chinese press in the Indies. For several years prior to 1917 a similar summary had been compiled under the auspices of the colonial government's Advisor for Native Affairs. The summaries are an invaluable historic source, as many of the original newspapers have disappeared. They were never without particular political biases and what attracted their attention was for the most part fairly predictable. The relative detail of the summaries often gives a reasonable idea of what was seen as a threat to the colonial regime. See Doris Jedamski, 'Balai Pustaka: A Colonial Wolf in Sheep's Clothing', *Archipel,* 44 (1992) pp. 34–5.

3   Two major bibliographies of material published in the Netherlands Indies exist. The first (J. A. van der Chijs, *Proeve eener Ned. Indische Bibliographie (1659–1870),* Batavia and The Hague: Bruining and Wijt, 1875), covers the period from the earliest Dutch presence in the seventeenth century to 1870. This lists a total of 2,641 items published by private publishers from the end of the Dutch East India Company's rule in 1799–1870. The second (G. F. Ockeloen, *Catalogus dari boekoe-boekoe dan madjallah-madjallah jang diterbitkan di Hindia Belanda, dari tahoen 1870–1937,* Batavia: G. Kolff, Bell and Howell, 1938), covers the period 1870–1937. Ockeloen's is some 600 pages long and each page has approximately twenty entries — this yields an approximate figure of 12,000-plus titles published in the final seventy years of colonial rule in the Netherlands East Indies.

4   Anthony Milner, *The Invention of Politics in Colonial Malaya* (Cambridge: Cambridge University Press, 2001). While Milner's direct examples relate to colonial Malaya under British colonialism, the broader points he makes about the invention of a discourse called 'politics' and, related to it, the creation of a new 'public sphere' also apply to the Netherlands East Indies.

5   Benedict Anderson, *Imagined Communities* (London: Verso, 1991).

6   The colonial government did, however, enforce strict regulations on the importation of printed material. Its fears here centred largely on pan-Islamic material and its apparent threat to European colonial power. On relatively rare occasions these regulations did ensnare Indonesian nationalists. In 1916 while on a brief visit to the Netherlands journalist and activist, Marco Kartodikromo, published a collection of political writings entitled *Boekoe Sebaran Pertama (The First Pamphlet Book).* As Ahmad Adam notes: 'After five months, Marco returned and arrived at (sic) Batavia on 12 February 1917. But barely ten days later he was put in preventive custody in the native gaol in Batavia. Again he was charge of (sic) committing *persdelict* and transgressing Article 66a — "arousing or fostering animosity, hate or contempt against the government of the Netherlands Indies"'. When the trial began, Marco was further charged with transgressing Articles 21 and 30 of the Indies Printing Press Regulation, accused of having printed and distributed seditious articles, and imprisoned (Ahmad Adam, 'Radical Journalism and Press Persecution in Java, 1914–1918', *Jebat,* 20 (1992), p. 100.).

7   Ibid., p. 94.

8   Ibid., pp. 94–5.

9   Semaoen, *Hikajat Kadiroen* (The Story of Kadiroen), (Semerand: Kantoor PKI, c.1920); Soemantri, *Rasa Merdika: Hikajat Soedjanmo* (The Experience of Freedom: The Story of Soedjanmo), (Semarang: VSTP, 1924).

10 Anderson, *Imagined Communities.*

11 I use the term 'East Indian' nationalist here because Indonesia as a political term had yet to come into existence in 1913 and, while virtually all of the activists in the campaign I describe have been absorbed into the pantheon of Indonesian nationalist leaders, at the time of this controversy all were members of a largely Eurasian political organization that few Indonesians would see as central to their national narrative. The party, *De Indische Partij* (The Indian/Indies Party), was radical and advocated independence for the East Indies, but was also a more multiracial party than was to characterize most later Indonesian nationalist organizations, perhaps with the exception of the Indonesian Communist Party.

12 Soewardhi Soerjaningrat, *Djika Saja Nederlander/Als ik eens Nederlander was* (*I ever was a Netherlander*), (Bandung: Comite Boemipoetra goena merajakan Pesta Seratoes Tahoen Keradjaan Belanda, 1913).

13 Adam, 'Radical Journalism', p. 94.

14 Abdul Muis, *Salah Asoehan* (Batavia: Balai Pustaka, 1928). In English, *Never the Twain* (trans. Robin Susanto) (Jakarta: Lontar, 2011).

15 Keith Foulcher, 'Biography, History and the Indonesian Novel: Reading *Salah Asuha*', *Bijdragen tot de taal-, land- en volkenkunde* 161.2/3 (2005): 247–68.

16 Sjafi Radjo Batuah, 'Di balik Salah Asuhan', *Pustaka dan Budaja* 5 (1964): 30–9.

17 Ibid., p. 31. ('*untuk mendjaga pemuda² sebangsa jang mendapat pendidikan barat supaja tetap bersifat timur, karena tindakan kebarat-baratan dari sebagian mereka sering mengagetkan anggota² keluarga mereka jang amat kolot (terutama di Sumatera Barat) dan mendjadi halangan bagi mereka dalam meperoleh pendidikan dan pengadjaran penting bagi anak-anak mereka. Selain itu kebanjakan perkawinan tjampur mendjerumuskan orang Timur kedalam bentjana dan djuga menjeret pula perempuan Barat dalam kekatjauan itu*')

18 Ibid., pp. 33–9. Reproduces the correspondence in Indonesian translation. All details of the original version of the work are derived from information contained in this correspondence.

19 Ibid., p. 38. ('I do not believe that anything educational will come out of this work').

20 Ibid., p. 38.

21 The phrase is derived from mid-nineteenth-century Dutch novelist, Eduard Douwes Dekker (pseudonym: Multatuli) and is used in his novel *Max Havelaar or the Coffee Sales of the Netherlands Trading Company*, first published in Dutch in 1860 (Multatuli, *Max Havelaar or the Coffee Sales of the Netherlands Trading Company*, New York: Knopf, 1927).

22 Takashi Shiraishi, 'The Phantom World of Digoel', *Indonesia*, 61 (1996), pp. 93–118.

23 For instance, Sutan Takdir Alisyahbana, *Lajar Terkembang*, (Batavia/Jakarta: Balai Pustaka, 1936). See C. W. Watson, 'Plus ça change…? A Comparison of Two Indonesian Feminist Novels: Suwarsih Djojpuspito's *Maryati* and Istiah Marzuki's *Sundus*', *Indonesian and Malay World*, 33.95 (2005): 67–95.

24 Quoted in Sutan Sjahrir, *Out of Exile* (New York: Greenwood, 1969), p. 112.

References

Adam, A., 'Radical Journalism and Press Persecution in Java, 1914–1918', *Jebat; Malaysian Journal of History, Politics and Strategic Studies*, 20 (1992): 91–105.

Alisjahbana, St. T., *Lajar Terkembang,* Batavia/Jakarta: Balai Pustaka, 1936.

Anderson, B. R. O'G., *Imagined Communities,* London: Verso, 1991.

Batuah, S. R., 'Di balik Salah Asuhan', *Pustaka dan Budaja,* 5 (1964): 30–9.

Chijs, J. A. van der, *Proeve eener Ned. Indische Bibliographie (1659–1870),* Batavia and The Hague: Bruining and Wijt, 1875.

Dekker, E. D., (pseudonym: Multatuli), *Max Havelaar or the Coffee Sales of the Netherlands Trading Company,* New York: Knopf, 1927.

Foulcher, K., 'Biography, History and the Indonesian Novel: Reading *Salah Asuhan*', *Bijdragen tot de taal-, land- en volkenkunde* 161 (2/3) (2005): 247–68.

Jedamski, D., 'Balai Pustaka: A Colonial Wolf in Sheep's Clothing', *Archipel,* 44 (1992): 23–46.

Milner, A., *The Invention of Politics in Colonial Malaya.* Cambridge: Cambridge University Press, 2001.

Muis, A., *Salah Asoehan,* Batavia/Jakarta: Balai Pustaka, 1928.

Muis, A., *Never the Twain,* Jakarta: Lontar, 2011.

Ockeloen, G. F., *Catalogus dari boekoe-boekoe dan madjallah-madjallah jang diterbitkan di Hindia Belanda, dari tahoen 1870–1937,* Batavia: G. Kolff, Bell and Howell, 1938.

Poeze, H. A., 'Political Intelligence in the Netherlands Indies', in R. Cribb (ed.), *The Late Colonial State in Indonesia: Political and Economic Foundations of the Netherlands Indies, 1880–1942,* Leiden: KITLV Press, 1994, pp. 229–44.

Semaoen, *Hikajat Kadiroen,* Semerand: Kantoor PKI, c.1920.

Shiraishi, T., 'The Phantom World of Digoel', *Indonesia,* 61 (1996): 93–118.

Sjahrir, St., *Out of Exile,* New York: Greenwood, 1969.

Soemantri, *Rasa Merdika: Hikajat Soedjanmo,* Semarang: VSTP, 1924.

Soerjaningrat, S., *Djika Saja Nederlander/Als ik eens Nederlander was,* Bandung: Comite Boemipoetra goena merajakan Pesta Seratoes Tahoen Keradjaan Belanda, 1913.

Watson, C. W., 'Plus ça change…? A Comparison of Two Indonesian Feminist Novels: Suwarsih Djojpuspito's Maryati and Istiah Marzuki's Sundus', *Indonesian and Malay World* 33 (95) (2005): 67–95.

6

Teaching Librarians to be Censors: Library Education for Francophones in Quebec, 1937–61

Geoffrey Little

The narrative of North American librarians as champions of intellectual freedom and advocates for unrestricted access to books in the twentieth century is challenged by the history of library education for Francophones in the Canadian province of Quebec. Between 1937 and 1961, French Canadian librarians who received their education at École de Bibliothécaires, or School of Librarianship, at Université de Montréal, were trained through mandatory courses on censorship and the Index of Prohibited Books to act as censors and gatekeepers to dangerous or immoral library materials. Historians of censorship and libraries in Quebec have situated this practice within the context of Quebec's pre-1960 history, when the Catholic Church controlled many of the province's social and educational institutions and dictated the boundaries of intellectual and cultural discourse within the province. What has received almost no attention, however, is the ways in which censorship was institutionalized through library education and librarianship in Quebec. This culture of censorship was both symptom and cause, and its legacy has frustrated both the development of libraries and the creation of a reading public in a province where the literacy rate is almost five per cent lower than the national average and which has one of the highest high school dropout rates in Canada.[1]

Quebec was established as a colony of France in 1608 and the first significant collections of books belonged to religious communities. It was only after the British conquest in 1759 that British administrators created secular, semi-public libraries, which were succeeded by literary societies and mechanics' institutes.[2] Home to a majority French-speaking population with significant English, Irish and Scottish communities, by the middle of the nineteenth century Quebec's Roman Catholic hierarchy believed that the province's Catholic, French character was under threat from neighbouring English Canada and the United States. At the same time, the Church expanded its role as a provider of social services in Quebec ranging from hospitals to schools to orphanages to poor relief. This coincided with the rise of Ultramontanism within the church, which, among other things, advocated for a strong role for the Church in civic life, including policing of public and cultural morality. This is evidenced in the way the Church dealt with Institut canadien, a French-Canadian literary society established in 1844, the library of which included titles listed in the Index of Prohibited Books. Relations between the Institut and the Church deteriorated to such a degree that the Bishop of Montreal eventually denied the sacraments, including Christian burial, to its members.[3] Yvan Lamonde has argued that mid- and late-nineteenth century Quebec was actually characterized by 'ecclesiastic censorship of books, newspapers, and libraries.'[4] Marcel Lajeunnese has written that, as early as the 1840s:

> Catholic clergy of Lower Canada [Quebec] seemed to fear that public education, and the increase in literacy that it would bring, would make French Canadians more vulnerable to a wide and sustained spread of Protestant or non-Orthodox printed material ... For the Catholic clergy, a parish library appeared to be a means of countering this danger. It was seen as a solution to bad books and bad reading material.[5]

Accordingly, parish libraries were promoted by church authorities as repositories for 'good' books and reading material. One parish library's catalogue stated that this local institution had an important social and moral role:

> [the library] must be a place of moral preservation, a place of intellectual edification, and moral recreation. In other words, its goal is to promote a taste in healthy reading, to combat impiety; to oppose dangerous books; to promote books that conform in all respects to the dogmas of religion; to conserve morality; to facilitate instruction by providing families and individuals with varied, enjoyable, and solid reading.[6]

Despite this high moral purpose, however, most parish libraries were poorly run and lacked the quantity of books and periodicals available to Canadians in the rest of the country, or even to English Protestants in Montreal who belonged to association libraries like the Mechanics' Institute (est. 1828) or the Fraser Library (est. 1885), or the ten English-language circulating libraries that operated in the city before 1900.[7] This, combined with a strictly demarcated Catholic and Protestant school system in Quebec, meant that everyday access to books and magazines for many French Canadians was regulated and controlled by religious, educational and civic authorities.

Given these restrictive conditions, and despite Montreal's position as Canada's largest city as well as its financial capital, the public library movement that flourished in North America in the late- nineteenth and early-twentieth centuries almost entirely bypassed Quebec. While communities in the rest of Canada were establishing libraries, many with the support of the Carnegie Corporation, only one city in Quebec – Westmount, a wealthy English-speaking enclave directly adjacent to Montreal – created a publicly-funded, free library.[8] Birdie MacLennan has described how the efforts of the Mayor of Montreal to secure a grant from the Carnegie Corporation in 1901–2 were opposed by the Catholic Archbishop, who condemned the public library, with its free, open stacks and the immoral English, Protestant and American materials it would likely contain, as a threat 'more dangerous than the most malevolent smallpox virus.'[9] The city council eventually passed a bylaw in 1902 creating a public library, but from its start it suffered from a poor collection, limited funds and no dedicated premises until 1917. Moreover, it faced competition from the Sulpician Library, a public library created by the Sulpician order of priests that was run according to Catholic principles, including adherence to the rules of the Index of Prohibited Books and its prohibition of works by authors like Sand, Stendhal, Voltaire, Zola, Balzac and Hugo.[10]

The state of Quebec's public libraries was revealed in 1933 by a commission of inquiry into Canadian library services sponsored by the American Library Association and the Carnegie Corporation. The chapter of the commissions' report on Quebec was subtitled 'A Language and Library Problem' and it reported that a majority of the province's 275 parish libraries were 'semi-moribund and, for purposes of information or recreation, negligible'.[11] Moreover, 118 of these libraries reported an annual expenditure of just $5 a year or less on books and periodicals, with an average budget of $50, within a total of $12,700 spent on books in the entire province for a population of 2.8 million.[12] By comparison, in 1933 the Saskatoon Public Library spent $12,000 a year on books for a population of just over 43,000.[13] In a meeting with Premier Louis-Alexandre Taschereau, the commissioners were warned that 'a public library is not without its perils to our modern generation ... They too often have access to books that they could not find in their homes'.[14] The state thus reinforced and approved of the church's attempts to limit access to materials it perceived as harmful or immoral. It is no surprise, then, that the commissioners concluded that 'the library problem in the Province of Quebec is one not capable of quick and easy, or happy and final solution'.[15]

The 'library problem' also extended to training for French-speaking librarians. Education for librarianship in Canada began in 1904 with a summer program at McGill University, an English-language institution founded in 1821. Offered annually, with breaks during the First World War, it became a diploma program in 1927 and a bachelor of library science degree in 1930, requiring an undergraduate degree for admission.[16] While McGill offered part of the 1932 summer session in French, there were no regular opportunities for Francophones to receive library training in their native language.

The creation of an entirely French language library school was the result of a conversation between Paul-Aimé Martin (1917–2001), a 21-year-old member of the Congregation of the Holy Cross and the editor of *Mes Fiches,* a serial publication featuring French and French Canadian book reviews, and Marie-Claire Daveluy (1880–1968), a librarian at the Montreal Municipal Library and a graduate of McGill's summer library program. According to Daveluy, during a discussion about a difficult cataloguing problem that Martin brought to her one day in 1937:

> We spoke about the need for professional training for our French Canadian librarians and bibliographers. The librarian [Daveluy] spoke from the heart and revealed that she had been cultivating a project precisely like this for almost twenty years. She wanted to spread library education in French amongst Quebec's intellectuals. Father Martin, a fervent apostle of the book, came out of the Municipal Library that morning, carrying, in addition to a solution of the

technical cataloguing problem, new convictions, and a project that needed to be achieved at all costs. [17]

Martin and Daveluy took their concept to Father Emile Deguire, headmaster of Collège Sainte-Croix, and Aegidius Fauteux, director of the Montreal Municipal Library and former director of Sulpician Library, which had closed in 1931. The group met with the rector of Université de Montréal, a Catholic university established in 1919 by a papal charter of Benedict XV, and proposed the creation of a French-language library school that would be affiliated with the university. The idea was apparently well received and the school was established on 13 May 1937 as 'École des bibliothécaires de l'Université de Montréal' or the Library School of the University of Montreal. [18] Despite the stated affiliation with the university, the School was constituted as an arm's-length private institution, neither under the jurisdiction of the university nor incorporated into its academic or administrative structures, an arrangement that would present a series of problems over the next quarter century.

The School began offering courses in July 1937. Students entering the two-year diploma programme in bibliography and library science registered for 20 courses over three week sessions in the summers of 1937 and 1938 held at the Montreal Municipal Library. The part-time teaching faculty, which included co-founders Fauteux and Daveluy, was made up of three women and twelve men, five of which, or a third of the entire faculty, were in holy orders. [19] The programme had no defined admissions requirements or criteria, but it was expected that applicants would have the equivalent of a high school diploma, compared to the bachelor's degree required for admission to the programme at McGill, and priority was given to applicants already working in libraries. In the midst of the Great Depression, the 1937 prospectus also explicitly stated that 'the School does not guarantee employment to students'. [20] The curriculum was divided into five modules, one of which was concerned with the use and appli-cation of censorship, with one course on the principles and generalities of censorship and another on the history and rules of the Index of Prohibited Books, both of which were taught by Abbé Philippe Perrier, a noted historian of French Canada. [21] The first year's student body reveals something of the role of the church in the provision of library services in Quebec: of fifty-five students, fourteen were nuns, eight were priests, and two were religious brothers. [22]

From 1938, courses were offered during the academic year rather than in the summer and in 1945 the School began to offer a bachelor's degree in library science and bibliography. [23] As at McGill, the admissions criteria became an undergraduate degree. At this point, the courses on censorship were integrated into the module on general bibliography. [24] To reinforce the religious nature of their studies, students also now took courses on the history of the Catholic Church, the history of the church in Canada, and English and American Catholic literature. The School's 1950–1 prospectus reveals that the censorship courses featured three components: 'principals and generalities'; 'preliminary censorship'; and the instruction on the application of the Index, including its history, legislation and 'conseil practique' or practical advice. [25] The course was taught entirely by priests until 1961 and, while there are no extant syllabi in the school's records, copies of the final exams for 1954, 1958 and 1959 have survived. In 1958, Abbé Vivalde Massé, a Franciscan priest, asked his students:

1. How do you learn about the moral dimensions of books?
2. Does the obligation of the Index apply to someone who believes that he can read a book without harm?
3. Can you prove that books can exert influence?
4. What kinds of books should be submitted to the censor before publication?
5. Name five categories of books condemned by general decrees.
6. Is there a difference between a book that has been placed on the Index by special decree and a book that has been placed there by general decree?
7. Is a book condemned because it has not been subjected to censorship when it should have been submitted [before being published]?[26]

In 1959, Father Jean Thorn, a canon lawyer and a future judicial vicar of the Archdiocese of Montreal, asked his students to reply to a series of yes and no questions:

1. Can a baptized layman read any Bible?
2. Do reprints need to be resubmitted to the censor?
3. If a film script is based on a book on the Index, do I sin by seeing the film?
4 André Gide has been condemned *opera omnia* [all works], but do I sin if I read his translation of Shakespeare's *Henry V*?
5. Is a student of literature obliged to ask permission from the ecclesiastical authorities to read books on the Index?
6. Is it true that a printer does not sin if he prints a history of the Church written by a monk who would not have had to submit his book to the censor and therefore did not receive the imprimatur?
7. Is it true that the law of censorship does not require *sub gravi* obligation?
8. Can I read a translation of a book on the Index?
9. Are Catholics the only ones subject to the laws of the Index?
10. If *The Mandarins* by Simone de Beauvoir has been placed on the Index, can I read her book *All Men are Mortal?*

The School's interest in the teaching and application of censorship was inextricably bound with its Catholic foundation, but also with its nationalist mission to promote and protect French Canadian culture. In its 1937 prospectus, the School advertised as its goal:

> The study of the indispensible knowledge for librarians, that is to say to all persons, religious or lay, committed to the custodianship of a repository of books in a public or private institution. This training gives students a general idea of the work in a library. It relies on French and American methods adapted for French-Canadians and Catholics.[27]

Co-founder Marie-Claire Daveluy also believed it was her task to promote professional library training and education in Quebec and in the French language. While the study of library science was flourishing in English Canada, Daveluy contended that in Quebec 'it thus became urgent for us to organise amongst ourselves, by ourselves, and for ourselves permanent technical instruction in librarianship'.[28] Before the founding of the School, she wrote that:

> French Canada kept looking with sadness at other countries of the world like South Africa, Bulgaria, Finland, Brazil, and China. Like these nations it [French Canada] now had technical training organized around its book repositories for librarians seeking professional competence.[29]

Like these other former colonies with linguistic and cultural minorities, Quebec could now stand with the cultures and nations of the world that provided libraries for their people. For others, like Omer Héroux, the editor of the Montreal daily newspaper *Le Devoir*, the creation of a library school for French Canadians was a matter of national pride and identity, which censorship of books helped to protect and preserve:

> It is a question of pride, a question of dignity, a question also of immediate use … As well, we cannot imagine that the same question—that of censorship, for example, and the Index, to which the program has consecrated six lessons, will be treated in exactly the same way by the two universities [McGill and Université de Montréal].[30]

Just as libraries could not be neutral and had a moral responsibility to protect readers from 'bad' books and direct them to 'good' ones, schools that educated librarians had a mission to produce vigilant, morally upstanding bibliographic guardians. Juliette Chabot, a professor at the School, wrote in 1939 that:

> Because of Canada's political and geographic situations, we are inundated with Anglo-American literature, too often imbued with Protestantism. It is necessary to distinguish these things from all sides and to be able to capture new ideas and Christianize them.[31]

At the same time, the existence of censorship courses at the School must be contrasted to increasing efforts against censorship and the promotion of free access to books by librarians in the rest of North America. In 1939 the American Library Association (ALA) adopted a Library Bill of Rights. Motivated, in part, by the banning of John Steinbeck's 1939 novel *The Grapes of Wrath* in a number of American cities, the Bill of Rights advocated for open stacks, free and unrestricted access to books, and the selection of library materials based on their value to the community rather than the political, social or religious views of their authors. In 1940, ALA established the Committee on Intellectual Freedom to Safeguard the Rights of Library Users to Freedom of Inquiry, and in 1953 the American Book Publishers' Council and ALA adopted the Freedom to Read Statement, which declared, 'The freedom to read is essential to our democracy'.[32] It rejected claims that 'censorship and suppression are needed to avoid the subversion of politics and the corruption of morals'.[33] The Catholic library community, however, disagreed. In 1946, the archbishop of Quebec City stated that, as 'integral parts of the education system, libraries themselves cannot be neutral any more than they can be non-confessional'.[34] In 1958, Harold C. Gardiner, the Jesuit literary editor of *America* magazine, published the Catholic Viewpoint on Censorship in response to the Freedom to Read Statement. Gardiner wrote: 'the Catholic Church does more firmly hold that some books can "seduce," that they are of grave danger to the faith and morals of the generality of the Catholic body. Holding that, she is compelled, by her own internal logic and constitution, to protect the faithful.'[35]

By the end of the 1950s, École des Bibliothécaires had reached a crisis point. The relationship with Université de Montréal remained ambiguous, and the school faced constant funding and space problems, which meant that it was ineligible for accreditation by the ALA, an increasingly essential professional qualification that required schools to be part of a university, employ full-time professors and have a dedicated technical library.[36] In 1961, however, the school was absorbed by Université de Montréal. Swift changes followed, mirroring the secularization and professionalization of education in Quebec. A new full-time director and professors were hired and the school's name was changed from École des Bibliothécaires to École de Biblioéconomie, or School of Library Science. None of the part-time professors, including co-founders Martin and Daveluy, returned to teach in the new school.

Changes at the new school were a reflection of massive social shifts in Quebec. In 1959 the provincial government finally passed legislation to permit the creation of municipal public libraries and a general election in June 1960 marked the start of the Quiet Revolution, a period of immense social and cultural change for Quebec. Changes were also taking place within the Catholic Church. In January 1959, Pope John XXIII announced his intention to convene the Second Vatican Council, a body that ultimately promulgated reform in the church, including the elimination of the Index as a tool for clerical censorship.

At the new École des Biblioéconomie the censorship courses were replaced by a class called 'Livrès et Lectuers,' taught by Edmond Desrochers, a Jesuit priest and a graduate of the library school at Columbia University. In 1964, Desrochers presented his students with the following question on their final exam:

> In anticipation of the third session of the [Second Vatican] Council, which is presumed will result in the suppression of the Index, the librarian of a Catholic classical college buys one hundred books listed on the Index, catalogues them, puts them on the shelves, and lends them to interested students.
>
> The authorities call you in and demand your opinion on the choice of books. Give your answer in writing.[37]

This evidence of a lingering concern with 'good' books into the mid-1960s demonstrates that, despite changes to Quebec society and increasing efforts to build the library profession and library infrastructure, the Quiet Revolution did not transform Quebec or its libraries overnight, nor did it create a mass literate society. For example, of the fifty-three students in the new School's 1963 summer session, twenty-six were nuns, seven were religious brothers and one was a priest. It has also taken decades for Quebec to build a public library system that can compare to English Canada. In 1959, 3.3 million municipal library loans were recorded in Quebec compared to 25 million in Ontario, 6.3 million in British Columbia and 3.3 million in Alberta, while the total budget for all public libraries in Quebec in 1968 was $5.1 million, or $1.50 per resident served, compared with $6.5 million in Ontario or $3.75 cents per resident.[38] Lajeuneese has reported that, by the end of the 1980s, 20 per cent of Quebec's public libraries did not have a single full-time employee and only 40 per cent were staffed by a trained librarian.[39] As late as 2011, Montreal, Canada's second largest city since the 1970s, was spending $46.59 per resident on library services compared to $54.09 in Ottawa, $70.52 in Toronto and $75.13 in Vancouver.[40] Although, as Birdie MacLennan points out, the creation of the Grand Bibliothèque in Montreal and the consolidation of Quebec's Bibliothèque et Archives nationales du Québec (BAnQ) have significantly improved library services in Quebec and Montreal in particular, the province still lags in funding, collections, services and resources.[41] Moreover, despite the provincial government's 2007 claim that over 95 per cent of the province's residents were served by a public library, in 2010 the *Globe and Mail* newspaper reported that there were close to one million functionally illiterate Quebecers.[42]

Despite its relatively short existence, École des Bibliothécaires speaks to a period in Quebec when the act of reading was seen as having the power to corrupt both morals and national character. Well-trained Catholic librarians could, through the promotion of good books and judicious application of the Index, introduce readers to uplifting, beneficial literature that would also aid in building a morally healthy culture. The founders of the school also wanted to promote librarianship in Quebec as a means of enriching the province's intellectual life and capabilities, yet they operated within and supported a larger system of censorship, observation and control. Only massive shifts in government policy and society would change and gradually dismantle this system, but it has taken decades to counter the effects of censorship on literacy and the creation of a reading public in Quebec.

Notes

1 Statistics Canada et al., *Skills in Canada: First Results from the Programme for the International Assessment of Adult Competencies (PIAAC), Table B.1.2 Literacy.* Ottawa, 2013; Employment and Social Development Canada, 'Indicators of Well-being in Canada: Learning – School Drop-outs', available at http://www4.hrsdc. gc.ca/.3ndic.1t.4r@-eng.jsp?iid=32#M_3 [accessed 28 October 2014].

2 Marcel Lajeunesse, 'Public Libraries and Reading in Quebec: A History of Censorship and Freedom,' *Library and Information History*, 28 (2012): 28.

3 For more on the history of the Institut canadien see Yvan Lamonde, *Gens de parole: conférences publiques, essais et débats à l'Institut canadien de Montréal 1845–1871* (Montreal: Boréal, 1990).

4 Yvan Lamonde, 'Social Origins of the Public Library in Montreal', *Canadian Library Journal* 38 (December 1981): 366–7.

5 Lajeunesse, 'Public Libraries and Reading in Quebec', p. 29.

6 Bibliothèque de la paroisse Ste-Anne. *Règlements et catalogue*, 1898 in Réjean Savard, 'Le discours sur la lecture et l'évolution des bibliothèques publiques au Québec de 1850 à 1950', *Argus*, 26 (1997): 20–1.

7 Lamonde, 'Social Origins of the Public Library in Montreal', pp. 364–5.

8 Lajeunesse, 'Public Libraries and Reading in Quebec', p. 30.
9 Birdie MacLennan, 'The Library and its Place in Cultural Memory. The Grand Bibliothèque du Québec in the Construction of Social and Cultural Identity', *Libraries & the Cultural Record*, 42 (2007): 353.
10 For a history of the Sulpician Library, see MacLennan, 'The Library and its Place in Cultural Memory', pp. 356–60.
11 *Libraries in Canada: A Study of Library Conditions and Needs* (Toronto and Chicago: Ryerson Press and American Library Association, 1933), p. 40.
12 Ibid.
13 Ibid., p. 77.
14 Ibid., p. 35.
15 Ibid., p. 39.
16 Stanley Brice Frost, *McGill University: For the Advancement of Learning, Volume II, 1895–1971* (Kingston and Montreal: McGill-Queen's University Press, 1984), p. 31; 302–3.
17 Marie-Claire Daveluy, 'L'École de Bibliothécaires de l'Université de Montréal', *Culture*, 1 (1940): 14.
18 'Chronologie des relations entre l'École des Bibliothécaires et l'Université de Montréal,' n.d., box 3215, file 9, Fonds de l'École de bibliothéconomie et des sciences de l'information, 1938–2010, E6, Division de la gestion de documents et des archives, Université de Montréal (afterwards Fonds d'EBSI).
19 *Programme et Prospectus de L'École de Bibliothécaires de l'Université de Montréal 1937*, p. 2, box 5944, Fonds d'EBSI.
20 'The School does not guarantee situations to students', *Programme et Prospectus de l'École de Bibliothécaires de l'Université de Montréal 1937*, p. 3, box 5944, Fonds d'EBSI.
21 Ibid., p. 7.
22 'Liste des Élèves Reguliers aux Cours de Bibliothécaires de l'Université de Montréal', n.d., box 3226, file 1, Fonds d'EBSI,
23 École de Bibliothé*caires – 1945–1946*, p. 7, box 2724, Fonds d'EBSI.
24 Ibid., 12.
25 École de Bibliothécaires de l'Université de Montréal: Programme et Prospectus, [1950–1], p. 8, box 2724, Fonds d'EBSI.
26 'Questions d'examen sur la censure des livres', 19 March 1958, box 3222, file 47, Fonds d'EBSI.
27 École de Bibliothecaires de l'Universite de Montreal Année 1942–1943, Programme et Prospectus, p. 1, box 3215, Fonds d'EBSI.
28 Marie-Claire Daveluy, 'L'École de bibliothécaires de l'Université de Montreal', n.d., p. 4, box 3225, file 39, Fonds d'EBSI.
29 Ibid.
30 Omer Héroux, 'On travaille tout de même', *Le Devoir*, 24 September 1951, p. 1.
31 'Juliette Chabot, 'Les bibliothèques françaises', *L'Action universitaire*, 6 (1939): 7.
32 'The Freedom to Read: A Statement by the American Library Association and the American Book Publishers Council', *Bulletin of the American Association of University Professors*, 39 (Summer 1953): 209. See further discussion of this statement in Loren Glass's chapter in this volume.
33 Ibid. For a history of ALA and censorship, see Louise S. Robbins, *Censorship and the American Library: The American Library Association's Response to Threats to Intellectual Freedom, 1939–1969* (Westport, CT: Greenwood Press, 1996).

34 Lajeunesse, 'Public Libraries and Reading in Quebec', p. 32.
35 Harold C. Gardiner, *Catholic Viewpoint on Censorship* (Garden City, NY: Hanover House, 1958), p. 51.
36 Paul-Aimé Martin to Mgr. Irénée Lussier, 19 February 1957. Fonds de Secretariat General, 1951–72, D35/C19.1, Division de la gestion de documents et des archives, Université de Montréal.
37 'Bibl. 514, Livres et Lectures, Examen Final, 1er semestre', 10 January 1964, box 3126, Fonds d'EBSI.
38 'Summary Statistics for All Public Libraries, 1959', *Canada Year Book 1961* (Ottawa: Dominion Bureau of Statistics, 1961), p. 370; 'Summary Statistics for All Public Libraries, 1968', *Canada Year Book 1970–71* (Ottawa: Information Canada, 1971), p. 458.
39 Marcel Lajuenesse, 'Public Libraries and Reading in Quebec' 33.
40 Canadian Urban Libraries Council, 2011 Canadian Public Library Statistics, Table G, p. 1, available at http://www.mississauga.ca/file/COM/2011CanadianPublicLibrarySta tistics-all.pdf [accessed 30 October 2014].
41 MacLennan, 'The Library and its Place in Cultural Memory', p. 376.
42 Observatoire de la culture et des commuications due Quebec. 'Importane progression des biblitheoques publiques du Quebec entre 1995 et 2007', (March 2010), p. 1; Sean Gordon, 'The Lost Boys of Quebec', *Globe and Mail*, 11 September 2010, p. F7.

References

Canadian Urban Libraries Council, '2011 Canadian Public Library Statistics, Table G, p. 1', available at http://www.mississauga.ca/file/COM/2011CanadianPublicLibrary Statistics-all.pdf [accessed 30 October 2014].
Chabot, J., 'Les bibliothèques françaises', *L'Action universitaire*, 6, 2 (1939): 6–7.
Commission of Inquiry into the Library Situation in Canada, *Libraries in Canada: A Study of Library Conditions and Needs*, Toronto and Chicago: Ryerson Press and American Library Association, 1933.
Daveluy, M. C., 'L'École de Bibliothécaires de l'Université de Montréal', *Culture* (1940): 13–18.
Dominion Bureau of Statistics, *Canada Year Book 1961*, Ottawa: Queen's Printer for Canada, 1961.
Fonds de l'École de bibliothéconomie et des sciences de l'information, 1938–2010, E6, Division de la gestion de documents et des archives, Université de Montréal.
Fonds de Secretariat General, 1951–72, D35/C19.1, Division de la gestion de documents et des archives, Université de Montréal.
'The Freedom to Read: A Statement by the American Library Association and the American Book Publishers Council', *Bulletin of the American Association of University Professors* 39 (1953): 209–14.
Frost, S. B., *McGill University: For the Advancement of Learning, Volume II, 1895–1971*, Kingston and Montreal: McGill-Queen's University Press, 1984.
Gardiner, H. C., *Catholic Viewpoint on Censorship*, Garden City, NY: Hanover House, 1958.
Gordon, S., 'The Lost Boys of Quebec', *Globe and Mail*, 11 September 2010, p. F7.

Héroux, O., 'On travaille tout de même', *Le Devoir*, 24 September 1951, p. 1.

Information Canada, *Canada Year Book 1970–71*, Ottawa: Queen's Printer for Canada, 1971.

Lajuenesse, M., 'Public Libraries and Reading in Quebec: A History of Censorship and Freedom', *Library & Information History*, 28 (2012): 26–40.

Lamonde, Y., 'Social Origins of the Public Library in Montreal', *Canadian Library Journal*, 38 (1981): 366–7.

Lamonde, Y., *Gens de Parole: conférences publiques essais et débats à l'Institut canadien de Montréal 1845–1871*, Montreal: Boréal, 1990.

MacLennan, B., 'The Library and its Place in Cultural Memory. The Grand Bibliothèque du Québec in the Construction of Social and Cultural Identity', *Libraries & the Cultural Record*, 42 (2007): 349–86.

Observatoire de la culture et des communications du Québec, 'Importante progression des bibliothèques publiques du Québec entre 1995 et 2007', available at http://www.bdso.gouv.qc.ca/docs-ken/multimedia/PB01691FR_progBiblio1995_2007H00F00.pdf (2010) [accessed 30 October 2014].

Robbins, L. S., *Censorship and the American Library: The American Library Association's Response to Threats to Intellectual Freedom, 1939–1969*, Westport, CT: Greenwood Press, 1996.

Savard, R., 'Le discours sur la lecture et l'évolution des bibliothèques publiques au Québec de 1850 à 1950', *Argus*, 26 (1997): 19–27.

Statistics Canada et al., *Skills in Canada: First Results from the Programme for the International Assessment of Adult Competencies (PIAAC), Table B.1.2 Literacy*, 2013, available at http://www4.hrsdc.gc.ca/.3ndic.1t.4r@-eng.jsp?iid=32#M_3 [accessed 28 October 2014].

7

Surrealism to Pulp: The Limits of the Literary and Australian Customs

Nicole Moore

Through the last two decades literary studies and literary theory have been compelled, in the surging wake of the so-called 'end of theory', and in response to the manifest diversification yet empirical objectification of literature as a subject of study, to return to the vexed question of the nature of the literary. At stake in that question, of course, are a set of powerfully unresolved concepts that continue to drive broad inquiry in the humanities and lie at the root of ongoing attempts to come to grips with the role of culture in the contemporary world. So, once more, critics confront the relationship between language and art, the status of representational truth, the problem of literary value, the experience of literary knowledge, the character of aesthetic engagement and also the quality of literary alterity; both the worldly 'uses' of literature, to inter-polate Rita Felski's expanded use of the term in these contexts, and its unworldly claims either to otherness or to a radical resistance to instrumentality. The place of literature as such is in question, as it becomes at once just a niche, high-brow genre in the globalizing book industries and an increasingly nebulous quality envisioned and lauded perhaps only in the disaggregating pages of literary review journals. In asking how literature now matters, critics and theorists have also had to ask: where is it and what is it? In what does it consist and persist?

Derek Attridge's 2004 book *The Singularity of Literature* was a key venture into this hermeneutic problematic, but it begins from the assertion that 'all attempts since the Renaissance to determine the difference between "literary" and "non-literary" language have failed – and this is a *necessary* failure, one by which literature as a cultural practice has been continuously constituted'.[1] For Attridge, failure consists in an inability to define the distinctive identity of the literary or its 'singularity' as cultural practice, and is identifiable in descriptions that seek to yet cannot capture this distinctiveness. So the ineffable becomes a defining quality of the literary, with his most assertive claim being that 'literature, or rather the experience of literary works, consistently exceeds the limits of rational accounting'.[2] This does not stop Attridge offering a set of descriptors of his own: a taxonomy of the literary that seeks to identify aspects or dimensions of the literary experience that 'lie at the heart of Western art as a practice'. Attridge's five descriptors are: innovation, or 'invention'; uniqueness, or 'singularity'; alterity or otherness; the work's 'occurrence as a particular kind of *event*', which he calls 'performance'; and, last, 'its participation in the realm we call "the ethical".[3] These categories map differentially onto those put forward by others, including Felski, Jonathan Culler and Charles Altieri, venturing into this debate within similarly theorized frames (while outside that frame, cognitive and new empiricist 'distant' or digital models for reading reconstitute the literary more radically).[4]

Attridge's description of a work of literature as an 'event' or 'performance' has been perhaps his most innovative categorical contribution, opening up discussion of the literary to temporal elements and repositioning it not as an object but as an experience that takes place in time and within certain nominal parameters, and that occurs as an event that must be understood as literary and is thus, perhaps necessarily, performative. This suggestive conception allows into the definition all manner of concrete and material elements that have traditionally remained outside text-based formulations, and reflects the recent, discipline-wide shift in literary studies towards re-valuing reading, understood as temporally bound and historically locatable, in understanding the work – we might say significance or value – of a text. This is even at the same time as it opens up the definitional question further, compelling us to ask not only where and what, but *when* is the literary; at which reading moment does it happen? Attridge's conception becomes particularly suggestive for attempts to identify the possibilities of a material history of the literary, and, if we step further than that, for what we might perceive as the institutional, even legal production of literature as a concept.

In that regard, it may also be a useful description for examining what historically can be recognized as the mutually-defining relationship between literature and censorship. Literature and print censorship are usually conceived as long-time adversaries, even mutually-exclusive opposites as concepts and forms of practice, each opposed to the very precepts of the other. As the introduction outlines, this volume seeks to understand the degree to which they have been dialectical terms, each producing the other, coeval and mutually constitutive. If we concede the work of this dynamic across the centuries – first, that the literary, in its confrontation with the regulation, prohibition, proscription and silencing of unsanctioned forms of speech, writing and representation, comes to a defensive understanding of itself as the opposite of what is targeted (by definition never obscene, blasphemous, seditious, as is asserted in the key legal defence of literary and artistic merit); and second, that censorship, in its aims to regulate, proscribe and contain offensive forms of speech and representation, must also work to identify and thus define offence as such, and in doing so, inevitably identifies, limits and polices what is not offence, or what can be seen to defend itself self-evidently against such charges, that is, literary merit – and if we concede the enacting of this dynamic in modern print censorship, in national and international regulatory regimes and legislative instruments that inherit Enlightenment models of state and subject, as well as British Victorian and French conceptions both of offence and merit, then we can see that this mutually-defining relationship can also be a key element, in turn, in any contemporary endeavour to establish the nature of the literary.

Via critics like Attridge, we might look for the literary experience as an event, a recognizable performance in which readerly cognition or meaning-making is the key form of action. Then the reading work of the censorship apparatus, with its elaborated legislative instruments and juridical doctrine enabling the legal adjudication of offence, can serve as a kind of performance arena or a bureaucratic stage, even an example of what psychoanalysis long ago called 'the scene of reading', on or in which institutionalized reading is enacted and as yet (un)sanctioned forms of the literary are witnessed, confirmed or rejected, and (we could say) made literary. And as this chapter seeks to demonstrate, what becomes apparent when working with bureaucratic records from 'successful' regimes of print censorship are their explicit address and workaday solutions to this notional conundrum of the literary. Censors of literature need to know what it is, and successful regimes of censorship can be seen to conscientiously set in place institutional and administrative taxonomies of classification that produce working definitions of literature, usually in line with principles drawn from scholarly, 'expert' advice.

Twentieth-century literary censorship in English-speaking countries often proceeded transparently from a Leavisite insistence on literature as a form of moral discourse and practice, or in the case of the busy South African apartheid censors in the mid-1950s, from the models of formalist American New Criticism, especially those offered by Cleanth Brooks' *The Well-Wrought Urn* and René Wellek's and Austin Warren's *Theory of Literature*. The latter defined the literary as an 'entity, a closely knit organisation which isolates itself from commonplace reality' and 'remains true to itself and its own legitimate rules'.[5] 'With these latest formalist tests', as Peter McDonald notes, the South African Publications Commission could argue in a Report from 1956 that, 'it was possible to "safeguard" genuine literary works'. McDonald's history of literary censorship under apartheid attends to the ways in which censorship, with literary critics at work as censors, functioned paradoxically as at once the guardian of the literary as well as its policeman,[6] and his chapter for this volume confronts the complex compromises of the censor critic directly. Regimes of publication censorship have had to produce 'successful' definitions of the literary, using as their measure of accomplishment the effective implementation of state-sanctioned, institutionally-construed versions of the literary on the reading of national populations.

Success and failure in these schemas can be seen to be measured oppositely than in Attridge's model. His definition of success is an actualization of the 'singularity' of literature, a positivist attribution of qualities to the experience or 'nature' of the literary, even as Attridge suggests that this is impossible, while censorship's measure of success is an actualization of a consensus on offence, notionally a negative attribution of qualities to that which cannot be countenanced. (It may be productive to think about this through anthropologist Michael Taussig's work on public secrecy and what he couches, via Žižek and through him via Hegel, as 'the labour of the negative'.) Censorship defines the literary only in the negative, as necessarily that which is not its primary object, but it is worth questioning whether such a definition of literature is inevitably a 'failed' definition. Censorship's legal proscriptions actively produce material manifestations of literature, as we buy, borrow, download, read and experience it, and cannot in that sense always be set aside as historically 'wrong'.

Other contemporary definitions of the literary offer alternatives to Attridge's taxonomy that are worth exploring against the institutional histories of censorship, including Rita Felski's account of the 'uses of literature'. In the name of literature's 'connectedness', rather than exceptionalism, and its epistemological, ideological and social rather than merely aesthetic functions, she nominates four quite different categories, or 'modes of textual engagement' to define the literary: *recognition, enchantment, knowledge* and *shock*.[7] Building transparently on what she acknowledges as 'venerable literary categories', including *anagnorisis* (for Aristotle a key plot device in Greek tragedy, in which the familiar is first rendered strange and then only recognized when it is too late), beauty, mimesis and the sublime, Felski's taxonomy invests not in the nature or character of the literary on the page but in its human effects, in that which it produces in us as we read, and so evidences perhaps even more clearly than Attridge an interest in the literary as experience rather than object. Given this, it is the final category that is of most particular import for examining literature's relations with the censor.

In positing 'shock' as symbolically central to contemporary literature and literary studies, Felski seemingly reverses the conventional understanding through which censorship as a practice of law has proceeded: that shock is an attribute or effect of offence rather than merit and, if a piece of representation shocks, it tips dangerously away from any characterization as art. One of the ways in which obscenity differs from pornography, for example, is that it encompasses what legal theory can call 'disliked mental states' – disgust, repulsion and shock.[8] In another example from South Africa, McDonald evidences the way in which 'moral repugnance – or, more accurately, racialised disgust', particularly of miscegenation and racial 'intermingling', figured conspicuously in forms of apartheid censorship.[9] Felski instead seeks to *valorize* 'literature's power to disturb', often discussed using specialized terms such as the sublime, transgression, trauma, dislocation, self-shattering, Shklovsky's *ostranenie* or 'defamiliarization', or Heidegger's *Stoss* – the idea that an artwork is a blow to consciousness, a rupturing of the taken for granted. Reading the modernists, in particular Beckett, Brecht and Sartre's *Nausea*, but also *The Bacchae*, Kleist's *Penthesilea*, African American novelist Gayl Jones' *Eva's Man*, and especially Baudelaire's *Les Fleurs du Mal*, Felski declares: 'Here, indisputably, was the literature of extremity, of what Foucault and others call "the limit experience", a bracing blend of solipsism, paranoia, brutality, and despair, where the standard supports and consolations of everyday life are ruthlessly ripped away'.[10] Felski's reanimation of the category of shock might place it exactly in the border zone of that defining dialectic between censorship and the literary being pursued here – at once at the limits of the literary and pushing the boundaries of offence.

The productive work of this dynamic can be exposed in two case studies, both from the Australian history of publications censorship – a history that paralleled administratively and legally the regimes of other British settler colonies, notably apartheid South Africa and Catholic Ireland, but was distinctive in its aims and effects.[11] The first instance plays out in tandem with Felski's conception; indeed the banned book was invoked as itself 'the limit of literature' by influential French critic Philippe Sollers[12] and remains an end point for phemonenological quests for aesthetic experience, such as those of André Gide, André Breton and other surrealists, and in their wake Maurice Blanchot. Through April and May 1944, the Australian Literature Censorship Board considered the 1868 French *symboliste* work *Les Chants du Maldoror* [*The Lay of Maldoror*] by 'Le Comte de Lautréamont', or Isidore Ducasse.[13] The Literature Censorship Board was a non-statutory body of appointed literary and legal experts, established in 1933 to provide advice to the federal Australian Minister for Customs, who was responsible under the 1901 Trade and Customs Act for the prohibition of obscene, blasphemous or seditious goods or articles, including books, and after the passage of regulations through 1938, for publications exhibiting an excessive representation of violence or crime. In 1944, Customs' Comptroller General, through the normal processes – that is, after having seized it from an importer, whether private or commercial – forwarded for the Board's inspection a copy of the 1924 edition of *The Lay of Maldoror*, published by the Casanova Society in its first English translation by John Rodker. The edition was a private printing, for only 100 subscribers, and contained three illustrative plates of surrealist lithographs by Odilon Redon. (A copy of this edition is now held in the Metropolitan Museum of Modern Art.[14]) The Board recommended passing it on 16 May 1944, but the Minister for Customs over-ruled the Board's decision and banned it on 9 September.[15] (It is worth noting that between these two decisions J. T. Kennedy, a practising Catholic and interventionist bureaucratic censor, took up the role of Comptroller General of the Department of Trade and Customs, administering the Customs Act for the Minister and controlling the material sent for the Board's consideration.) Without a clause in the Act allowing for literary or artistic merit, the Board's role was technically merely advisory, with the identification of offence resting finally and powerfully in the Minister's legally indisputable 'opinion'; it was exceptional, nevertheless, for the Board's advice to be countered so directly.

Lautréamont died mysteriously in 1870 at just 24, two years after publishing the first part of this 'extraordinary work of Satanic obscenity', as the Australian censors termed it. It is still a highly influential, perhaps notorious example of the *roman noir*; in its nightmarish, disjointed and hallucinatory surrealism at once the apex and the nadir of the supernatural Romantic Gothic. Maldoror 'is the blasphemous, remorseless opponent of God and man' who treats 'the Romantic aspiration for the divine and transcendental with Supreme irony', as Paul Knight outlines, while God is portrayed as a visitor to brothels or a drivelling cannibal.[16] Superlatively self-conscious, the work anticipates its own censorship in France under the Second Empire, interpellating its intrepid reader as, effectively, an accomplice in its crime, warning as well as tempting us with the dangers of reading itself:

> May it please heaven that the reader, emboldened and having for the time being become as fierce as what he is reading, should, without being led astray, find his rugged and treacherous way across these sombre and poison-filled pages; for, unless he brings to his reading a rigorous logic and a tautness of mind equal at least to his wariness, the deadly emanations of this book will dissolve his soul as water does sugar. It is not right that everyone should read the pages which follow; only a few will be able to savour this bitter fruit with impunity.[17]

Lautréamont, as Maldoror, requires and thus conjures a distinctively 'wary' reader, at once rational and fierce, and in this figuration ironically, self-consciously, echoes the characteristics required by the censor himself – reading despite the danger of harm and corruption and with a fierce commitment, despite evil, to the greater good. Thus, the Australian censors couldn't say they hadn't been warned and, indeed, 'reading Maldoror is a vertigo', as Maurice Blanchot declares, in his lengthy essay extrapolating what he nominates as 'the experience of Lautréamont'. This is an experience made of 'absolute lucidity and thick darkness, consciousness that knows everything and knows not where it goes, so as to feign the illusion of a commentary entirely conscious of not being able to explain anything and at the same time uniquely preoccupied with making everything reasonable'.[18]

As Chairman of the Board, classicist and poet Dr L. H. Allen furnished a closely written, four-page report defending *The Lay of Maldoror* as a work of artistic interest and distinction. His approach was to insert Lautréamont into an elaborate web of poetic influence, marshalling as evidence of his work's literary character its relations to the writings of Shelley, Byron, Southey, Blake, Swift, Thomas Moore, Baudelaire, Gérard de Nerval (whom Allen notes translated Goethe's *Faust* into French in 1828), and Goethe's spirit of negation, drawing on Allen's 1907 doctorate on Shelley from the University of Leipzig. In his report, the literary emerges as a collective agglomeration, the text imbricated into a tapestry of legitimacy in which the quantity and quality of literary associations are what must be emphasized, and the originality – for Attridge the 'singularity' – of the obviously highly *outré*, incontestably 'shocking' work must be suppressed.

Allen says:

> The author was a Satanist, a rebel against the order of the world; but he avers that he 'sings of evil only to oppress the reader and make him desire the good as a remedy' (xvii). He recognises himself that his pitch is exaggerated; and as Byronism at that time raged through Europe with its overdone sentimentalities it is not surprising that so young a man should have taken a perverted pleasure in hiding his personality behind sulphurous clouds.[19]

The drama of his reading restages Maldoror's own – reading Lautréamont as Maldoror, as Satan, performs the text as elaborated script, redacted and sanitized for the Department of Customs, the censor critic mollifying the Comptroller with the author's youth, precursors and good intentions. Customs is also given explicit direction in *how to read* such a text:

> In estimating a book such as this, the reader is dealing with an intellect steeped in the revolutionary period of his time (he was born only two years before the European revolutionary year of 1848), influenced by Satanism, and building a symbolic world where figures must not be understood in a literal sense.

Allen acknowledges that 'there are passages which reach the very verge of horror, even though they are symbolic'. The vocabulary of boundaries or verges signals that he is defending the categorical here – the limits of the literary against the obscene – while 'horror' conveys something very close to Felski's lauded 'shock', conjuring the Gothic complex of bodily or bestial transgression and abjection in Lautréamont's text only to back away and to divest it of its literal, visceral force. As 'horror' it is not literary but, interestingly, neither is it explicitly obscene. To finish his defence, Allen turns explicitly to the tested, juridical concept of aesthetic value:

> There are striking flashes of genius in his work, and the vividness of his imagination is at times astounding. He must, therefore, be regarded as an element in French literature and in that of symbolism, to be reckoned with. Horrible as some of its passages are (e.g. XLVII, p. 205 ff.), the book must have value for literary students. Moreover psychiatrists, alienists and all students of mental phenomena would be likely to find in the wild and fantastic figures, valuable material for their work.

His decision is to pass this edition, published in 1924 with only 100 copies. He notes that, in 1944, before the end of the war, not many copies of it are likely to make it to Australia in any case, but that a cheaper edition for indiscriminate reading 'would not be advisable, without special consideration'.[20]

The only other member of the Board to comment was J. F. Meurisse Haydon, Professor of French and German at Canberra's new University College, and the Board's long-serving expert in French literature. He recommended passing *Maldoror* too, but for distinctly different reasons.

> This extraordinary work gives us the disordered visions of a mind which is the victim of hallucinations and nightmare excursions into the realm of the illogical, the inconsequent, the horrible and the grotesque. It contains passages which are definitely obscene. Yet these are so completely submerged under the mass of hysterical detail that they become harmless. The seeker after pornography would be hopelessly bored and would soon cast the book aside as providing too unsatisfactory a field for his appetites.

Far from evincing aesthetic or intellectual 'genius' or 'astoundingly' vivid imagistic literary achievement, *Maldoror* for Haydon is of quite limited merit: bad, and pathologically so – delusional and hysterical. It is 'definitely obscene', but this obscenity is so poorly rendered and 'submerged under detail' that it proves 'unsatisfactory'. Lautréamont's obscenity is just too boring to be pornographic – effectively, in a sardonic, reversed evaluation not atypical for Haydon, dismissed as not good enough. Neither pornography nor literature, *Maldoror* is yet acknowledged to occupy 'a place of its own among the more freakish products of French literature of the Second Empire', and to be of some limited influence, if only on writers 'who will be forgotten in 100 years' time'. So, Haydon almost sighs, since it matters so *little*, it can pass.

As censors, Allen and Haydon produce opposite readings, though agreeing to pass the book for importation. Allen mounts an argument that Maldoror is highly literary and exceptionally so; at the limits of literature and a revealing an example of its extremities, partly based on its power to shock. There is some sense here

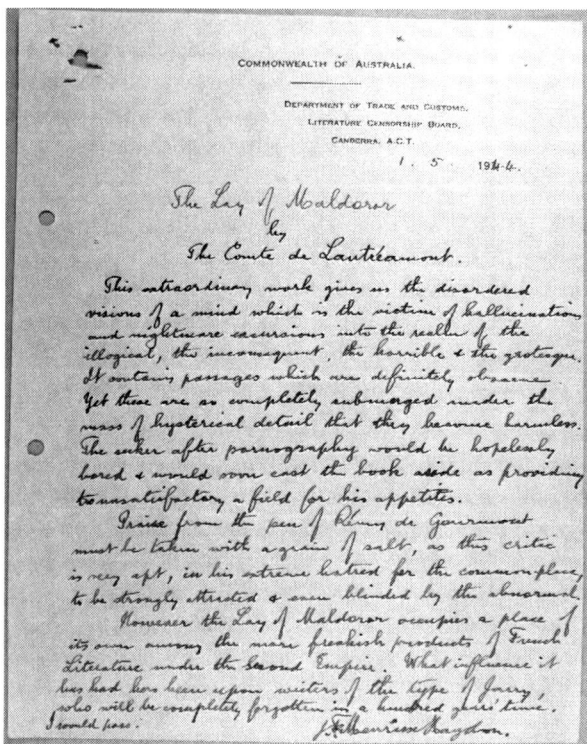

Fig. 7.1: Report by J. F. Meurisse Haydon to the Australian Literature Censorship Board on comte de Lautréamont's *The Lay of Maldoror*, 1944 (NAA A3023 Folder 1941/44).

that Lautréamont's obscenity is itself literary, pre-empting what becomes the later twentieth-century consensus on his work. Haydon downplays this power, for him explicitly located in obscenity, and does this by characterizing the literary as boringly-detailed inconsequence that overwhelms the obscene. The book is just literary enough to pass, for Haydon, and not shocking enough to ban.

In this attempt to gauge what can be couched as the limits of literature for censorship, we can compare *The Lay of Maldoror* with a contrasting instance of the Board's deliberations on the nature or the manifestation of the literary. Examined in 1936, this title drew from the Board a very different verdict on the work's merit and a recommendation to ban. As one of many in that very active year for Australian censorship, *Furnished Room* by prolific pulp novelist James Noble Gifford was presented to the Board, sent to Australia by the provocative, later notorious New York publisher Greenberg.[21] (Notably, it circulated too through the Fiction Lover's Library, available for borrowing: 'We rent books, we do not sell them'.) Gifford sustained a high-volume career across the middle decades of the century, releasing titles like *Made for Love*, *Never Forget Love*, *Bride to Be* and *The Bride Wore Overalls* under a large clutch of pseudonyms and with a number of different paperback publishers through the 1930s, 1940s and into the 1950s. This title was unexceptional in his output and is unremembered even by vintage genre fiction specialists. A contemporary review on

Amazon describes it: 'Book is set in New York and is about a young man arriving in the city and his chase of excess. May well have been risqué for the time.'

In recommending it be passed, Haydon's comments are clear, brief and relatively undeliberated: 'A story of no particular merit. Several of the incidences are treated with considerable "realism" but I think the book is honest in purpose.'[22] Allen similarly weighed merit against intent, but with opposite outcomes:

> This story of syphilis is honest enough in its purpose but so crude in its execution that it is better put away among the rubbish. The seduction scenes are just the average pseudo-passion, and would not, in themselves, matter one way or the other in a better book. The intention of the book is not so much the question as the effect; and while I think that effect may be good or bad according to the reader, yet I think that such matters should be treated with more power and personality. There is not a character in the book worth a name, nor an incident worth the ink, and I think it is better to keep a barrier against such crude and amateurish handling of a subject like this.[23]

Here the literary is loudly present in the verdict of its absence; this book can be banned because it is judged just not good enough not to be. And it is striking that Allen explicitly concedes that 'in a better book' the obscenity, perhaps even as such, would not be offensive. What that comment illuminates is that for him the literary's defining

Fig. 7.2: Endpapers of Gifford's *Furnished Room* (Greenberg, 1934) with stamps from the New York Fiction Lover's Library (Photograph by the author).

opposite is not, in fact, obscenity or offence, transgressive shock or unspeakable indecency, but popular mundanity, the average and the fake. In this case, his criteria are aesthetic, elitist, technical, or, as Felski would couch it, 'theocratic', reserving the right to be obscene for those who preserve its aesthetic powers against the 'amateur'.

Hayden references the main character's diagnosis, the novel's 'honest purpose', but won't name it: Allen presents the novel as centrally a 'story of syphilis'. A flag to the censors, with their long-established role in the history of literary obscenity, STDs and syphilis marked any book as already excluded from claims to the literary. With precedents from Ibsen's *Ghosts* to Joyce's *Ulysses*, however, *Furnished Room* draws most directly on Eugène Brieux's educative 1913 Broadway play *Damaged Goods* (originally *Les Aviaries*), then 'the most forthright discourse on syphilis to reach American audiences'.[24] Similarly set in rooming houses around Broadway, and following an out-of-work actor facing destitution in the depression years, Gifford's novel even restages the play's scenes in the Doctor's office, though his main character refrains from marrying because of the danger of infection, thus taking the moral line of action refused by Brieux's George Dupont.[25] And Allen's report echoes the objections of vocal opponents to the play, who separated it, too, from claims to the literary: 'The theatre's mission is aesthetic, not ethical ... When the stage tries to teach, particularly when it tries to teach seriously of subjects generally considered too delicate for common conversation, it may accomplish some good, but it invariably causes harm, too, by its general appeal to the merely curious and morbid minds'.[26] Alexander Butler's 1919 UK film adaptation had been prosecuted in Melbourne and banned from screening, the appeal judge notably exempting film as a medium from any defensive claim to literary merit.[27] Allen's determining condemnation in 1936 was similarly wary of 'harm', under the Hicklin ruling, but did not separate the aesthetic from the ethical. In his report, adequate aesthetic achievement is a prerequisite for the ethical: without it, sexual content is dangerous and immoral.

In the introduction to his elaboration of the provocations provided by *Lautréamont and Sade* in 2004, Maurice Blanchot ends by declaiming, like Attridge and Felski, about the character of the literary, but in an assertive attempt to separate it from 'the notion of value':

> criticism—literature—seems to me to be associated with one of the most difficult, but important, tasks of our time, played out in a necessarily vague movement: the task of preserving and of liberating thought from the notion of value, consequently of opening history up to what all these forms of value have already released into it and to what is taking shape as an entirely different—still unforeseeable—kind of affirmation.[28]

Contrarily, John Frow argues that 'there is no escape from the discourse of value', drawing on the influential work of liberal critic Barbara Herrnstein Smith.[29] We see from the deliberations of these censors that value is also not merely a discourse in censorship practice, but a regulatory legal concept, an adjudicated fact or absence that determines the legal status of a work as a prohibited object or otherwise, within the work of legal instruments like the Australian Customs Act or Customs Regulations, and even, I'd argue, the contemporary Australian state and federal publications Acts, even if they include no address to such a concept. Value adjudicates merit; merit weighs against, defends against offence.

This is not a new place or problematic within which to end up, as legal historians of censorship know, but it is nevertheless where one very determining material history of the literary has been and continues to be played out. What can be added to consideration of this problematic is a clearer understanding of how censors' articulation of both 'the literary' and reading itself has constructed that value as an adjudged fact. More than this, perhaps, from the records of censorship, we can also demonstrate that the literary is not simply equivalent to value or merit, even in as much as it must be given such or formalized as such in the bureaucratic juridical frame. Censorship's *reading* is recorded in these reports as both a performed event and as a manifestation of affect. The censors are first witness to the texts' ability to provoke or produce felt meaning (to 'degrade and corrupt', to shock and exalt, to repulse and shame, to astound and console, to pleasure and excite, to bore and disappoint), and their own reading is an exercise of the Hicklin test for obscenity, since obsenity remained the principal offence for the Australian federal regime until the 1970s. And in this way they construct the literary, as does Felski, as an *experience*, as the feeling of affect or a response to textual stimuli produced by reading. Allen asks for 'more power and personality' from *Furnished Room*, and Blanchot seeks this too, surely, in his lengthy expository excursion into the almost impossible *Maldoror*, sustained for one of his longest essays – to experience its qualities, to feel its elaborated effects, to study the structures of the consciousness it requires.

Second, in outlining the adjudication of possible offence, the censors perform the literary as *event*. It is not the reading that is the literary event, nor of course is it the action of censorship, the moment (the inscription of dates on the memorandum) of banning. It is the searching for and finding, the identification and reporting, the readerly recognition (parse Felski) of the literary and its subsequent descriptions that constitute its performance. In this way, absenting or denying the literary from Gifford's book performs the literary in negative, even in as much as it may ignore or misrecognize the claims such a text might make. The censors' reading – manifest in their considered, highly-strategic reporting, in their expository roles as simultaneously witnesses, critics and judges, and in their deliberative reasoning and rationalized desires – brings the literary into institutionalized form, negatively as well as positively. Censorial regulation of print culture is discursive in its enactment; itself rhetorical, as is the law, and thus in its character assertively literary.

Censorship at once delimits literature for readerships and provokes questions about its limits, and so perhaps what proves to be at stake in this dynamic, at least from these instances, is whether its definitions ultimately are final or stable. We have to acknowledge that, effectively, what censorship does *do*, or did do, is definitive – prohibiting entry to both of these books, and denying to readers whatever forms of the literary or non-literary may be at play. In that sense the literary *is* made, denied or defined in the *action* or event of banning, ultimately, even if it does not inhabit that moment. For if it is not here, not there, to be read, how can any writing be literary? Such forms of institutional regulation enact a state's instrumental power through language, in rhetorical forms delegated from the wording of legislation and regulatory agencies that are in their turn delegated from judicial and executive power. This is not to misrecognize the exercise of power, vis-à-vis the work of Bourdieu on the literary field, but to identify its literary nature or character in such control.

And what does it mean to identify the imbrication of the literary within such exclusionary structures of sovereign nation-making as Australian federal Customs? Long-standing parallels with the regimes of apartheid South Africa and Catholic Ireland are important pointers to the kind of white, (post-)colonial modernity aspired to by this form of biopolitical government, troping Christian notions of moral purity to enforce hegemonic models of population uniformity, cordoned off from the upheaving, non-literary (that is, non-English) Asia-Pacific stretching around it and an Indigenous Australia hidden from view. Australia itself continues to figure as a limit or an extremity in a globalizing world view – a global stretch too far, into the 'paraperiphery', and perhaps especially for the literary. The metropolis has a tendency to wonder what one could expect anyway. But the fact of this imbrication – the embedding of literary expertise into the heart of these structures and exactly as a marker of their modernity, in a leavening of hegemony by professionalism in response to public concern, as it was in South Africa and in New Zealand – demonstrates the centrality of formulations of the literary to the regulatory success of the modern postcolonial nation state.

Notes

1 Derek Attridge, *The Singularity of Literature* (London and New York: Routledge, 2004), p. 1. I would like to acknowledge invaluable feedback on this chapter from participants in the Literary Trials in the World Republic of Letters workshop at the University of Oldenburg in March 2014, especially Ralf Grüttemeier, Elisabeth Ladenson, Peter McDonald and Gisèle Sapiro.
2 Ibid., p. 3.
3 Ibid.
4 See Jonathan Culler, *The Literary in Theory* (Stanford, CA: Stanford University Press, 2007); Rita Felski, *Uses of Literature* (Oxford: Blackwell, 2008); Elizabeth Beaumont Bissell (ed.), *The Question of Literature* (Manchester: Manchester University Press, 2002), and the 2013 (44, 4) issue of *New Literary History* edited by Felski.. See also the 2010 issue of *PMLA* on 'Literary Criticism in the Twenty-first Century', the 2014 (28, 1–2) issue of *Australian Literary Studies*, and Paul Jay, *The Humanities 'Crisis' and the Future of Literary Studies* (London and New York: Palgrave/Macmillan, 2014), on the current state of literary studies as an academic discipline.
5 Quoted in Peter D. McDonald, *The Literature Police* (Oxford: Oxford University Press, 2009), p. 27.
6 Ibid.
7 Felski, *Uses of Literature*, p. 14.
8 Quoted in J. M. Coetzee, *Giving Offence* (Chicago: University of Chicago Press,

1996), p. 20; cf. Nicole Moore, *The Censor's Library* (Brisbane, Qld: University of Queensland Press, 2012), p. 10.

9   McDonald, *The Literature Police*, p. 23.

10   Felski, *Uses of Literature*, pp. 106–7.

11   See Moore, *The Censor's Library*, for a full history of Australian federal publication censorship.

12   Quoted in Paul Knight, 'Introduction', comte de Lautréamont, *Maldoror and Poems* (London: Penguin, 1978), p. 26.

13   The records of the Literature Censorship Board are held, with the records of the Department of Trade and Customs, in the National Archives of Australia as NAA Series A3023.

14   Purchased in 1979. Available at http://www.metmuseum.org/collection/ the-collection-online/search/352999?rpp=30&pg=1&ft=maldoror&pos=2 [accessed June 2014].

15   NAA A3023 Folder 1941/1944. Details of all federal Customs bans executed through the Literature Censorship Board, in its differing forms from 1933 to 1973, are collected in the *Banned in Australia* bibliographic dataset hosted by the *AustLit* e-resource (Bullock and Moore, *Banned in Australia*, http://www.austlit.edu.au/ specialistDatasets/Banned, AustLit, 2008).

16   Knight, 'Introduction', p. 18.

17   Lautréamont, *Maldoror*, p. 29.

18   Maurice Blanchot, *Lautréamont and Sade* (Stanford, CA: Stanford University Press, 2004), p. 48.

19   NAA A3023 Folder 1941/1944.

20   A similar discussion by the Board in 1946 concerned popular libertine poet and writer Pierre Louÿs' *Collected Works*, released by Liveright Publishers in New York in 1926, 1927 and 1932. The LCB again recommended restricted circulation and again that advice was ignored by the Minister, who declared the title a prohibited import (26.8.1946; NAA A3023 Folder 1945/1947). Famous for his sympathetic inclusion of erotic lesbian themes, Louÿs, like Lautréamont, was still almost completely unread in Australia. Allen's report for the Board embarked on a lengthy discussion of Louÿs' place in the French canon, again via Allen's particular training in the classics and the Romantics, and again what was at issue or what was produced in his exposition was literary value.

21   Cf. Loren Glass, *Counterculture Colophon* (Stanford, CA: Stanford University Press, 2013).

22   NAA A3023 Folder 1935/1936.

23   Ibid.

24   John H. Houchin, *Censorship of the American Theatre* (Cambridge: Cambridge University Press, 2003), p. 63.

25   Writing on 'America's pulp modernism', Paula Rabinowitz observes that 'the rooming house remains, in fiction, film and art, a sinister place filled with wild women and brutal men' ... 'an iconic zone of danger and defeat', *Black & White & Noir* (New York: Columbia University Press, 2002), p. 32.

26   'That Moral Play', *New York Times*, 2 March 1913, 111, p. 6. Quoted in Houchin, *Censorship of the American Theatre*, p. 663.

27   Ina Bertrand, *Film Censorship in Australia* (Sydney: Australian Film and Television School, 1981), pp. 86–7.

28   Blanchot, *Lautréamont and Sade*, p. 6.
29   John Frow, *Cultural Studies and Culture Value* (Clarenden Press, 1995), p. 134.

References

Attridge, D., *The Singularity of Literature*, London and New York: Routledge, 2004.
Beaumont Bissell, E. (ed.), *The Question of Literature: The Place of the Literary in Contemporary Theory*, Manchester: Manchester University Press, 2002.
Bertrand, I., *Film Censorship in Australia*, Sydney: Australian Film and Television School, 1981.
Blanchot, M., *Lautréamont and Sade*, Stanford, CA: Stanford University Press, 2004.
Bullock, M. and N. Moore, *Banned in Australia*, AustLit, 2008. Available at http://www.austlit.edu.au/specialistDatasets/Banned [accessed June 2014].
Coetzee, J. M., *Giving Offence: Essays on Censorship*, Chicago: University of Chicago Press, 1996.
Culler, J., *The Literary in Theory*, Stanford, CA: Stanford University Press, 2007.
Felski, R., *Uses of Literature*, Oxford: Blackwell, 2008.
Frow, J., *Cultural Studies and Cultural Value*, Clarenden Press, 1995.
Glass, L., *Counterculture Colophon: Grove Press, the* Evergreen Review *and the Incorporation of the Avant-Garde*, Stanford, CA: Stanford University Press, 2013.
Houchin, J. H., *Censorship of the American Theatre in the Twentieth Century*, Cambridge: Cambridge University Press, 2003.
Jay, P., *The Humanities 'Crisis' and the Future of Literary Studies*, London and New York: Palgrave Macmillan, 2014.
Knight, P., 'Introduction', in comte de Lautréamont, *Maldoror and Poems*, London: Penguin, 1978, pp. 7–26.
Lautréamont, comte de, *Maldoror and Poems* (trans. with introduction by P. Knight), London: Penguin, 1978.
McDonald, P. D., *The Literature Police: Apartheid Censorship and Its Cultural Consequences*, Oxford: Oxford University Press, 2009.
Moore, N., *The Censor's Library: Uncovering the Lost History of Australia's Banned Books*, Brisbane, Qld: University of Queensland Press, 2012.
Rabinowitz, P., *Black & White & Noir: America's Pulp Modernism*, New York: Columbia University Press, 2002.
Taussig, M., *Defacement: Public Secrecy and the Labour of the Negative*, Stanford, CA: Stanford University Press, 1999.

8

'That Monstrous Thing': The Critic as Censor in Apartheid South Africa

Peter D. McDonald

Literary criticism is censorship.
Literary critics are censors.

On the face of it, these two claims seem at best rhetorically extravagant, at worst wildly implausible. Can it really be the case that literary criticism, which we might provisionally think of as a special form of public commentary on literary works, is censorship, which we might for now define as the official regulation of public expression? And is it really plausible to think that the academics, journalists, broadcasters, bloggers and writers, the diverse community of professional literary critics in today's complex multimedia world, belong in the same company as the shadowy group of authorized inspectors who have banned all manner of things over the centuries? The answer to both these questions, in my view, is no, but it is worth recalling that in the very recent past others have thought differently. In fact, on some measures, it could be argued that the linkage between literary criticism and censorship, critics and censors, became something of an orthodoxy in the 1980s and 1990s, especially among literary critics who were also university teachers.

One of the most emphatic early proponents of this orthodoxy was the British academic Chris Baldick. In *The Social Mission of English Criticism* (1983), his classic study of the English critical tradition from Matthew Arnold to F. R. and Q. D. Leavis, Baldick insisted that 'there is no impassable gulf between censorship and criticism; the former may often be seen as the paradigm of the latter, or, so to speak, its armed wing'.[1] To give this claim some historical depth, he then went on to cite approvingly some comments Sainte-Beuve made in a column for the French newspaper *Le Constitutionnel* in 1850 about the statist, even reactionary politics of literary critics as a class. 'Every time political order restores itself and resumes its regular course,' Sainte-Beuve remarked, uncannily prefiguring the direction of his own newspaper under the Second French Empire, 'literary order tends to fall into line and follow suit as best it can.' In his view, the tendency of criticism to ally itself to the forces of 'restoration' was unsurprising because it was literary critics, 'intelligent people of sound understanding, judicious, learned, and more or less acute, who gathered together in agreement, who re-established order in intellectual life and acted as a literary police.'[2] To reinforce this connection, and lend further authority to the language of policing, Baldick could also have turned to Hazlitt, resurrecting his repudiation of William Gifford, the ferocious Tory critic and editor of the *Anti-Jacobin* and the *Quarterly Review*, whose critical opinions allegedly sent Keats to an early grave. In an open letter of 1819, Hazlitt wrote of Gifford: 'Your clandestine connexion with persons high in office constantly influences your opinions, and alone gives importance to them. You are the Government Critic, a character nicely differing from that of a government spy—the invisible link that connects literature with the police.'[3] Unlike Sainte-Beuve, Hazlitt was, of course, attacking an individual critic, or at most a particular style of criticism, not all critics, a difference we shouldn't forget and to which I shall return. On this issue, however, Baldick was with Sainte-Beuve. 'Criticism from Plato onwards has', he noted, underscoring his own more expansive claim, 'presupposed censorship, banishment, and official persecution in the very language of its "judgements" and in its images of its own authority'.[4]

A decade later Michael Holquist took up Baldick's theme in terms that were, if anything, even more expansive. Introducing a special issue of the *PMLA* on censorship in 1994, Holquist rightly challenged the moralistic, often Manichean terms in which discussions of censorship are regularly framed, showing, among other things, that relations between writers and censors have always been more complex than the popular 'persecutor-victim model' suggests and that censorship always has the perverse effect of 'focusing attention on that which it denies'.[5] His main argument, however, centred on the claim that 'censorship' is 'pervasive and insistent in all disciplines that mediate language'.[6] It followed that, for Holquist, 'to be for or against censorship as such is to assume a freedom no one has'. 'Censorship *is*', he asserted: 'One can only discriminate among its more and less repressive effects.'[7] This pervasiveness was evident in what he called the 'unsettling filiation' not just between censorship and literary criticism, but between censorship and translation, literary history, textual criticism and even certain modes of writing itself.[8] 'Poets not only are prey to the thought police who wear uniforms', he commented, 'but must also contend with suppression by critics and with the vicissitudes of self-censorship'.[9] According to Holquist, Peter Temes's article on Laura (Riding) Jackson, which featured in the *PMLA* special issue, made the last point about self-censorship in a particularly powerful way. Temes showed how (Riding) Jackson's self-censoring decision to abandon the supposed indeterminacies of poetry for the supposed transparencies of prose was driven by a desire to 'gain absolute control' over the meanings of her oeuvre. 'She became that monstrous thing,' Holquist remarked, 'a poet turned censor'.[10]

I should make it clear that I am not disputing Baldick and Holquist's right to extend the meaning of the term 'censor' in the way they do, making it effectively signify any effort to fix or at least control the meaning of words or the question of value. After all, the endless figural or other refashioning of words is an inescapable and welcome feature of any living language. Moreover, given what they felt themselves to be up against, extensions of this kind were good for polemical purposes. In my view, however, the price of such Foucauldian rhetoric is too high in this case. At one level, by deliberately, and, of course, provocatively, eliding the difference between banning a book and offering a dubiously definitive reading or evaluation of it, their inventive extension of the word opens up a range of questions about the ethics, or perhaps just the sobriety, of literary criticism as a profession. Holquist was, after all, addressing his fellow critics in what is perhaps the leading professional journal in the English-speaking world. More worryingly, by expanding the conception of censorship in the way he does, Holquist betrays the actual victims of sometimes brutal regimes. He conjures up a frankly bizarre world in which, say, William Gifford's attack on Keats is somehow morally equivalent to the Soviet Union's treatment of Solzhenitsyn or the apartheid regime's suppression and exiling of Es'kia Mphahlele. At another level, by pointing out the 'unsettling filiation' between censors and critics, which they see primarily in intellectualized terms, Baldick and Holquist oblige us to accept an oddly immaterial, or, more accurately, non-institutional analysis of the situation. Focusing as they do on the supposed links between the way censors and critics *think*, they both ignore the very different institutional positions they ordinarily occupy: critics, say, as accredited guardians of a civic 'Republic of Letters'; censors, say, as the state-appointed gatekeepers of a wider public sphere.

For these reasons, I wish to defend the distinction the latest online edition of the *OED* draws between what it calls the 'transferred' and the 'specific' meanings of the word 'censor'. While recognizing that the noun can be applied to anyone 'who exercises official or officious supervision over morals and conduct', and so perhaps even over meaning and value in Holquist's endlessly transferrable sense, the *OED* also now gives the specific sense as 'an official in some countries whose duty it is to inspect all books, journals, dramatic pieces, etc., before publication, to secure that they shall contain nothing immoral, heretical, or offensive to the government'.[11] This is not to suggest that lexicographers should have the last word. It is worth noting, for instance, that this definition, given the emphasis on scrutiny before publication, fails to capture the apartheid censors who, for the most part, inspected books after publication. In fact, on this issue, the *OED* is unintentionally complicit with the apartheid regime, which also believed that censorship proper happened before publication. That is why its defenders denied that they had a censorship system at all. What happened in apartheid South Africa was for this reason always officially euphemized as 'publications control'. So, if critics may sometimes be censors in the transferred sense, as Holquist and Baldick suggest, they are evidently not censors in the *OED*'s specific sense.

What is most worrying about the stronger formulations Baldick and Holquist advocate, however, is that they distract from what is, arguably, a more plausible, though no less sobering, pair of claims, namely that:

Censorship is literary criticism.
Censors are literary critics.

As I argued in *The Literature Police*, both claims hold true in the case of apartheid South Africa, and, as others have shown, something similar can be said for Australia, the GDR and many other censoring regimes.[12] Ever since the advent of print and the governmental anxieties it fuelled, 'intelligent people of sound understanding, judicious, learned, and more or less acute', as Sainte-Beuve put it, have given the lie to the popular image of the censor as philistine bureaucrat by serving as Hazlitt's 'Government Critic', even more literarily than Gifford did. Given the specific complexities of the South African situation, notably the tangled histories of Afrikaans literature and white South African liberalism, the apartheid censors, many of whom were leading writers, critics and academics, occupied an especially perverse position. They did not simply inspect books and other publications with a critically-informed eye, they saw themselves as the guardians of a civic 'Republic of Letters', working within the censorship system and committed to protecting from it works they identified as literary. Since they could, and often did, effectively ban books that failed to meet their literary standards, they enjoyed powers well beyond the dreams of even the most megalomaniacal critics of the ordinary kind.

So what exactly happens when critics are given the power to ban and censors make literary judgements when separating the 'undesirable' from the 'not undesirable', as the apartheid terminology had it? For one thing, you find copious reports like the one on J. M. Coetzee's second fiction *In the Heart of the Country* (1977, see Fig. 8.1). H. Merwe Scholtz, a professor of Afrikaans literature and a minor poet, and Anna Louw, an eminent Afrikaans novelist, effectively wrote mini-essays in criticism in their roles as censors – Louw subsequently reworked hers into a newspaper review. Importantly, neither made specific reference to the precise terms of the law. For another thing, you find instances of what can only be called paranoid reading, in which the censors allow their own anxieties, or perhaps the anxieties engendered by the role they are performing as censors, to get the better of their critical acumen. The leading Afrikaans poet and critic, T. T. Cloete, for instance, who was also known for introducing the more subtle forms of literary theory into Afrikaans criticism in the 1970s, insisted that Wopko Jensma's Dadaist-inspired anti-poem 'Only the best', a cryptically savage indictment of Afrikaner self-righteousness, had to be banned because it was 'a clear case predicting revolution ("brandishing flags of blood", "the drumming of our feet", "slit throats") – and the rebels are surely the Bantu (the drum gives the decisive clue)'. In fact, the blood-thirsty crowd in the poem is really the Afrikaner, understood as a vengeful volk that believes in and is prepared to kill for, its 'one and only holy dream' of white supremacy.[13]

Most conspicuously, what you find when censors are critics is that the numerous individual decisions they make are guided by a series of assumptions about literary merit and, more generally, about what constitutes literature as such. Based on the detailed analysis of over 500 decisions, which served as a foundation for my argument in *The Literature Police*, I felt able to identify three main assumptions underlying the apartheid censors' thinking:

1. Literature, which is governed by its own rules and unities, constitutes a privileged aesthetic space set apart from more mundane forms of discourse, including pornography, mass-market fiction, journalism and political writings.
2. Though it belongs, first and foremost, to a volk, that is, to a nation understood as a racialized ethno-linguistic community, it is not narrowly local or patriotic. A

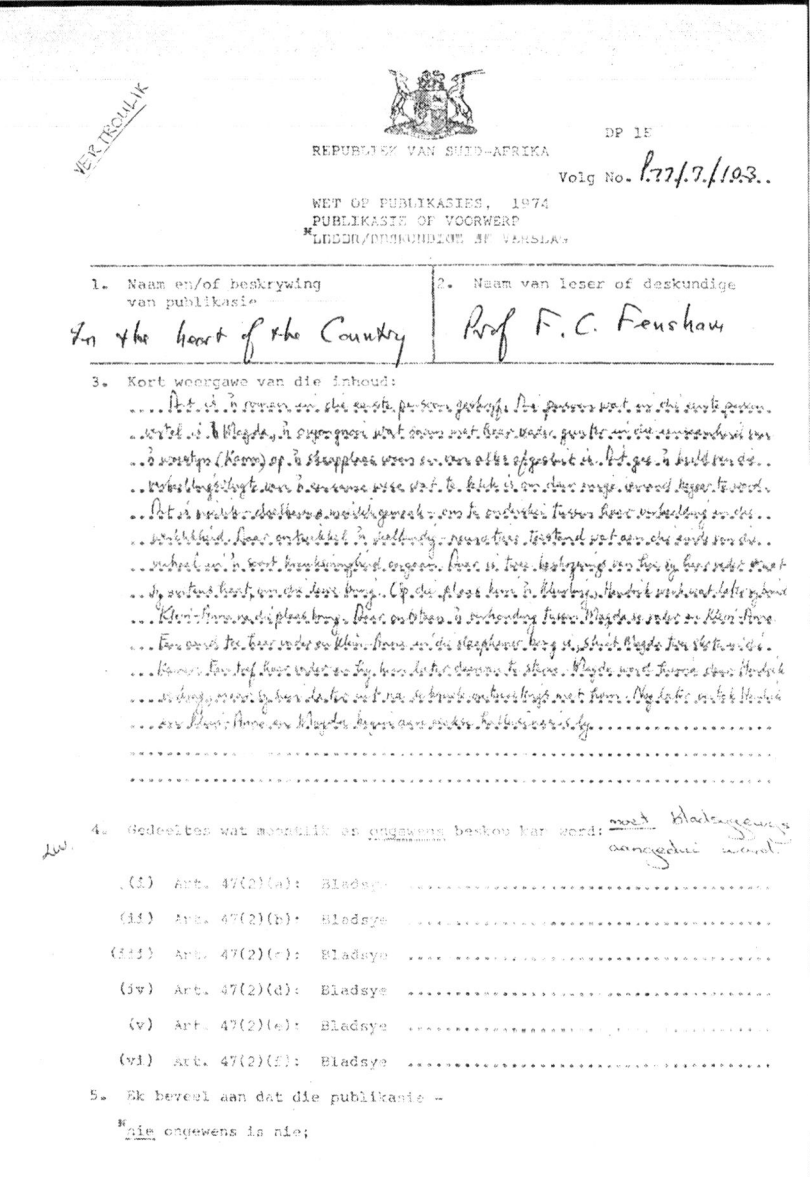

Fig. 8.1: Report from the South African censors on J. M. Coetzee's second fiction *In the Heart of the Country* (1977) (Source: Western Cape Provincial Archives and Records (WCPAR), Cape Town).

particular literature achieves greatness only when it takes its place within a series of larger spheres, construed variously as 'European', 'Western' or, ultimately, the 'universal'.

3. Literature does not appeal to a mass readership. It can be appreciated only by a limited and sophisticated public or, in effect, to make the circularity clear, only by literary readers.

A heady amalgam, in other words, in which nineteenth-century aestheticism fused with New Critical formalism, nationalism collided less predictably with a universalistic idea of Western humanism, and where everything was overlaid with a more familiar set of prejudices against mass culture. On these grounds, the censors decided that J. M. Coetzee and Mafika Gwala, for instance, were legitimate citizens of their Republic of Letters, despite their obvious offensiveness towards the government; whereas Ingoapele Madingoane and Wilbur Smith were not. The former, in their view, wrote versified Black Consciousness propaganda for a young black readership, while the latter produced morally corrupting pulp fiction for the masses.

That these assumptions persisted over the three decades of apartheid censorship – the 1960s, 1970s and 1980s – is remarkable, though it can be explained fairly easily. Throughout this period, and despite various structural changes in the bureaucracy, the censorship personnel remained fairly consistent. The most influential literary censors were mostly university-educated, white, mainly Afrikaans-speaking men who came of age intellectually in the 1940s and 1950s. Though a number of them, like Cloete and Merwe Scholtz, kept up with the latest developments in literary theory, the majority took their cue from Wellek and Warren's *Theory of Literature* (1948), and, more broadly, from the traditions of American New Criticism and Prague linguistics out of which that classic collaborative study emerged. Various well-known formulations from Wellek and Warren permeate their reports: they prized works that had a 'complex, close-knit organization', insisted on the determinative importance of 'fictionality' and the 'aesthetic function', and, as we have seen, argued that 'universal and national literatures implicate each other'.[14] Yet it was not just these particular formulations that mattered. What the censors also took from Wellek and Warren was a specific understanding of theory as 'an *organon* of methods'.[15] Wellek and Warren's ambition to outline a 'general' and 'systematic' set of protocols that would elevate literary criticism, which, in their view, routinely concerned itself with particulars, to 'a species of knowledge' shaped the idea the censors had of the foundations on which their role and authority as guardians of the literary was based.[16]

Wellek and Warren's own project can be traced back to classical poetics, but they were themselves most directly indebted for their conception of theory as systematic knowledge to I. A. Richards's *Principles of Literary Criticism* (1924), a work they cited approvingly on a number of occasions, despite reservations about its psychologism. As is well known, Richards's own ambition as a theorist was to put the evaluative judgements of the literary-critical elite on a secure (that is, for him, a principled) scientific footing. Intellectually, this initiative was needed because, in his view, the normative and the descriptive aspects of literary criticism, the evaluative questions of merit and the supposedly scientific questions of literariness, were co-dependent. 'The two problems "What is good?" and "What are the arts?" reflect light upon one another', he said. Indeed, 'neither ... can be fully answered without the other'.[17] This intellectual project also had a broader social and cultural purpose, however. Formulating 'a general theory of value' based on an 'explicit set of principles' was essential, Richards claimed, in order to bolster the authority of the 'expert in matters of taste' and 'to habilitate the critic'.[18] Given a proper theoretical 'stronghold' and provided with the right 'weapons' – militarism was as much a part of Richards's lexicon as scientism – the literary-critical elite would, he believed, not only be properly qualified but able to confront the many forces allegedly rallied against it in the 1920s.[19]

According to Richards, these forces included the general threat of 'commercialism' and mass culture, the 'damaging attacks' of anti-elitists like Tolstoy – Richards found Tolstoy's 'What is Art?' (1897) especially objectionable – and, most importantly for the purposes of my argument, the 'blunderings' of the clergy, the police and the censors.[20] In fact, for Richards, it was 'the errors exemplified by censorship' – above all, its crude moralism – that made his own theoretical project necessary.[21] In the face of this particular challenge, it was, he insisted, vital to go beyond the outmoded and inadequate formulas of art for art's sake, still favoured by most critics in the anti-censorship polemics of the 1920s, which, for all their importance, were, Richards felt, too unworldly, too disengaged. 'So loath have [critics] been to be thought at large with the wild asses that they have virtually shut themselves up in a paddock.' Shifting figures, and reinforcing his argument about professionalism, he added 'it is as though medical men were all to retire because of the impudence of quacks'.[22] His 'general theory of value' was, then, intended not just to 'show the place and function of the arts in the whole system of values', thereby giving criticism a central role in public life, but to empower professionally-accredited critics in their struggle against the censorious quack-critics by enabling them to defend 'a wider and subtler definition of health'.[23] Rejecting the 'comic, stupefying, enraging interferences' of the censors, who were fixated on the health of public morals, and the quietest aestheticism of the established literary critics, who had retreated, like some pedigree race horses, into their 'paddock', Richards once again looked to science, medicine specifically, to find a language for his new theoretically-grounded critic as anti-censor.[24] This new kind of professional critic would, he said, be 'as closely occupied with the health of the mind as the doctor with the health of the body'.[25]

Seen against this background, the perversity of the apartheid censors' position is, if anything, only more pronounced. If they were censors in the OED's specific sense – that is, if we discount the claims about scrutiny before publication – they were also critics in the Richards-Wellek-Warren mould, for whom a robustly theoretical knowledge was the means not just of identifying literature but of protecting it from the censorship system, and thereby of ministering to the mental health of the nation. As the chief censor put it in a secret briefing of 1963, 'it is my belief that censorship is a double-edged sword if it is not applied with regard for what in Western civilization is considered the most precious possession of the individual and the community: genuine mental freedom. Seen in this way our task is a national calling in the broadest sense of the word'.[26] The censors' commitment to this idea of the critic, and of theory, gives the detailed history of their numerous decisions a significance beyond the particular circumstances of apartheid South Africa. While their blink-eredness and crude arbitrariness might speak to the peculiarities of that history, their manifest lack of consensus, reflected in their numerous internal disputes and about-turns, tells us something about the model of theoretical knowledge on which their self-understanding as critics depended. What the archives of the apartheid censorship bureaucracy unexpectedly – even absurdly – provide, in other words, is an overwhelming body of documentary evidence to support the critique of early twentieth-century theory that was among the primary achievements of what we now think of as the 'age of theory' from the 1960s to the mid-1990s. Perhaps too often we forget that much so-called Theory was in fact anti-theory. To those who remain unper-suaded by the writings of Maurice Blanchot or Jacques Derrida, possibly the two most forceful critics of the systematizing, scientist ambitions of much earlier theory, I can recommend a week's study in the dusty outbuildings of the Western Cape Provincial Archives in Cape Town; or, for that matter, among the court records of literary trials in just about any jurisdiction in the world. The experience would, I am sure, cure even the most tenacious believer in theory as 'a species of knowledge' once and for all.

And yet, as Baldick and Holquist's own language unintentionally reveals, freeing literary criticism from the assumptions on which this particular form of professional hubris is based is never easy. Baldick, for instance, has no difficulty challenging the ridiculous side of Richards's supposedly 'scientific' certitudes. He refers to the exercises in 'practical criticism' Richards developed in Cambridge as a seemingly rigorous test of 'a candidate's unaided sensibility', and exposes the unexamined political assumptions underpinning his Arnoldian faith in the critic's self-assured expertise as a disinterested guardian of 'culture' and 'value'.[27] What seems most striking about Baldick's analysis today, however, is the extent to which his critical stance as a hard-headed debunker of all claims to disinterested knowledge preserves the episte-mological assumptions he set out to question. Adopting the voice of a clear-eyed political realist, Baldick frequently looks askance at the 'Cold War sophistry' of much liberal-minded humanistic criticism and champions areas of research considered 'too sordid and worldly to have been treated by the theories and histories of criticism'.[28] On this model, real knowledge replaces bogus knowledge just as materialism trumps idealism. A similar logic surfaces in Holquist. Despite making short shrift of what he calls 'all proponents of certainty', principally by invoking the traditions of scepticism associated with Bakhtin and de Man, he, too, appeals to scientific modes when challenging what he calls 'a commonsensical faith in one's perceptions of the world'.[29] 'The world of appearance', Holquist says, 'is just that: a layer of obviousness concealing the counterintuitive subtleties of subatomic particles and their oxymoronic relations with one another.'[30] Whether it is the critic as worldly realist or the critic as quantum physicist, Baldick and Holquist both want, at some level, to distinguish themselves and the enterprise of literary criticism as they see it, by appealing to an idea of superior, perhaps even authentic knowledge. It is not difficult to see Plato's ghost hovering in the background of this vision.

This particular legacy haunts Holquist's closing remarks in his introduction to the *PMLA* special issue, which also raise a number of other questions I would like to address by way of conclusion. Writing at a time (January 1994) when yet another 'wave of attacks on the academic study of literature' seemed to be 'receding', Holquist rightly predicted that 'those who perceive literariness as dangerous' would rise again, like some monster of the deep, to 'name it' as 'a menace to certainty'.[31] He had in mind the censorious champions of the Western canon and its supposed values who were leading the culture wars in the US in the early 1990s. Given the wider attacks on the university and the humanities today, it is difficult not to credit his prescience. Yet, on this issue, there was, for Holquist, really not much to worry about. After all, the reactionary defenders of the canon and its supposedly radical destroyers both agreed that literariness was dangerous. The only difference was that the latter, among whom Holquist included himself, saw this as a good thing. Teaching the sceptic's anti-censorious lessons about the indeterminacy of value and meaning was, he noted, the primary aim of all those 'who profess literariness' simply because they were 'in the business of teaching others and themselves to read'.[32] Reading was, he said, 'an act of resistance', specifically to 'what the censor wants', namely, texts 'that can be read in only one way'.[33] As these formulations suggest, Holquist was at this point primarily indebted to Paul de Man, especially the de Man of 'The Resistance to Theory'. Earlier he had quoted de Man's observations about literature's capacity to offer 'negative knowledge about the reliability of linguistic utterance' and his characterization of criticism as 'a powerful and indispensable tool in the unmasking of ideological aberrations, as well as a determining factor in accounting for their occurrence'.[34] By pitting knowledge against 'ideological aberrations', and by appealing to the language of 'unmasking', this self-consciously Marxist formulation, which de Man directed against those who saw his own style of criticism as culpably apolitical, once again reveals the tenacity with which neo-Platonic assumptions persist in debates of this kind.

As a response to those who sought to control literature's energies, not least by seeing it as a simple expression of pre-defined moral or political values, Holquist and de Man's emphasis on the importance of reading and the disruptiveness of literary language was clearly salutary. It is also worth noting, especially given some of the other attitudes then in vogue, that they both remained firmly committed to defending literature as a mode of public intervention in its own right. Despite their scepticism about the more censorious forms of literary criticism, and the attitudes of some cultural guardians, neither endorsed the flight from literary into cultural studies, or the dogmas of suspicion associated with the less interesting forms of Marxist, feminist or post-colonial analysis that were current in the 1980s and 1990s. Though Baldick was more sympathetic to these traditions, it is clear that most of his own suspicions were directed against particular styles of literary criticism, not against the literary as such. I should perhaps add that in saying this I am not questioning the motives of those who discredited literature as a category and saw literary studies as a lost cause. Among other things, *The Literature Police* provides ample evidence for anyone anxious to expose the bogus disinterestedness of a literary-critical elite or to discredit any overblown claims about literature's mystical powers. What I am questioning, however, are the terms in which that particular form of socio-political critique was articulated and the consequences it had for how we understand the role of literary critics. It is not just that the otherwise laudable assault on traditional criticism too often fostered a cynicism about the literary as such, but that it promoted an approach to reading, based primarily on a predisposition towards suspicion, that missed too much, perhaps not even just too much, but everything. Given this, Marjorie Garber's somewhat surprising recent observations about the prospects for literary studies can only be welcomed. 'It is high time to take back the term *literature*', she argued in *The Use and Abuse of Literature* (2011), not as a word designating 'an instrument of moral or cultural control, nor yet as an infusion of "pleasure", but rather as a *way of thinking*'.[35] Coming as it does from a former champion of cultural studies, Garber's remarks constitute a radical re-alignment, which, in my view, bodes well for the future.

Clearly knowledge, whether in Wellek and Warren's positive sense, or de Man's negative one, is going to play a vital part in this future. No one is saying that knowing as much as possible about the history of literature in all its aspects will not remain indispensable to literary critics and students alike. What is equally clear, however, is that any effort to establish a secure epistemological foundation for literary criticism, and so for the authority of literary critics, on a scientific or neo-Platonic claim to *knowledge* is going to founder. This is in part because, as a matter of principle, Richards's tangled questions 'What is good?' and 'What are the arts?' can, as the apartheid censorship archives reveal and the 'age of theory' has taught us, never be asked or answered once and for all. It is also because literature, considered as a highly labile way of thinking, relentlessly puts our own acquired competence, modes of reading and categories, including any prior understanding we might have of the literary itself, in question. Like an endlessly evolving computer virus, any writing worth taking seriously as literature reconfigures knowledge, remixes modes of understanding and obliges us to reboot. In the face of these unpredictable challenges, I would argue it is better not to think of those who 'profess literariness', as Holquist put it, as being 'in the business of teaching others and themselves to read', but as teaching others and themselves how to keep learning how to read. This is perhaps the most surprising, general and enduring lesson contained in the apartheid censorship archives.

Notes

1 Chris Baldick, *The Social Mission of English Criticism* (Oxford: Oxford University Press, 1983), pp. 8–9.
2 Ibid., pp. 12–13.
3 Alexander Ireland (ed.), *William Hazlitt: Essayist and Critic* (London: Frederick Warne, 1889), p. 93.
4 Baldick, *Mission*, p. 9.
5 Michael Holquist, 'Corrupt Originals: The Paradox of Censorship', *PMLA*, 109, 1 (1994), pp. 15–16. For related reflections on Holquist's analysis, see Nicole Moore, 'Censorship Is', *Australian Humanities Review*, 54 (May 2013), available at http://

www.australianhumanitiesreview.org/archive/Issue-May-2013/moore.html [accessed 8 September 2014].

6 Ibid., p. 17.
7 Ibid., p. 16.
8 Ibid., p. 18.
9 Ibid., p. 20.
10 Ibid., p. 21.
11 'censor, *n.2*.' *OED online*, 1889, Oxford University Press, available at http://www.oed.com/ [accessed 19 December 2013].
12 See Robert Darnton, *Censors at Work* (New York: W. W. Norton, 2014); and Nicole Moore, *The Censor's Library* (St Lucia: Queensland University Press, 2012).
13 Peter D. McDonald, *The Literature Police: Apartheid Censorship and its Cultural Consequences* (Oxford: Oxford University Press, 2009), pp. 299–301.
14 René Wellek and Austin Warren, *Theory of Literature* (1948; London: Penguin Books, 1993), pp. 24–5, 53.
15 Ibid., p. 19.
16 Ibid., p. 15.
17 I. A. Richards, *Principles of Literary Criticism* (1924; London: Routledge, 1995), p. 27.
18 Ibid., p. 26.
19 Ibid., p. 25.
20 Ibid., p. 26.
21 Ibid., p. 25.
22 Ibid.
23 Ibid.
24 Ibid., p. 24.
25 Ibid., p. 25.
26 McDonald, *Literature Police*, p. 40.
27 Baldick, *Mission*, p. 197.
28 Ibid., p. 9.
29 Holquist, 'Corrupt Originals', pp. 16, 22.
30 Ibid., p. 16.
31 Ibid., 23.
32 Ibid.
33 Ibid., p. 22.
34 Ibid.
35 Marjorie Garber, *The Use and Abuse of Literature* (New York: Pantheon Books, 2011), p. 7.

References

Baldick, C., *The Social Mission of English Criticism*, Oxford: Oxford University Press, 1983.

Darnton, R., *Censors at Work*, New York: W. W. Norton, 2014.

Garber, M., *The Use and Abuse of Literature*, New York: Pantheon Books, 2011.

Holquist, M., 'Corrupt Originals: The Paradox of Censorship', *PMLA*, 109 (1) (1994): 14–25.

Ireland, A. (ed.), *William Hazlitt: Essayist and Critic*, London: Frederick Warne, 1889.

McDonald, P. D., *The Literature Police: Apartheid Censorship and its Cultural Consequences*, Oxford: Oxford University Press, 2009.

Moore, N., *The Censor's Library*, St Lucia: Queensland University Press, 2012.

Moore, N., 'Censorship Is', *Australian Humanities Review* 54 (May 2013), available at http://www.australianhumanitiesreview.org/archive/Issue-May-2013/moore.html [accessed 8 September 2014].

OED online, Oxford University Press, available at http://www.oed.com/ [accessed 19 December 2013].

Richards, I. A., *Principles of Literary Criticism*, London: Routledge, 1995.

Wellek, R. and Warren, A., *Theory of Literature*, London: Penguin Books, 1993.

Part III

Diabolical Evasion of the Censor in Mikhail Bulgakov's *The Master and Margarita*

Ilona Urquhart

In Stalinist Russia, only one form of literature was allowed to be written and published: socialist realism. The Soviet government required complete acceptance of sanctioned forms of Marxist ideology so that its vision of the culmination of history – communism – could become a reality. Early Soviet policies regarding literature were shaped by the ideas of Andrei Zhdanov, who believed that literature had a powerful influence over readers, claiming at the first Soviet Writers' Congress that socialists were writing 'a literature which has organized the toilers and oppressed for the struggle to abolish once and for all every kind of exploitation'.[1] As a consequence, Zhdanov was wary of literature that might encourage dissenting views. Socialist realism, therefore, had to be unambiguous and avoid techniques used in modernism, which was founded on an entirely different interpretation of history, modernity and progress. In addition to this hortatory literary proscription, book production was regulated by the government-approved compulsory art organization, the Union of Artists, and widespread state censorship. Nevertheless, during the 1930s a major work of modernism was written in secret in Moscow, only to be published after the deaths of both Joseph Stalin and the author, Mikhail Bulgakov.

By a writer of satires critical of the success of the revolution, Bulgakov's plays and literary works were frequently banned by Soviet censorship. He begged the government to allow him to leave the Soviet Union in 1930, asserting that 'for me, not being allowed to write is tantamount to being buried alive'.[2] Stalin interceded and arranged a job for him at the Moscow Arts Theatre, however, and Bulgakov stayed within the grasp of the censor. In response, he spent the next ten years, until his death in 1940, writing the novel now hailed as his masterpiece, *The Master and Margarita*. The subversive nature of this work meant that it was censored on its first appearance in Russian in 1966–7 and only appeared in full in 1973.[3]

In this work, the devil, given the name Woland, comes to Moscow with a demonic retinue to test, at a Black Magic show, the Muscovites' commitment to their professed ideology; to harass the staff of the Variety Theatre and the members of the literary organization MASSOLIT, all of whom compliantly produce socialist realism; and to redeem the author of a politically subversive novel about Pontius Pilate, the Master, from a mental institution and reunite him with his lover Margarita. The accounts of events in Moscow are interspersed with chapters dedicated to the story of Pontius Pilate, initially appearing as a story told by the devil and later purporting to be the Master's novel. Woland is atypical for a devil character, as his machinations appear playful compared to the reality of Stalinist Russia. Surprisingly, he also encourages belief in the existence of Jesus and appears to be working towards the same goal as the Jesus-figure of the novel. Thus, the support the devil gives to heterodox art, in the conflict between art sanctioned by the government and art prohibited by the government, suggests that Bulgakov is working with an inverted value system in which what is 'evil' is that which is opposed to the Soviet government.

Having been forced into the role of diabolical adversary by the censor, Bulgakov embraces his characterization through the language of *The Master and Margarita*. In addition to the centrality of his devil character, the techniques of the novel are devilish in the dual sense of being opposed to the permitted genre of socialist realism and recalling the ambiguous devil of the Orthodox tradition. As Simon Franklin has explained, the Orthodox devil is an amalgamation of different understandings: 'an extrapolation, a field of possibilities, a set of interwoven traditions'.[4] As with other interpretations of the devil in modernity, its inherent irreconcilability with scientific and rational discourse makes definitions hard to determine. The novel's narratorial voice shares this elusiveness and, by constructing a world that is profoundly ambiguous, promotes the suspicion that the devil has not only authored the internal narrative recounting the decisions of Pontius Pilate but the entirety of the novel.

The ambiguity associated with the devil is put to work in *The Master and Margarita* as a strategy to resist censorship. This, as Leo Strauss's *Persecution and the Art of Writing* argued in 1941, is a well-established technique used by writers desperate to share heterodox views in repressive societies. In this essay, I apply Strauss's insights to explore how censorship can produce a form of discourse in which the transgressive content is protected by layers of ambiguity. As *The Master and Margarita* is stylistically different from Strauss's examples, this will provide an opportunity to consider how modernist literary techniques provide a new means of resisting the demands of censorship, even as these are shaped by censorship.

A German-Jewish émigré to the US, Strauss praised the constitution's protection of the rights of Americans, and wrote his essay at a time, as Georges Van den Abbeele notes, 'when another wave of explicit attacks on writers shocked the intellectual world'.[5] He looked at writings from epochs as disparate as Classical Athens, several medieval Muslim countries, seventeenth-century Holland and England, as well as eighteenth-century France and Germany to determine how heterodox views could pierce the hegemony of orthodoxy.[6] According to Strauss, the same strategy was practised throughout these historical periods, enabling dissident writers to suggest alternative forms of society without putting themselves at risk of repercussions by explicitly advocating such. 'Persecution', Strauss explained, 'gives rise to a peculiar technique of writing, and therewith to a peculiar type of literature, in which the truth about all crucial things is presented exclusively between the lines. That literature is addressed, not to all readers, but to trustworthy and intelligent readers only'.[7] To elaborate on the concept of 'writing between the lines' he provides the example of a writer transmitting a subversive view while appearing, to the careless reader, to attack the subversive view. The writer would do this by elaborating the subversive view in great detail and a disinterested tone, before attracting the attention of the reader with a dramatic shift in tone: '[t]hat central passage would state the case of the adversaries more clearly, compellingly and mercilessly than it had ever been stated'.[8] Having signalled the author's true perspective in this 'esoteric' content, the piece would then turn to the accepted view, written with such bombast and verbosity as to repulse the reader. The benefit of such a textual strategy is that its esoteric meaning can never be proven definitively, protecting the writer from the censor.

Strauss's conservatism and the mobilization of his ideas in the foreign policy of George W. Bush's administration have resulted in a popular interpretation of his work that suggests it advocates deceiving the masses through this technique of 'writing between the lines'.[9] Recent studies of Strauss and his work argue that this is a garbled interpretation of his theories, explaining that his interest was never contemporary politics, but political philosophy of the ancient world.[10] Rather than outlining an elitist scheme to keep esoteric or secret information within a select group, Strauss actually wrote of 'esoteric' content that can be understood by a reader who fully grasps the implications of the 'exoteric' or surface content, an interpretation far more amenable to works produced under censorship. As such, though modern critics might shy away from Strauss in light of how his theories have influenced world politics, his work can still be used constructively – creating a parallel with Bulgakov's novel, in the ways in which it is shaped by censorship and the idea of the devil.

A possible consequence of censorship, therefore, is providing incentive for the production of writing concerned with evading censorship. Although Bulgakov's *The Master and Margarita* had been written by 1941, its delayed publication meant that Strauss could not have been aware of its existence. Nevertheless, this work utilizes the technique of 'writing between the lines' in order to present a subversive view while distancing itself from that view. *The Master and Margarita* has rarely been considered in this light, because Bulgakov's biography has popularized an understanding of him as a writer who 'could, probably, in all honesty say about himself: in the day I write rubbish, and at night – a novel for posterity,' as Marietta Chudakova has said.[11] *The Master and Margarita* is largely understood as an unequivocally transgressive novel that proved Bulgakov could not be silenced. After all, Bulgakov was open about his opposition to Soviet censorship and socialist realism, stating in his 1930 letter to the Soviet government that, '[t]o struggle against censorship, whatever its nature, and whatever the power under which it exists, is my duty as a writer, as are calls for freedom of the press'.[12]

However, circumstances often meant that Bulgakov had to put aside his principles in order to survive as a writer in the Soviet Union. His last play, *Batum*, was a positive treatment of Stalin's early years, and was written as a commission for the Moscow Arts Theatre.[13] This play would ostensibly come under the rubric of the 'rubbish' that Bulgakov spent his days writing, intended to please Stalin and the censor. The binary that Chudakova constructs between the day's conformist writing and the night's transgressive writing implies that *The Master and Margarita* is unequivocally subversive. However, although I maintain that the work is ultimately subversive, Bulgakov's use of ambiguity means that alternative readings are not impossible.

It is imperative, therefore, to explore the means by which the novel puts forward its subversive message in order to assess with a degree of certainty whether *The Master and Margarita* 'offers a deliberate … debunking of the socialist realist myth'.[14] The ambiguity of the novel is so pervasive that a case *could* be made that Woland is actually a traditional devil, so that his treatment of the Muscovites and his support for the Master are works of evil. The text's openness to contradictory readings is made clear by the existence of critical interpretations that deviate dramatically from common consensus, such as Katherine Sirluck's assertion that Woland's intention is to 'prevent the completion of [the Master's] novel' when it is typically accepted that Woland saves the Master's novel.[15] In this essay I will demonstrate why the subversive message perceivable amongst the ambiguity of the novel is more plausible than reading *The Master and Margarita* as ambivalent about Soviet ideology or even supportive of it. I do this by exploring the significance of the centrality of the devil in the novel, and its pervasive association of the devil with the written word. Strauss's theorization of literature written under threat of persecution offers an ideal historical starting point for addressing the ambiguities in Bulgakov's novel, without being forced to conclude that the novel is in fact ambivalent about Soviet society.

The practice of presenting subversive views while protecting oneself from charges of sedition is far more elaborate in Bulgakov's novel than in the typical esoteric work described by Strauss. Like other modernist writers, Bulgakov tried to 'make it new,' in Ezra Pound's words. Unlike other modernist writers, though, his interest in testing the limits of formal experimentation seems to have been secondary to his desire to devise new means of evading the censor. Regardless of his motivations, the end result was a unique form of modernism shaped by the threat of censorship. Instead of using tone and word choice to mask his views, as earlier writers did, Bulgakov utilized elements of the supernatural, satire and irony to criticize the Soviet Union, while leaving open the possibility that he was criticizing those who were criticizing the Soviet Union.

The Master and Margarita even has a similar frame to the subversive 'attacks' Strauss discusses, for the events of the novel can be interpreted 'as carnival,' with the attention-grabbing central action of the novel bookended by representations of order under Soviet rule.[16] Maria Kisel asserts that Bulgakov was writing for an imagined Soviet reader who might not be open to heterodox sentiments. So, he 'utilizes tantalizing literary tricks to retain his audience's attention. The combination of humour, mystery, romance, and the supernatural creates an undisputable page-turner'.[17] These 'literary tricks' are interspersed with scenes in which the devil and his retinue test the commitment of the Muscovites to their professed Soviet ideals, exposing their insincerity, while the writers of Soviet realism are punished and the Master, a writer of heterodox literature, is rewarded. However, the narrator brings into question the events of the novel, so that 'Bulgakov grants his readers the power of free will by providing the option of dismissing the uncanny happenings as mass hypnosis and thereby rejecting the author's educational efforts … Having glimpsed a wider

the thunderstorm would only come towards evening, and cowardice was, undoubtedly, one of the most terrible vices. Thus spoke Yeshua Ha-Notsri. No, philosopher, I disagree with you: it is the most terrible vice! [45]

Curtis notes that although it is possible that the personal pronoun could be Pilate, '[a] subjective narratorial interjection seems to be inserted' here.[46] It is plausible that this is the authorial persona – Woland – highlighting the key message of his gospel, or even Bulgakov as himself. The claim that cowardice is the most terrible vice is formally ambiguous, because the identity of the speaker is not obvious. That this is a major concern of the novel, however, is clear.

Pilate, not Jesus, is the focus of the Jerusalem narrative because Woland is concerned with authenticity, and the courage it often requires. Pilate's guilt is so strong that he cannot rest for thousands of years because he cowardly followed his socialized ideals and sentenced Yeshua to death for treason, betraying his spiritual need for Yeshua's teachings and conscience in the process. Pilate's sin is that of almost all the Muscovites, except the Master and Margarita – acquiescing to the values of their tyrannical society even though this means ignoring their values, needs and desires.

Beyond the benefits that the techniques of modernism offered him for evading the censor, *The Master and Margarita* suggests that Bulgakov shared a view of the world commonly associated with modernism. David Punter notes that modernism has often been framed as a reaction to Enlightenment faith in progress and rationality.[47] Having rejected the revolution's necessity and desirability as it was enshrined in socialist realism, Bulgakov wrote a novel in which the devil is concerned with testing Muscovites' true satisfaction with life in the Soviet Union and exposing their insincerity. From this perspective, Bulgakov's use of the supernatural and thematization of religion within the text is also an attempt to represent the human condition 'in ways more real than realism', to use a phrase from Peter Childs's discussion of modernism.[48] *The Master and Margarita* proposes that the communist claim that the USSR had reached the point in history where reason could eradicate irrationality failed to see that faith, imagination and love were an essential complement to reason, and could not be excluded from society.

Even without acknowledging the content of the novel, then, the literary movement the novel most closely aligns with indicates that *The Master and Margarita* is intentionally subversive. The complexity of modernism means that, even in places where the novel's meaning is ambiguous (or especially in such places), Bulgakov's work is in conflict with Soviet demands for art. Jan Plamper explains that by the 1930s, the censors were concerned not only with eradicating heterodox sentiments, but ambiguous statements where heterodox sentiments might be hiding.[19] Despite the techniques he used in *The Master and Margarita* to mask his critique, Bulgakov's work was still unpublishable in the Soviet Union. The Soviet expectations of art meant that even his attempts to hide subversive sentiment would have been considered subversive.

Rather than its representation of the Soviet Union, it is the multiplicity of ways Bulgakov challenged the doctrine of socialist realism – through ambiguity, modernist literary techniques and the association between the devil and the heterodox writer – that marks *The Master and Margarita* as autonomous art. Richard Shusterman's comment 'that most (perhaps all) of the great art we have was created under very real and definite constraints or limitations' suggests that literary innovations are often responses to real world conditions.[50] The cryptic way in which Bulgakov's attack on Soviet society is presented demonstrates that censorship can produce new ways of writing as determined writers continue to attempt to circumvent censorship.

Notes

1 Andrei Zhdanov, 'Soviet Literature – The Richest in Ideas, The Most Advanced Literature', in H. G. Scott (ed.), *Problems of Soviet Literature: Reports and Speeches at the First Soviet Writers' Congress* (Moscow: Co-Operative Publishing Society of Foreign Workers in the U.S.S.R., 1935), p. 17. I would like to thank my doctoral supervisor, Geoff Boucher, and Nicole Moore for their comments on earlier drafts of this chapter, and to also thank Geoff for introducing me to Strauss's work and, much earlier, *The Master and Margarita*.

2 Cited in J. A. E. Curtis, *Manuscripts Don't Burn: Mikhail Bulgakov: A Life in Letters and Diaries* (London: Bloomsbury, 1991), p. 109.

3 Ibid., p. x.

4 Simon Franklin, 'Nostalgia for Hell: Russian Literary Demonism and Orthodox Tradition', in Pamela Davidson (ed.), *Russian Literature and Its Demons* (New York: Berghahn Books, 2000), p. 33.

5 Georges Van den Abbeele, 'The Persecution of Writing: Revisiting Strauss and Censorship', *Diacritics*, 27 (2) (1997): 5.

6 Leo Strauss, *Persecution and the Art of Writing* (Chicago: The University of Chicago Press, 1952), p. 33.

7 Ibid., p. 25.

8 Ibid., p. 24.

9 Thomas L. Pangle, *Leo Strauss: An Introduction to His Thought and Intellectual Legacy* (Baltimore: John Hopkins University Press, 2006), p. 2.

10 Ibid., p. 4; Catherine Zuckert and Michael Zuckert, *The Truth about Leo Strauss: Political Philosophy and American Democracy* (Chicago: The University of Chicago Press, 2008), p. 2.

11 Cited in Maria Kisel, 'Feuilletons Don't Burn: Bulgakov's *The Master and Margarita* and the Imagined "Soviet Reader"', *Slavic Review*, 68 (3) (2009): 583.

12 Cited in Curtis, *Manuscripts Don't Burn*, p. 106.

13 Ibid., pp. 229–30. Despite Bulgakov's best efforts, this play still did not meet the censor's approval and was never performed.

14 David Gillespie, *The Twentieth-Century Russian Novel: An Introduction* (New York: Berg Publishers, 1996), p. 3.

15 Katherine Sirluck, '*The Master and Margarita* and Bulgakov's Antiauthoritarian Jesus', in Paul C. Burns (ed.), *Jesus in Twentieth Century Literature, Art, and Movies* (London: Continuum International Publishing, 2007), p. 95.

16 John Bushnell, 'A Popular Reading of Bulgakov: Explication des Graffiti', *Slavic Review* 47 (1988): 511.

17 Kisel, 'Feuilletons Don't Burn', p. 594.

18 Ibid., p. 598.

19 Vladimir Tumanov, 'Diabolus ex Machina: Bulgakov's Modernist Devil', *Scando-Slavica*, 35 (1989): 56, 61.

20 Laura D. Weeks, 'What I Have Written, I Have Written', in Laura D. Weeks (ed.), *The Master and Margarita: A Critical Companion* (Evanston, IL: Northwestern University Press, 1996), p. 30.

21 Mikhail Bulgakov, *The Master and Margarita* (Dana Point: Picador, 1995), p. 124.

22 Ibid., p. 124.

23 Ellendea Proffer, 'Commentary', in M. Bulgakov, *The Master and Margarita* (Dana Point: Picador, 1995), p. 346.

24 Bulgakov, *The Master and Margarita*, p. 181.

25 Ibid., pp. 181, 326.

26 The other chapters of the Jerusalem narrative appear as Bezdomny's dream and the Master's novel respectively, but seeing as they form a coherent narrative we can assume a single author. Of all of them, only Woland has the supernatural power required to inspire the story in others.

27 Neil Cornwell, *The Literary Fantastic: From Gothic to Postmodernism* (New York: Harvester Wheatsheaf, 1990), p. 168.

28 Ibid., p. 168.

29 Bulgakov, *The Master and Margarita*, p. 216.

30 Proffer, 'Commentary', p. 352.

31 Bulgakov, *The Master and Margarita*, p. 295.

32 Ibid., p. 298.

33 Ibid., p. 45.

34 Ibid., p. 46.

35 Ibid., pp. 33, 12.

36 Laura D. Weeks, 'In Defense of the Homeless: On the Uses of History and the Role of Bezdomnyi in *The Master and Margarita*', *Russian Review* 48 (1989): 64.

37 Bulgakov, *The Master and Margarita*, p. 18.

38 Ibid., p. 34.

39 J. A. E. Curtis, *Bulgakov's Last Decade: The Writer as Hero* (Cambridge: Cambridge University Press, 1987), p. 135.

40 Ibid., p. 263.

41 Ibid., p. 274.

42 Ibid., p. 274.

43 Richard W. F. Pope, 'Ambiguity and Meaning in *The Master and Margarita*: The Role of Afranius', *Slavic Review* 36 (1977): 5–15.

44 Ibid., p. 16.

45 Bulgakov, *The Master and Margarita*, p. 272.

46 Curtis, *Bulgakov's Last Decade*, p. 155.

47 David Punter, *Modernity* (Houndmills, Basingstoke: Palgrave Macmillan, 2007), p. 36.

48 Peter Childs, *Modernism* (London: Routledge, 2008), p. 3.

49 Jan Plamper, 'Abolishing Ambiguity: Soviet Censorship Practices in the 1930s', *Russian Review* 60 (4) (2001): 526.

50   Richard Shusterman, 'Aesthetic Censorship: Censoring Art for Art's Sake', *The Journal of Aesthetics and Art Criticism* 43 (1984): 176.

References

Bulgakov, M., *The Master and Margarita*, Dana Point: Picador, 1995.

Bushnell, J., 'A Popular Reading of Bulgakov: Explication des Graffiti', *Slavic Review*, 47 (1988): 502–11.

Childs, P., *Modernism*, London: Routledge, 2008.

Cornwell, N., *The Literary Fantastic: From Gothic to Postmodernism*, New York: Harvester Wheatsheaf, 1990.

Curtis, J. A. E., *Bulgakov's Last Decade: The Writer as Hero*, Cambridge: Cambridge University Press, 1987.

Curtis, J. A. E., *Manuscripts Don't Burn: Mikhail Bulgakov: A Life in Letters and Diaries*, London: Bloomsbury, 1991.

Franklin, S., 'Nostalgia for Hell: Russian Literary Demonism and Orthodox Tradition', in Pamela Davidson (ed.), *Russian Literature and Its Demons*, New York: Berghahn Books, 2000.

Gillespie, D., *Twentieth-Century Russian Novel: An Introduction*, New York: Berg Publishers, 1996.

Kisel, M., 'Feuilletons Don't Burn: Bulgakov's *The Master and Margarita* and the Imagined "Soviet Reader"', *Slavic Review*, 68 (2009): 582–600.

Pangle, T. L., *Leo Strauss: An Introduction to His Thought and Intellectual Legacy*, Baltimore: John Hopkins University Press, 2006.

Plamper, J., 'Abolishing Ambiguity: Soviet Censorship Practices in the 1930s', *Russian Review*, 60 (2001): 526–44.

Pope, R. W. F., 'Ambiguity and Meaning in *The Master and Margarita*: The Role of Afranius', *Slavic Review*, 36 (1977): 1–24.

Proffer, E., 'Commentary', in M. Bugakov, *The Master and Margarita*, Dana Point: Picador, 1995.

Punter, D., *Modernity*, Houndmills, Basingstoke: Palgrave Macmillan, 2007.

Shusterman, R., 'Aesthetic Censorship: Censoring Art for Art's Sake', *The Journal of Aesthetics and Art Criticism*, 43 (1984): 171–80.

Sirluck, K., '*The Master and Margarita* and Bulgakov's Antiauthoritarian Jesus', in P. C. Burns (ed.), *Jesus in Twentieth Century Literature, Art, and Movies*, London: Continuum International Publishing, 2007.

Strauss, L., *Persecution and the Art of Writing*, Chicago: The University of Chicago Press, 1952.

Tumanov, V., 'Diabolus ex Machina: Bulgakov's Modernist Devil', *Scando-Slavica*, 35 (1989): 49–61.

Van den Abbeele, G., 'The Persecution of Writing: Revisiting Strauss and Censorship', *Diacritics*, 27 (1997): 2–17.

Weeks, L. D., 'In Defense of the Homeless: On the Uses of History and the Role of Bezdomnyi in *The Master and Margarita*', *Russian Review*, 48 (1989), pp. 45–65.

Weeks, L. D., 'What I Have Written, I Have Written', in L. D. Weeks (ed.), *The Master and Margarita: A Critical Companion*, Evanston, Illinois: Northwestern University Press, 1996.

Zhdanov, A., 'Soviet Literature – The Richest in Ideas, The Most Advanced Literature', in H. G. Scott (ed.), *Problems of Soviet Literature: Reports and Speeches at the First Soviet Writers' Congress*, Moscow: Co-Operative Publishing Society of Foreign Workers in the U.S.S.R., 1935.

Zuckert, C. and Zuckert, M., *The Truth about Leo Strauss: Political Philosophy and American Democracy*, Chicago: University of Chicago Press, 2008.

10

Reading the Enemy: East German Censorship across the Wall

Christina Spittel

It is May 1991, and they lie abandoned in their thousands, all brand-new, all untouched, except by the elements, on a tip outside Leipzig. There are glossy coffee-table celebrations of Dresden, shrivelling in the sun, and essays by Stefan Heym, blacklisted only years before and unwanted now. Alongside them, fables by Gaius Julius Phaedrus, novels by Heinrich Mann, Leo Tolstoy, Heinrich Böll and Volker Braun, poetry by Jaroslav Seifert, the Czech Nobel Prize winner of 1984.[1] Issued by East German presses in the closing years of the German Democratic Republic (GDR), all these books have proved unsellable in the newly-reunited Federal Republic. There they lie, dumped by a wholesaler keen to be rid of stock that booksellers were returning in bulk, often in unopened parcels.

For some East Germans, this was deeply personal – a dismantling of the libraries from which lives might be sourced. 'After the fall of the wall', recalled prominent actor Peter Sodann, 'tons of books from GDR publishers were pulped. Nobody wanted them anymore. But I won't let people take my past away from me!'[2] For others, the literary itself was at stake. Literary scholar Werner Mittenzwei remembers 1989 as a defeat, when a citizenry largely abandoned its writers for other pursuits, relegating literature from its privileged role as key cultural force and state-protected social good to one source of pleasure and knowledge among many.[3] He evokes a dystopia of unregulated reading, where literary value, once determined by the state, was being radically redefined. As real estate was being privatized and rents rose, publishing houses that used to 'occupy entire buildings and floors', Mittenzwei wrote, 'had to retreat under the rooftops. They even had to rid themselves of their archives and libraries'. The literary was being crowded out, he felt, by 'books about tax law, travel guides, Konsalik, Rosamunde Pilcher and memoirs of all shades', as West German publishers began supplying bookshops previously beyond their reach: 'It was the most humiliating time *belles lettres* had ever experienced.'[4]

A committed Marxist and card-carrying member of the Socialist Unity Party (SED), Mittenzwei was making a spirited if belated intervention into the 1990s German *Literaturstreit* (literature debate), a heated, even vitriolic 'stock take' of East German claims to German letters in the light of newly-emerging details about writers' entanglements with the state, particularly the *Ministerium für Staatssicherheit*.[5] Scholars have since nuanced the stark, black-and-white image created at that moment, of a censorious, repressive regime, sustained by a literary elite who sacrificed their art to *Gesinnungsästhetik*, an aesthetic of ideology. For Mary Fulbrook, the GDR was not so much a totalitarian state as a 'participatory dictatorship', its citizens 'active participants in a ... complex maze of practices, and inhabit[ing] a ... complex moral and political universe'.[6] Sara Jones has demonstrated that relationships between writers and the state were more fluid and ambiguous than epithets such as 'functionary' and 'chief dissident' suggest.[7] Book historians, most notably Siegfried Lokatis and more recently Robert Darnton have used oral histories and archival records to document how censorship was, as Darnton puts it, 'Top of Form an essential aspect of the process for transforming a manuscript into a book', highlighting, in other words, the ways in which the East German censorship regime *made* books and produced literary meaning, rather than merely suppressing such.[8]

Building on this work, this chapter considers the relationship between East German power and culture as mutually constitutive as well as repressive. It enquires into the meaning the socialist state enabled *and* prevented, as a self-proclaimed reading nation (*Leseland*) or culture reserve (*Kulturschutzgebiet*) – a regime that prized and protected literature as an important tool in the construction of socialism. There were no videos to compete with books, no PCs, no computer games, no strong press and most importantly for the context of this chapter, there was no free publishing industry.[9] As Eberhard Brüning, professor of English literature at Karl Marx Universität Leipzig, explained in 1978, 'the principles of socialist publishing policy are not determined by the constraint of the market, bestseller hysteria, the manipulation of taste or the striving for profit, but by the effort to create a holistically educated socialist person, shaped by the ideals of real humanism'.[10]

This 'educational dictatorship' critically relied on the state's commitment to read on behalf of its citizens, to curate their bookcases by limiting imports, screening their mail and their luggage, and insisting on licensing each book printed in the GDR as well as every publishing house operating there. To conceive of literature itself as a regime, as literary scholar John Frow has done, and of 'reading [a]s indeed always organized in advance' (by various semiotic but also socio-technical relations that structure encounters with a text), is a particularly illuminating way of approaching the GDR's state-directed literary production.[11] Indeed, Frow's conception of a regime of reading resonates with the vision for a literary society (*Literaturgesellschaft*) developed by East German writer (and first Minister of Culture) Johannes R. Becher, and with East German writer Joachim Walther's image of the 'Sicherungsbereich Literatur' (security area literature). In the 1950s, Becher envisaged literature as a network of relationships between readers, writers, publishers, film-makers and texts. Forty years later Walther, following extensive research in the Stasi archives, described the actualization of Becher's vision: the state's relentless efforts to monitor and shape these relationships and to patrol the creation of literary meaning as such.[12]

According to Frow, '[r]egimes can best be examined at their edges, the point at which they come into conflict with other regimes'.[13] This chapter revisits one such moment of collision: the publication in 1964 of the first East German anthology of West German short stories. The import of German-language literature into the GDR was always a 'hot iron', East German editor Roland Links recalled in the early 2000s,[14] while the German-German border remained 'entrenched terrain', as his former colleague Werner Liersch put it, as one of the faultlines of the Cultural Cold War, especially in the early 1960s, when the building of the Berlin Wall cemented the separation of the two states.[15] Liersch and Links prepared their anthology not only in the shadow of the Wall, but also at a time when the authorities in charge of controlling East German literary production underwent a significant restructure.

After two decades of disputes over competences between various authorities, and vocal complaints from book sellers demanding quality offerings and a timely, demand-based delivery, the *Hauptverwaltung Verlage und Buchhandel* (HV, Central Administration of Publishing Houses and the Book Trade) was founded in 1963 to safeguard the state's ideological *and* economic interests in the world of books.[16] Until 1989, it co-ordinated the means of literary production and distribution, most of which (printers, publishers, bookshops) were in fact owned by the state (or the party). The HV was not only charged with sanctioning ideological offence, although the guidelines for assessment, formulated in 1960 and in place until 1989, certainly and predictably clarified what needed to be suppressed in the national interest:

> Given that in the western zones a clerical-militarist regime exercises power and seeks to disrupt the building up of the GDR with all possible means, including ideological ones, we are forced to take every security measure. Literature which speaks up against the construction of socialism in the GDR, against the preservation of peace, against the principles of proletarian internationalism and against the unity of the socialist bloc, antihumanist and revisionist literature which falsifies Marxism-Leninism must not appear in the GDR.[17]

Rather than merely curbing book production and stifling readers' desires, the state sought to define model reading – to place the 'right book in the right hands at the right time', as the HV's guidelines put it.[18] A dense web of libraries 'enable[d] access to the good book', even in distant rural areas, observed East German literary scholar Arno Hochmuth.[19] In a socialist literary society, he argued, the state's task was to take care of the 'ensemble of relationships between literature and the people, i.e. the mental atmosphere that allows for literary excellence and diversity as well as the formation of a discerning readership'.[20] Indeed, the HV's guidelines insisted that 'promoting and preventing literature constitute a unity'.[21]

Under close supervision from the *Politbüro* and the *Ministerium für Staatssicherheit*, the HV organized the nation's reading by steering a text's entire life. It approved ideas for publication as part of short and longer-term plans; allowed them to materialize by issuing the compulsory imprimatur, as well as the required paper stock and (potentially) foreign currency, based on clearly-defined quotas; and finally, it monitored a book's social life. The department for *Literaturpropaganda* signed off on all public readings and, where necessary, steered reviews in the media.[22] The HV's key task was to issue the permission required to unlock any East German printer.

The *Kulturpolitisches Wörterbuch*, or *Dictionary of Cultural Policy*, which contained no entry for 'censorship', defined an imprimatur (*Druckgenehmigung*) as a tool for 'quality control', and elaborated: 'In essence, the imprimatur is a cultural-political and legal means used by the state to plan and steer various printed goods depending on political, cultural, economic and individual needs.'[23]

Officially, then, the HV was not to censor, but to *assess*, and to guide publishing houses in their work towards manuscripts worthy of approval. Erich Wendt had complained in 1960 that publishers were still irresponsibly sending in 'test balloons',[24] despite the clear instructions on the Ministry's application form: 'Only submit complete manuscripts that are ready to go to the printer's! Applications for printing need no covering letters!'[25] The full manuscript, complete with illustrations, prefaces or afterwords had to speak for itself, supported only by two assessments, also supplied by the publisher (usually one internal appraisal and one external reader's report). With his/her signature on the form, the head of a publishing house, as the guidelines put it, 'confirms that the publication of the book is a political and scholarly necessity and that content and form meet the highest possible standards.'[26] The East German regime of reading was thus very much a participatory dictatorship in Fulbrook's sense: publishers and censors collaborated so well that the HV rejected no more than 1 to 2 per cent of all applications.[27] As a result, German scholars Martina Langermann, Simone Barck and Siegfried Lokatis have been able to describe the GDR as 'a book writing "combine" of writers, editors, officials and censors of unprecedented dimensions',[28] and Joachim Walther to refer to the HV's director as 'simultaneously the GDR's chief publisher and head censor with considerable executive power'.[29]

A product of this combine, Werner Liersch's edited *Erkundungen: 19 westdeutsche Erzähler* (*Explorations: 19 West German Authors*) took three years to appear. On the cover of the slim white paperback, each author's name features, as if stamped in black and purple ink. Lothar Reher's graphic design cleverly signals that this crossing of the German-German border had official approval, and yet, underneath and in-between the names, traces of what seem further names appear: had not everyone made it safely across, into East German bookshops, in 1964? Frow has argued that any text that is read 'beyond the bounds of its own culture, will in some sense not be the "same" text; its value and standing, the interpretive possibilities it is seen to offer, ... and the uses to which it can appropriately be put all shift unstably in this passage.'[30] The Ministry's thick file on the volume, preserved today in the Bundesarchiv Berlin, documents censors' and assessors' attempts to ground these West German stories in an East German regime of reading, to stabilize and secure their meaning, and thus to both scout and delimit the volume's interpretive possibilities. It also shows how the HV sought to educate its *professional* readers – the staff at Volk und Welt, in this case – to read responsibly.

Right at the beginning of this file is the request for permission to print, which reached the Ministry on 9 October 1963, with a full manuscript and a record five assessments; the request, the form shows, was granted on 7 November that year. A short note from Walter Czollek, then Volk und Welt's director, is typed on the back:

Fig. 10.1: Cover of *Erkundungen: 19 westdeutsche Erzähler* (Volk und Welt, 1964), [edited by Werner Liersch, cover design by Lothar Reher].

> This title … had been completed years ago. For political reasons, the selection had to be changed several times. The volume was up for debate for some time at the Ministry. It has now been updated with new contributions. It is of greatest importance to the publisher to publish as soon as possible. An agreement about this has been reached with Mr Gruner.[31]

Volk und Welt's records, now held at the Akademie der Künste Berlin, reveal the volume's backstory: editor Werner Liersch signed his contract on 16 May 1961 and negotiations with West German publishers began soon after. Letters document hopeful exchange with the West right across the portfolio of the GDR's lead publisher for international literature. Intermingled with requests for West German stories are inquiries about other work from around the world for which West German publishers were holding translation rights: could Fischer Verlag grant permission to reprint Ryūnosuke Akutagawa's 'Rashomon', for another volume in a series of international stories? 'We are very keen to give the floor to West German authors, too, in this series', Roland Links' letter of 8 August 1961 continued, asking for rights to Luise Rinser's work, among others. 'Surely we don't need to stress just how important the German stories in particular are to us.' Could Suhrkamp Verlag please resend their German translation of Marcel Proust's *Swann in Love*, as it was missing from the parcel, and give Volk und Welt an unlimited option for this difficult author? ('We have told you already that we will need time for Proust.') Could they also grant rights to stories by Wolfgang Hildesheimer and Martin Walser, Links inquired, on 7 August – just six days before the Berlin Wall was built, only a few blocks away from his office in Glinkastraße.[32] On 9 August, the project was shelved: 'in the current political situation, detailed deliberations with the Ministry will need to be factored in.'[33]

The Wall seriously disrupted German-German literary exchange. When East German writers Franz Fühmann, Erwin Strittmatter and Stephan Hermlin expressed support for the Wall, Fischer Verlag cancelled their contracts for West German editions, even pulping 25,000 copies of a Strittmatter novel. East German publisher Rütten & Loening put on ice projects with West Germany's Wolfdietrich Schnurre and Günther Grass, following their protests against the GDR's government.[34] Once relationships had normalised, Volk und Welt worked in line with the HV, sending in a revised manuscript in October 1962. Hardly ready for the printers, this substantial version represented instead a catalogue of options, 'a maximum', as editor-in-chief Georgina Baum explained in her covering letter, 'taking into account West Germany's most renowned and significant authors. In our discussion, we would need to clarify whether these authors can be included with these works.' Readers' reports, she added, would be forwarded as soon as they arrived. Delays in securing permissions had required several changes to the selection.[35]

Ticks, crosses and question marks show the HV's censor working through two external assessments that arrived early in 1963. One came from Günther Cwojdrak, himself a writer, with expertise in West German literature. (He had published the polemical study, *The Literary Re-armament* (1957), and was now helping Aufbau Verlag justify the publication of one of Martin Walser's novels.[36]) The second was provided by the more obscure Hans Otto Lauterbach; like Cwojdrak, a migrant from the West.[37] The censor agreed with Cwojdrak's comment that Klaus Roehler's 'Silvester alle Tage' ('New Year's Eve Every Day'), a bitter satire of the middle-class aspirations of two West German businessmen and their wives, 'captures important symptoms of West German reality in a critical and precise manner'.[38] She was less convinced, however, that the bored teenagers who eventually escape from their parents' drawn-out party, 'already depicted the signs of a coming rebellion', as Lauterbach suggested.[39] In fact, her own notes reveal that she found the story poorly resolved: 'completely misses a punchline'.[40] Interspersed among the typed letters and reports, these hand-written notes record her own responses to her reading, in a frank, unguarded voice. Even at the headquarters of the GDR's centralized production of the literary, they provide a glimpse of what Frow has called 'the multifarious reality of uses rather than norms of good practice'.[41]

The Ministry's norms are observed, certainly: what grinds into motion at the censor's desk was 'the well-oiled machine of ideology critique, the x-ray gaze of symptomatic reading', to use Rita Felski's phrase.[42] Political attitudes are pigeonholed as 'bourgeois' or 'petit-bourgeois', 'anti-fascist' and 'critical of society' ('gesellschaft-skritisch'). This is not the only basis on which some stories appear 'OK' ('in Ordnung') or at least 'possible', however, while many remain unclassified, and two are 'very redundant' ('sehr überflüssig'). Of the latter, Ingeborg Drewitz's 'The dog' ('Der Hund'), is criticized for its bleakness. The other, Siegfried Lenz's satirical 'The hyenas' favourite food' ('Lieblingsspeisen der Hyänen') is summarized easily enough ('The trip to Europe of an American soldier who wants to revisit places he remembers from the war but is prevented from doing so because his wife and daughter want to shop for shoes') but its purpose does not disclose itself to the censor's X-ray gaze: 'Shoe shopping. What is that supposed to mean?'[43] One fifth of the stories disappointed in this way; others at least caused the censor to doubt herself. And yet this anonymous censor also yearned to do more than 'just' understand: she wanted to be enchanted, to cite one of the modes of textual engagement that Rita Felski identifies. 'To be enchanted is to be rendered impervious to critical thought, to lose one's heads and one's wits, to be seduced by what one sees...'.[44] Yet the stories proved inhospitable, refusing to entertain or move, registering instead as 'sehr kühl' ('stand-offish', 'reserved') or at least 'cold, not humanist'. Luise Rinser's 'A dark story' ('Eine dunkle Geschichte') 'lacks any real tragedy', blankly refusing her emotional engagement: it 'leaves one cold, because so eccentric'. Editor Werner Liersch's proposed commentary proved unhelpful: 'Blathering on. A few reasonable ideas at the end. Who are these writers? All good citizens? To whom are such stories addressed?' A small, separate note, in pencil, sums up the experience: 'Not very pleasant to read, the emanations of a society in decline. A few good things in there, a few possibilities, but cut energetically. Think of readership, save foreign currency and paper'.[45]

In their reports, both Cwojdrak and Lauterbach had conceived of this East German readership as potentially grateful for these useful stories, yet further reassurance was needed. In the early 1960s, East German academics had begun to research West German writing, and in consultation with the Ministry, Volk und Welt turned to Hans-Jürgen Geerdts, Professor of German Literature at Greifwald, who had written on West German realism. Geerdts, too, was positive, but some stories remained controversial. After a meeting with the censors, Volk und Welt staff were sent away to draw their own conclusions, and submit a reworked selection to another reader – this time, from the Party Academy itself. When that assessor ultimately declined to review, it was agreed that East German writer Hermann Kant would have the final say. Kant brought expertise on West German writing, and the (then) unblemished copybook of a trusted party functionary and Stasi informant.[46] His short, bold appraisal offered unconditional support, commending the editor's unflinching, even utopian outlook in the face of the 'artificial deserts of Modernism':

> The editor … wanted to show the oases in the desert, the gardens in all the dust; [he] wanted to let us know: things do not always have to be the way they are now, and they have not always been this way. There existed and there exists, even there, a literature worthy of the name and from which things might develop further, must develop further. The editor has the task of a teacher who reads out the best student essay to the class, not to say: this is what this class is like, but to say: this is what this class should be like.[47]

Significantly, Kant refrained from adding further to the diversity of interpretations that the volume had already garnered. Indeed, the Ministry's file preserves a range of views on the stories' value for their East German readership: for Kant, the selection offered 'absolutely fair information' about the best of West German writing; for external assessor Günther Cwojdrak, the Ministry's other expert in the Federal Republic's literary culture, it presented a sharp picture of West German realities, and a conviction that social criticism exists in West German literature; and for Volk und Welt's Roland Links, whose report reached the HV in October 1963, the volume signalled an East German standpoint on German literary matters, not least to the West, and countered images of ignorant, disengaged East German readers whose reading was limited by the border.[48] Professor Hans Jürgen Geerdts anticipated that the anthology might strengthen the GDR's own literature, by highlighting effective 'Allies', and commended the editor for undertaking this 'necessary and important, yet, from a cultural-political perspective, complicated task'.[49] H. Otto Lauterbach alone insisted on the need to sharpen the book's political edge by combing the journals of the Left for stories about the economic struggle of the industrial worker and the trade unions.[50] And only one person – a female staff member from the Ministry, perhaps the disenchanted censor – demanded 'highly emotional, positive stories, such as love stories' during a meeting. The latter, Roland Links assured the HV on behalf of Volk und Welt, was 'impossible to find in West German literature', and as for the few stories obtainable of West German industrial life, these were 'of insufficient literary quality' and often 'indefensible politically' as well, he explained.[51]

The political atmosphere, meanwhile, remained charged. The Ministry noted, in late 1962, that East German writers were complaining about the GDR's narrow approach to literature from the West, including West Germany.[52] In May 1963, the minister himself, Kurt Hager, addressed delegates of the German Writers' Union, many of whom had hoped that the Wall would bring some liberalization. Now they were told that the Wall's work was far from done: 'This antifascist wall of protection has to exist in everybody's head,' he exclaimed, using the state-approved term: *antifaschistischer Schutzwall*.[53] Clearly, the West German short stories in Liersch's volume needed a *Schutzwall* also: fortifications that delimited their reach, offering protocols for safe and productive engagement, but also protection from criticism for those responsible for the volume. Such paratextual additions were common practice in the East German regime of reading, and each of Liersch's assessors offered advice on this. They all highlighted the stories' need to be grounded more firmly in the specific artistic and political contexts from which they hailed, and asked for bio-bibliographical details and an Afterword that identified each author's political and aesthetic standpoint. Geerdts felt that 'the reader in our republic is entitled to these explanations and directions'.[54] Cwojdrak recommended further safety measures. He feared that some of the volume's authors might be misreading what were really the symptoms of late capitalism, and 'equate the decay of bourgeois society with the decay of the world, with human existence as such: this would need more detailed discussion in the Afterword.'[55]

So important was this built-in reading aid that revisions continued even after the HV's approval. In the 1950s, Becher had argued that to unlearn the (bad) habits of late bourgeois literature, readers needed to be addressed 'with much love, much patience …, in a language which shows these people that one respects them, considers them one of one's own.'[56] This is exactly what the HV asked of Liersch. He needed to become 'even more explicit, more intelligible to all' in conveying the East German standpoint, critically distancing himself from the authors' world views while emphasizing commonalities also.[57] Liersch's Afterword is built around the question of realist writing, and employs what David Bathrick has called 'the official, "monosemic" mode of discourse', articulated in black-and-white terms, as a set of binary opposites.[58] Liersch identifies the collection's commitment to 'the voices dedicated to realism in West German literature', to those who share some of the 'sense of narrative responsibility' that characterizes socialist writing, but remain marginalized in their own country.[59] In this way, the GDR itself emerges as a hospitable, progressive regime of reading, where literary meaning can unfold safely, without threat. Indeed, Liersch proceeds to paint the Federal Republic's literary culture in swift, bold and contrasting brushstrokes, as dominated by the absurd on the one hand, and the mass-produced, formulaic low-brow on the other – characterizing both as predictable, boring and dangerous manifestations of a regressive society.[60] And yet, while Liersch identifies the thematic concerns of his stories, he refrains from pointing his readers in precise directions: the title of his anthology – *Erkundungen* (explorations) – is suggestive of adventure, inviting perhaps what Frow has called 'readings in all their wildness'.[61] Indeed, the blurb admits (perhaps to the confused censor, perhaps to East German book-buyers, who were rejecting overly didactic fare by the early 1960s), that 'not all these explorations are explicit and unambiguous'.

When the Central Administration's guidelines for assessments were drafted in 1960, one staff member suggested they condemn outright 'all manifestations of routine, of forbearance and liberal attitudes towards literary assessment', and threaten non-compliant assessors, editors and censors with disciplinary measures. The proposal went unheard.[62] Indeed, much of the Department's work *was* routine: if the publication of West German literature in the early 1960s challenged the HV, and showed a Ministry keen to parcel out the responsibility for its decision, the publication of much other writing was quiet and unsensational, closely surveilled but undisturbed by the authorities. Yet they were always reading along: patrolling and delimiting a nation's experience of the literary, and securing it at the same time.

Notes

1 See Werner Mittenzwei, *Die Intellektuellen: Literatur und Politik in Ostdeutschland, 1945–2000* (Berlin: Aufbau, 2003), pp. 442–7. The incident was widely reported in the German media. Lutheran pastor Martin Weskott eventually took the books to Katlenburg near Göttingen (in the former West), where they continue to be sold for charity. Unless stated otherwise, all translations from German are the author's.

2 Susanne Schneider, 'Peter Sodann', *Süddeutsche Zeitung Magazin*, 11, 14 March 2014, available at http://sz-magazin.sueddeutsche.de/texte/anzeigen/41676/Peter-Sodann [accessed 1 September 2014]. Sodann has opened his library of GDR books to include such books abandoned by others, and now claims to own 4–5 million titles.

3 Mittenzwei, *Die Intellektuellen*, pp. 361–2. See also Alison Lewis, 'The Writers, Their Socialism, the People and Their Bad Table Manners: 1989 and the Crisis of East German Writers and Intellectuals', *German Studies Review*, 15 (2) (1992): 243–66.

4 Mittenzwei, *Die Intellektuellen*, pp. 443–4.

5 The *Literaturstreit* began with hostile reviews of Christa Wolf's *Was bleibt* (1990, *What remains*), accusing the author (previously valued in East and West Germany) of publishing her account of a writer's surveillance by the state, written in the 1970s, only when it was safe to do so. A broader debate unfolded when Sascha Anderson, of the Prenzlauer Berg's avant-garde, was unmasked as a Stasi spy, and the various entanglements of Monika Maron, Heiner Müller, Christa Wolf and many others with the Stasi became apparent. See Stuart Parkes, *Writers and Politics in Germany, 1945–2008* (Rochester: Camden House, 2009), pp. 150–63.

6 Mary Fulbrook, *The People's State: East German Society from Hitler to Honecker* (New Haven, CT: Yale University Press, 2005), pp. 12, 13.

7 Sarah Jones, *Complicity, Censorship and Criticism: Negotiating Space in the GDR Literary Sphere* (Berlin: de Gruyter, 2011).

8 Robert Darnton, *Censors at Work: How Censors Shaped Literature* (New York: W. W. Norton, 2014), p. 191.

9 See Jochen Hörisch, who also draws attention to the barely-developed telephone network. Jochen Hörisch, 'Verdienst und Vergehen der Gegenwartsliteratur', in Christian Döring (ed.), *Deutschsprachige Gegenwartsliteratur: wider ihre Verächter* (Frankfurt: Suhrkamp, 1995), pp. 36–7.

10 Eberhard Brüning, 'Australische Literatur in der DDR: Ein Überblick', *Zeitschrift für Anglistik und Amerikanistik*, 26 (2) (1978): 102.

11 John Frow, *The Practice of Value: Essays on Literature in Cultural Studies* (Perth: University of Western Australia Publishing, 2013), p. 10.

12 Johannes R. Becher, *Von der Größe unserer Literatur* (Berlin: Aufbau, 1956). Joachim Walther, *Sicherungsbereich Literatur: Schriftsteller und Staatssicherheit in der Deutschen Demokratischen Republik* (Berlin: Links, 1996). In 1983 problems with the censorship authority forced Walther to resign from his position as editor for Buchverlag Der Morgen Berlin, which he had held since 1968.

13 Frow, *The Practice of Value*, p. ix.

14 Roland Links, 'Der Umgang mit deutschsprachiger Literatur von 1954 bis in die siebziger Jahre', in Siegfried Lokatis and Simone Barck (eds), *Fenster zur Welt: Eine Geschichte des DDR Verlags Volk und Welt* (Berlin: Links, 2005), p. 97.

15 Werner Liersch, 'Erkundung der *Erkundungen*', in Monika Estermann and Edgar Lersch (eds), *Deutsch-deutscher Literaturaustausch in den 70er Jahren* (Wiesbaden: Harrassowitz, 2006), p. 34.

16 Siegfried Lokatis, 'Die Hauptverwaltung Verlage und Buchhandel', in Simone Barck, Martina Langermann and Siegfried Lokatis, (eds), *Jedes Buch ein Abenteuer': Zensur-System und literarische Öffentlichkeiten in der DDR bis Ende der sechziger Jahre* (Berlin: Akademie Verlag, 1998), p. 189.

17 Quoted in Lokatis, 'Die Hauptverwaltung Verlage und Buchhandel', p. 191.

18 Lokatis, 'Die Hauptverwaltung Verlage und Buchhandel', p. 192.

19 Arno Hochmuth et al., 'Der Aufbau der sozialistischen Literaturgesellschaft in der DDR und die Aufrechterhaltung des spätbürgerlichen Literaturbetriebs in Westdeutschland', in Arno Hochmuth (ed.), *Literatur im Blickpunkt* (Berlin: Dietz, 1967), pp. 39, 40.

20 Ibid., p. 42.

21 Gabriele Thomson-Wohlgemuth, *Translation under State Control: Books for Young People in the German Democratic Republic* (London: Routledge, 2009), p. 97.

22 Beate Müller, 'Censorship and Cultural Regulation: Mapping the Territory', in Beate Müller (ed.), *Censorship & Cultural Regulation in the Modern Age* (Amsterdam, New York: Rodopi, 2004), p. 22.

23 'Druckgenehmigung' in Manfred Berger et al. (eds), *Kulturpolitisches Wörterbuch* (Berlin: Dietz, 1978), pp. 149–50.

24 Lokatis, 'Die Hauptverwaltung Verlage und Buchhandel', p. 189.

25 Application for permission to print form for *Anthologie westdeutscher Erzählungen*, 4 October 1963, BArch DR1/5129/130.

26 Quoted in Lokatis, 'Die Hauptverwaltung Verlage und Buchhandel', p. 193.

27 Siegfried Lokatis, 'Paradoxien der Zensur in der DDR', in M. Sabrow (ed.), *Der geteilte Himmel: Literatur und ihre Grenzen in der DDR* (Leipzig: Akademische Verlagsanstalt, 2004), p 81.

28 Simone Barck, Martina Langermann and Siegfried Lokatis, 'The German Democratic Republic as a "Reading Nation": Utopia, Planning, Reality and Ideology', in M. Geyer (ed.), *The Power of Intellectuals in Contemporary Germany* (Chicago: University of Chicago Press, 2001), p. 90.

29 Joachim Walther, *Sicherungsbereich Literatur*, p. 39.

30 Frow, *The Practice of Value,* p. 16.

31 Application, 'Anthologie westdeutscher Erzählungen', 4 October 1963, BArch DR1/5129/128 R.

32 Roland Links, Volk und Welt, to S. Fischer Verlag, 8 August 1961 and Roland Links to Suhrkamp Verlag, 7 August 1961, Akademie der Künste Berlin, Archiv Volk und Welt, 1246. Similar letters went to Kiepenheuer & Witsch, Rowohlt, etc.

33 Links, File note, 9 August 1962, ibid.
34 Julia Frohn, *Literaturaustausch im geteilten Deutschland: 1945-1972* (Berlin: Links, 2014), pp. 108-9.
35 Georgina Baum, Volk und Welt, to Dr Anneliese Kocialek, Ministerium für Kultur, 24 October 1962, BArch DR1/5129/161.
36 See Frohn, *Literaturaustausch im geteilten Deutschland*, pp. 113 and 186-7, and Irene Charlotte Streul, *Westdeutsche Literatur in der DDR: Böll, Grass, Walser und andere in der offiziellen Rezeption, 1949-1985* (Stuttgart: Metzler, 1988), p. 55.
37 See Liersch, 'Erkundung der *Erkundungen*', p. 39.
38 Günther Cwojdrak, 'Anthologie westdeutscher Erzähler', 10 December 1962, DR1/5129/152-153, 152.
39 H. Otto Lauterbach, 'Anthologie westdeutscher Erzählungen', 27 November 1962, DR1/5129/145-151, 147.
40 File note, 'Anthologie westdeutscher Erzähler', DR1/5129/156-159, 156.
41 Frow, *The Practice of Value*, p. 39.
42 Rita Felski, *Uses of Literature* (Oxford: Blackwell, 2008), p. 1.
43 File note, 'Anthologie westdeutscher Erzähler', ca. February 1962, DR1/5129/157.
44 Felski, *Uses of Literature*, p. 56.
45 File note, 'Anthologie westdeutscher Erzähler', DR1/5129/156, 158, 159.
46 See Frohn, *Literaturaustausch im geteilten Deutschland*, p. 113, but also Jones, *Complicity, Censorship and Criticism*, esp. pp. 50-71, on Kant's later difficulties with the HV.
47 Hermann Kant, 'Anthologie westdeutscher Erzähler', no date, BArch DR1/5129/162-163, 162.
48 Kant, 'Anthologie westdeutscher Erzähler', DR1/5129/162; Cwojdrak, 'Anthologie westdeutscher Erzähler', DR1/5129/146; Roland Links, 'Anthologie westdeutscher Erzählungen' (Publisher's Report), undated, DR1/5129/164-169, 165.
49 Geerdts, 'Anthologie westdeutscher Erzählungen', DR1/5129/138.
50 Lauterbach, 'Anthologie westdeutscher Erzählungen', DR1/5129/145.
51 All quotes from Links, 'Anthologie westdeutscher Erzählungen', DR1/5129/165. Liersch's Afterword reiterates: 'We did not find a single work of significance in our genre in which working people are depicted with their questions of and answers to West German everyday life.' Werner Liersch, 'Nachwort', in Werner Liersch (ed.), *19 westdeutsche Erzähler* (Berlin: Volk und Welt, 1964), p. 278.
52 Quoted in Frohn, *Literaturaustausch im geteilten Deutschland*, p. 112.
53 Quoted in Streul, *Westdeutsche Literatur in der DDR*, p. 17.
54 Geerdts, 'Anthologie westdeutscher Erzählungen', DR1/5129/142.
55 Cwojdrak, 'Anthologie westdeutscher Erzähler', DR1/5129/152.
56 Quoted in Hochmuth et al., 'Der Aufbau der sozialistischen Literaturgesellschaft', p. 50.
57 Hoffmann, File note, 18 November 1963, DR1/5129/137.
58 David Bathrick, *The Power of Speech: The Politics of Culture in the GDR* (Lincoln: University of Nebraska Press), p. 15.
59 Liersch, 'Nachwort', pp. 273, 274, 278.
60 Liersch, 'Nachwort', pp. 273-4.
61 Frow, *The Practice of Value*, p. 39.
62 Lokatis, 'Die Hauptverwaltung Verlage und Buchhandel', p. 174.

References

Bathrick, D., *The Power of Speech: The Politics of Culture in the GDR*, Lincoln: University of Nebraska Press, 1995.

Barck, S., M. Langermann and S. Lokatis, 'The German Democratic Republic as a "Reading Nation": Utopia, Planning, Reality and Ideology' (trans. M. Latham and D. Pendas), in M. Geyer (ed.), *The Power of Intellectuals in Contemporary Germany*, Chicago: University of Chicago Press, 2001, pp. 88–112.

Becher, J. R., *Von der Größe unserer Literatur*, Berlin: Aufbau, 1956.

Brüning, E., 'Australische Literatur in der DDR: Ein Überblick', *Zeitschrift für Anglistik und Amerikanistik*, 26, 2 (1978), pp. 101–14.

Darnton, R., *Censors at Work: How Censors Shaped Literature*, New York: W. W. Norton, 2014.

'Druckgenehmigung', in M. Berger et al. (eds), *Kulturpolitisches Wörterbuch*, Berlin: Dietz, 1978, pp. 149–50.

Emmerich, W., *Kleine Literaturgeschichte der DDR*, Leipzig: Kiepenheuer, 1997.

Felski, R., *Uses of Literature*, Oxford: Blackwell, 2008.

Frohn, J., *Literaturaustausch im geteilten Deutschland: 1945–1972*, Berlin: Ch. Links, 2014.

Frow, J., *The Practice of Value: Essays on Literature in Cultural Studies*, Perth: University of Western Australia Publishing, 2013.

Fullbrook, M., *The People's State: East German Society from Hitler to Honeker*, New Haven: Yale University Press, 2005.

Hochmuth, A. (ed.), 'Der Aufbau der sozialistischen Literaturgesellschaft in der DDR und die Aufrechterhaltung des spätbürgerlichen Literaturbetriebs in Westdeutschland', in Arno Hochmuth (ed.), *Literatur im Blickpunkt*, Berlin: Dietz, 1967, 2nd rev. edn, pp. 38–51.

Hörisch, J., 'Verdienst und Vergehen der Gegenwartsliteratur', in Christian Döring (ed.), *Deutschsprachige Gegenwartsliteratur: wider ihre Verächter*, Frankfurt: Suhrkamp, 1995, pp. 30–48.

Jones, S., *Complicity, Censorship and Criticism: Negotiating Space in the GDR Literary Sphere*, Berlin: de Gruyter, 2011.

Lewis, A. 'The Writers, Their Socialism, the People and their Bad Table Manners: 1989 and the Crisis of East German Writers and Intellectuals', *German Studies Review* 15(2) (1992): 243–66.

Liersch, W. (ed.), *Erkundungen: 19 westdeutsche Erzähler*, Berlin: Volk und Welt, 1964.

Liersch, W., 'Erkundung der *Erkundungen*', in Monika Estermann and Edgar Lersch (eds), *Deutsch-deutscher Literaturaustausch in den 70er Jahren*, Wiesbaden: Harrassowitz, 2006, pp. 34–41.

Links, R., 'Der Umgang mit deutschsprachiger Literatur von 1954 bis in die siebziger Jahre', in S. Lokatis and S. Barck (eds), *Fenster zur Welt: Eine Geschichte des DDR Verlags Volk und Welt*, Berlin: Links, 2005, pp. 97–102.

Lokatis, S., 'Die Hauptverwaltung Verlage und Buchhandel', in S. Barck, M. Langermann and S. Lokatis, *'Jedes Buch ein Abenteuer': Zensur-System und literarische Öffentlichkeiten in der DDR bis Ende der sechziger Jahre*, Berlin: Akademie Verlag, 1998, pp. 173–205.

Lokatis, S., 'Paradoxien der Zensur in der DDR', in M. Sabrow (ed.), *Der geteilte Himmel:*

Literatur und ihre Grenzen in der DDR, Leipzig: Akademische Verlagsanstalt, 2004, pp. 75–99.

Mittenzwei, W., *Die Intellektuellen: Literatur und Politik in Ostdeutschland, 1945–2000*, Berlin: Aufbau, 2003.

Müller, B., 'Censorship and Cultural Regulation: Mapping the Territory', in B. Müller (ed.), *Censorship and Cultural Regulation in the Modern Age*, Amsterdam, New York: Rodopi, 2004, pp. 1–31.

Parkes, S., *Writers and Politics in Germany, 1945–2008*, Rochester: Camden House, 2009.

Schneider, S., 'Peter Sodann', *Süddeutsche Zeitung Magazin*, 11, 14 March 2014, available at http://sz-magazin.sueddeutsche.de/texte/anzeigen/41676/Peter-Sodann [accessed 1 September 2014].

Streul, I. C., *Westdeutsche Literatur in der DDR: Böll, Grass, Walser und andere in der offiziellen Rezeption, 1949–1985*, Stuttgart: Metzler, 1988.

Thomson-Wohlgemuth, G., *Translation under State Control: Books for Young People in the German Democratic Republic*, London: Routledge, 2009.

Walther, J., *Sicherungsbereich Literatur: Schriftsteller und Staatssicherheit in der Deutschen Demokratischen Republik*, Berlin: Links, 1996.

11

Wild Spiders Crying Together: Confessional Poetry, Censorship and the Cold War

Tyne Daile Sumner

I do not think a 'headline poetry' would interest more people any more profoundly than the headlines.

Sylvia Plath, 'Context'[1]

When American confessional poet Robert Lowell was prosecuted for draft evasion before a United States district court in New York on 13 October 1943, the concurrent implications of political dissidence were irrefutable. The indictment came approximately one month after Lowell sent his 'Declaration of Personal Responsibility' to President Roosevelt, affixed to a letter that opened with an uncharacteristically explicit pronouncement: 'I very much regret that I must refuse the opportunity you offer me in your communication of August 6, 1943, for service in the Armed Forces.'[2] Lowell's reasons for non-participation were comprehensive and he was resolute. In categorical recognition of the pervasive public concerns with American cold-war containment culture and in direct opposition to unprecedented levels of state surveillance, Lowell's fervent and compelling diatribe criticized fundamental contradictions in America's strategic policies, asserting that 'wars are won not by irrational valor but through the exercise of moral responsibility'.[3] Contending that 'modern wars had proved subversive to the Democracies and history', Lowell charged that US hostile acts such as 'the bombings of the Dams and of Hamburg were not mere isolated acts of military expediency but marked the inauguration of a new long-term strategy, endorsed and coordinated' by America's Chief Executive.[4] This provocative articulation of Lowell's beliefs, including that obedience to conscription was synonymous with a 'Machiavellian contempt for the laws of justice and charity between nations',[5] as well as his consequent objection to saturation bombing in Europe and other American military tactics, resulted in a 12-month prison sentence. The then-26-year-old poet served the first ten days of his confinement in New York's West Street jail.

In addition to illustrating Lowell's apparent gift for political critique, the letter subscribes unmistakably to a long and particular tradition of American sociopolitical dissent: a form of rebellion that prioritizes, above all else, the sanctity of individual autonomy. This attitude to the state and the self is perhaps expressed best in Henry

David Thoreau's 'Resistance to Civil Government' (1849) where he declares, 'I was not born to be forced, I will breathe after my own fashion'.[6] Although Lowell was jailed, he served only five months of the year-long sentence and went on to publish poems critical of the war in his collections *Land of Unlikeness* (1944) and *Lord Weary's Castle* (1946). A quarter of a century later, he produced more anti-war poems in the collections *Life Studies*, *Near the Ocean* and finally *Notebook* in 1969.

What becomes apparent through the alignment of Robert Lowell's outspoken public persona with his lyric poetry is not necessarily the synchronicity of public activism and poetic works, but rather the capacity for an intriguing disjunction between the two. Certainly, Lowell's lyrical mode was not as direct as the notorious Ginsbergian boldness applied in often-censored anti-war proclamations such as those in 'America' (1956), where Ginsberg writes:

America when will we end the human war?
Go fuck yourself with your atom bomb.[7]

However, the personal focus and revelatory style shared by Lowell and several of his fellow confessionals achieve a remarkably subtle balance between artistic perplexity and anti-government protest. Thus, while much confessional poetry appears to eschew, perhaps even satirize, the exercise of political commentary, upon closer inspection, many mid-twentieth century confessional poems can be seen to engage in a distinctive practice of political protest, in many cases characterized by shrewd and aesthetically-driven censorship-avoidance. The poetry of Robert Lowell, Sylvia Plath and Anne Sexton utilizes a subjective, autobiographic style that yet seeks to condemn the repressive state policies it simultaneously evades. While outspoken political objection risked censorship (and, in Lowell's case, incarceration), a delicate artistic balance between personal disclosure and public commentary could work to criticize American cold-war suspicion and anxiety from *within* the structures the American government sought to contain. The substratum of the American government's approach to post-war atomic anxiety was an emphasis on the security of the domestic American lifestyle and, while many viewed confessional poetry as an inward-looking, even narcissistic form, a closer examination of several key poems reveals that this apparent emphasis on sheltered domesticity could be used to subvert the public rhetoric of the cold-war period.

An examination of confessional poetry in relation to cold-war domesticity requires not only an assessment of the intersection of literary and cultural approaches, but an appraisal of the status of the home within the period's ideological structures more broadly. George Kennan's influential containment doctrine of 1946 meant that American foreign policy focused on preventing the spread of Soviet-backed Communism was paramount; an advancement of the proverbial Red Scare. By the end of the twentieth century, however, several critics had begun to conceptualize the specifically domestic resonance of Kennan's policy. Elaine Tyler May's *Homeward Bound: American Families in the Cold War Era* (1988) is a fundamental text on the connections between public policy and private life during the Cold War because it unearths containment's domestic equivalent. May writes: 'More than merely a metaphor for the cold war on the homefront, containment aptly describes the way in which public policy, personal behaviour, and even political values were focused on the home.'⁸ With other key texts, especially Thomas Schaub's *American Fiction in the Cold War* (1991) and Alan Nadel's *Containment Culture: American Narratives, Postmodernism, and the Atomic Age* (1995), May's work represented a cultural turn in Cold War studies. After Frances Stonor Saunders' *The Cultural Cold War: The CIA and the World of Arts and Letters* (2000), today these belong to an expansive body of work that foregrounds literature in its reassessment of the Cold War.

With this raft of new critical intersections between cold-war ideology and literature came an increased interest in the ways in which post-war American private life was shaped by geopolitical dynamics. More specifically, critics began to examine the American home as a site of ideological security amid a tumultuous cold-war setting. As Beatriz Colomina has written of the militarized, post-war kitchen space in her book *Domesticity at War* (2006): 'As we all know but rarely publicize, the house is a scene of conflict. The domestic has always been at war. The battle of the family, the battle of sexuality, the battle of cleanliness, for hygiene, and more recently, the ecological battle. With recycling, even the waste of the house is subject to classification. Domesticated.'⁹ As the American Government's propaganda campaign succeeded in replacing missiles with washing machines, bombs with automobiles, images of American domestic bliss transformed war into living.

As a result, much of the ideological rhetoric of US cold-war politics focused on the 'home' and the 'family,' insisting that 'the "model" home, with a male breadwinner and a full-time female homemaker, adorned with a wide array of consumer goods, represented the essence of American freedom'.¹⁰ Parallel to this hypothetical were real and significant changes in the consumption patterns of American households. In the decade following the Second World War, the household appliance and furnishing purchases of American families climbed by over 200 per cent, reflecting the United States' position as the world's most productive economy.¹¹ Inspired not only by advertising but also by a general national ethos that claimed 'More is Better', wage-earning families embraced suburban life, the majority purchasing expensive domestic appliances for the very first time. The famous 'Kitchen Debate' between Vice-President Richard Nixon and Soviet Premier Nikita Khrushchev exemplifies the preoccupation with high-quality consumer goods and the powerful domestic ideologies that underpinned post-war America's social and political approach to the atomic age.¹² Ultimately, the Cold War irrevocably revised America's understanding of the domestic realm, emphasizing its significance as a secure space, free from the intrusions into private life that had become synonymous with threats to America's democratic liberty. Yet, as the themes of confessional poetry suggest, the family home could also be a menacing channel for, and source of, personal expression. Speaking from *within* the home, confessional poets inverted America's embrace of domestic surveillance, revealing the paradoxical and often frightening double-bind generated by an overemphasis on security.

Sylvia Plath's 1962 'A Secret' mocks the illusionary power of secrecy in this mode, sarcastically questioning the worth of information that exists only in so far as it is publicly inaccessible. She writes:

A secret! A secret!
How superior.
You are blue and huge, a traffic policeman,
Holding up one palm[13]

The outlandishly blue, phantasmagorical policeman-secret depicted in this poem sets the tone as a peculiarly hallucinatory, dreamlike witch-hunt for the truth, subscribing to a style for Plath's poems that, as Rosenthal describes, 'make a weirdly incantatory black magic against unspecified persons and situations'.[14] In ways comparable to many of Plath's later poems, 'A Secret' interrogates the methods and motives of a controlled, dystopian world, calling attention to the nightmarish US reality of comprehensive surveillance and oppressive regulatory governance. It becomes unclear, as the poem unfolds, who is repenting, as the identity of the speaking 'I' assumes perhaps greater secrecy than the 'secret' itself. Yet, despite this blurring of accuser with penitent, guilty with guiltless, the vehemence of the confession remains intact. Confession becomes a dual-act: uttered by the poet but also enacted or 'stamped' within the narrative of the poem:

A difference between us?
I have one eye, you have two.
The secret is stamped on you,
Faint, undulant watermark.

Will it show in the black detector?
Will it come out
Wavery, indelible, true
Through the African giraffe in its Edeny greenery,

The Moroccan hippopotamus?
They stare from a square, stiff frill.
They are for export,
One a fool, the other a fool.[15]

As Sarah Churchwell has noted, '"A Secret" is, implicitly, about revealing secrets, about, as it were, publishing them: the eponymous secret, in its very nature, seeks disclosure'.[16] It is difficult, of course, to deny the biographical quality of the poem; it is almost certainly motivated in part by Ted Hughes's affair with Assia Wevill, which was a traumatic period in Plath's life around which several of her poems revolve. Biographical context aside, however, 'A Secret' remains one of Plath's most ambiguous and cryptic poems: the lines, 'Will it show in the black detector? / Will it come out' are a teasing reminder of the difficulty of locating the poem's ultimate meaning. Yet, despite the 'morbid secretiveness'[17] that Rosenthal argues prevents a clear and immediate reading of the poem, when placed alongside Plath's other surveillance-focused poetry 'A Secret' occasions an intriguing reflection upon its turbulent twentieth-century context. All written in 1962, poems such as 'The Other', 'Eavesdropper', 'Words Heard, by Accident over the Phone', 'The Detective', 'The Courage of Shutting-Up', 'The Jailer' and 'The Secret' not only illustrate Plath's personal preoccupation with surveillance, they also reflect the hugely controversial stance that confessional poetry took in relation to post-war government policy.[18] Of this intriguing group of later poems, Christina Britzolakis remarks, 'these "weird" scenarios recycle key motifs of Gothic popular culture, drawing on cinematic as well as literary texts, to probe the nightmarish underside of the Cold War suburban dream of normality. Their satirical target, like that of many contemporary thrillers and horror films, is the stifling family-centred and ethnocentric conformity of the 1950s small-town idyll.'[19]

'The Secret' takes the purified, surreal rhetoric of the 'ideal' suburban existence, with its model couple, perfect home and stash of hyper-commercial women's magazines, and enacts a horrifying distortion process. The African animals printed over a child's bed-quilt come to life and become terrified: 'They stare from a square, stiff frill. / They are for export.' Nothing in the once-sacred family home is safe: 'One a fool, the other a fool.'[20] The years immediately preceding the construction of 'A Secret' saw an escalation of the Cold War. Both the Soviet Union and the United States commenced a series of disconcerting atmospheric H-bomb tests and the perceived 'missile gap' had entered mainstream American political rhetoric as an ostensible indication of the quantity and power of the USSR's military apparatus in comparison with America's own. Plath's feelings about nuclear disquiet surface in a letter to her mother from 1960, where she describes her reaction to an Easter protest march:

> I saw the first of the 7-mile-long-column appear—red and orange and green banners, 'Ban the Bomb!' etc., shining and swaying slowly. Absolute silence. I found myself weeping to see the tan, dusty marchers, knapsacks on their backs— Quakers and Catholics, Africans and whites, Algerians and French—40 percent were London housewives. I felt proud that the baby's first real adventure should be as a protest against the insanity of world-annihilation.[21]

The dreamlike policeman that haunts 'The Secret' appears again in 'The Other', where Plath links surveillance and confession, emphasizing that the former must always result in the latter. The implication in this poem, at least for Plath, is that one can, of course, surveil without censoring – watching everything and stopping nothing. However, the *necessity* to confess seems to arise from the notion that a literary privatization of publicly-expressed dissent may distort the very sentiments that are being surveiled. Thus, in complicating the relationship – or distance – between poet and persona, Plath neatly evades censorship via the literary confessional mode. 'The Other' (1965) reveals the outpouring of speculation, or suspicion, that surfaces in resistance to being watched. Plath writes:

> Smilingly, blue lightning
> Assumes, like a meathook, the burden of his parts.

> The police love you, you confess everything.
> Bright hair, shoe-black, old plastic[22]

The poem presents a succession of surreal yet associated notions: interrogation, assumption, crime, detection, surveillance and confession, intertwining the roles of interrogator and interrogated so as to undo the division between the two. As Deborah Nelson has written, in response to the surveillance-fuelled fury of 'The Other', 'there may be no crime to confess to ... but it does not matter; everything—"bright hair, shoe-black, old plastic"—constitutes evidence of a crime, everything contributes to the confession'.[23] Reverting to the role of the 'watched' as opposed to the 'watcher', Plath questions:

> Is my life so intriguing?
> Is it for this you widen your eye-rings?
>
> Is it for this the air motes depart?
> They are not air motes, they are corpuscles.[24]

These lines, though characteristically sardonic, reveal the terrorizing results of over-surveillance, where 'eye-rings' spy and 'motes depart', yet they do not know what for or why; surveillance for surveillance's sake becomes the overriding principle. This sentiment also resonates in 'Eavesdropper', where the government-led initiative of 'good-neighbourliness', in which citizens enact a penetrating yet seemingly protective suburban watch upon one another, becomes an insidious act of undercover work. Beneath the surveillance of the 'big blue eye', the citizens of 'Eavesdropper' become:

> cow people
> Trundling their udders home
> To the electric milker, the wifey, the big blue eye[25]

In Plath's dystopian narrative of surveillance, the all-powerful eye of the observer 'melts the skin' of its people, turning them into 'gray tallow, from bone and bone'.[26] The effect is disturbing, the poem's 'schizophrenic perspective ... producing a quasi-Brechtian alienation effect, confronting the reading with a world locked into the frozen grimace of cliché'.[27]

Plath's keen awareness of the rhetoric of McCarthyism resonates not only in her poetry. In a journal entry taken from her early years at Smith College in the 1950s, Plath prefigures the infiltrating effect that the dominant male political rhetoric of the era would have over the collective American consciousness. She writes: 'school children will sigh to learn the names of Truman and Senator McCarthy. Oh, it is hard for me to reconcile myself to this'.[28] In his 2003 work *Cold War, Cool Medium*, Thomas Doherty reflects on this sentiment, explaining how McCarthy dominated the era, 'propelled high on the atmosphere of external threat, internal insecurities, and nuclear tremors'. Doherty conjures a moment in American political history where the Senator 'swirled with cyclone force across newspaper headlines, newsreels, and television screens: McCarthy, the great ogre of Cold War America, who as noun and adjective earned his dictionary entry as part of the language'.[29] Though less overtly politically active than Lowell, Plath nevertheless harboured a strong anti-war outlook, writing to her mother in 1955 of her desire to 'counteract McCarthy and much adverse opinion about the United States'.[30] Thus, Plath's poems, in subscribing to the distinctly 'confessional' style that fused personal revelation with incisive public commentary, can be studied for their astute capacity to slip neatly under the radar of increasingly-repressive state policies. In thinking about the links between surveillance and censorship, two central motivations invariably surface: control over citizens and the restriction of freedom. Although they do not necessarily provide anonymity, confessional poems nevertheless afford a sense of pseudonymity: the poet and the persona become indistinguishable. A passage from her 1962 essay, 'Context', provides a chilling example of what is perhaps Plath's deliberately equivocal effort to reveal, yet also conceal, her true poetic motive. She writes: 'My poems do not turn out to be about Hiroshima, but about a child forming itself finger by finger in the dark. They are not about the terrors of mass extinction, but about the bleakness of the moon over a yew tree in a neighbouring graveyard.'[31]

Anne Sexton's poetry, though less obviously sensitive to surveillance, treads a similar path to Plath's work in terms of its resistance to the rhetoric of America's idealized suburban home. In Sexton's verse, the institution of the home is rendered a paradoxical space, incapable of security due to the fallibility of mass-produced privacy, yet never entirely public in its own right. In Sexton's poetry, the home is always conceived of as 'misrepresented' by the cold-war political propaganda that advertised it as the pinnacle of American democratic confidence. Poems such as 'Housewife', 'Self in 1958', 'Man and Wife: to Speke of Woe that Is in Marriage', 'For John Who Begs Me Not to Enquire Further', 'Live' and 'Unknown Girl in the Maternity Ward' figure both the ultimate impossibility of privacy and the various myths that plague the concept of 'the suburban'. As Deborah Nelson has noted, one of Sexton's shorter poems, 'Housewife', transforms the woman, literally, into a house, marking a direct connection between the invasion of domestic security and a raid upon personal, bodily privacy.[32] The fusing of 'house' and 'wife' in the poem's title leads to the house becoming a living, breathing woman:

> Some women marry houses.
> It's another kind of skin; it has a heart,
> a mouth, a liver and bowel movements.[33]

The 'house' depicted in the poem, while accessible to the public – 'Men enter by force' – is also a form of prison: 'See how she sits on her knees all day, / faithfully washing herself down.' The home's caretaker, the woman who paradoxically *is* also the home, is both protected and exploited by the 'permanent and pink' walls of her own suburban space. Nelson summarizes this contention, noting how 'this disconnection of the woman from public discourse was one of the results of marking the threshold of the home as the border between public and private and then idealizing privacy'.[34] Ultimately – and insofar as my reading of 'Housewife' renders it at least partially satirical – Sexton's poem works to belittle the entire concept of nationwide internal security. The incestuous undertone, marked by a disturbing image of sexual engagement between a man, his wife and mother, coupled with the removal of the housewife's personal and domestic autonomy – 'A woman is her mother' – reduces the home to a mere playpen, a juvenile resting-place where mothers and their children are deprived of their privacy by an invasive, omnipresent 'Jonah'.[35] The satirical irony that inflects Sexton's poem affords it an almost political dubiety; while on the one hand she parodies cold-war discourse, she also appears to evade any political accountability through the mode of personal confession.

As all these poems illustrate, Plath and Sexton wrote about the home from within the home, developing a formula that marks the most characteristic confessional poems, namely locating 'the pressure in family life, specifically in the relations of parents and children'.[36] Importantly, this preoccupation with confessional poetry reflected a much wider socio-political anxiety, one perhaps best expressed by J. Edgar Hoover in a well-known speech to new graduates at St Johns University in Brooklyn in 1942, where he stated: 'The home is the first line of defense of our Democracy … When the home is destroyed, everything in our civilization crashes to its doom'.[37] Hoover's speech, aptly entitled 'A Nation's Call to Duty: Preserve the American Home', summarized the intense focus on domestic security that marked the American government's post-war effort to identify and remove communists from American public life.[38] Hoover believed that the key to national security lay in the institution of the family, the inexorable foundation of which was the family home, epitomizing American culture's insistence on privacy.

An assessment of this anxiety-fuelled period, however, is incomplete without reference to the powerful and pervasive effect of America's booming technologies. The arrival of regular commercial television network programming in America by the early 1950s, for example, played a significant role in dissolving the tensions between public and private life that preoccupied the nation.[39] Marketed as a new domestic device that would strengthen family ties among, predominantly, white middle-class families, television acted to propagate its large-scale agenda of goods-advertising while maintaining the illusion of social and cultural intimacy; the emergence of the term 'family room' in the post-war period eponymously illustrates the ideology that aligned household spaces with family togetherness.[40] In this sense, television not only acted to marshal public opposition to communism during the Cold War, it also helped to mobilize the onset of consumer society, often through a productive synthesis of familiar, 'everyday' domesticity with advertising and politically-motivated material.[41] Such an agreement was intensified by the growing interest in confession more generally, contributing to publicists' realization that 'the more intimate a star's confession, the more widely his or her image could be disseminated'.[42]

As these examples illustrate, despite sharing an equivalent investment in tensions between public and private, confessional poetry was able to resist and invert public assumptions about the sanctity of the home. By doing so, poets such as Plath, Sexton and Lowell were able to engage closely with and eventually undermine the foundations of cold-war discourse constructed out of privacy. The 'sphere of psychosocial formation' that existed in the middle-class home's 'bedrooms, bathroom, staircases, and kitchens' provided a foundation from which the confessionals could participate in 'the concerns with social hygiene that inflected popular culture'.[43] Importantly, confessional poetry's powerful yet subtle critique of privacy also couched a political dissidence that would likely have otherwise been censored.

In poetic response to these tensions, Robert Lowell's poetry operates at perhaps the most intriguing junction of all the confessionals. As Adam Beardsworth has suggested, despite Lowell's distinctive 'insular, even narcissistic aesthetic', his key confessional poems reveal that 'he sought expression of atomic anxiety through the figure of the abject pathological self', insofar as 'his subjective autobiographic style allowed him to express an implicit dissent that evaded the surveillance of increasingly repressive state policies'.[44] Simultaneously, Lowell's poetry situates its wider cultural crises inside the framework of his own family, 'consistently viewing [experience] as neither merely personal, nor merely history'.[45] The 'I' of his poetry, therefore, negotiates an alluring status that is situated halfway between the anxieties and concerns of a post-war American collective consciousness and the manufactured intimacy that characterizes confessional poetry. In 'Memories of West Street and Lepke', Lowell presents a domestic lifestyle that is both sedated and anxious, characterized by morbid infantilization, as the poem's speaker examines his experience as a conscientious objector during the Second World War:

> Only teaching on Tuesdays, book-worming
> in pajamas fresh from the washer each morning,
> I hog a whole house on Boston's
> 'hardly passionate Marlborough Street',
> where even the man
> scavenging filth in the back alley trash cans,
> has two children, a beach wagon, a helpmate,
> and is a 'young Republican'.
> I have a nine month's daughter,
> young enough to be my granddaughter.
> Like the sun she rises in her flame-flamingo infants' wear.
>
> These are the tranquillized *Fifties*,
> and I am forty.[46]

This passage is arguably the nucleus of *Life Studies* and, at a stretch, perhaps forms the nucleus of Lowell's career. The opening of the poem – a sequence William Doreski has described as 'a kind of post-war L'Allegro'[47] – contrasts the idealized representative American with the social and political shortcomings of his own affluent, mid-century reality. A blurring of the boundaries between public and private comes to realization in, of all things, Lowell's contrast of pajamas. The speaker's pajamas, 'fresh from the washer each morning' appear absurd, pathetic alongside the rising 'flame-flamingo' garment exhibited by his daughter, 'young enough to be [a] granddaughter'. Here, Lowell conflates an assessment of the self-deprecating ethos of an individual grasping for vitality in a disconcerting, maladjusted world, with the blithe liveliness of a child. Similarly, the calm, social confidence and access to leisure afforded by 'book-worming' and 'whole house' hogging are simultaneously numbing, the speaker conceding a state of tranquilization identical to that of his era.

Unlike the scores of early critics who connected *Life Studies* inextricably with Lowell, reducing the poems, as Daniel Hoffman did, to a mere study of Lowell's 'own family',[48] Richard Fein's assessment connects them, first and foremost, to the social and political chaos of the 1950s. Of the state of national life revealed in 'Memories of West Street and Lepke', Fein notes:

> At the end of the poem, we come across the mentally tough slogan 'agonizing reappraisal', a phrase that during the tenure of Secretary of State John Foster Dulles in the Eisenhower years of mental vapidity was used to describe a supposedly painful rethinking of American foreign policy. In employing the phrase himself, Lowell not only indicates how *Life Studies* grew out of the atmosphere of the 1950s, but uses his own plight to rescue the phrase from its fate as a political cliché. At the same time, he ambiguously connects himself to the deceptive language of the time.[49]

The 'ambiguity' described by Fein situates Lowell's poems, especially those written during the Eisenhower years, on the fringes of satire, from where he consistently parodies and subverts cold-war discourse yet circumvents political accountability through the guise of personal confession. 'Fall 1961', Lowell's foremost poem of the Kennedy years,[50] blurs public discourse with the intricacies of family life in order to appropriate the political rhetoric surrounding the tensions between the United States and the Soviet Union over above-ground nuclear explosions during November 1961. Contextually, the poem is situated amidst one of the greatest outpourings of print media hyperbole experienced throughout the cold-war period, yet its poetic outlook is individual and reflexive. Ironically, it delivers a far more disturbing depiction of the threat of nuclear warfare than any journalistic endeavour:

> All autumn, the chafe and jar
> of nuclear war;
> we have talked our extinction to death.
> I swim like a minnow
> behind my studio window.
>
> Our end drifts nearer,
> the moon lifts,
> radiant with terror. [51]

The speaker, paddling back and forth 'like a minnow' behind the glass of his private studio, imitates the 'state', which similarly hovers inside its glass covering, able to see out yet compelled by force to stay in. The poem's powerfully dissenting tone requires little elaboration. The danger-seeking state, submerged under a glass bell, is held fundamentally responsible for the risk of nuclear drift; the line 'our end drifts near' plays into an anxious and obsessive public discourse about the dangers of nuclear explosion. Set in the months following the Bay of Pigs invasion, the famous U-2 incident, the start of the Space Race, widespread anxiety over the assumed 'missile gap' and a global nuclear arms race, 'Fall 1961' deliberately exploits an already-menacing public anxiety about the possibility of imminent annihilation.

Yet Lowell's political dissent falls under the rubric of confessional poetry and thus neatly evades literary censorship. Careful to overlap public rhetoric with the language of domestic, private life, the poem mocks the language of America's wartime victory narrative through the obscuring lens of an abject, self-deprecating father figure: 'A father's no shield / for his child.' Significantly, the poem concludes with lines that caused outrage amongst many readers when the poem was published. Lowell's assertion: 'We are like a lot of wild / spiders crying together, / but without tears' provides one of the most disturbing images of post-war America, the lines suggesting a state of histrionics in which the nation, while never actually under direct threat of nuclear attack, reacted as though it were. Furthermore, as Josh Schneiderman points out, the spider metaphor is also important in and of itself. Spiders are solitary creatures. The image parodies the illusion of America as an impenetrable cohesive force, presenting the nation instead as 'an indistinguishable mass of preterits',[52] a 'confused swarm of crawling insects too terrified to emote',[53] joined only by the perceived threat of nuclear destruction. Yet, for all the subversive weight behind these seemingly methodically-crafted lines, the spider image derives neither from public discourse nor from the poet's personal aesthetic but rather from domestic speech: the lines are direct quotations from Lowell's four-year-old daughter, effortlessly interlaced into the politically-charged rhetoric of the poem.

Notes

1   Sylvia Plath. 'Context', *Johnny Panic and the Bible of Dreams* (London: Faber and Faber, 1979). p. 92.
2   Robert Lowell, *Collected Prose* (London: Faber, 1987), p. 367.
3   Ibid., p. 368.
4   Ibid.
5   Ibid.
6   Henry David Thoreau, 'Resistance to Civil Government', in Nancy L. Rosenblum (ed.), *Thoreau: Political Writings* (Cambridge: Cambridge University Press, 1996), p. 14.
7   Allen Ginsberg, *Collected Poems, 1947–1997* (New York: Harper Collins, 2006), p. 154.
8   Elaine Tyler May, *Homeward Bound: American Families in the Cold War Era* (New York: Basic Books, 1988), p. 14.
9   Beatriz Colomina, *Domesticity at War* (Barcelona: Actar, 2007), p. 296.
10 Tyler May, *Homeward Bound*, p. 16.
11 See Edward Denison and Jean-Pierre Poullier, *Why Growth Rates Differ: Postwar Experience in Nine Western Countries* (Washington: Brookings Institution, 1967); James Patterson, *Grand Expectations: The United States, 1945–1974* (New York: Oxford University Press, 1996), p. 312; Stephanie Coontz, *The Way We Never Were: American Families and the Nostalgia Trap* (New York, NY: BasicBooks, 1992), pp. 24–5; Lizabeth Cohen, 'From Town to Shopping Centre: The Reconfiguration of Community Marketplaces in Postwar America', *The American Historical Review*, 101, 4 (1996); Daniel Seligman, 'The New Masses', *America In the Sixties: The Economy and the Society* (New York: Harper & Row, 1960), p. 108; Shelley Nickles, 'More is Better: Mass Consumption, Gender, and Class Identity in Postwar America', *American Quarterly*, 54 (4) (2002).

12 For a summary of this 'debate', see Tyler May, *Homeward Bound*, pp. 16–18.
13 Sylvia Plath, *Ariel: The Restored Edition* (New York: Harper Collins Publishers, 2004), p. 21.
14 M. L. Rosenthal, *The New Poets: American and British Poetry Since World War II* (New York: Oxford University Press, 1967), p. 88.
15 Plath, *Ariel*, p. 21.
16 Sarah Churchwell, 'Secrets and Lies: Plath, Privacy, Publication and Ted Hughes's "Birthday Letters"', *Contemporary Literature* 42 (2001): 106–7.
17 M. L. Rosenthal, 'Poets of the Dangerous Way', in L. Wagner-Martin (ed.), *Sylvia Plath* (London: Routledge, 1988), p. 61.
18 Here I take up Deborah Nelson's assertion that many of these poems use the body as a means of investigating the rhetoric of privacy. Through their incorporation of policemen, surgeons, judges, priests and psychoanalysts, Sexton's poems place confession within the context of external pressures on individual privacy, an anxiety intimately tied to post-WWII government policy. See Nelson, 'Beyond Privacy: Confessions Between a Woman and Her Doctor', *Feminist Studies*, 25 (5) (1999): 284.
19 Christina Britzolakis, *Sylvia Plath and the Theatre of Mourning* (Oxford: Clarendon, 1999), p. 143.
20 Plath, *Ariel*, p. 21.
21 Sylvia Plath, *Letters Home* (ed. Aurelia Schober Plath) (London: Faber, 1975), p. 378.
22 Plath, *Ariel*, p. 41.
23 Deborah Nelson, *Pursuing Privacy in Cold War America* (New York: Columbia University Press, 2002), p. 81.
24 Plath, *Ariel*, p. 41.
25 Sylvia Plath, *Collected Poems* (ed. T. Hughes) (London: Faber, 1981), p. 261.
26 Ibid., p. 261.
27 Britzolakis, *Sylvia Plath and the Theatre of Mourning*, p. 145.
28 Sylvia Plath, *The Journals of Sylvia Plath, 1950–1962* (ed. Karen V. Kukil) (London: Faber, 2000), p. 32.
29 Thomas Doherty, *Cold War, Cool Medium: Television, McCarthyism, and American Culture* (New York: Columbia University Press, 2003), p. 13.
30 Plath, *Letters Home*, p. 163.
31 Plath, *Johnny Panic and the Bible of Dreams*, p. 92.
32 Deborah Nelson's discussion of 'Housewife' is perhaps the most insightful to date. See Nelson, *Pursing Privacy in Cold War America*, p. 96.
33 Anne Sexton, *All My Pretty Ones* (Boston: Houghton Mifflin, 1962), p. 48.
34 Nelson, *Pursuing Privacy in Cold War America,* p. 98.
35 Ibid., p. 96.
36 Diane Wood Middlebrook, 'What Was Confessional Poetry?', in J. Parini (ed.), *Columbia History of American Poetry* (New York: Columbia University Press, 1993), p. 635.
37 Edgar J. Hoover, 'A Nation's Call to Duty: Preserve the American Home', *Vital Speeches of the Day*, 8 (18) (1942): 555.
38 Fred J. Cook's *The FBI Nobody Knows* (1964) was a best-selling account of Hoover and the FBI, and a controversial attempt to link debates over widespread surveillance in America with cold-war anti-communism.
39 Lynn Spigel, *The Revolution Wasn't Televised: Sixties Television and Social Conflict* (New York: Routledge, 1997), p. 50.

40   Lynn Spigel, *Make Room for TV: Television and the Family Ideal in Postwar America* (Chicago: University of Chicago Press, 1992), p. 39.
41   For a discussion of television's relation to cold-war politics, see Fred J. MacDonald, 'The Cold War As Entertainment in Fifties Television', *Journal of Popular Film and Television*, (4/7/1) (1978): 3–31; Russell E. Shain, 'Hollywood's Cold War', *Journal of Popular Film* 3 (1974): 334–50; and Erik Barnouw, *Tube of Plenty: The Evolution of American Television*, 2nd edn (New York: Oxford University Press, 1990), pp. 112, 213. Stuart Ewen's *Captains of Consciousness* (1976) provides an important assessment of the arrival of television entertainment and consumerism in American life after World War II.
42   Elaine Kendall, 'Success (?) Secret of the Starmakers', *New York Times Magazine*, September (1962): 38.
43   Middlebrook, 'What Was Confessional Poetry?', p. 647.
44   Adam Beardsworth, 'Learning to Love the Bomb: Robert Lowell's Pathological Poetics', *Canadian Review of American Studies*, 40 (2010): 96–7.
45   Daniel Hoffman, 'Arrivals and Rebirths', *The Sewanee Review*, 68 (1960): 132.
46   Robert Lowell, *Life Studies* (London: Faber & Faber, 1959), p. 57.
47   William Doreski, *Robert Lowell's Shifting Colors* (Athens: Ohio University Press, 1999), p. 76.
48   Hoffman, 'Arrivals and Rebirths', p. 130.
49   Richard Fein, *Robert Lowell* (New York: Twayne Publishers, 1970), p. 61.
50   Lowell was a keen supporter of Kennedy. For the specificities of this support, see Alvarez, 'A Talk with Robert Lowell', in Jeffery Meyers (ed.), *Robert Lowell: Interviews and Memoirs* (Ann Arbor: University of Michigan Press, 1988), pp. 99–108; and Steven Gould Axelrod, 'Robert Lowell and the Cold War', *The New England Quarterly*, 72 (3) (1999): 348.
51   Robert Lowell, *For the Union Dead* (England: Faber and Faber, 1964), p. 11.
52   Josh Schneiderman, '"Pilgrim's Blues": Puritan Anxiety in Robert Lowell's "For the Union Dead"', *Journal of Modern Literature*, 31 (2008): 69.
53   Selim Sarwar, 'Robert Lowell: Scripting the Mid-Century Eschatology', *Journal of Modern Literature*, 25 (2002): 126.

References

Alvarez, A., 'A Talk with Robert Lowell', in Jeffery Meyers (ed.), *Robert Lowell: Interviews and Memoirs*, Ann Arbor: University of Michigan Press, 1988, pp. 99–108.

Axelrod, S., 'Robert Lowell and the Cold War', *The New England Quarterly*, 72 (3) (1999): 339–61.

Barnouw, E., *Tube of Plenty: The Evolution of American Television*, 2nd edn, New York: Oxford University Press, 1990.

Beardsworth, A., 'Learning to Love the Bomb: Robert Lowell's Pathological Poetics', *Canadian Review of American Studies*, 40 (2010): 95–116.

Britzolakis, C., *Sylvia Plath and the Theatre of Mourning*, Oxford: Clarendon, 1999.

Churchwell, S., 'Secrets and Lies: Plath, Privacy, Publication and Ted Hughes's "Birthday Letters"', *Contemporary Literature*, 42 (2001), 106–7.

Cohen, L., 'From Town to Shopping Centre: The Reconfiguration of Community,

Marketplaces in Postwar America', *The American Historical Review,* 101 (4) (1996): 1050–81.

Colomina, B., *Domesticity at War,* Barcelona: Actar, 2007.

Cook, F., *The FBI Nobody Knows,* New York: Macmillan, 1964.

Coontz, S., *The War We Never Were: American Families and the Nostalgia Trap,* New York, NY: Basic Books, 1992.

Denison, E. and Jean-Pierre Poullier, *Why Growth Rates Differ: Postwar Experience in Nine Western Countries,* Washington: Brookings Institution, 1967.

Doherty, T., *Cold War, Cool Medium: Television, McCarthyism, and American Culture,* New York: Columbia University Press, 2003.

Doreski, W., *Robert Lowell's Shifting Colors,* Athens: Ohio University Press, 1999.

Ewen, S., *Captains of Consciousness: Advertising the Social Roots of the Consumer Culture,* New York: McGraw-Hill, 1976.

Fein, Richard, *Robert Lowell,* New York: Twayne Publishers, 1970.

Ginsberg, A., *Collected Poems, 1947–1997,* New York: HarperCollins, 2006.

Hoffman, D., 'Arrivals and Rebirths', *The Sewanee Review,* 68 (1960): 118–37.

Hoover, E. J., 'A Nation's Call to Duty: Preserve the American Home, *Vital Speeches of the Day,* 8 (18) (1942): 554–6.

Kendall, E., 'Success (?) Secret of the Starmakers', *New York Times Magazine,* September 1962: 38

Lowell, R., *Life Studies,* London: Faber & Faber, 1959.

Lowell, R., *For the Union Dead,* England: Faber and Faber, 1964.

Lowell, R., *Collected Prose,* London: Faber, 1987.

MacDonald, F. J., 'The Cold War as Entertainment in Fifties Television', *Journal of Popular Film and Television,* 7 (1) (1978): 3–31.

Middlebrook, D. W., 'What Was Confessional Poetry?', in J. Parini (ed.), *Columbia History of American Poetry,* New York: Columbia University Press, 2003.

Nelson, D., 'Beyond Privacy: Confessions Between a Woman and Her Doctor', *Feminist Studies,* 25 (5) (1999): 279–306.

Nelson, D., *Pursuing Privacy in Cold War America,* New York: Columbia University Press, 2002.

Nickles, S., 'More is Better: Mass Consumption, Gender, and Class Identity in Postwar America', *American Quarterly,* 54 (4) (2002): 581–622.

Patterson, J., *Grand Expectations: The United States, 1945–1974,* New York: Oxford University Press, 1996.

Plath, S., *Letters Home* (ed. A. S. Plath), London: Faber, 1975.

Plath, S., *Johnny Panic and the Bible of Dreams,* London: Faber and Faber, 1979.

Plath, S., *Collected Poems* (ed. T. Hughes), London: Faber, 1981.

Plath, S., *The Journals of Sylvia Plath, 1950–1962* (ed. Karen V. Kukil), London: Faber, 2000.

Plath, S., *Ariel: The Restored Edition,* New York: Harper Collins Publishers, 2004.

Rosenblum, N. (ed.), *Thoreau: Political Writings,* Cambridge: Cambridge University Press, 1996.

Rosenthal, M. L., *The New Poets: American and British Poetry Since World War II,* New York: Oxford University Press, 1967.

Rosenthal, M. L., 'Poets of the Dangerous Way', in L. Wagner-Martin (ed.), *Sylvia Plath,* London: Routledge, 1988.

Sarwar, S., 'Robert Lowell: Scripting the Mid-Century Eschatology', *Journal of Modern Literature,* 25 (2002): 114–30.

Schneiderman, J., "'Pilgrim's Blues": Puritan Anxiety in Robert Lowell's "For the Union Dead'", *Journal of Modern Literature*, 31 (2008): 58–80.

Seligman, D., 'The New Masses', in *America In the Sixties: The Economy and the Society*, New York: Harper & Row, 1960.

Sexton, A., *All My Pretty Ones*, Boston: Houghton Mifflin, 1962.

Shain, R., 'Hollywood's Cold War', *Journal of Popular Film*, 3 (4) (1974): 334–50.

Spigel, L., *Make Room for TV: Television and the Family Ideal in Postwar America*, Chicago: University of Chicago Press, 1992.

Spigel, L., *The Revolution Wasn't Televised: Sixties Television and Social Conflict*, New York: Routledge, 1997.

Tyler May, E., *Homeward Bound: American Families in the Cold War Era*, New York: Basic Books, 1988.

12

Freedom to Read: Barney Rosset, Henry Miller and the End of Obscenity

Loren Glass

One afternoon in the fall of 1940, Barney Rosset, then a freshman at Swarthmore College, walked into the legendary Steloff's Gotham Book Mart on 47th Street in New York City and purchased a pirated copy of Henry Miller's notorious novel *Tropic of Cancer*. Barney was feeling bereft – his girlfriend, a freshman at Vassar College, had just broken up with him – and he found solace reading Miller's stream-of-consciousness account of his solitary struggles as an unknown expatriate writer in Depression-era Paris. Thus began a lifelong literary relationship between a marginal modernist and a revolutionary publisher that would transform literary history, when two decades later Barney Rosset, then owner of Grove Press and publisher of *The Evergreen Review*, would stake his reputation and his livelihood on legally publishing Miller's underground masterpiece.

Though Rosset would eventually acquire a reputation as a dealer in dirty books, his interest in Miller was neither salacious nor pecuniary. When I interviewed him some years ago for my history of Grove, he told me: 'I didn't even notice the obscenity … I noticed two things: one, he'd had a terrible breakup with a girlfriend. And that struck home to me … And also Henry's anti-American stance: All Americans looked alike, talked alike … etcetera.'[1] Then he handed me a copy of a paper he wrote at Swarthmore called 'Henry Miller vs. "Our Way of Life"'. Written on the eve of America's entry into WWII, when 'drums are rolling' and 'men are marching', the paper openly ponders what in 'our way of life' is worth fighting for.[2] Noting that Miller, as an expatriate, might have a singular insight into this question, Rosset focuses on Miller's comparison between Paris, where he found 'greater independence' and became 'a completely self-sufficient being',[3] and New York, 'a land of the dead' where he saw 'only automatons'.[4] Rosset approves of the critique, but takes exception to Miller's individualism, claiming 'we must participate in action with our neighbors if we ever wish to achieve any of the freedom which Miller so covets'. He therefore provocatively concludes, 'perhaps our salvation lies in all of us becoming artists'.[5]

Barney gave me a copy of this paper, which he had once used as evidence in court that his interest in Miller was not pecuniary, in order to refute yet another argument: mine. In an article for *Critical Inquiry* called 'Redeeming Value: Obscenity and Anglo-American Modernism', I had argued that 'the end of obscenity was also a triumph for modernist formulations of the literary, insofar as texts previously valued by an elite intelligentsia were finally being granted mainstream cachet'.[6] Much of my article focused on Grove's legendary battles against censorship in the 1960s, which I argued had brought late modernism into the mainstream; I intended this argument to be central to my history of Grove Press and the *Evergreen Review*. Barney would have none of it. 'This is based on aesthetics', he argued, shaking his copy of my article in the air disdainfully. 'To me it's like quibbling between Catholicism and Protestantism ... None of them really interest me ... I looked at *Tropic of Cancer* from a political, and social, point of view'.[7] But, as his conclusion affirms, Rosset wanted to make the freedoms Miller found in art available to everyone.

The story of Rosset's battles, a central strand in the larger historical transformation that his lawyer Charles Rembar dubbed the 'end of obscenity', has been told many times, first by the lawyers who participated in it, and then by scholars and historians (including me) invested in framing the process in less triumphalist terms.[8] In this discussion, I'd like to focus on an underappreciated component of the story that is nevertheless crucial to understanding its larger literary and legal significance. Since the landmark case of *The United States v. One Book Called 'Ulysses'* (1933), a key strategy for defending material deemed obscene under US law involved the solicitation of 'expert' testimony to establish that the material in question has literary value. The juridical legitimacy of this testimony was, ultimately, based on the rights guaranteed by the First Amendment of the Constitution, usually glossed as 'freedom of expression'.

However, over the course of Rosset's campaign to publish *Tropic of Cancer*, which was far more extensive than his battles over any other single author or title, the language of the defence shifted from the author's (or publisher's) individual freedom of expression to the reader's collective right to read. Inaugurated by the American Library Association's 'Freedom to Read Statement' in 1953 and confirmed by the National Council of Teachers of English pamphlet 'The Students' Right to Read' in 1962, the concept of a collective right of access, as opposed to an individual right to expression, gradually gained ground in the post-war era. The campaign to exonerate *Tropic of Cancer*, and especially the landmark Chicago case of *Franklyn Haiman v. Robert Morris* (1962), was a tipping point in this transformation, after which the significance of expert testimony as to literary value diminished in the face of more democratic claims of access. This change, I intend to conclude, paralleled a shift away from authorial intention and toward readerly reception as a guide to literary interpretation, a shift that, ironically, mortally damaged Miller's reputation at the very moment that it was reaching a kind of apex of acclaim.[9]

When Rosset purchased Grove Press for $3,000 (US) in 1951, publishing *Tropic of Cancer* was already part of his long-term plan. Miller's less explicit writing had been published by New Directions, but owner Jay Laughlin was unwilling to publish the *Tropics*, which were only available in English through Maurice Girodias' notorious Olympia Press 'Traveler's Companion' Series in France; they remained banned across the Anglophone world. Rosset was determined to bring them out, but he proceeded cautiously, well aware of the risk involved in the endeavour. His reputation for impulsiveness notwithstanding, Rosset planned his decade-long battle against censorship with both deliberation and determination; in one unpublished autobiographical fragment, he calls it 'a carefully planned campaign, much like a military campaign'.[10]

Rosset's campaign was crucially bolstered by the passage of *Roth v. US* in 1957, the first case in which the US Supreme Court directly addressed whether obscenity constitutes an exception to First Amendment protection for freedom of speech and the press. The notorious booklegger Samuel Roth in fact lost his case, but in the landmark ruling Associate Justice William Brennan Jr had defined obscenity as 'utterly without redeeming social importance', indicating that lawyers had only to establish social importance (the term would later be changed to 'social value') in order to defend against charges of obscenity.[11] *Roth* represented the initial articulation of what Rosset's lawyer Edward de Grazia would later call the 'Brennan Doctrine', a developing definition of obscenity formulated by Supreme Court Justice William Brennan that would make it easier for 'defense lawyers to demonstrate that the works of literature or art created by their clients were entitled to First Amendment Protection'.[12] As de Grazia's far-ranging study, *Girls Lean Back Everywhere: The Law of Obscenity and the Assault on Genius*, affirms, 'experts' such as literary critics, authors, journalists, publishers and college professors were central to this legal demonstration. Indeed, according to de Grazia, 'the only significant breakthrough to freedom that was made over the past century by authors and publishers ... was made when the courts were required by law ... to admit and give weight to the testimony of "expert" authors and critics concerning a challenged work's values'.[13]

Shortly after the passage of *Roth*, Rosset decided to launch his campaign with *Lady Chatterley's Lover*, since D. H. Lawrence, unlike Henry Miller, was a well-established and widely-taught author whose work was already recognized as having value. Indeed, Rosset didn't much like the novel, and only used the case as an opening wedge for his campaign to publish Miller. After the widely-publicized exoneration of *Lady Chatterley's Lover* in the US in 1959 (it would be exonerated the following year in the UK in an equally prominent case), Rosset felt ready to publish *Tropic of Cancer*. But Miller did not. As Barney recounted to me, 'I had tried to get Miller and totally failed. I'd gone to California, to Big Sur ... and he said no ... He said he couldn't stand the idea. If I published it, it would be read by college students'.[14] But Rosset persisted, and with the help of Maurice Girodias, whose father Jack Kahane had originally published both *Tropics*, and Miller's German publisher, Heinrich Ledig-Rowohlt, he finally managed to get Miller to agree to publication in the United States in 1961, with an advance of $50,000. The hardcover caused little controversy, and indeed was celebrated in the *New York Times Book Review* as at last 'available in the author's native country', in a glowing review by Harry Moore aptly titled 'From Under the Counter to the Front Shelf'.[15] But the paperback, distributed by Dell in 1962 for 95 cents and put up for sale in drugstores and corner markets across the country, was suppressed and confiscated in numerous venues, while simultaneously enjoying many months on bestseller lists in those same venues. Henry Miller became both a *cause célèbre* and a *succès-de-scandale*, and the strategies of both his accusers and defenders illustrate how the elite aesthetics of modernism collapsed into a popular politics of identity over the course of the 1960s.

For the elitist experts whose job it would be to defend *Tropic of Cancer*, Henry Miller had never been easy to categorize or evaluate. His biography, and particularly his expatriation in the 1930s, tended to align him, albeit somewhat belatedly, with the modernist 'lost generation', but his unseemly and unwavering focus on this biography (almost all of Miller's fiction is patently autobiographical) tended to violate the evaluative protocols critics used to canonize the work of that generation. Edmund Wilson, reviewing the then unavailable *Tropic of Cancer* for the *New Republic* in 1938, called it 'an epitaph for the whole generation of American artists and writers that migrated to Paris after the war' and 'the lowest book of any literary merit that I ever remember to have read'.[16] In both his bohemian lifestyle and his literary experimentation Miller seemed to fit, if somewhat awkwardly, into the lost generation category. Certainly Miller's literary aspirations were modernist; as one biographer describes, he wanted to be 'a working-class Proust, a Brooklyn Proust'.[17]

However, as *Partisan Review* editor Philip Rahv would affirm, 'with few exceptions the highbrow critics, bred almost to a man in Eliot's school of strict impersonal aesthetics, are bent on snubbing him'.[18] Rahv comments quite trenchantly on the socioeconomic and psychosexual underpinnings of Miller's objectionable 'personality':

> So riled is his ego by external reality, so confused and helpless, that he can no longer afford the continual sacrifice of personality that the act of creation requires, he can no longer bear to express himself implicitly by means of the work of art as a whole but must simultaneously permeate and absorb each of its separate parts and details.[19]

Miller seemingly can't afford, both literally and figuratively, to practise Eliot's 'impersonal' act of creation, but his own aesthetic is clearly a dialectical response to that act, with whose Proustian protocols Miller was deeply familiar. Miller's gargantuan personality, his maddening mix of garrulous charm and aggravating arrogance, emerges in ambivalent resistance to the figure of the modernist genius he can't quite be.

Miller was not only too personal to be considered high modernist; he was also too popular, despite the difficulty in obtaining his work. As Kenneth Rexroth, writing on the eve of Miller's American apotheosis, proclaimed: 'Henry Miller is really a popular writer, a writer of and for real people, who, in other countries, is read, not just by highbrows, or just by the wider public which reads novels, but by common people, by the people who, in the United States, read comic books'.[20] Much of Miller's initial popularity was enabled not by the scattering of critical accolades but by the widespread smuggling of his banned books into the United States by American tourists and GI's returning from the Second World War. Unlike Lawrence, around whom a critical consensus had been established, Miller posed a problem for mid-century arbiters of literary taste.

Nevertheless, Rosset armed himself with an enormous battery of critical endorsements, since he knew that only they could prove that a text had redeeming social value. He solicited written comments from an impressive roster of critics, writers and publishers, including Jacques Barzun, Marianne Moore, Lawrence Durrell, Archibald MacLeish, W. H. Auden, T. S. Eliot, Arthur Miller, Thornton Wilder, Vladimir Nabokov, Alfred Kazin, Malcolm Cowley and many others. And he was wise to prepare, as he was almost immediately engulfed in a firestorm of controversy; US obscenity law at the time was a frequently contradictory patchwork of innumerable state and local ordinances, and *Tropic of Cancer* precipitated over thirty court cases and over fifty instances of extrajudicial suppression across the country. Since he had agreed to indemnify booksellers against any fines or court costs and to handle all legal cases arising from the sale of Miller's book, Rosset found himself battling for the very financial survival of Grove Press.

The challenge of establishing the literary value of *Tropic of Cancer* is neatly summed up in the epigraph to Miller's *Black Spring*, the lesser known second volume in the trilogy that begins with *Cancer* and ends with *Tropic of Capricorn*: 'What is not in the open street is false, derived, that is to say, *literature*.' This dig at the very modernism with which Miller would simultaneously strive to associate himself would receive an inverse ironic commentary in the trials of *Tropic*, as experts in literature attempted to prove they had the street credentials to evaluate the book. The first trial, somewhat inevitably, was in Boston, for which Barney hired the renowned first amendment lawyer Ephraim London, who assembled an illustrious cast of experienced expert witnesses, including Mark Schorer, Harry Moore and Harry Levin. However, Judge Arthur Goldberg was not impressed by the credentials of these scholars, interrupting Schorer's testimony with the quip: 'all that was necessary in this case was to offer the book in evidence and then leave it to me, who knows everything about how the ordinary man feels and what his reaction would be.'[21] Assistant Attorney General Leo Sontag agreed and he attempted to establish that Schorer and the other witnesses for the defence were not in touch with the American public, and therefore could not be expected to represent the book's effects on an ordinary reader. Sontag proclaimed, 'it's said that a rarified atmosphere exists on the campus at the University of California at Berkeley'. Judge Goldberg then required clarification: 'do you feel he is in an "Ivory Tower" and therefore has no contact with ordinary human beings?' Sontag affirmed, 'That is correct, your honor. The Professor is on a shelf by himself with others'. Schorer then quipped, 'I'd like to tell you sometime the non-"Ivory Tower" aspects of my life'.[22] London attempted to come to the rescue by reminding the court that 'the judge's life is, if anything, more of an "Ivory Tower" existence than that of a college professor'. And the judge crankily responded, 'We are on the street just the same as and as much as any ordinary being'.[23]

Who's in the Ivory Tower and who's on the street, and from which position is it most legitimate to judge a book like *Tropic of Cancer*? The courtroom would have to wait for Harry Levin's testimony for an ironic resolution, although this was not fully recognized in the trial itself. London introduced him with the claim that 'Professor Levin's qualifications are so many that I would like to save a great deal of time by merely reading a few of them in the record and having the professor acknowledge that these are his accomplishments'.[24] Judge Goldberg was unimpressed until London concluded that Levin was the Irving Babbitt Professor of Comparative Literature at Harvard University. He and Levin then discovered that they both studied under Babbitt as undergraduates. Although Judge Goldberg would in the end disregard the expert testimony and find the book obscene, this incidental exchange affirms the degree to which Grove's campaign initially depended upon the professional class solidarity of the judges, academics and publishers who participated in these trials, a solidarity which was fractured by the ultimate success of their efforts.

The Boston trial was handled *in rem*, which is to say that the case was against the book itself. In the Chicago trial of *Franklyn Haiman vs. Robert Morris*, handled by Elmer Gertz, the demographic alignments of the adversaries were clearer. *Tropic of Cancer* was being suppressed and confiscated across suburban Illinois, and the case pitted Grove against an array of small-town police departments, including Arlington Heights, Skokie, Glencoe, Lincolnwood, Morton Grove, Niles, Des Plaines, Mount Prospect, Winnetka and Evanston. Rosset grew up in Chicago, where his father had been president of the Metropolitan Trust Company; Gertz surely must have felt reassured when Judge Samuel Epstein opened the proceedings with the claim, 'I doubt if any lawyer, who is old enough, hasn't had some sort of business relationship with Barney Rosset'.[25]

Rosset saw this case as a 'peak moment' of his career and his affidavit provides a convenient snapshot of his strategy for exonerating his favourite author.[26] On the first page he affirms that 'many Grove Press books are in use in colleges and universities throughout the country', after which he lists some of these institutions, including Bard, Columbia, Harvard, Johns Hopkins, Princeton, Smith and Vassar.[27] Rosset then cites the decision in the *Lady Chatterly* case, affirming that 'Grove is a reputable publisher with a good list which includes a number of distinguished writers and serious works'.[28] After recounting the complicated publication history of *Tropic of Cancer,* he concludes that 'Grove Press published Henry Miller's *Tropic of Cancer* in the belief that it is a serious work of literature. This belief is confirmed by the opinions of scholars and critics'.[29] A series of reviews, including Moore's review for the *Times,* are attached as exhibits.

Judge Samuel Epstein's ruling, issued on 21 February 1962, marked a turning point not only in the struggle to exonerate *Tropic of Cancer* but also in the larger battle over literary and legal obscenity in the post-war United States. Epstein concedes that, when it comes to the question of literary value, he must depend 'upon the expert testimony as well as the documentary evidence' and he cites both that testimony and the evidence provided by the exhibits in Rosset's affidavit.[30] He also notes that *Tropic of Cancer* 'is to be found on the shelves of many of the libraries of American universities' and that 'In some universities, studies of the book are part of the course in English literature'.[31] However, in his conclusion he pursues another line of reasoning, arguing 'as a corollary to the freedom of speech and the press, there is also a freedom to read. The right to free utterances becomes a useless privilege when the freedom to read is restricted or denied'.[32] Based on this reasoning, Epstein rules that '"Tropic of Cancer" is not obscene as defined in the law, and that interference by the police in its free distribution should not be enjoined'.[33]

Rosset in turn made Judge Epstein's landmark ruling into the basis of a nationwide campaign. Grove printed and circulated thousands of copies of the decision, and published a 'Statement in Support of Freedom to Read' on the front cover of the July-August 1962 issue of the *Evergreen Review*, which also included *Chicago Sun-Times* book reviewer Hoke Norris's account of the Chicago trial. The statement, which runs over from the front cover into the flyleaf, is followed by a long alphabetical list of signatories, including James Baldwin, Ian Ballantine, Saul Bellow, Louise Bogan, Richard Ellmann, Arnold Gingrich, Hugh Hefner, Jack Kerouac, Carson McCullers, Marianne Moore, Lionel Trilling, Robert Penn Warren and many others. It significantly shifts the terms of defence from elite endorsement to democratic access, affirming, 'the issue is not whether *Tropic of Cancer* is a masterpiece of American literature', but rather 'the right of a free people to decide for itself what it may or may not read'.

Rosset and his lawyers were unable to appeal either of these cases to the Supreme Court, and thus while Miller's book remained a bestseller across the country in 1963, it was also unavailable in many locations, and Grove's coffers continued to be drained by litigation. Finally, Edward de Grazia (one of the many lawyers Rosset had retained to handle the multiple cases against *Tropic*) managed to appeal the Florida case of *Grove Press v. Gerstein,* using the argument that the Supreme Court had not yet determined 'whether the Constitutional guarantees of free expression are not violated by the application of local, rather than national, "contemporary community standards" to the question of whether a literary work may be suppressed as "obscene"'.[34] Further on in his petition, De Grazia clarified that the issue of national standards concerns both 'free artistic expression and freedom to read', revealing his desire to incorporate Epstein's formulation into the Supreme Court's interpretation of the First Amendment.[35]

On 22 June 1964, the Supreme Court overturned the *Gerstein* decision and, in the attached case of *Jacobellis v. Ohio,* affirmed that 'the constitutional status of an allegedly obscene work must be determined on the basis of a national standard. It is, after all, a national Constitution we are expounding'.[36] It had been three years almost to the day since Grove had first issued *Tropic of Cancer,* and over that brief period the company had not only revolutionized the publishing industry by rapidly dismantling a regime of literary censorship that had been in place since the nineteenth century, it had also mobilized a cadre of publishers, academics and artists in a successful effort to transform the cultural field itself by incorporating the literary underground into the mainstream.

The 1960s were Miller's decade, as Grove was finally able to publish not only the *Tropics* but also his Proustian magnum opus, the *Rosy Crucifixion*. And his books sold well; in June 1965, Miller occupied the top four positions on the *New York Post*'s bestseller list, and he remained on bestseller lists across the country for the remainder of the decade. *Tropic of Cancer* alone would eventually sell more than 2.5 million copies in Grove's mass-market edition. Furthermore, something of an academic industry emerged around his work, as professors and critics strove to legitimate and account for his popularity.

It was, as Miller himself anticipated, a brief apotheosis, as the right to read that Epstein had proclaimed became exercised by students less sympathetic to Miller's (and Rosset's) sexual politics. The shift can be marked by a somewhat different legal battle, really more of a skirmish, that began in May 1969, when Grove Press received a letter from Ellen Krieger at Doubleday stating that 'we are planning to publish, early next year, a trade book entitled *Sexual Politics* by Kate Millett ... In our book, we are quoting from several of your books ... May we have permission to use these quotes in our book?'[37] Grove promptly sent a copy of the letter to Miller, explaining that 'enclosed is a letter from Doubleday and the material to which they refer. The author, Kate Millett, is quoting rather extensively from SEXUS and BLACK SPRING. We would normally give such permission for inclusion of quotes in a critical work. However, since this is not 'exactly' literary criticism, I would like to know whether or not you agree to quotations'. Miller sent the letter back, with his response scrawled across it: 'I refuse to give permission to quote from my books'.[38]

Then, in June, Grove received a review copy of 'Sexual Politics: Miller, Mailer, and Genet', a version of Millett's book's introduction, which was to appear as the opening essay in the upcoming *New American Review*, Theodore Solotaroff's resuscitation of the New American Library's groundbreaking journal *New World Writing*. In his cover letter, Solotaroff notes that 'Miss Millett's essay has been adapted from a Ph.D. dissertation which she is doing at Columbia. This might seem to be an unlikely source for writing that is as candid, partisan, and witty as Miss Millett's attack on the sexual attitudes of Henry Miller and Norman Mailer ... Considering, however, the outspokenness emanating from the campuses, Miss Millett's scholarly but devastating analysis of the cult of masculinity in two of our supposedly liberated writers is perhaps not so unexpected after all'.[39]

Emily Jane Goodman, Grove's recently-hired house counsel, warned that Miller's refusal was on shaky legal ground: 'Doubleday takes the position that Miss Millett's book is a critical work and that their excerpts from our authors would be within fair usage. We would have a very difficult time disputing this'.[40] Millett's methodological reliance on extensive quotation attests to the degree to which Rosset's determination to make these texts legally available and democratically accessible was a condition of possibility for the political critique she launched.

Millett opens with what could arguably be a methodological and political credo for the next generation of literary critics:

> It has been my conviction that the adventure of literary criticism is not restricted to a dutiful round of adulation, but is capable of seizing upon the larger insights which literature affords into the life it describes, or interprets, or even distorts. This essay, composed of equal parts of literary and cultural criticism, is something of an anomaly, a hybrid, possibly a new mutation altogether. I have operated on the premise that there is room for a criticism which takes into account the larger cultural context in which literature is conceived and produced. Criticism which originates from literary history is too limited in scope to do this; criticism which originates in aesthetic considerations, 'New Criticism', never wished to do so.[41]

The connection between Millett's critical agenda and the freedom to read is evident in the texts she chooses as illustrations of her argument. Her first chapter opens with a quote from Miller's *Sexus*, published by Grove in 1965, that, a decade earlier, would have resulted in Millet's own text being censored. After the lengthy quote, Millett affirms, 'What the reader is vicariously experiencing at this juncture is a nearly supernatural sense of power, should the reader be male'.[42] She leverages her argument, then, through specifying Miller's predominantly male readership, rendering the subject of masculine literary subversion as an object of feminist ideological critique. Thus she overturns the critical celebration of Miller as sexually liberatory: 'Miller is a compendium of American sexual neuroses, and his value lies not in freeing us from such afflictions, but in having had the honesty to express and dramatize them'.[43] In exposing the personal, and sexual, investments of Miller's earlier readers, Millett confirms that literary critics are just another interpretive community whose values are susceptible to ideological critique. Indeed, it is no coincidence that Stanley Fish's highly influential essay, 'Literature in the Reader: Affective Stylistics', came out in the same year as *Sexual Politics*. As Jane Tompkins would later proclaim of that now-classic essay, 'the reader's activity is declared to be *identical* with the text and therefore becomes itself the source of all literary value'.[44] She concludes, 'the net result of this epistemological revolution is to repoliticize literature and literary criticism'.[45] The passage from Millett to Tompkins affirms that the exoneration of *Tropic of Cancer* precipitated a shift in the culture of expertise from an evaluative focus on the literary text to a political focus on the contexts of reception, based not in the freedom of expression but in the freedom to read.

Notes

1 Rosset Interview Transcripts, Barney Rosset Papers, Columbia University Special Collections (BRP).
2 Barney Rosset, 'Henry Miller vs. "Our Way of Life"', *Nexus: The International Henry Miller Journal*, 2 (1) (2005): 1.
3 Ibid., p. 2.
4 Ibid., p. 4.
5 Ibid., p. 5.
6 Loren Glass, 'Redeeming Value: Obscenity and Anglo-American Modernism', *Critical Inquiry*, 32 (2) (2006): 342.
7 Rosset Interview with Author, 5 October 2009.
8 See, for example, Charles Rembar, *The End of Obscenity: The Trials of Lady Chatterley, Tropic of Cancer, and Fanny Hill* (New York: Random House, 1968), pp. 163–211; Earl Hutchison, *Tropic of Cancer on Trial: A Case History of Censorship* (New York: Grove, 1968); Edward De Grazia, *Girls Lean Back Everywhere: The Law of Obscenity and the Assault on Genius* (New York: Random House, 1992), pp. 366–97; Rosa Eberly, *Citizen Critics: Literary Public Spheres* (Urbana: University of Illinois, 2000), pp. 62–102; Elisabeth Ladenson, *Dirt for Art's Sake: Books on Trial from Madame Bovary to Lolita* (Ithaca, NY: Cornell University Press, 2007), pp. 157–86; and Loren Glass, *Counterculture Colophon: Grove Press, the* Evergreen Review, *and the Incorporation of the Avant-Garde* (Stanford, CA: Stanford University Press, 2013), pp. 111–17.

9   Miller had himself used the phrase 'Freedom to Read' in his letter protesting the Norwegian ban on *Sexus*, 'Defence of the Freedom to Read,' published in *ER*, 3 (9) (1959): 12–20.

10 Barney Rosset (nd), 'A Few Steps from the Long March', Barney Rosset Papers, Columbia University Special Collections (BRP).

11 *Roth v. United States*, 354 U.S. 476 (1957), p. 483.

12 Edward De Grazia, *Girls Lean Back Everywhere: The Law of Obscenity and the Assault on Genius* (New York: Random House, 1992), p. xii.

13 Ibid., p. 686.

14 Rosset Interview with Author, 5 October 2009.

15 Harry Moore, 'From Under the Counter to Front Shelf', *New York Times Book Review*, 18 (18 June 1961): 5.

16 Edmund Wilson, (1952), 'Twilight of the Expatriates', in G. Wickes (ed.), *Henry Miller and the Critics* (Carbondale: Southern Illinois University Press, 1963), pp. 25–30.

17 Robert Ferguson, *Henry Miller: A Life* (New York: W. W. Norton, 1991), p. 149.

18 Philip Rahv, 'Sketches in Criticism: Henry Miller', in George Wickes (ed.), *Henry Miller and the Critics* (Carbondale: Southern Illinois University Press, 1963), p. 76.

19 Ibid., p. 82.

20 Kenneth Rexroth (1959), 'The Reality of Henry Miller', in George Wickes (ed.), *Henry Miller and the Critics* (Carbondale: Southern Illinois University Press, 1963), p. 119.

21 Trial Transcript: *Attorney General vs. A Book Named, 'Tropic of Cancer'*, Grove Press Papers, Syracuse University Special Collections Library (GPP), p. 89.

22 Ibid., p. 88.

23 Ibid., p. 90.

24 Ibid., p. 218.

25 Trial Transcript: *Franklyn S. Haiman v. Robert Morris* (GPP), p. 15.

26 Rosset Interview Transcripts (BRP), p. 16.

27 Barney Rosset, (1961), 'First Affidavit of Barney Rosset in Support of Motion for Temporary Injunction', *Franklyn S. Haiman v. Robert Morris* No. 61 S 19718 (21 February 1962), p. 1.

28 Ibid., p. 2.

29 Ibid., p. 6.

30 Samuel Epstein, 'Opinion of the Honorable Samuel B. Epstein', *Franklyn S. Haiman v. Robert Morris* No. 61 S 19718 (21 Feb 1962), p. 9 (GPP).

31 Ibid., p. 13.

32 Ibid., p. 14.

33 Ibid., pp. 14–15.

34 Edward De Grazia, 'Petition for a Writ of Certiorari to the District Court of Appeal', Third District, State of Florida. October 1963, p. 4 (GPP).

35 Ibid., p. 11.

36 *Jacobellis v. State of Ohio*, 84 S. Ct. 1676 (1964), p. 426.

37 Krieger, Ellen to Judith Schmidt, 13 May 1969, GPP.

38 Schmidt, Judith to Henry Miller, 14 May 1969, GPP.

39 Solatoroff, Theodore to Grove Press, 23 June 1969, GPP.

40 Goodman, Emily Jane to Judith Schmidt, 29 July 1969, GPP.

41 Kate Millet, *Sexual Politics* (New York: Equinox, 1970), p. xii.

42 Ibid., p. 6.

43 Ibid., p. 295.

44 Jane Tompkins, *Reader-Response Criticism: From Formalism to Post-Structuralism* (Baltimore: Johns Hopkins, 1980), p. xvi.
45 Ibid., xxv.

References

Attorney General v. A Book Named, 'Tropic of Cancer. 184 N.E. 2d 328 (1962) GPP.
Barney Rosset Papers, Columbia University Special Collections (BRP).
De Grazia, E., Petition for a Writ of Certiorari to the District Court of Appeal, Third District, State of Florida. October 1963.
De Grazia, E., *Girls Lean Back Everywhere: The Law of Obscenity and the Assault on Genius,* New York: Random House, 1992.
Eberly, R., *Citizen Critics: Literary Public Spheres,* Urbana: Illinois, 2000.
Epstein, S., 'Opinion of the Honorable Samuel B. Epstein', *Franklyn S. Haiman v. Robert Morris* No. 61 S 19718 (21 February 1962), GPP.
Ferguson, R., *Henry Miller: A Life,* New York: W. W. Norton, 1991.
Fish, Stanley, 'Literature and the Reader: Affective Stylistics', *New Literary History,* 2 (1) (Autumn 1970): 123–62.
Franklyn S. Haiman v. Robert Morris No. 61 S 19718 (21 Feb. 1962). Trial transcript, GPP.
Glass, L., 'Redeeming Value: Obscenity and Anglo-American Modernism', *Critical Inquiry,* 32 (2) (Winter 2006), pp. 341–61.
Glass, L., *Counterculture Colophon: Grove Press, the* Evergreen Review, *and the Incorporation of the Avant-Garde,* Stanford, CA: Stanford University Press, 2013.
Goodman, Emily Jane to Judith Schmidt, 29 July 1969, GPP.
Grove Press Papers, Syracuse University Special Collections Library (GPP).
Hutchison, E. R., *Tropic of Cancer on Trial: A Case History of Censorship,* New York: Grove, 1968.
Jacobellis v. State of Ohio, 84 S. Ct. 1676 (1964).
Krieger, Ellen to Judith Schmidt, 13 May 1969, GPP.
Ladenson, E., *Dirt for Art's Sake: Books on Trial from* Madame Bovary *to* Lolita, Ithaca: Cornell University Press, 2007.
Miller, H., 'Defence of Freedom to Read', *ER* 3.9 (1959), pp. 12–20.
Miller, H., *Black Spring,* New York: Grove, 1963.
Millett, K., *Sexual Politics,* New York, Equinox, 1970.
Moore, H., 'From Under the Counter to Front Shelf', *New York Times Book Review* 18 (18 June 1961): p. 5.
Rahv, P., 'Sketches in Criticism: Henry Miller', in George Wickes (ed.), *Henry Miller and the Critics,* Carbondale: Southern Illinois University Press, 1963.
Rembar, C., *The End of Obscenity: The Trials of Lady Chatterley,* Tropic of Cancer *and* Fanny Hill, New York: Random House, 1968.
Rexroth, K., (1959), 'The Reality of Henry Miller', in George Wickes (ed.), *Henry Miller and the Critics,* Carbondale: Southern Illinois University Press, 1963.
Rosset, B., (1959), Affidavit. *Grove Press, Inc., v. Robert K. Christenberry,* 10 June 1959, GPP.
Rosset, B., (1961), First Affidavit of Barney Rosset in Support of Motion for Temporary Injunction. *Franklyn S. Haiman v. Robert Morris* No. 61 S 19718 (21 February 1962), GPP.

Rosset, B., 'Henry Miller vs. "Our Way of Life"', *Nexus: The International Henry Miller Journal*, 2, 1 (2005): 1–7.

Rosset, B., (n.d.) 'A Few Steps from the Long March', BRP.

Rosset Interview Transcripts, BRP.

Schmidt, Judith to Henry Miller, 14 May 1969, GPP.

Solatoroff, Theodore to Grove Press, 23 June 1969, GPP.

'Statement in Support of Freedom to Read', *Evergreen Review*, 6 (25) (1953), front cover and flyleaf.

Tompkins, J., *Reader-Response Criticism: From Formalism to Post-Structuralism*, Baltimore: Johns Hopkins, 1980.

Wickes, G. (ed.), *Henry Miller and the Critics*, Carbondale: Southern Illinois University Press, 1963.

Wilson, E., (1952), 'Twilight of the Expatriates', in G. Wickes (ed.), *Henry Miller and the Critics*, Carbondale: Southern Illinois University Press, 1963.

Part IV

13

Out of the Shadows: The Emergence of Overt Gay Narratives in Australia

Jeremy Fisher

For most of the twentieth century, as it remained in much of the world, homosexuality was illegal in Australia. The country was also subject to publication censorship relatively draconian for an English-speaking nation. This combination ensured overt homosexual works were comparatively unknown in Australia, even as titles imported from other English-speaking countries. In the late 1960s and early 1970s, however, publications of the homosexual rights and gay liberation movements began to appear. These were soon joined by more commercial publications aligned to an increasingly overt gay subculture. While censorship continued to be imposed on these publishers and publications under State jurisdictions, and many struggled economically, a few managed to eke out an existence. While gay-targeted newspapers and magazines documented the emerging gay subculture and provided entertainment, a number of newly-established small presses concentrated on more literary endeavours and produced a considerable number of novels, poetic works and play scripts. A number of writers published by these gay presses were taken up by more established publishers and have since gone on to mainstream success. Newspapers and magazines are still a feature of the gay media in Australia, but have now been supplemented by online publications. In light of the lessening of targeted censorship in Australia, this chapter explores the emergence of overt gay narratives and recounts their evolution from that date.

Australia in the 1950s was another country, as James Baldwin might have noted: a place where men wore hats and were firmly in charge, and Anglo-Celtic women wore dresses and looked after the home that everyone aspired to own. Indigenous Australians lived out of sight on reserves, with little access to health or education, and were unable to vote. The government decided what people could read and view. Homosexuality was against the law and, as historian Graham Willett has documented, police rounded up hundreds of men each year for indecent acts, with over 3,000 convicted of such offences between 1945 and 1960.[1] At the same time, the Australian Security Intelligence Organisation (ASIO) successfully argued that homosexuals should not be employed in sensitive public service positions, while the FBI kept a close eye on the fledgling gay movement in the United States.[2] Willett, and in his wake censorship historian Nicole Moore, have also noted that strict censorship restricted the circulation of 'books and films and plays with homosexual themes (few though they were)'.[3]

The English-speaking world slowly shifted its perception and treatment of homosexuals and homosexuality in the latter half of the twentieth century. The United Kingdom permitted the Wolfenden Commission to investigate the legal status of homosexuality in 1957, though law reform did not occur until 1967. In the United States, in 1962 Illinois became the first state to decriminalize homosexuality, but other states were slow to follow, and it took a Supreme Court decision in 2003 (Lawrence *v.* Texas) to decriminalize homosexuality nationwide. In Australia in 1958, the then New South Wales Police Commissioner, Colin Delaney, described homosexuality as the 'greatest menace facing Australia',[4] his views undoubtably shaped by the fact that homosexuality had not been subject to much discussion at all. My own studies of Australian medical and psychiatric literature show a small interest in the reporting of international research, but that is the extent of the evidence of medical discussion of homosexuality.[5] Works published both overseas and in Australia that did discuss homosexuality or offer representation of its practice were targeted for banning or their circulation curtailed.[6] Nicole Moore notes that 'frequently and secretly, Australian censorship ... banned any material with real or identifiable hints of homosexuality'.[7] Historian Deana Heath claims that successive Australian governments considered their censorship activity:

> an issue of national security. The system was designed to enforce a strict class division (by keeping out cheap editions and allowing only certain members of the public access to banned books), and to deny the freedom of information to the public. The system kept out knowledge of what was going on elsewhere in the world (particularly in relation to changing notions of sexual morality, and to alternative political models), and, possibly most importantly, it promoted (albeit within prescribed grounds) rather restricted Australian sexuality.[8]

The Book Censorship Board was the first national censorship authority with any scholarly expertise and was set up in 1933. As Moore's work establishes, the first book the Board reported on, *The Magnificent* by English writer Terence Greenidge, was banned in a unanimous decision because, in the words of the various members, it was 'an attempt to delineate the homosexual mind' that not only condoned 'the ways of homosexualists but appear[ed] to regard such persons as belonging to a select class of elite', while '[h]alf of the characters are homosexual, with a habit of telling their friends and acquaintants so'.[9] Novelist Kenneth Seaforth Mackenzie's *The Young Desire It* received a different reception from the Board. Despite the book featuring a schoolmaster who attempts, but ultimately refrains from, physical contact with a pupil, a board member still reported that 'the love passages between the boy and girl are of extreme beauty and leave no doubt as to the supremacy of the natural instincts'; because of this the book was permitted entry into Australia.[10] The book was based on Mackenzie's experiences at Guildford Grammar School in Perth and a new edition in 2013 features a foreword by prominent Australian writer David Malouf, who describes it as 'very nearly perfect'.[11] As was the case with many Australian writers of that period,

Mackenzie's work was first published in the United Kingdom while British publishing interests continued to dominate the Australian market, and so as an import, it was subject to federal Customs restrictions.

Gore Vidal's *The City and the Pillar* was banned in 1950, a decision upheld in 1958, 1963 and 1965. In his 1950 report on this book, board member Kenneth Binns noted '[t]hat the practice of homosexuality is a criminal offence',[12] as it was in most Australian states until the 1980s.[13] Since Item 14 of the Customs regulations under which the board worked dictated that censorship ought to prevent incitement to crime, and because the book was likely to be popular with readers and perhaps encourage homosexual practice, Binns argued it should be banned. The board recommended that Vidal's book be restricted in circulation, but that was overruled by the Customs Minister who banned the book completely. It was not released until 1966.[14]

In 1953, three books from Greenberg, a New York publisher founded in 1924 and with a history of publishing gay and lesbian titles, were banned in Australia primarily because they were written for a homosexual readership.[15] Greenberg faced similar problems in the United States. In the early 1950s, principals of the firm were indicted on a charge of sending obscene materials through the mail,[16] including Nial Kent's *The Divided Path* (1949), one of the titles the Australian board banned in 1953. By the 1950s the thriving US pulp fiction industry was producing books aimed directly at gay readers. There were, however, distribution problems because, like Australian Customs, 'the American postal system could rule that anything homosexual was immoral just because it was homosexual and thereby cause arrests for publishers and distributors'.[17] However, after the October 1954 issue of the homosexual magazine *One* was declared 'non-mailable' (or obscene) by the US postal service because it contained, amongst other things, an advertisement for see-through pajamas and a story about a successful lesbian love affair, the publishers took the matter to court.[18] Justice Brennan's decision in the US Supreme Court in January 1958 declared that obscenity was devoid of any 'redeeming social importance', thus clearing the way for legal defences that could establish social worth in the representation of sexuality, as Loren Glass's chapter in this volume recollects.

However, the severe restrictions placed on both male and female homosexual literature in Australia prohibited even scholarly or literary titles: James Baldwin's *Another Country* was banned from 1963 until 1966, Clifford Allen's academic work *Homosexuality* was banned in 1958 and Australian G. M. Glaskin's *No End to the Way* (published under the pseudonym Neville Jackson) was banned for 13 months through 1965 and 1966.[19] This last work is generally regarded as the first Australian openly homosexual novel,[20] whose history and impact I have described elsewhere.[21] Other banned books included Vidal's *The City and the Pillar* (published in 1948) and possibly James Barr's *Quatrefoil* (1950), both of which were early representations of a gay underworld, and both apologist (at least in the original version of Vidal's book, which notoriously ended with the death of the homosexual protagonist). In both the United States and the United Kingdom, a tragic ending was a means by which authors and publishers could argue they were not promoting a homosexual lifestyle (which was one reason why E. M. Forster chose to publish *Maurice* only after his death, as 'the lovers get away unpunished and consequently recommend crime'[22]), but this strategy did not succeed in Australia.

Pulp fiction from the United Kingdom, the United States and Canada was routinely targeted for importation bans when Customs defined titles as unduly emphasizing matters of sex or crime, or as calculated to encourage depravity (while further restrictions on mass-produced US publications remained through tariff controls left over from the Second World War). But some books published in the 1950s and 1960s with homosexual content were being read in Australia. For example, elsewhere I have recorded how gay activist Ron Austin, now in his mid-eighties, recalled being given a copy of *Quatrefoil,* which he understood to have been banned, around 1954, when he came to Sydney from the Hunter Valley to study.[23]

Publications from the United Kingdom were more accessible for Australia. Through much of the twentieth-century, British and American publishers had a gentlemen's agreement in place that divided the English-speaking world up as territorial markets into which they would sell each other the rights to publish their own books. British publishers assumed 'Empire' (later, Commonwealth) rights to American editions (though Canada could be an exception) when they purchased the rights. Books that were not sold on to a British publisher could be brought into Australia only if the American publisher had the rights to sell in Australia and a distributor was willing to take stock. This is why the edition of Vidal's *The City and the Pillar* banned in 1950 was the UK John Lehmann edition. The US edition, published two years before, was not licensed for sale in Australia, although individuals could bring in copies of books for their own use if they had the ability to pay for books in the US, then a difficult procedure from Australia. These books were still subject to Customs supervision, of course, and Customs retained the right to seize offending books sent by international mail or found in the luggage of persons arriving in Australia.[24] Author Gerry Glaskin, who moved back and forth between Amsterdam and his home town of Perth, Western Australia, complained to his London publisher, John Bunting of Barrie & Rockliff, that his six author copies of *No End to the Way* 'had to be returned to you by the Australian Customs Department'.[25] He also had his copies of John Rechy's *City of Night* and James Baldwin's *Another Country* seized by Customs when they were sent to him through the post.[26] Dennis Altman has described how in 1969 Customs removed from his luggage copies of Vidal's *Myra Breckenridge* and Sanford Friedman's *Totempole,* a low-brow novel set in the Korean War. After the subsequent court case, *Totempole* was released, but *Myra Breckenridge* remained prohibited.[27]

But there were some signs of change by this time. In 1969, the list of banned books was somewhat reduced after a review by the Customs Minister, Senator Don Chipp, following the landmark case *Crowe v. Graham*[28] and the Altman case and Penguin's successful defence of its publication of *Portnoy's Complaint* followed soon after. In July 1970, homosexual men and women in Sydney formed the group Campaign Against Moral Persecution (CAMP), the first openly homosexual rights organization in Australia, and this organization published its newsletter *Camp Ink* four months later.[29] While Sydney-based, *Camp Ink* set out to educate a national readership, both gay and straight, about homosexuality. It was a serious magazine with serious intent and was sent to parliamentarians and other influential people. By December 1973, the list of banned literary works had been reduced to zero. In an environment where censorship was greatly lessened and where there was open discussion of the decriminalization of homosexuality, it was inevitable that openly gay works of literature began to be published. While *Camp Ink* retained its educative role throughout its irregular five-year existence, poetry was introduced in February 1972 (vol. 2, no. 4, p. 13) under the editorship of Stefanie Bennett, who continued as poetry editor for a number of the following issues and is still writing poetry.[30] The first short story, 'A knock on the door' by Werner Probst, appeared in 1972 (Volume 2, number 10) and tells of the Gestapo knocking on the door of the flat of a German gay couple to remove them to a concentration camp.

The fact that *Camp Ink* escaped censorship opened the door for other publications and books targeted at the gay market or a more liberal readership. These publications sought to make money in one form or another and some were sometimes connected with sex shops or gay commercial businesses, which they shamelessly promoted. Gold Star, a paperback publisher briefly extant in Melbourne with its titles available in such venues as well as newsagents and convenience stores, brought out Wal Watkins's *Wayward Warriors* in 1972. Watkins's novel describes a homosexual romance on board an Australian destroyer in World War II. Its cover, completely unrelated to the story, must have tested State censorship authorities for whom pictures of naked men were still a bit risqué. The magazine *William & John* had to publish a special issue in the state of Victoria, 'censoring our full frontal nudes', but its erotic stories scraped through.[31]

One of the first commercial gay publications was *Little Butch: Mr Groovy*, a tabloid newspaper first published in 1972 (a date its title virtually screams). The content was poorly laid out and edited and filled with advertisements for newly visible gay venues, but amongst the pictures of naked men, readers could find short stories and occasional poems.

William & John commenced publication in Sydney for proposed national distribution in April 1972. It was a one-colour magazine with a full-colour cover. Its contents featured male nudes and a range of theatre, music and literature reviews and interviews. However, as referred to earlier, the publishers encountered problems with State licensing authorities regarding the photographic content, and were subject to bans in different states. Throughout the twentieth century, and to some extent still, each of the six State and two Territory jurisdictions in Australia asserted and enforced its own definition of obscenity. As Griffith notes, 'If the banning of works by Nabokov and D. H. Lawrence was the work of the Commonwealth Customs Minister, regulation of the magazine *Oz* was a matter for the State courts',[32] and State courts regularly heard cases relating to what police officers, in the main, considered 'obscene'. The definition of obscenity revolved around the Hicklin case's 'tendency of material to deprave and corrupt', but, after the previously-mentioned High Court of Australia case *Crowe v Graham* in 1969, gradually moved towards a community standards test. This was accepted by an in-principle agreement between the Commonwealth and State Attorneys General in 1974, building on a number of previous agreements.[33]

The single issue of *William & John* retained in the State Library of New South Wales (volume 1, number 3) contains a short story, 'Last summer' by 'Steve Peregrin Took' (p. 37), which is an unhappy tale of two boys who die after a night of love together. The tragic plotting and the Tolkien reference in the author's name show the literary memes of the past being embedded in the counter culture: *The Lord of the Rings* was required hippie reading.

Stallion commenced publication as a tabloid newspaper in 1973. Its first issue contained a short story, and there were others, some with humourous intent, in the issues that followed. More complex themes, such as a rape enjoyed by the victim, also featured indicating that the writers of these stories were engaging with other gay literature such as Vidal's *Myra Breckenridge* in which rape is treated as a transformative experience.

Whether or not influenced by the works of the patrician Vidal, homosexuality was finding a place in these scenes and plebeian magazines in ways that have not been considered within the figuration of Australian literature. So far, researchers have appeared to ignore the considerable amount of fiction published in the more commercial gay publications that followed *Camp Ink*'s lead. Within five years of the banning of Glaskin's *No End to the Way*, the first 'out' Australian work, prominent Sydney writer Frank Moorhouse was incorporating homosexual characters into his discontinuous narratives. Moorhouse also had a story, 'The cup and the wand (& the Magician)', printed in a 1974 edition of *Gayzette* (pp. 16–17), a tabloid newspaper that continued the pedigree of *Stallion*. In this story an older man seduces a younger man through the use of Tarot.[34] *Gayzette* first appeared on 5 September 1974 and set itself a mission. Notably, in a reply to a letter to the editor in the 19 September 1974 issue, the editor, Martin Smith, wrote 'we believe one of the roles of *Gayzette* is to develop gay literature in this country' (p. 2). Two issues later *Gayzette* republished a short story written by the English writer Robin Maugham, but included a very short story, 'The face in the fire', by Roly Nash (p. 15); this little piece tells of a couple, one of whom has drowned. Tragic endings were proving difficult to shake, but were completely absent from 'The first call', a short story by 'Geoffrey' in the issue of 31 October 1974. This is the story of a young Australian diplomatic officer in Bangkok who is seduced by a young Thai man, in a happy tale of fulfilled desire, with an interesting cross-cultural twist. It has some similarities with G. M. Glaskin's Asian novels, *A Lion in the Sun* and *The Beach of Passionate Love*. The 14 November 1974 issue contained 'Extracts from Zimmer's essay' by recognized poet and writer Robert Adamson and journalist Bruce Hanford. *Zimmer's Essay* was published in full by Sydney publisher Wild & Woolley in 1974, but had first appeared in an expurgated form in the counter-cultural newspaper *The Digger* in 1972. The poetic work documents and fictionalizes Adamson's sexual and drug experiences in prison.

Other book publishers were also emboldened enough to commission books with gay themes, though it is questionable whether they were aimed at a gay market. Horwitz's Scripts Publications brought out *The Gay Way* in 1974. The cover announced: 'Men craved his body ... A woman needed his passion ... His choice was her or ... *The Gay Way*'. Ultimately, he chose the woman. The story concerns 19-year-old Danny who 'had gone to bed with men before many times, but in a rather fizzy, party sort of way' (back cover blurb). It is by 'Mark Harris', one of the many pseudonyms used by Carl Ruhen, who wrote numerous titles for Horwitz including *The Violent Ones* (1966), *The Naked Vampires* (1971), *The Naked Voyeur* (1971), *Lesbian Love-Slave* (1972) and *Porno Girls* (1974). Ruhen also wrote novelizations for popular Australian televisions series and movies, including *The Road Warrior* (*Mad Max 2*) (1981), which introduced Mel Gibson to North American audiences.

The early gay magazines and newspapers faced distribution and financing obstacles and publication often ceased abruptly. In September 1975 the most influential and long-lasting of the gay tabloids, *Campaign*, was launched. Like its predecessors, it included fiction as part of its offerings and the first issue contains a piece of science fiction, 'Parting gift', by Trevor Nielsen (p. 12), in which a 'Terran' visitor to an unnamed planet leaves with a beautiful, loving male robot. Nielsen had another science fiction story, 'Christmas future', in the December 1975 issue. In February 1976, *Campaign* published the first instalment of Kevin Dowling's amusing epistolary series 'Dear Barrie: Some gentlemen prefer gentlemen'. This chronicled the adventures in the Sydney gay world of a naive fictional character called Bob from the small New South Wales town of Temora. Short fiction continued to appear in *Campaign* from time to time. A short story competition, with a AU$50 first prize, was announced in May, with winning entries to be published in July. Potential entrants were warned: 'Please note that the "unrestricted" classification of the newspaper does not permit us to print pornography or anything which could corrupt' (p. 28). The June 1976 issue features a somewhat pederastic story, 'David' by C. William (p. 28) and also a note indicating only four entries, all of poor quality, had been received in the story competition. While the July 1976 *Campaign* is missing from the Mitchell Library collection, the August 1976 issue contains 'yet another' entry in the *Campaign* short story competition, Dusty Wyatt's 'Eloise ... and the stud club' (pp. 14, 45): this is a mystical account of a sex club.

Campaign also offered its readers a comprehensive coverage of the arts. For instance, the December 1976 issue featured an interview with the US gay author Joseph Hansen, active in the gay movement in Los Angeles, by Martin Smith, former *Gayzette* editor and soon to be editor of *Campaign*. *Campaign* lasted until 2000. Over the years it had a number of different editors, one of whom was Dave Sargent, involved with the more academic journal *Gay Information* and the Sydney Gay Writers Collective, which published *InVersions* 1 and 2, booklet collections of prose and poetry in 1980. The collective also published the first openly homosexual anthology in Australia, *Edge City on Two Different Plans*, in 1982, with Sargent one of the editors. Unfortunately, Sargent died in 1985 as the AIDS epidemic began to take its toll.

As I have recounted elsewhere, after the radical emergence of open homosexuality in Australia in the early 1970s, the late 1970s and early 1980 saw attempts to consolidate the gains that had been made.[35] While *Campaign* dominated the commercial market, magazines and journals such as *Gay Liberation Press* (later *GLP*) in Sydney (1974–6), *Gay Changes* in Adelaide (1977–9), *Ganymede: Journal of Gay Poetics* in Sydney (1979–80), *The Star* (later *Star Observer*, *Sydney Star Observer* and *SSO*, 1979) in Sydney, *Gay Information* (later *Journal of Gay Studies*) in Sydney (1980–7) and *Queensland Pride* in Brisbane (1991) provided venues for emerging gay writers. All of these publications took a political stance, supporting the gay liberation movement.[36] They encouraged gay writers to contribute stories and, to a lesser extent, poems.

Writers began to produce larger works. Gary Dunne's *If Blood Should Stain the Lino* (1983) is an early, long gay narrative, with a central character called Simon Byrne who visits sex clubs, works as a dishwasher and otherwise engages in life in the inner-city.[37] Written in the first-person, Dunne's urgent telling of a gay existence in Sydney in the late 1970s and early 1980s aims as much as to record as to recount. Dunne was only 29 when the book was published and a member of the previously-mentioned Sydney Gay Writers Collective. With both men and women members, the collective had a political mission to produce and publish openly gay works, to overcome repression and encourage gay writers to express themselves. In that period, the collective was

Fig 13.1 Cover of *GLP: A Journal of Sexual Politics,* Issue 8 [Photograph by the author – no copyright traceable].

publishing material in both *InVersions* and the anthology *Edge City on Two Different Plans* that may well have been the subject of obscenity charges just a decade before. Police were still harassing and arresting homosexuals in Sydney. In perhaps the most infamous instance, in June 1978, 53 people participating in the first Gay and Lesbian Mardi Gras were arrested, and some severely beaten.

The shift from a hidden world to one that recognized, if not accepted, homosexuals is reflected in Simon Payne's long-form narrative *The Beat* (1985), which is set in Melbourne and formally interesting – each of its chapters gives a viewpoint from one of the various men who had been in a toilet block (a beat, or homosexual pick-up place) the night a young man was killed there. The young man proves to have been a 'poofter basher': the poofters (an Australian slang term for homosexuals equivalent to queer or faggot) come together in a silent pact and retaliate. While it was obviously written before any awareness of AIDS, it covers the diverse range of types well, each character revealed as a recognizably different kind of Australian gay man. Some of them are quite horrible people and there is a degree of stereotyping, but the aim is to show that there is no one type of homosexual. The joining together of these men in an attack on the basher is presented as spontaneous and, even though they are all in different relationships, not necessarily sexual, with each other, their conspiracy of silence ensures no-one discovers their involvement in the killing. This now out-of-print book thus assertively reverses the tradition of the 'tragic ending' and demonstrates the narrative possibilities available in a less restricted publishing environment. G. H. Payne noted in *Campaign*: 'As a novel it is first rate … but what a pity it had to be published abroad and not by some bold local publishing house'.[38] It was ranked number five in *Campaign*'s paperback bestseller list in that issue.[39]

Another book that emerged from the post-liberation milieu was Sasha Soldatow's *Private – Do Not Open* (1987), an unusual diversion undertaken by the mainstream publisher Penguin. The book was championed within the publishing company by its editor, Bruce Sims, who was a friend of Soldatow's and made it on to the list, according to Penguin publisher Brian Johns, because '[q]uite simply we were making the list as broad as possible'.[40] While, like Dunne's work, the story is a first-person recounting, unlike Dunne, Soldatow uses little humour. *Private – Do Not Open* is a visceral work, full of death, bodies and sex. The self-referential narrative links places and people and illuminates an inner-city world of drugs and drink. At times, the text is reflective, explicitly examining some of the issues that seemed important in the sexual liberation movements of the 1970s in a way characteristic of this writer's later work. Despite its claim to be a series of stories about a career made of falling in love, *Private – Do Not Open* is nihilistic. The fact that it was published in the middle of the AIDS crisis is not an influence on this, moreover, since much of the book was written well before HIV made itself known. Bruce Sims and freelance editor Jane Arms crafted it into a coherent manuscript from a number of pieces written by Soldatow. Sims had this editorial freedom at Penguin, where he says 'the whole environment in the company was very liberal'.[41] As it is, the book could easily fit on the list of one of the small gay presses operating in the 1970s and 1980s, when most mainstream Australian publishers continued to avoid gay titles. It affirms the liberationist mantra that the personal is political, but its overall self-indulgent tone perhaps reflects also the closeness between editors and author.

Such self-indulgence disappeared as HIV emerged to have a broad and inevitable impact on the development of homosexual narrative in Australia, though less immediately in works of fiction – as critic Michael Hurley noted in 1996: 'Non-fiction and the visual arts dominate innovative attempts to reorder both the social representations of HIV and AIDS and the way those representations are given narrative shape'.[42] These works were also regrettably tragic enough in character to appeal outside the small gay market. American anthropologist Eric Michaels' *Unbecoming: An AIDS Diary* (1990) and Tim Conigrave's posthumous memoir *Holding the Man* (1995) are both written by men influenced by liberationist ideology within the gay subculture overt after Stonewall and the period of Gay Liberation. Given the fact they are memoirs from men who can see their own imminent deaths, it is not surprising that the works are intently self-reflective. Their candour and simplicity, too, derive from this urgency. The narratives are tragic once again, but now not because of any need to meet with legal or editorial approval.

Today, while AIDS is still endemic, thanks to retroviral drugs it is no longer a death sentence. As science has transformed the treatment of a disease, so technology has changed media. Print is no longer the dominant means of communication. Digital media in all its forms provides an incessant stream of news and trivia, and even allows potential romantic or sexual partners the opportunity to meet. Newspapers and magazines struggle to survive in this new environment. So far, books continue to sell in print form, though sales of digital versions have risen dramatically. In this environment, gay print publications have suffered. The online editions of journals provide no place for literature. However, the transformed social and cultural environment in Australia brought about by the changes in the 1970s and 1980s has permitted some of the writers who were first published in the early gay media to develop careers as accomplished and admired storytellers. Graeme Aitken, author of *50 Ways of Saying Fabulous, Vanity Fierce* and *The Indignities*, and Christos Tsiolkas, author of *Loaded, The Jesus Man, Dead Europe, The Slap*, amongst others, are prime examples. The stories each tells could never have been told without the perseverance and tenacity with which those who came before them struggled against the strictures of censorship and its particular focus on homosexuality.

Notes

1 Graham Willet, 'The Darkest Decade: Homophobia in 1950s Australia', *Australian Historical Studies*, 28 (109) (1997): 127.
2 Ibid., p. 26; Douglas M. Charles, 'From Subversion to Obscenity: The FBI's Investigations of the Early Homophile Movement in the United States, 1953–1958', *Journal of the History of Sexuality*, 19 (2) (2010), p. 262.
3 Graham Willett, 'Minorities can Win: The Gay Movement, the Left and the Transformation of Australian Society', *Overland*, 149 (1997): 64; Nicole Moore, *The Censor's Library* (Brisbane, University of Queensland Press, 2012).

4 'Homosexual menace in Australia', *Sydney Morning Herald,* 11 June 1958, p. 5.

5 Jeremy Fisher, 'Interface: Medicine and Homosexuality in Australia', *Gay Information* Summer (1982), pp. 44–8.

6 Marita Bullock and Nicole Moore, 'Introducing Australia's Bibliography of Banned Books', *Banned in Australia* (AustLit, 2008), available at http://www.austlit.edu.au/specialistDatasets/Banned/bullockMoore [accessed 21 December 2013].

7 Moore, *Censor's Library,* p. 14.

8 Deana Heath, 'Literary Censorship, Imperialism and the White Australia Policy', in Martin Lyons and John Arnold (eds), *A History of the Book in Australia 1891–1945: A National Culture in a Colonised Market* (St Lucia, Qld: University of Queensland Press, 2001), p. 82.

9 Moore, *Censor's Library,* p. 130.

10 Ibid., p. 148.

11 Helen Trinca, 'Letter from the heart inspired Mackenzie's nearly perfect novel', *Weekend Australian* (17–18 August 2013), p. 3.

12 Moore, *Censor's Library,* p. 152.

13 New South Wales, the most populous state, did not repeal laws criminalizing homosexuality until 1984; in 1997, Tasmania became the last state to do so. Melissa Bull, Susan Pinto and Paul Wilson, 'Homosexual law reform in Australia', *Trends and Issues in Australian Crime and Criminal Justice 29* (Canberra: Australian Institute of Criminology, 1991), available at http://www.aic.gov.au/documents/F/2/E/%7BF2ED9BD3-0314-4EAA-AD03-410635E620DE%7Dti29.pdf. [accessed 21 December 2013]; Rodney Croome, 'Homosexuality', in Alison Alexander (ed.), *The Companion to Tasmanian History* (Centre for Tasmanian Historical Studies, 2006), available at http://www.utas.edu.au/library/companion_to_tasmanian_history/G/Gay%20Law%20Reform.htm [accessed 21 December 2013].

14 Moore, *Censor's Library,* p. 154.

15 Ibid., p. 150.

16 Drewey Wayne Gunn, 'Testing the Limits: Six Greenberg Authors', in Drewey Wayne Gunn (ed.), *The Golden Age of Gay Fiction* (Albion, NY: MLR Press, 2009), p. 55.

17 Drewey Wayne Gunn, 'The Golden Age of Gay Fiction: For, By, About & Out!', in Drewey Wayne Gunn (ed.), *The Golden Age of Gay Fiction* (Albion, NY: MLR Press, 2009), p. iv.

18 Charles, 'From Subversion to Obscenity', pp. 280–5.

19 Bullock and Moore, *Banned in Australia;* Moore, *The Censor's Library,* p. 261.

20 Michael Hurley, *A Guide to Gay and Lesbian Writing in Australia* (Sydney: Allen & Unwin/Australian Lesbian and Gay Archives, 1996), p. 190.

21 Jeremy Fisher, 'An End to the Way: Pulp Becomes Classic Down Under', in Drewey Wayne Gunn and Jaime Harker (eds), *1960s Gay Pulp Fiction: The Misplaced Heritage* (Amherst: Massachusetts University Press, 2013), pp. 292–311.

22 E. M. Forster, *Maurice* (New York: W. W. Norton, 1971), p. 250.

23 Jeremy Fisher, 'Cuddling the Wrong Characters: Reading, Writing and Gay Self-identity', *Overland* 176 (2004): 63.

24 Moore, *The Censor's Library,* p. 31.

25 Gerald Glaskin, Letter to John M. Bunting, 17 May 1965 (Random House Archives).

26 Gerald Glaskin, Letter to J. B. Pattison, 5 March 1965 (Random House Archives).

27 Dennis Altman, *Defying Gravity* (Sydney: Allen & Unwin, 1997), p. 102.

28	Gareth Griffith, *Censorship in Australia: Regulating the Internet and other Recent Developments.* Briefing Paper No. 4/02 (Sydney: New South Wales Parliamentary Library Research Service, 2002), available at http://www.parliament.nsw.gov.au/prod/parlment/publications.nsf/0/49793fb0b8a24337ca256ecf00074d64/$FILE/04-02.pdf [accessed 29 August, 2014].

29	David Hilliard, 'Sydney Anglicans and Homosexuality', *Journal of Homosexuality* 33 (2) (1997): 106.

30	The poems published in *Camp Ink* are not as yet listed in *AustLit*, the Australian literature bibliographical database.

31	Bill Calder, *The Origins of Gay Media in Australia 1969–78,* Postgraduate Diploma Thesis, Monash University (2011), available at http://gaymediahistory.wordpress.com/ [accessed 3 September 2014].

32	Griffith, *Censorship*, p. 7. *Oz* magazine was first published in Sydney, New South Wales, and faced charges of obscenity in *Neville v. Lewis* (1965) NSWR 1571. After losing, the editors moved the magazine to London where they successfully defended more charges in the British courts.

33	Ibid., p. 7.

34	This work doesn't (yet) appear to be listed in Moorhouse's extensive *AustLit* bibliography.

35	Jeremy Fisher, 'Sex, Sleaze and Righteous Anger: The Rise and Fall of Gay Magazines and Newspapers in Australia', *TEXT*, 25 (2014), available at http://www.textjournal.com.au/speciss/issue25/Fisher.pdf [accessed 2 September 2014].

36	Shirleene Robinson, 'The Queer Press and the Fight against Homophobia', in Shirleene Robinson (ed.), *Homophobia: An Australian History* (Sydney: Federation Press, 2008), pp. 193–217.

37	The title plays on the final line ('If blood should stain the wattle') of 'Freedom on the Wallaby', a poem by iconic Australian writer Henry Lawson, published in *The Worker*, Brisbane (16 May 1891), as a call to arms for the Australian working class.

38	G. H. Payne, 'Snippets', *Campaign*, August (1985): 33.

39	*Campaign*, August (1985): 50.

40	Brian Johns, Personal communication, 1 September 2014.

41	Bruce Sims, Personal communication, 8 September 2014.

42	Hurley, *A Guide*, p. 130.

References

Adamson, R. and B. Hanford, *Zimmer's Essay*, Sydney: Wild & Woolley, 1974.

Aitken, G., *50 Ways of Saying Fabulous*, Sydney: Vintage Random House, 1995.

Aitken, G., *Vanity Fierce*, Sydney: Vintage Random House, 1998.

Aitken, G., *The Indignities*, Melbourne: Clouds of Magellan, 2010.

Allen, C., *Homosexuality,* London: Staples Press, 1958.

Altman, D., *Defying Gravity*, Sydney: Allen & Unwin, 1997.

Baldwin, J., *Another Country*, New York: Dial Press, 1962.

Bradstock, M., G. Dunne, D. Sargent, and L. Wakeling (eds), *Edge City on Two Different Plans*, Sydney: InVersions, 1983.

Bull, M., S. Pinto, and P. Wilson, 'Homosexual Law Reform in Australia', *Trends and Issues in Australian Crime and Criminal Justice*, 29 (1991), Canberra: Australian Institute of Criminology, available at http://www.aic.gov.au/documents/F/2/E/%7BF2ED9BD3-0314-4EAA-AD03-410635E620DE%7Dti29.pdf [accessed 21 December 2013].

Bullock, M. and N. Moore, *Banned in Australia: Federal Book Censorship 1900–1973*, AustLit, 2008, available at www.austlit.edu.au/specialistDatasets/Banned [accessed 21 December 2013].

Calder, B., *The Origins of Gay Media in Australia 1969–78*, Postgraduate Diploma Thesis, Monash University (2011), available at http://gaymediahistory.wordpress.com/ [accessed 3 September 2014].

Charles, D. M., 'From Subversion to Obscenity: The FBI's Investigations of the Early Homophile Movement in the United States, 1953–1958', *Journal of the History of Sexuality*, 19 (2) (2010): 262–87.

Conigrave, T., *Holding the Man*, Melbourne: McPhee Gribble, 1995.

Croome, R., 'Homosexuality', in Alison Alexander (ed.), *The Companion to Tasmanian History*, Centre for Tasmanian Historical Studies, 2006, available at http://www.utas.edu.au/library/companion_to_tasmanian_history/H/Homosexuality.htm [accessed 3 September 2014].

Dunne, G., *If Blood Should Stain the Lino*, Sydney: InVersions, 1983.

Fisher, J., 'Interface: Medicine and Homosexuality in Australia', *Gay Information* Summer (1982), pp. 44–8.

Fisher, J., 'Cuddling the Wrong Characters: Reading, Writing and Gay Self-Identity', *Overland*, 176 (2004): 61–6.

Fisher, J., 'An End to the Way: Pulp Becomes Classic Down Under', in D. W. Gunn and J. Harker (eds), *1960s Gay Pulp Fiction: The Misplaced Heritage*, Amherst: Massachusetts University Press, 2013.

Fisher, J., 'Sex, Sleaze and Righteous Anger: The Rise and Fall of Gay Magazines and Newspapers in Australia', *TEXT*, 25 (2014), available at http://www.textjournal.com.au/speciss/issue25/Fisher.pdf [accessed 2 September 2014].

Forster, E. M., *Maurice*, New York: W. W. Norton, 1971.

Friedman, S., *Totempole*, New York: Dutton, 1965.

Glaskin, G. M., *A Lion in the Sun*, London: Barrie & Rockliff, 1960.

Glaskin, G. M., *The Beach of Passionate Love*, London: Barrie & Rockliff, 1961.

Glaskin, G. M., Letter to J. B. Pattison, 5 March 1965 (Random House Archives).

Glaskin, G. M., Letter to John M. Bunting, 17 May 1965 (Random House Archives).

Greenidge, T., *The Magnificent*, London: Fortune Press, 1933.

Griffith, G., *Censorship in Australia: Regulating the Internet and other Recent Developments*, Briefing Paper No. 4/02, Sydney: New South Wales Parliamentary Library Research Service, 2002, available at http://www.parliament.nsw.gov.au/prod/parlment/publications.nsf/0/49793fb0b8a24337ca256ecf00074d64/$FILE/04-02.pdf. [accessed 29 August, 2014].

Gunn, D. W., 'Testing the Limits: Six Greenberg Authors', in D. W. Gunn (ed.), *The Golden Age of Gay Fiction*, Albion NY: MLR Press, 2009.

Gunn, D. W., 'The Golden Age of Gay Fiction: For, By, About & Out!', in D. W. Gunn (ed.), *The Golden Age of Gay Fiction*, Albion NY: MLR Press, 2009.

Harris, M., *The Gay Way*, Sydney: Script Publications, 1974.

Heath, D., 'Literary Censorship, Imperialism and the White Australia Policy', in M. Lyons and J. Arnold (eds), *A History of the Book in Australia 1891–1945: A National Culture in a Colonised Market*, St Lucia, Qld: University of Queensland Press, 2001.

Hilliard, D., 'Sydney Anglicans and Homosexuality', *Journal of Homosexuality*, 33, 2 (1997): pp. 101–23.

'Homosexual Menace in Australia', *Sydney Morning Herald*, 11 June 1958, p. 5.

Hurley, M., *A Guide to Gay and Lesbian Writing in Australia*, Sydney: Allen & Unwin/Australian Lesbian and Gay Archives, 1996.

Jackson, N., (G. M. Glaskin) *No End to the Way*, London: Barrie & Rockliff, 1965.

Kent, N., *The Divided Path*, New York: Greenberg, 1949.

Michaels, E., *Unbecoming: An AIDS Diary*, Sydney: Empress Publishing, 1990.

Moore, N., *The Censor's Library: Uncovering the Lost History of Australia's Banned Books*, Brisbane: University of Queensland Press, 2012.

Payne, S., *The Beat,* London: GMP Publishers, 1985.

Robinson, S., 'The Queer Press and the Fight against Homophobia', in S. Robinson (ed.), *Homophobia: An Australian History*, Sydney: Federation Press, 2008.

Soldatow, S., *Private: Do Not Open,* Melbourne: Penguin, 1987.

Trinca, H., 'Letter from the heart inspired Mackenzie's nearly perfect novel', *Weekend Australian*, 17–18 August 2013, p. 3.

Tsiolkas, C., *Loaded*, Sydney: Vintage Random House, 1995.

Tsiolkas, C., *The Jesus Man,* Sydney: Vintage Random House, 1999.

Tsiolkas, C., *Dead Europe*, Sydney: Vintage Random House, 2005.

Tsiolkas, C., *The Slap*, Sydney Allen & Unwin, 2008.

Vidal, G., *The City and the Pillar*, London: John Lehmann, 1950.

Vidal, G., *Myra Breckenridge*, Boston: Little, Brown, 1968.

Watkins, W., *Wayward Warriors,* Melbourne: Gold Star, 1974.

Willet, G., 'Minorities can Win: The Gay Movement, the Left and the Transformation of Australian Society', *Overland* 149 (1997): 64–8.

Willet, G., 'The Darkest Decade: Homophobia in 1950s Australia', *Australian Historical Studies*, 28 (109) (1997): 127.

14

Silenced Lives: Censorship and the Rise of Diasporic Iranian Women's Memoirs in English

Sanaz Fotouhi

My maternal grandmother never learned to read or write. Living into her seventies, she always relied on others to read things to her. It always fascinated us to know why her parents had not insisted on her education when she herself had made sure all her children received adequate schooling. When I was a teenager, I asked her once why she had not gone to school. She looked at me and said that parents of her generation did not like girls to receive an education because if they did, they would start communicating. They would start writing and sharing things with the world. Families did not like this. What happened in the family was to stay in the family.

I did not fathom the cultural and societal gravity of my grandmother's statement until years later, when I became exposed to narratives by women from across the globe. It was then that I noticed the missing voices of Iranian women in Persian literature and realized the sad reality that many women of my grandmother's generation, and prior, had never really had a chance to express themselves. In their illiteracy they had not authored any books. When they did appear as subjects of men's books, it was often in passing, and as symbolic characters who aided the male hero in his quest. Even Sufi Persian poetry, for instance – the literature loved by everyone in Iran – has always been a male-dominated form of expression. It was not only in Iran, however, that these women's voices and stories had remained absent. When Iranian women did appear in Western literature, their presence was marred with Oriental mystery, as passive subjects of a Western male gaze and often victims of patriarchal oppression.

My initial awareness of the historically-absent voices of Iranian women in literature, coincided with the cusp of a revolutionary period for Iranian women's literature, particularly outside Iran, in the early 2000s. Ever since the Islamic revolution of 1979 and the mass migration of Iranians to other countries, the Iranian diaspora has been constructing a body of literary work in English. Of this body of work, which to date includes over 200 titles, women's memoirs form almost a third. These books, often written with intimate detail, explore and expose aspects of Iranian women's lives never previously represented.

Given the private and highly-censored nature of Iranian society that has, until very recently, enforced the general silencing of women's voices, the question is, 'why have so many women begun to explore the deepest and most intimate aspects of their lives in such an uncensored and public manner'? More importantly, why have so many women writers chosen the revealing form of the memoir over fictional accounts in which they could explore issues while withholding their own personal and private lives?

This chapter sets out to examine the reasons for the popularity of the memoir form for Iranian women writers in diaspora. It situates diasporic Iranian women's memoirs in relation to the historical and social contexts of censorship that has governed women's expression in Iran. It argues that the popularity of memoir today can be traced back to the various historical and social aspects of censorship that have existed in Iran for women. It draws on psychological theories of identity, narrativity and subjectivity, and examines how the memoir, because of the very nature of its form, has become a prominent medium of expression through which Iranian women can renegotiate and reconstruct their individual identities, in the face of those silences and censorships that have previously ruled their lives.

Historical understanding

If we look at Iranian social history, my grandmother's inhibition and belief that women's stories were never to be told was not unique. Iranian history reveals a society with distinct public/private segregation, in which the imparting of personal stories was not only taboo but could also have detrimentally negative consequences. As Farzaneh Milani observes, in Iran the autobiographical form as we know it today, based on the disclosing of private and personal information, has not been a favoured form of expression historically. Among many reasons for the autobiography's disfavour, rooted deep in Iranian history and culture, has been the 'fear that the information revealed [...] can be used, or rather, misused against their authors'.[1] This, Milani argues, stems from the strict censorship exercised by the various regimes that have ruled thousands of years of Persian literature and culture.

Milani goes on to argue that, although censorship has been externally imposed, gradually it has become a structural part of Iranian communication, in which people eventually self-censor for fear of the consequences of revealing too much information. A cultural tradition emerged that purposely censors or hides disputes, scandals and the involvement of family members with criminal and political activities. Consequently, 'avoiding voluntary self-revelation and self-referentiality, most Iranian writers have turned their backs on autobiography'.[2] This is not to say, however, that Iranians have never written about their lives. In fact, through recent Iranian literary history one does encounter a genre that calls itself autobiography. But examples of this are normally written by male public figures, in an impersonal manner, avoiding self-importance, and revolving around their public offices, thus lacking any depth about private affairs.

While Iranian men with a public presence have had the chance to write about their lives, until recently that opportunity did not exist for Iranian women. Milani relates the lack of a public voice for women to the concept of veiling. She writes that histori-cally the majority of Iranian women 'were suppressed physically and verbally by the conventions of the veil and public silence'.[3] If we look at the characteristics of Iranian society, traditionally and until recently, it has been highly gender-segregated: men have belonged to the public sphere and women to the private. In this culture, women's domain 'was a private world, where self-expression, either bodily or verbally, was confined within the accepted family circle'.[4] Within this tradition, propriety demanded that 'a woman's body be covered, her voice go unheard, her portrait never painted, and her life story remain untold'.[5] Milani blames this segregation for the lack of women's autobiographical accounts in Persian. She writes:

> Erased from the public scene and privatized, the Iranian woman has for long been without autobiographical possibilities. Textual self-representation of individuals is not divorced from their cultural representation; and in a culture that idealizes feminine silence and restraint, not many women can or will opt for breaking the silence. Most will not name the formerly unnamed, or move beyond the accepted paradigms of female self-representation. In a sexually segregated society where access to a woman's world and word is limited, and the concept of honour is built around woman's virginity (proof of her inaccessibility) women's autobiographies, with their assertive self-attention and self-display, cannot easily flourish, and they have not.[6]

Although in recent years the situation has changed for women and they have gained a greater voice in Iran's literary scene, as Milani observes in her latest book *Words Not Swords* (2011), it was this social dynamic, coupled with the general lack of women's education until Reza Shah's modernization scheme in the 1930s, that led to the historical absence of women's autobiographical voices in Persian literature.

Added to this, the trauma of the Iranian Revolution in 1979, which replaced the Pahlavi monarchy with a new Islamic republic, not only brought even stricter censorship, but also reinforced gender dichotomy, resulting in even fewer opportu-nities for women to write autobiographically. As Haleh Esfandiari argues in her book *Reconstructed Lives* (a book which played a part in her later imprisonment in Iran):

> [T]he Islamic revolution had a marked and transforming impact on all areas of Iranian life. But for women, its consequences were especially profound—legally, socially, professionally, psychologically, both in the home and in society. [...] The state set out deliberately and consciously to reconstruct and redefine the place of women under the law and in the public and the private spheres.[7]

Such a legal transformation, as has been established, was not towards freedom. If women's inability to write about their life experiences had been mostly due to family and self-censorship prior to the revolution, after the revolution censorship became state-sponsored. Consequently, the Islamic revolution had a traumatic impact on the lives of many Iranian women; while those who stayed in Iran had to live with everyday oppressions and silences, those who left faced the dislocating trauma of exile.

Despite this situation, however, the decades since the revolution have seen an increase in Iranian women's literary presence internationally. As Geoffrey Nash argues, 'It has often been pointed out that in spite of the Islamic Republic of Iran's turning back of the clock in respect of obvious areas of women's presence in the public arena, writing by Iranian women has increased exponentially since 1979'.[8] This expansion of women's writing in Iran, glossed over by some Western readers because of language barriers and Western stereotypical constructions of Iranian women as continuously silent, is the result of numerous social and cultural factors.[9] However, despite an upsurge in Iranian women's literature, women's voices and narratives have continued to be highly censored by the Islamic government to ensure adherence to the laws of the state. It is in response to the historical absence of autobiographical accounts, particularly women's narratives, that diasporic Iranian writers have chosen the memoir as a favourite medium of expression. Distanced by time and space from the divided society that had held many in silence until recently, diasporic Iranian writers are 'free, at last, to shape the boundaries of [their] own story'.[10]

Writing beyond censorship and the therapeutic effects of the memoir

The young girls and women who migrated from Iran took with them memories of the silences that had ruled their lives and the lives of their foremothers. In this context, the memoir, as opposed to other forms of expression, has been an effective therapeutic medium for many authors. In *Shattered Subjects* (2000), Suzette Henke argues that all autobiographical forms of writing have the potential to be what she calls 'scriptotherapy'. Scriptotherapy is 'the process of writing out and writing through traumatic experiences in the mode of therapeutic reenactment'.[11] Henke, who looks at the role of narrativity and subjectivity in relation to traumatized subjects, believes:

> the authorial effort to reconstruct a story of psychological debilitation could offer potential for mental healing and begin to alleviate persistent symptoms of numbing, dysphoria, and uncontrollable flashbacks. [It] [...] might provide a therapeutic alternative for victims of severe anxiety and, more seriously, of post-traumatic stress disorder.[12]

This therapeutic potential has to do with the very form of the memoir, which by its nature offers possibilities to express realities of a distant, traumatic or, at times, censored past that otherwise may not have been documented. It is the process of writing, the very act of narrating or constructing narrative that allows the form to operate as a therapeutic space of expression. As Kelly Oliver argues about the psychology of oppression, individuals and groups who have been tortured, traumatized and discriminated against have been objectified and their sense of identity and agency has been taken away. One of the means through which such people can regain a sense of identity is through the process she calls 'bearing witness to oppression and subordination'.[13] She suggests that those affected can heal themselves and 'repair damaged subjectivity by taking up a position as speaking subjects', and by being recognized by others as sharing the same human feelings.[14]

In this process, because of its emphasis on recalling and engaging with very personal, often traumatic experiences, and its ability to provide a space for revelation, the memoir can provide the perfect formal space through which this kind of private/public interaction can play out. According to Gillian Whitlock, one of the significant elements of the memoir is that it can mediate 'between the public and private'.[15] It 'is a cultural space where relations between the individual and society are thought out intensely and experienced intersubjectively'.[16] Psychologically, for many, breaking the taboos surrounding private or individual experiences and locating them in the public sphere can be an important process in reconstructing and negotiating personal or group identity.

In this way, most post-revolutionary, diasporic Iranian women's memoirs serve as a form of 'scriptotherapy' for their authors: as individual, uncensored exercises of healing and reconstruction from trauma and oppression. In her essay 'From Tehran to Tehrangeles', Gillian Whitlock argues that most diasporic Iranian women's memoirs 'share experience and articulation of the revolution as a traumatic event, as a wound inflicted during a key period in the author's personal development'.[17] Looking at the body of diasporic Iranian women's memoirs, it is clear that the lives of each and every one of these writers have been affected dramatically by the revolution. The restrictive Islamic codes of conduct relegated many to the margins of society and discriminated against many minority groups, eventually forcing some into exile. It is to this sense of oppression and discrimination, and the inability to speak about it publicly, that many have responded in their memoirs. Perhaps the oppression unleashed by the revolution is best summed up in the words of Azar Nafisi who, in her memoir *Reading Lolita in Tehran,* complains 'of a loss, the void in our lives that was created when our past was stolen from us, making us exiles in our own country'.[18] By controlling and censoring expression, 'they invaded all private spaces and tried to shape every gesture, to force us to become one of them, and that in itself was [a] form of execution'.[19] This is why, as Whitlock observes, these memoirs 'constitute a "gathering of the wounded," a working-through of revolutionary trauma, and the disclosure of memory marked by the events of the revolution: the loss of home and culture, shaped by the nostalgia that scars life in the diaspora'.[20]

It is through Whitlock's observation of the revolution as a traumatic experience that this chapter situates the memoir as a form of scriptotherapy for writers. These memoirs bear uncensored witness to painful personal experiences of alienation, loss, dismay and ultimately exile. This can be seen, in various forms, from the earliest and more obscure memoirs emerging in the late 1980s to better-known accounts published recently. For instance, in *Out of Iran* (1987), one of the first memoirs by an Iranian woman in English, Sousan Azadi bears witness to the individual subordination that she was subjected to following the revolution. A great-granddaughter of a Qajar King, she narrates her life from her husband's death and her subsequent difficulties in obtaining child custody from her in-laws in the Islamic regime, to her imprisonment and eventual escape through Turkey to Canada. The book begins with the narrator recalling the discrimination her family faced immediately after the revolution. She begins:

> The *taughout*. Satan. A ruler who has transgressed the limits of his authority. Such was Ayatollah Rhollah Khomeini's title for Mohammad Reza Pahlavi, King of Kings, Shah of Iran. And we, the Shah's loyal subjects, were condemned by Khomeini as the *taughouti*, the followers of Satan [...] We were the rich of Iran, the ruling elite, the nation's leaders. We didn't want to accept a vengeful religious leader as our new master. In his view, because we were Westernized, we must have been immoral. I have known what it is like to be hated just because I wanted basic rights as a woman in a Moslem country. Within three years I found myself an unwilling exile, purged by a society that I barely recognized as my own...[21]

By explaining her own position and political beliefs, which she would not have been able to express had she been in Iran, Azadi uses the autobiographical form to become a speaking subject: to reinvent herself anew, and not as a 'taughouti' but as an educated, honourable member of Iranian society.

The memoir allows her to freely reconstruct her own sense of subjectivity against an historically-imposed image – the 'taughouti'. She becomes a speaking subject by bearing witness to objectification at the hands of the newly-established regime. To put it in Henke's words, the autobiographical form provides a space in which the writer can 'rebel against the values and practices of the dominant culture and [...] assume an empowered position of political agency in the world'. [22]

For those writers who encountered the revolution as children, the memoir allows them to tap into childhood memories, and to recount and bear witness to the horrors of that era, with perhaps more understanding as adults. Afschineh Latifi, in *Even After All This Time* (2005), for example, recounts the traumatic story of the execution of her father, who was a high-ranking colonel under the Shah's regime, and follows her family's difficult journey into exile. Similarly, Banafsheh Serov, one of the first Iranian-Australians to write a memoir, remembers her family's illegal and dangerous escape after the revolution through Turkey and eventually to Australia in *Under a Starless Sky* (2008). In *Journey from the Land of No* (2004), Roya Hakakian recalls the discrimination her Jewish family faced after the revolution, provoking their eventual journey to America.

Recalling these traumatic experiences as adults can be healing, as it not only allows repressed memories to come to the fore but also offers authors a sense of closure. As Eve Zibart writes in an online interview with Hakakian, 'the word is the expression of the essential self, and the manner in which we re-create our universe'.[23] Zibart writes that Hakakian had 'thought she had understood pretty well the upheaval of the late 1970s and early '80s in her native Iran [...] but once she began to write about that time, the act of writing both clarified and reshaped those events'. Indeed, Hakakian confirms the therapeutic effects of writing – once she started writing, 'everything came into focus and I was able to make sense of things I thought were unconnected'.[24]

While it can be suggested that writing is a kind of scriptotherapy for many of these writers (even without the narrator necessarily acknowledging it openly), for a few it is the therapeutic effects that have attracted them most of all. For instance, in Marina Nemat's *Prisoner of Tehran* (2007), which deals with her imprisonment and forced marriage to her interrogator at the age of 16, Nemat overtly addresses the therapeutic effects of writing in regaining her subjectivity. *Prisoner of Tehran* opens with Nemat's arrival in Canada. She writes, 'there is an ancient Persian proverb that says: "The sky is the same color wherever you may go",[25] but quickly recasts it, as she continues:

> But the Canadian sky was different from the one I remembered in Iran: it was a deeper shade of blue and seemed endless, as if challenging the horizon [...] the vastness of the landscape astonished me. [...] we had to build a new life in this strange country that had offered us refuge when we had nowhere to go. I had to concentrate all my energy on survival.[26]

This opening establishes that it is distance from Iran that has allowed Nemat to survive and eventually bear witness to the traumas of her imprisonment. In fact, as Sydney columnist Paul Sheehan observed, 'had she written this book in her native Iran, she would have been executed by the state'.[27] The opening lines set the tone of the entire memoir. Set in a new land with an endless horizon, we immediately know this is a personal narrative of survival, healing, reconstruction, new beginnings and possibilities. This self-consciousness, which becomes even more obvious as the narrative proceeds, forms a running theme throughout Nemat's memoir. In the early pages of the book, Nemat recounts the moment when, after nearly 20 years of silence, and after becoming a 'proud middle-class Canadian', she decided to speak. She writes:

> This is when I lost the ability to sleep.
> It began with snapshots of memories that flashed into my mind as soon as I went to bed. I tried to push them away, but they rushed at me, invading my daytime hours as well as the night. The past was gaining on me, and I couldn't keep it at bay; I had to face it or it would completely destroy my sanity. If I couldn't forget, perhaps the solution was to remember. I began writing about my days in Evin—Tehran's notorious political prison—about the torture, pain, death, and all the suffering I had never been able to talk about. My memories became words and broke free from their induced hibernation.
> I believed that once I put them on paper, I would feel better—but I didn't. I needed more. I couldn't keep my manuscript buried in a bedroom drawer. I was a witness and I had to tell my story.[28]

Although the above words reveal Nemat's writing as a conscious therapeutic exercise to keep her own sanity, her emphasis on the feeling that her healing is not complete without sharing her manuscript points to the need for intersubjective recognition to fully reconstruct her sense of subjectivity, in the manner that both Oliver and Henke observe. Here, readers and the recognition that writers may gain from them, play an integral part in the healing process. And this suggests that, when someone like Nemat writes a memoir, a significant part of their healing takes place only when they are read and acknowledged by others.

However, in reading these memoirs, we must keep in mind that they transcend any particular woman's experience. Through the narration of their individual stories, these writers are also bearing witness and responding to larger, often generational, historical and socio-political forces that had censored and silenced their voices. As Oliver argues, those traumatized 'do not merely articulate a demand to be recognized or to be seen [...] they bear witness to a pathos beyond recognition and to something other than the horror of their objectification'.[29] Seen in this light, these memoirs, too, though articulated in and through personal accounts, should be read as forms of witness with motivations beyond the personal desire for recognition. They witness a larger socio-political and historical pathos, and their narratives ask for recognition of groups and individuals marginalized and objectified under various oppressive forces.

Breaking vows of silence

One recurrent issue with which many diasporic Iranian memoirs engage is the silence caused by years of censorship and oppression. The historical dichotomy of public/private domains and the social forces that generally silenced women's narratives in Iranian society have resulted in a kind of gradual self-censorship. As Milani argues, 'external restrictions sustained over time eventually generate[d] internal ones'.[30] This created a kind of individual/family dichotomy, or a form of self-censorship. It separated the individual, especially one who had been in a traumatizing or harmful situation such as imprisonment, from the rest of the family – the individual and family censor themselves and their expression with a veil of silence. Such silence fails to recognize the trauma of the oppressed person, so that as 'these private, sacred precincts protect, they also imprison', because 'the sophisticated mechanisms that shield the inner self from exposure and intrusion also amputate and silence part of the self'.[31]

This silence forms one of the central themes of diasporic Iranian women's memoirs. Among the silences, one of the most dramatic has been that of ex-prisoners, particularly between the prisoner and their family. Ex-prisoners, especially female political prisoners, have had an invisible existence. Fuelled by rigid and self-imposed censorship that protects the boundaries between public and private, their silence frequently stems from fear that personal information revealed can be used or misused by the regime against the authors and their families. Unable to speak about their experiences, ex-prisoners are frequently doubly oppressed, received back into silent families who are fearful of both knowing what has happened and the consequences of such knowledge. Ex-prisoners often complain about being received into shrouds of silence upon their return home. For example, Zarah Ghahramani, a young political activist who was imprisoned for a month in Evin during the student protests of 2001, recounts her ordeal in her memoir *My Life as a Traitor* (2007). The narrative reveals the silence into which she walked after being released. In an interview she speaks of her experiences after being picked up by her father from the side of the road where prison guards had dropped her off blindfolded:

> He came, and we hugged and cried and all that, and then we went home. My sisters came over, and my father made breakfast for us, like when we were kids. It was all really normal. I was expecting them to ask me what had happened, where I had been, but we just had normal, everyday breakfast. Then I went to have a shower and I saw my face for the first time after a month. It was really scary. I hardly stopped myself from screaming, wondering what my family was going through seeing me like that, and not even saying anything. It was really frustrating for me – I really wanted to talk. But when I think about it now, it was the best thing they did. It was hard enough for them, what happened to me. I'm sure they didn't want to know any more.[32]

While the very act of writing can be liberating and therapeutic for those who have experienced such silence, for some, writing has become a deliberate and conscious attempt to break it down. In *Prisoner of Tehran,* for instance, Nemat is driven to write deliberately and self-consciously on the social pathos caused by silencing and self-censorship. When she is freed after two years, she is received into a web of silence. Instead of asking her about what has happened, her family and friends require her to dress in fine clothes, and attend parties. Like Ghahramani, no one, not even her family, asks about, acknowledges or wants to know what happened. Frustrated by this silence, she confronts her grandmother:

> "Why doesn't anyone ask me anything about the last two years?" I asked.
>
> "The answer is very simple. We're afraid to ask because we're afraid of knowing. I think this is some kind of a natural defence. Maybe if we don't talk about it, and maybe if we pretend it never happened, it will be forgotten."
>
> I had expected my homecoming to make things simple again, but it hadn't. I hated the silence surrounding me. I wanted to feel loved. But how could love find its way through silence? Silence and darkness were very similar: darkness was the absence of light and silence was the absence of sound, voices. How could one navigate through such oblivion?[33]

Nemat, too, would have lived with these stories only in her heart, as she had for 20 years, had it not been for the sudden realization that there are many such women whose voices needed to be heard. Her decision to break this silence comes after an encounter with another ex-prisoner. Nemat tells of an event that inspired her narrative. In 2005, she met a girl, Parisa, who had been an inmate at Evin at the same time. Talking to Nemat, Parisa realizes that she had not, until then, 'talked to anyone about her prison experiences' because 'people just don't want to talk about it'.[34] It is this to which Nemat responds:

> This was the very silence that had held me captive for more than twenty years.
>
> When I was released from Evin my family pretended that everything was all right. No one mentioned the prison. No one asked, "what happened to you?" I ached to tell them about my life in Evin, but I didn't know where to start. I waited

for them to ask me something, anything that would give me a place to begin. I guessed that my family wanted me to be the innocent girl I had been before prison. They were terrified of the pain and horror of my past, so they ignored it.[35]

After this meeting, she contends, 'if I had doubts about speaking out, they vanished'.[36] It is Nemat's recognition of Parisa, and the similarity of their silences, coupled with the significance of Zahra Kazemi's death (the Canadian-Iranian photojournalist who was captured and beaten to death in Evin in 2003), that makes her break her own silence. She speaks to heal herself, but also to bear witness to the larger socio-political situation that had affected others similarly. Nemat's last words in the postscript to her work reveal her intentions:

> I knew what I had gone through in Evin was still happening behind its walls, but seeing Zahra's picture, and her beautiful smile gave this knowledge, a painful and shocking power that cut through me. [...] The world had now taken notice because Zahra was a Canadian. If the world had paid attention, if the world had cared, Zahra would not have died; many innocent lives would have been saved. But the world had remained silent, partly because witnesses like me had been afraid to speak up. But enough was enough. I was not going to let fear hold me captive any longer. [...]
>
> I had a story to tell. Zahra had given Iran's political prisoners a name and a face; now it was my turn to give them words.[37]

Memoirs like Nemat's, which highlight oppressive silences and censorships also experienced by others through their own personal stories, recuperate silenced experiences on multiple levels. On a personal level, they allow the narrator to bear witness to trauma. Narration, thus, becomes a form of scriptotherapy: a way of gaining personal recognition and regaining subjectivity. On another level, these narratives articulate something beyond the narrator's need for personal recognition. They bear witness to a social and historical pathos caused by silence and censorship, and allow the voices of those who otherwise might not have a chance to express themselves to be recognized. As such they are important contributions in helping those who have been oppressed historically to regain their subjectivity, as they 'render human the dehumanized and convey the fullness of voice and presence to those denied their rights'.[38]

While, beyond doubt, the memoir in diaspora has, as Stephen Kaufman suggests, provided Iranian women with 'the opportunity to tell their own stories, [by] taking advantage of new freedoms and an increased feeling of comfort in their new societies',[39] it seems that they cannot escape the socio-political predicaments of the diasporic society into which they are received. Although, as we have seen, many of these narratives are written freely and without much relative self-censorship, it does not necessarily mean that the cycles of silence have been broken. These memoirs, which are written and consumed in the West, are received within stereotypes and already existing predefined spaces of reception for Middle East narratives. Although this allows for the uncensored voices of many women to be heard, it may silence them further by placing them within restrictive and stereotypical spaces of recognition through which these accounts are read in the West. As Amireh and Majaj put it in their complaint about contemporary Western interest in Middle Eastern women's narratives, 'our identities [as Muslim and Middle Eastern Women] [...] served to silence us at a time when we most felt the need to speak'.[40] It is within this context that we need to begin to understand the complexity of these narratives, as stories that have emerged from centuries of censorships and silences in Iran.

Notes

1 Farzaneh Milani, *Veils and Words: The Emerging Voices of Iranian Women Writers* (Syracuse: Syracuse University Press, 1992), p. 209.
2 Ibid., p. 202.
3 Ibid., p. 46.
4 Ibid.
5 Ibid.
6 Ibid., p. 201.
7 Haleh Esfandiari, *Reconstructed Lives: Women and Iran's Islamic revolution* (Washington, DC: John Hopkins University Press, 1997), p. 1.
8 Geoffrey Nash, *Writing Muslim Identity* (New York: Continuum, 2012), p. 56.
9 For an analysis of the reasons for this popularity see Kamran Talattof, *The Politics of Writing in Iran* (Syracuse, NY: Syracuse University Press, 2000), Chs 4 and 5.
10 Azar Nafisi, *Things I've been Silent About* (New York: Random House, 2010), p. xxi.
11 Suzette Henke, *Shattered Subjects: Trauma and Testimony in Women's Life-writing* (New York: St. Martin's Press, 2000), p. xii.
12 Ibid.
13 Kelly Oliver, *Witnessing: Beyond Recognition* (London: University of Minnesota Press, London, 2001), p. 7.
14 Ibid.
15 Gillian Whitlock, *Soft Weapons: Autobiography in Transit* (Chicago: University of Chicago Press, 2007), p. 16.
16 Ibid., p. 11.
17 Gillian Whitlock, 'From Tehran to Tehrangeles: The Generic Fix of Diasporic Iranian Memoirs', *ARIEL* 39 (1–2) (2008), p. 80.
18 Azar Nafisi, *Reading Lolita in Tehran* (New York: Fourth Estate, 2004), p. 76.
19 Ibid., p. 77.
20 Whitlock, 'From Tehran to Tehrangeles', p. 80.
21 Sousan Azadi, *Out of Iran: One Woman's Escape from the Ayatollahs* (London: Macdonald, 1987), p. 1.
22 Henke, *Shattered Subjects,* p. xvi.
23 Eve Zibart, 2004, 'The Power of the Word: An Iranian writer recalls her youth in "The Land of No"', *Book Page*, available at http://bookpage.com/review/journey-from-the-land-of-no/the-power-of-the-word [accessed November 2014].
24 Ibid.
25 Marina Nemat, *Prisoner of Tehran* (New York: Free Press, 2008), p. 1.
26 Ibid., pp. 1–2.

27 Paul Sheehan, 'The unattainable feminist dream', *Sydney Morning Herald*, 28 May
    2007, available at http://www.smh.com.au/news/opinion/the-unattainable-feminist-
    dream/2007/05/27/1180205070029.html [accessed 12 March 2011].
28 Nemat, *Prisoner of Tehran*, p. 2.
29 Oliver, *Witnessing*, p. 8.
30 Milani, *Veils and Words*, p. 212.
31 Ibid.
32 See her interview with Keira Butler, 'Thirty days in Iran's worst prison', *Mother Jones*,
    available at http://motherjones.com/politics/2008/01/thirty-days-irans-worst-prison
    [accessed 5 March 2009].
33 Nemat, *Prisoner of Tehran*, p. 212.
34 Ibid., p. 3.
35 Ibid., p. 4.
36 Ibid., p. 3.
37 Ibid., p. 301.
38 Whitlock, 'From Tehran to Tehrangeles', p. 81.
39 Stephen Kaufman, 'Iranian women in exile finding voices through literature', *Payvand
    News Iran*, 6 July 2006, available at http://www.payvand.com/news/06/nov/1079.html
    [accessed 9 July 2006].
40 Amal Amireh and Lisa Suhair Majaj, *Going Global: The Transnational Reception of
    Third World Women Writers* (New York: Garland, 2001), p. 2.

References

Amireh, A. and L. S. Majaj, *Going Global: The Transnational Reception of Third World
    Women Writers*, New York: Garland, 2001.
Azadi, S., *Out of Iran: One Woman's Escape from the Ayatollahs*, London: Macdonald,
    1987.
Butler, K., 'Thirty days in Iran's worst prison', *Mother Jones*, available at http://motherjones.
    com/politics/2008/01/thirty-days-irans-worst-prison [accessed 5 March 2009].
Esfandiari, H., *Reconstructed Lives: Women and Iran's Islamic Revolution*, Washington,
    DC: John Hopkins University Press, 1997.
Gharamani, Z., *My Life as a Traitor*, New York: Farrar, Straus, and Giroux, 2008.
Hakakian, R., *Journey from the Land of No*, Auckland: Bantam, 2004.
Henke, S., *Shattered Subjects: Trauma and Testimony in Women's Life-writing*, New York:
    St. Martin's Press, 2000.
Kaufman, S., 'Iranian women in exile finding voices through literature', *Payvand News
    Iran*, 6 July 2006, available at http://www.payvand.com/news/06/nov/1079.html
    [accessed 9 July 2006].
Latifi, A., *Even After all this Time: A Story of Love, Revolution, and Leaving Iran*, New
    York: Ragen Books, 2005.
Milani, F., *Veils and Words: The Emerging Voices of Iranian Women Writers*. Syracuse, NY:
    Syracuse University Press, 1992.
Milani, F., *Words Not Swords: Iranian Women Writers and the Freedom of Movement*,
    Syracuse, NY: Syracuse University Press, 2011.
Nafisi, A., *Reading Lolita in Tehran*, New York: Fourth Estate, 2004.

Nafisi, A., *Things I've been Silent About*, New York: Random House, 2010.

Nash, G., *Writing Muslim Identity: The Construction of Identity*, London: Continuum, 2012.

Nemat, M., *Prisoner of Tehran*, New York: Freedom Books, 2008.

Oliver, K., *Witnessing: Beyond Recognition*, London: University of Minnesota Press, 2001.

Serov, B., *Under a Starless Sky: A Family's Escape from Tehran*, Sydney: Hachette Livre, 2008.

Sheehan, P., 'The Unattainable Feminist Dream,' *Sydney Morning Herald*, 28 May 2007, available at http://www.smh.com.au/news/opinion/the-unattainable-feminist-dream/2007/05/27/1180205070029.html [accessed 12 March 2011].

Talattof, K., *The Politics of Writing in Iran: A History of Modern Persian Literature*. Syracuse, NY: Syracuse University Press, 2000.

Whitlock, G., *Soft Weapons: Autobiography in Transit*. Chicago: University of Chicago Press, 2007.

Whitlock, G., 'From Tehran to Tehrangeles: The Generic Fix of Diasporic Iranian Memoirs', *ARIEL*, 39 (1–2) (2008): 7–27.

Zibart, E., 'The Power of the Word: An Iranian writer recalls her youth in "The Land of No"', *Book Page* (2004), available at http://bookpage.com/review/journey-from-the-land-of-no/the-power-of-the-word [accessed March 2006].

15

Egypt's Facebook Revolution: Arab Diaspora Literature and Censorship in the Homeland

Jumana Bayeh

This chapter explores the role of literary texts in the 2011 Egyptian uprising against President Hosni Mubarak. It illustrates the importance of literature to the revolution and questions the assumed centrality of new media forms like Facebook and Twitter. In the period of Egypt's republic, from the time of President Nasser's rule in the 1950s to President Mubarak's fall, literature was the space where resistance to the regime could be maintained, and this was because, unlike the work of journalists, the work of writers and artists remained largely free of state censorship, interference and monitoring. However, the focus on the role of digital media during the uprising has led many commentators to overlook the importance of literature. This is evident in the terms used to describe the revolutions. *The Guardian*'s Middle East editor, Ian Black, characterized the Arab Spring as '[s]pontaneous, unforseen and contagious … [It] took everyone by surprise'.[1] Alain Badiou argues that such characteristics of spontaneity and surprise explain why the recent events in the Arab world should not be referred to simply as 'revolts' or 'revolutions'. They are, in his assessment, better described as '*uprisings*' because this term implicitly registers the Arab people's abrupt transition from inertia to action. As Badiou argues, '*The inexistent has arisen* [*L'inexistant est relevé*] … people [who] were [once] lying down, submissive … were [now] getting up, picking themselves up, rising up'.[2] Alongside 'uprising', the not-too-dissimilar term 'awakening' was also deployed. *The Economist* editorialized that Egypt, Tunisia, Libya and Syria were undergoing nothing short of an 'awakening', exemplified by a new, youthful generation that had 'suddenly found its voice' and had just as spontaneously 'become intoxicated with the possibility of change'.[3] This seemed all the more unexpected because it occurred in 'a region that had [for years] rotted under repression' where people 'felt doomed' and had 'long despaired about the possibility of change'.[4]

Such spontaneity and the demand for swift change are seen to have been facilitated and accelerated by new social media platforms. Ease of access to these media forms for a large number of activists, especially the ability to immediately broadcast information, along with the short-text format of applications like Facebook and Twitter, are cited as factors that align with the speed and impromptu nature of the uprisings.[5]

This is why, as literary critic Julian Murphet observes, '[v]irtually every liberal media pundit tried to convert the revolution into another episode in the conquest of the world by digital technology',[6] and why the revolution in Egypt was quickly dubbed the 'Facebook Revolution'. Most assessments of this revolution have focused on how the Internet helped an array of Egyptian activists, like Zyad el-Elaimy, Walid Rachid and the so-called hero of the Egyptian revolution, Wael Ghonim, to organize what was deemed a leaderless uprising. Halim Rane and Sumra Salem, scholars of media and the international relations of the Middle East, argue exactly this, suggesting that social media, particularly Facebook, were vital because they 'enabled protestors to function as citizen journalists by disseminating information about the protests and transmitting news'.[7] Likewise, Philip Howard and Muzammil Hussain (professors of global media and public policy) stress that without digital technology 'virtual networks' would not have transformed with such speed into masses of people on the streets. Noting the impact of new social media in Egypt specifically, Howard and Hussain stress that such technologies became 'tools' in the hands of activists that 'not only set off a cascade of civil disobedience across Egypt, but made for a unique means of civic organising'.[8]

While such observations regarding the organizational capacity of digital technology may seem innocuous, for media and communications scholar Miriyam Aouragh they are politically charged. This is because it is the Internet and its affiliated forms of digital technology, rather than the Arab people, that have been deemed not only to have facilitated the revolution but also to have provoked the Arab awakening.[9] Howard's and Hussain's study of the role of digital technology during the uprisings exemplifies this view. While their work notes that the discontent expressed by many Egyptians during the revolution was not 'ready-made but [had to] gestate' for years, it still insists that in 'the last few years, this gestation process has gone forward via new media'.[10] Sociologists Xiaolin Zhuo, Barry Wellman and Justine Yu express a similar view but in more strident terms. While they, like Howard and Hussain, argue that it was 'clear that social media such as Facebook played important roles in transforming … informal networks' into organized activism, they also insist that without the use of digital media Egyptian society would not have 'develop[ed] the sense of modernity' required.[11] Modernity is aligned with the West by these writers and counterpoised with 'tradition'. As they state, 'much like Western societies, parts of Egyptian society are transforming away from traditional groups and towards more loosely structured [modern forms of] "networked individualism"' that are facilitated by online inter-action.[12] From the perspective of Zhuo, Wellman and Yu, it was Facebook and, more generally, digital media that allowed Egypt to evolve from its pre-modern or traditional ways to a modern and politically-active society.

This is not the first time that Egypt has been seen to have entered the modern period thanks to the introduction of a Western-invented form of media technology. In *Colonising Egypt*, Timothy Mitchell writes about the arrival of the printing press to Egypt in 1798, during Napoleon's short-lived occupation of Egypt, when French Orientalists installed the first Arabic printing press in the Middle East. The signifi-cance of this, from a contemporary perspective, is not so much that the French were able 'to conquer Egypt with a printing press' but more that 'the absence of printing over the preceding centuries has often been cited as evidence of the backwardness and isolation of the Arab world'.[13] Given that in the twenty-first century the printing press has been superseded by newer forms of technology, it is social media that Egypt now needs to acquire in order to embrace modernity. According to Zhuo, Wellman and Yu, it is no surprise that the youth who led the uprising 'pronounced themselves as "the Facebook generation"', signifying 'that they were no longer the pre-modern Egyptians of the past'.[14] Pre-modern Egyptians supposedly accepted their marginalization from the political process, the control of all forms of media and the oppressive measures practiced by the state. Modern Egyptians, however, used social media 'to establish an alternative public sphere' that neither the state nor the Mubarak regime could effectively control.[15]

It is widely assumed that Egypt's contemporary history is marked by the censorship of all forms of media, starting with newspapers and later extending to radio and television. But this censorship did not go unchallenged. Ghada Talhami, a professor of politics, tracks this history of censorship and notes that Egypt's presidents were 'often … locked in a confrontational embrace' with the media and press establishment because the latter 'championed campaigns of anti-censorship laws'.[16] Egypt's first two presidents, Gamal Abdel Nasser and Anwar al-Sadat, exercised their control over the media in different ways. Nasser's predominant approach was to appoint newspaper editors and journalists who were favourable to his regime's political views. His direct interference was made possible by the 1956 constitution, which gave the president, as head of the executive branch, greater powers than the legislative arm of the state, allowing him to assert his authority while simultaneously maintaining the illusion of a separation of powers. Nasser was therefore able, as journalism professor Orayb Aref Najjar suggests, to 'insist that the press was free' even as 'he was censoring certain types of speech', particularly speech that did not conform 'to the socialist system he had created'.[17]

While Sadat also appointed editors he favoured to prominent positions, he was more inclined to exercise his control of the press through legislated regulation. This may seem unlikely given that his presidency was marked by a general atmosphere of liberalization, in which the 1980 constitution recognized the press as 'the Fourth Estate', designating it independent and free of government interference.[18] Despite this, in practice freedom for journalistic reporting was not realized, nor the separation between press and state. Various clauses were added to the declaration ensuring that the independence of the press could be undermined,[19] Talhami concluding that it 'remained captive to the ruling party'.[20]

This captivity was only reinforced by Mubarak. Like Sadat, Mubarak altered legislation or introduced new laws to ensure he retained a tight grip on the press, but he imposed harsher punishments on journalists if they were found guilty of defamation. In 1996 the Higher Council of the Press was established to monitor news content for defamation against political figures, along with the activities of journalists, the Mubarak government thus awarding itself a degree of power over the press that no previous president had achieved.[21] This was most acutely displayed in relation to the War on Terror. After promising liberalization reforms to reporters between 2001 and

2006, Mubarak exploited the post-9/11 environment and the rhetoric associated with the War on Terror to delay changes, which, at the point of his very public demise in February 2011, had still not been initiated.[22]

This strengthening of press regulation, the appointment of favoured editors to top media positions and the monitoring of news content all converged to strengthen censorship in Egypt. Censorship laws and practices were largely impenetrable to scrutiny and meant that very little public debate could take place within traditional media outlets. But because social media and the Internet did not belong to this 'pre-modern' Egypt, they effectively allowed Egyptian revolutionaries to 'bypass the state control of information and discuss politics and democracy' as well as to organize the uprising.[23] As Murphet suggests, 'while established powers were … [left] napping in old media environments', activists were co-ordinating 'mass events with unprecedented speed' with the help of new media technologies.[24] This is why Howard and Hussain claim that, despite the fact that in 'the Middle East and North Africa, dissent existed long before the Internet', it was nevertheless 'the Internet, mobile phones and social media sites … [that] made the difference' during the events of 2011.[25]

There is little denying that social media was pivotal for the Egyptian uprising. However, it is wrong to assume that it is *only* through new social media that resistance to the severe censorship exercised by the Egyptian regime could be mounted. This fixation with the power of social media and the Internet explains why most critics and scholars, much like Howard and Hussain, fail to explore instances of dissent that were not facilitated by digital technology. Commenting on this oversight, Murphet suggests that we need to study the 'roles different [forms of] media play in the generation and propagation of [revolutionary] ideas'.[26] For Murphet this different media includes the literary texts produced by Egyptian writers like Nawal Saadawi and Naguib Mahfouz.

While the impact of such texts on the Arab Spring is not immediately apparent, an examination of the most popular slogan chanted during the Egyptian uprising illustrates literature's significant role in the revolution. The slogan *ash-shab yurid isqat an-nizam,* or 'the people want to topple the regime', was adapted from the poem 'The Will to Live', written in 1933 by Tunisian-born Abu al-Qasim al-Shabbi, which achieved iconic status in the 1950s as part of an effort to Arabize Tunisia after decades of French colonial rule. For the Egyptians, the 1940s and 1950s were equally marked by struggles against colonialism and so al-Shabbi's poem resonated with the Arab nationalist aspirations of Nasser and his followers. 'The Will to Live' and its opening line, 'If, one day, the people want to live, then fate will answer their call', are, as Elliot Colla explains, 'more than famous' and are 'known by any educated person anywhere in the Arab world'.[27] Its appropriation in the recent uprising demonstrates that literary texts form the basis of the 'deeper ideological saturation of the body politic' that precedes – by decades – the dissemination of wall posts and videos on Facebook.[28] Literature's temporal primacy, as outlined here, exposes one reason why it needs to be examined; it has shaped the language of the revolution. But a more important reason, particularly for Egypt, relates to the degree of autonomy that the State extended to its writers and artists, as opposed to the censorship it exercised against the press. This 'double standard' on the part of the State had, as Arabic literature professor

Richard Jacquemond indicates, 'complicated effects on the literary field and literary production'.[29]

In his book *Conscience of the Nation: Writers, State, and Society in Modern Egypt*, Jacquemond examines these 'complicated effects', establishing that the literary field was intensely political. Because reporters were unable to criticize the state openly, writers responded by bringing 'debates that could not take place freely in the political field into the cultural field under a different guise'.[30] This 'different guise' ranged from masking criticism of the state behind allegory, metaphor and poetic language, to publically defending a right to free speech. For Samia Mehrez, professor of Arabic literature, the masking of criticism calls into question the supposed independence of writers that Jacquemond stresses, however. Mehrez argues that the modern Egyptian state has been responsible for producing the literary establishment – what she refers to as the 'secular literati'.[31] This group has always 'been historically dominated by the political field and [has] consistently been dependent on it for status and power'.[32] Such dependence explains why writers felt compelled to temper their criticism but it does not mean that every writer was wedded to the state. Though Jacquemond concedes that some writers, like the celebrated author Mahfouz, cultivated close relations with ministries of culture and sought special permissions to release potentially controversial work, this did not negate the fact that 'literary writing ... was an important channel for political and social criticism'.[33] In fact for many writers 'literature and literary criticism [were viewed] as substitutes for political action or natural extensions of it'.[34]

In such an environment it comes as no surprise that Egypt's cultural scene, from the 1950s to Mubarak's fall in 2011, contained an abundance of dissident and politically-engaged writers, poets and artists, with the Nobel laureate Naguib Mahfouz a notable example. While some argue that his criticism of the regime was compromised by his close ties to it, most of his novels address controversial issues like political corruption and the failure of political leaders to address the declining socio-economic conditions. *Midaq Alley* (1966) and *The Cairo Trilogy* (1956–7) showcase the harsh political and social conditions that afflict destitute Egyptians and lay the blame for these conditions at the feet of the ruling elite.[35] The novels of Saadawi are just as politically engaged, with particular emphasis on Egypt's patriarchal system. Her most famous title, *Woman at Point Zero* (1975), explores the question of women's freedom in a male-dominated society by focusing on the life of one character, Firdaus, sentenced to death for murdering her pimp. Despite being offered an opportunity to appeal for clemency, Firdaus refuses to do so on the grounds that she has committed no crime, and explains her position by narrating her life-story, defined by poverty and prostitution. Having worked as a high-end prostitute for Egypt's political elite, Firdaus recounts the crimes of the very men that have condemned her to death. She 'spit[s] with ease on [these men's] lying faces ... on their lying newspaper [stories about her]' and elects to face death rather than engage with a system that defines her as a criminal.[36] Such sharp critiques of Egypt's political class earned Saadawi the ire of President Sadat. In 1981 she was imprisoned by him for committing crimes against the state and not released until after his assassination later that year.

While Mahfouz and Saadawi expressed their political views in their literary work, two of their contemporaries, Sheikh Imam Issa and Ahmad Fouad Nigm, did so through music and poetry. In the 1960s and 1970s, Imam and Nigm worked together (the former composing the music for the latter's protest poems), and were considered the icons of political dissent. Their fame was cemented after the 1967 war, when Arab armies were overpowered by Israel. Disillusioned by defeat, Egyptians formed what Marilyn Booth describes as 'a broad, loud, and student-led critique of the Nasser regime' aided by 'the force of a symbiotic artistic partnership' between Imam and Nigm.[37] Pieces like *al-Hamdu lillah* (1967; '*Thanks to God*') and *Is-Samt* (1968; '*Silence*') took aim at Nasser's regime for its lack of self-critique. These songs became anthems for protesting Egyptians and were highly popular among students and unionized workers. After 1967, the lyrics and music of this duo continued to accompany instances of civil unrest and protest, like the student-dominated uprising in 1972 and the bread riots in 1977. Although their artistic output ended in the mid-1980s, Imam and Nigm continue to serve as inspiration for numerous Egyptian writers and artists. This is evident in the establishment of the Writers and Artists for Change movement in 2005, when various high-profile writers and artists gathered to hear Nigm deliver the movement's founding statement, which stressed the long-standing role of Egyptian writers and artists as agitators for political change. The statement called for an array of reforms, including the democratization of the political system, and linked this to the movement's demand for the end of censorship practiced against writers, artists and academics. Accord to Mehrez, the statement's position echoes the very sentiments and political ideals conveyed in the earliest pieces by Imam and Nigm.[38]

Mahfouz, Saadawi, Imam and Nigm represent only four of many politically-engaged artists in Egypt. Others include Sonallah Ibrahim and Yusuf Idris, as well as more contemporary figures such as Alaa al-Aswany. Like the artists discussed above, the work of these writers is politically charged and further illustrates how political resistance has been intrinsic to Egyptian literature. Moreover, what is notable is that all of these artists reside in Egypt, and have successfully exploited the freedom extended to them by the state or found ways to circumvent censorship laws. Given this, their participation in the push for reform in modern Egypt is undoubtedly significant. And yet, as already noted, their contribution has barely featured in the assessments of the 2011 uprising by communications experts and journalists. Interestingly, where the contribution of these artists and writers is best acknowledged and actively documented is in the current literary work of Egyptian and Arab diasporic writers. Although they are displaced from their homeland and publish their work in their countries of settlement, Egypt's diaspora writers, such as Leila Aboulela, Leila Ahmed, Samia Serageldin and Ahdaf Soueif, remain invested in the cultural and political history of their homeland and compose stories that engage with events that occur there. As most of these writers have settled in the Anglophone world they write in English and are therefore well placed to communicate to readers beyond the Arab world.

Diaspora writers can describe or, as Waïl Hassan suggests, culturally 'translate' the political, social and cultural history of the homeland within their English-language novels. Hassan notes that authors in this category straddle two geographical spaces and are fluent in two, if not more, languages: by being both 'of the "Orient" by virtue of their background ... [and] of the "Occident" by reason of immigration' these Arab immigrant writers are able to interpret their original culture to their readers.[39] Layla Al Maleh extends Hassan's notion of 'cultural translation' by suggesting that these writers also produce literature that is necessarily and consciously informative for its Western readership. Al Maleh asserts that novels written by Arabs in English function as a '*medium* through which [readers] can gain better knowledge of the intellectual and spiritual make-up of Arabs'.[40] She compares literary texts with more traditional forms of media and concludes that 'literary works ... offer plausible interpretation and humanization of Arabs better than journalism ... or political memoir'.[41]

While many Egyptian diaspora authors are engaged in writing novels that represent the homeland in the way Al Maleh and Hassan outline, the London-based writer Ahdaf Soueif has been most prominent in recent years. During the Egyptian revolution, Soueif's articles and media appearances became a regular fixture in *The Guardian* and on BBC news programs. Her views were widely accessible on the Internet and were dispersed across the Anglophone world through broadcast and print syndication. Since 2011, Soueif has also delivered numerous public lectures addressing Egypt's revolution and has published a memoir of the uprising titled *Cairo: My City, Our Revolution* (2012). Despite being hailed by the *London Review of Books* as 'a political analyst and commentator of the best kind', Soueif is primarily a writer of fiction. Well before she became *The Guardian*'s political commentator, Soueif had published several works of fiction, the most substantial being her two novels, *In the Eye of the Sun* (1992) and *The Map of Love* (1999). These have contributed significantly to her profile in the West, particularly *The Map of Love*, which was shortlisted for the Man Booker Prize in 1999 and has been translated into over 20 languages. Soueif's newspaper articles are significant because they document the uprising's events as they unfolded in Cairo, but it is her novels that are indispensable to anyone trying to make deeper sense of the uprisings, because they outline the conditions and issues that preceded the events in early 2011.

This is done in two key ways: first, Soueif incorporates cultural works by various Egyptian and Arab artists extensively within her novels and, second, she deploys Arabic in her English-language texts in highly distinctive, even unique ways. While the former approach interweaves references to Egyptian cultural and literary production, the latter is a form of linguistic appropriation. These different approaches are nonetheless united by the same goals: not just to translate aspects of the Arabic language and Egyptian cultural work and life to an English-reading audience, but also to showcase how this language use and cultural output are necessarily political acts and committed to resisting oppression. The following two examples demonstrate this. The first, from *In the Eye of the Sun*, records the lyrics written by Nigm and performed by Sheikh Imam. In the scene the central character, Asya al-Ulama, residing in northern England while completing her doctoral thesis, attempts to explain Nigm's lyrics to several English friends but finds herself unable to do so by merely translating the words. The lyrics, as sung by Sheikh Imam, are concerned with the impact of

President Nixon's foreign policy on the Arab world. From the song's very opening line – 'Sharrafat ya Nixon Baba, Ya bta' el-Watergate' – Asya finds herself struggling to translate without also explaining the political context of the 1970s when the song was released, the multiple meanings of the words and the signification of those meanings. As the passage below demonstrates, it proves impossible to translate the song without resorting to laboured explanations:

> "You've honoured us, Nixon Baba" – "Baba" means "father" but it is also used, as it is used here, as a title of mock respect – as in "Ali Baba" … but the thing is you could also address a child as "Baba" as an endearment – a sort of inversion: like calling him Big Chief because he is so little – and so when it's used aggressively … it carries a … belittling signification … "You've honoured us Nixon/ O you of Watergate".[42]

This difficulty in translation continues with the next couplet: 'Amaloulak eema w seema/ Salateen el-fool wez-zeit'.

> 'Ok well,' Asya takes a deep breath. "'Eema" is "worth" or "value". So he says, "They made an eema for you": to make an "eema" for someone is to behave towards them as though they have value when they in fact have none. So, "They've put on a show that gives you value" – "seema" is always used as an idiom with "eema" because of the rhyme. It means appearance. So: "the appearance of a thing of value".[43]

These opening three lines are scathingly critical of Nixon but Sheikh Imam's and Nigm's strongest criticism and ridicule are reserved for those who are giving Nixon the appearance of value, in this case the Arab leaders. The second line of the couplet, 'Salateen el-fool wez-zeit' expresses this.

> 'The Sultans of "fool" and "zeit". "Fool" – that is one thing that everybody knows about Egypt – that "fool" is the basic diet of Egyptians. Particularly those from the more traditional or poorer sectors of society … It's brown beans stewed for a long time over a very low fire. It's the cheapest food you can get, and so to be a "sultan" of "fool" argues massive poverty and backwardness. This "fool" can be dressed in various ways. The simplest and cheapest is with oil – "zeit" – and lemon. So "fool" and "zeit" come together – but "zeit" also, like "oil" in English, means petrol oil. So if you take that meaning, then there are two categories of "Sultan" being referred to: the sultans of "fool" and poverty etc. and the sultans of wealth and oil.'[44]

Asya's act of translation continues for about five more pages in the novel, revealing not just the complexity of the Arabic language and its cultures but also the overt and sophisticated forms of political resistance that dominated the Egyptian cultural scene in the 1960s and 1970s.

The second example is taken from Soueif's second novel *The Map of Love* and showcases the author's ability, as a trained linguist, to explore the intricacies of Arabic grammar. *The Map of Love* interweaves two plotlines from different fin-de-siècle periods. The first is set at the end of the nineteenth century and details Egyptian nationalist resistance to British occupation. The second takes place at the end of the twentieth century and focuses on a modern form of imperialism – American-imposed neo-liberalism.[45] While the novel is replete with cross-lingual references, one particular scene connects the issue of political resistance, as a key feature of *The Map of Love*'s two plotlines, with the Arabic language. Here the novel's American character, Isabel Parkman, is given a short Arabic lesson by her distant relative, the protagonist Amal al-Khalidi. Amal explains that, in the Arabic language:

> 'Everything stems from a root. And the root is mostly made up of three consonants – or two. And then the word takes different forms. Take the root q-l-b, qalb. Qalb: the heart, the heart that beats, the heart at the heart of things. Then there's a set number of forms – a template almost – that any root can take. So in the case of "qalb" you get "qalab": to overturn, overthrow, turn upside down, make into the opposite, hence "maqlab" a dirty trick, a turning of the tables and also a rubbish-dump. "Maqloub": upside-down, "mutaqallib": changeable and "inqilab": a coup – So at the heart of all things is the germ of their overthrow, the closer you are to the heart, the closer to the reversal. Nowhere to go but down. You reach the core and then you're blown away'.[46]

By including this detailed explanation of the inner workings of Arabic, Soueif demonstrates that resistance is deeply embedded within the language itself. In that sense she reclaims, even if anachronistically, revolutionary action, or the 'Arab awakening', for Egypt and its own literary history.

These two examples from Soueif's work illuminate the centrality of literature and language to the Egyptian uprising. Text messages, wall posts on Facebook and pithy Tweets certainly represent social media's ability to circumvent Egypt's harsh censorship measures, but the censorious nature of the regime has a longer history than the digital age we currently inhabit. That history, despite Mubarak's overthrow, remains a part of Egypt today. The current military-led government has, by many assessments, sharpened its focus on the media well beyond the censorship practices of the outgoing regime.[47] News stories are heavily monitored and journalists, both Egyptian and foreign reporters working within Egypt, are targeted by the state with a new level of brutality. It is indeed a bitter irony that approximately 150 Egyptian writers publicly supported the military counter-coup against the democratically elected Muslim Brotherhood.[48] Despite the irony, what this means is that the censorship of the press that compelled Egypt's artistic practitioners to take up deeply political questions, off-limits for traditional media outlets, is likely to re-emerge. It is for this reason that the literature composed by Egypt's writers, rather than Facebook, Twitter and other forms of digital technology, needs to be carefully and actively examined. As a diaspora writer, Ahdaf Soueif has acted as a 'cultural translator', incorporating the work of Egyptian-based artists and explaining the inner workings of the Arabic language within her English-language novels. In doing so she conveys to her Western readership the long history and nuanced forms of resistance that exist in a country like Egypt.

Notes

1 Ian Black, 'Introduction', in T. Manhire (ed.), *The Arab Spring: Rebellion, Revolution and a New World Order* (London: Guardian Books, 2012), p. vii.
2 Alain Badiou, *The Rebirth of History: Times of Riots and Uprisings* (trans. G. Elliott) (London: Verso, 2012), p. 56; author's italics.
3 Editorial, 'The Awakening', *The Economist*, 17 February 2011, available at http://www.economist.com/node/18180416 [accessed 28 November 2013], para. 3.
4 Ibid.
5 See, for instance, Julian Murphet, 'Forget Twitter and Facebook, Literature Provides the Revolutionary Spark', *The Conversation*, 11 April 2011, available at http://theconversation.com/forget-twitter-and-facebook-literature-provides-the-revolutionary-spark-501 [accessed 21 November 2013], para. 3 and Philip N. Howard and Muzammil M. Hussain, 'The Role of Digital Media', *Journal of Democracy*, 22 (3) (2011): 35–6.
6 Murphet, 'Forget Twitter and Facebook', para. 4.
7 Halim Rane and Sumra Salem, 'Social Media, Social Movements and the Diffusion of Ideas in the Arab Uprisings', *Journal of International Communication*, 18 (1) (2012): p. 103.
8 Howard and Hussain, 'The Role of Digital Media', p. 39.
9 Miriyam Aouragh, 'Facebook Revolution? Social Media as Orientalist Mediator', paper delivered at *The Egyptian Revolution, One Year On* (Oxford University), 25 May 2011, 10:50mins.
10 Howard and Hussain, 'The Role of Digital Media', p. 41.
11 Xiaolin Zhuo, Barry Wellman and Justine Yu, 'Egypt: The First Internet Revolt?', *Peace Magazine* (Jul–Sept 2011), available at http://peacemagazine.org/archive/v27n3p06.htm [accessed 30 September 2013], para. 2.
12 Zhuo, Wellman and Yu, 'Egypt', para. 3.
13 Timothy Mitchell, *Colonising Egypt* (Berkeley: University of California Press, 1988), p. 133.
14 Zhuo, Wellman and Yu, 'Egypt', para. 15.
15 Zhuo, Wellman and Yu, 'Egypt', para. 16.
16 Ghada Talhami, *Palestine in the Egyptian Press: From al-Ahram to al-Ahali*, (Plymouth: Lexington Books, 2007), p. 278. For further details on censorship prior to 1952, including British imperial attitudes toward freedom of the press in Egypt and the evolution of press censorship during World Wars I and II, see Talhami, *Palestine in the Egyptian Press*, pp. 272–78.
17 Orayb Aref Najjar, 'Media Policy and Law in Egypt and Jordan: Continuities and Changes', in K. Hafez (ed.), *Arab Media: Power and Weaknesses* (New York: Continuum, 2008), p. 225.
18 Talhami, *Palestine in the Egyptian Press*, p. 281.
19 See Talhami, *Palestine in the Egyptian Press*, pp. 281–8 and Najjar, 'Media Policy', pp. 225–6 for further discussion of the 1980 constitution and Sadat's regulation of the press.
20 Talhami, *Palestine in the Egyptian Press*, p. 288.
21 Najjar, 'Media Policy', p. 227.
22 Najjar, 'Media Policy', p. 228; Augustus Richard Norton, 'The New Media, Civic Pluralism, and the Struggle for Political Reform', in D. F. Eickelman and J. W.

Anderson (eds), *New Media and the Muslim World: The Emerging Public Sphere,* (Bloomington, IN: Indiana University Press, 1999), p. 30.

23 Zhuo, Wellman and Yu, 'Egypt', para. 16.

24 Murphet, 'Forget Twitter and Facebook', para. 3.

25 Howard and Hussain, 'The Role of Digital Media', p. 35.

26 Murphet, 'Forget Twitter and Facebook', para. 7.

27 Elliot Colla, 'The People Want', *Middle East Research and Information Project* 263 (2012), available at http://www.merip.org/mer/mer263/people-want [accessed 1 December 2013], para. 12.

28 Murphet, 'Forget Twitter and Facebook', para. 9.

29 Richard Jacquemond, *Conscience of the Nation: Writers, State, and Society in Modern Egypt* (trans. D. Tresilian), (Cairo: American University of Cairo, 2008), p. 35.

30 Jacquemond, *Conscience of the Nation*, pp. 35–6.

31 Samia Mehrez, *Egypt's Culture Wars: Politics and Practice* (London: Routledge, 2008), p. 9.

32 Mehrez, *Egypt's Culture Wars*, p. 9.

33 Jacquemond, *Conscience of the Nation*, p. 36.

34 Jacquemond, *Conscience of the Nation*, p. 36.

35 Naguib Mahfouz, *Midaq Alley* (trans. T. Le Gassick), (New York: Anchor Books, 1992); *The Cairo Trilogy: Palace Walk, Palace of Desire, Sugar Street* (trans. O. E. Kenny, L. M. Kenny and A. Botros Samaan), (London: Everyman's Library, 2001).

36 Nawal Saadawi, *Woman at Point Zero*, (trans. S. Hatata), (London: Zed Books, 1983), p. 133.

37 Marilyn Booth, 'Exploding into the Seventies: Ahmad Fu'ad Nigm, Shaykh Imam, and the Aesthetics of a New Youth Politics', *Cairo Papers in Social Science*, 29 (2–3) (2009): 19.

38 Mehrez, *Egypt's Culture Wars*, pp. 1–2.

39 Waïl Hassan, *Immigrant Narratives: Orientalism and Cultural Translation in Arab American and Arab British Literature* (New York; Oxford: Oxford University Press, 2011), pp. 32, 28–9.

40 Layla Al Maleh, 'Preface', in L. Al Maleh (ed.), *Arab Voices in Diaspora: Critical Perspectives on Anglophone Arab Literature* (Amsterdam: Rodopi, 2009), p. x.

41 Al Maleh, 'Preface', p. x.

42 Ahdaf Soueif, *In the Eye of the Sun* (London: Bloomsbury, 1992), p. 496.

43 Soueif, *In the Eye of the Sun*, p. 497.

44 Soueif, *In the Eye of the Sun*, pp. 497–8.

45 For information on the impact of neo-liberalism on Egypt and its imposition as a form of economic imperialism see Joel Beinin, 'Underbelly of Egypt's Neoliberal Agenda', *Middle East Research Information Project*, 5 April 2008 and 'Workers' Protest in Egypt: Neo-liberalism and Class Struggle in 21st Century', *Social Movement Studies* 8 (4) (2009), pp. 449–54.

46 Ahdaf Soueif, *The Map of Love*, (London: Bloomsbury, 1999), pp. 81–2.

47 See Emad Shahin, 'Opinions are Dangerous as Egypt Cracks Down on Dissent', *The Conversation*, 7 March 2014, available at http://theconversation.com/opinions-are-dangerous-as-egypt-cracks-down-on-dissent-24039 [accessed 10 September 2014] for an examination of the compromised freedoms Egyptian reporters now face.

48   For details on the implications of this for literary criticism see Elliott Colla, 'Revolution on Ice', *Jadaliyya*, 6 January 2014, available at http://www.jadaliyya.com/pages/index/15874/revolution-on-ice [accessed 31 August 2014].

References

Al Maleh, L., 'Preface', in L. Al Maleh (ed.), *Arab Voices in Diaspora: Critical Perspectives on Anglophone Arab Literature*, Amsterdam: Rodopi, 2009.

Aouragh, M., 'Facebook Revolution? Social Media as Orientalist Mediator', paper delivered at The Egyptian Revolution, One Year On (Oxford University), 25 May 2011.

Badiou, A., *The Rebirth of History: Times of Riots and Uprisings* (trans. G. Elliott), London: Verso, 2012.

Beinin, J., 'Underbelly of Egypt's Neoliberal Agenda', *Middle East Research Information Project*, 272 (2008), available at http://www.merip.org/mero/mero040508 [accessed 1 December 2013].

Beinin, J., 'Workers' Protest in Egypt: Neo-liberalism and Class Struggle in 21st Century', *Social Movement Studies*, 8 (4) (2009): 449–54.

Black, I., 'Introduction', in T. Manhire (ed.), *The Arab Spring: Rebellion, Revolution and a New World Order*, London: Guardian Books, 2012.

Booth, M., 'Exploding into the Seventies: Ahmad Fu'ad Nigm, Shaykh Imam, and the Aesthetics of a New Youth Politics', *Cairo Papers in Social Science*, 29 (2–3) (2009): 19–44.

Colla, E., 'The People Want', *Middle East Research and Information Project*, 263 (2012), available at http://www.merip.org/mer/mer263/people-want [accessed 1 December 2013].

Colla, E., 'Revolution on Ice', *Jadaliyya* (2014), available at http://www.jadaliyya.com/pages/index/15874/revolution-on-ice [accessed 31 August 2014].

Editorial, 'The Awakening', *The Economist*, 17 February 2011, available at http://www.economist.com/node/18180416 [accessed 28 November 2013].

Hassan, W., *Immigrant Narratives: Orientalism and Cultural Translation in Arab American and Arab British Literature*, New York; Oxford: Oxford University Press, 2011.

Howard, P. N. and M. H. Hussein, 'The Role of Digital Media', *Journal of Democracy*, 22.3 (2011): 35–48.

Jacquemond, R., *Conscience of the Nation: Writers, State, and Society in Modern Egypt* (trans. D. Tresilian), Cairo: American University of Cairo, 2008.

Mahfouz, N., *Midaq Alley* (trans. Trevor Le Gassick), New York: Anchor Books, 1992.

Mahfouz, N., *The Cairo Trilogy: Palace Walk, Palace of Desire, Sugar Street* (trans. O. E. Kenny, L. M. Kenny and A. Botros Samaan), London: Everyman's Library, 2001.

Mehrez, S., *Egypt's Culture Wars: Politics and Practice*, London: Routledge, 2008.

Mitchell, T., *Colonising Egypt*, Berkeley: University of California Press, 1988.

Murphet, J., 'Forget Twitter and Facebook, Literature Provides the Revolutionary Spark', *The Conversation*, 11 April 2011, available at http://theconversation.com/forget-twitter-and-facebook-literature-provides-the-revolutionary-spark-501 [accessed 21 November 2013].

Najjar, O. A., 'Media Policy and Law in Egypt and Jordan: Continuities and Changes', in K. Hafez (ed.), *Arab Media: Power and Weaknesses*, New York: Continuum, 2008.

Norton, A. R., 'The New Media, Civic Pluralism, and the Struggle for Political Reform', in D. F. Eickelman and J. W. Anderson (eds), *New Media and the Muslim World: The Emerging Public Sphere*, Bloomington, IN: Indiana University Press, 1999.

Rane, H. and S. Salem, 'Social Media, Social Movements and the Diffusion of Ideas in the Arab Uprisings', *Journal of International Communication*, 18 (1) (2012): 97–111.

Saadawi, N., *Woman at Point Zero* (trans. S. Hatata), London: Zed Books, 1983.

Shahin, E., 'Opinions are Dangerous as Egypt Cracks Down on Dissent', *The Conversation*, 7 March 2014, available at http://theconversation.com/opinions-are-dangerous-as-egypt-cracks-down-on-dissent-24039 [accessed 10 September 2014].

Soueif, A., *In the Eye of the Sun*, London: Bloomsbury, 1992.

Soueif, A., *The Map of Love*, London: Bloomsbury, 1999.

Talhami, G., *Palestine in the Egyptian Press: From* al-Ahram *to* al-Ahali, Plymouth: Lexington Books, 2007.

Zhuo, X. and B. Wellman, J. Yu, 'Egypt: The First Internet Revolt?', *Peace Magazine* (Jul–Sept 2011), available at http://peacemagazine.org/archive/v27n3p06.htm [accessed 30 September 2013].

16

China's Elusive Truths: Censorship, Value and Literature in the Internet Age

Lynda Ng

Censorship is usually regarded in a negative light, especially in Western reports on the repressiveness of non-Western regimes. The strict censorship laws in China, for instance, are widely regarded as being in violation of its citizens' rights to freedom of speech, as legislated under Article 19 of the *Universal Declaration of Human Rights*. Nevertheless, totalitarian governments have always recognized the power of literature and, paradoxically, strict and overt censorship laws in a country such as China implicitly attest to literature's capacity to challenge and destabilize the larger regulatory and disciplinary frameworks of a governing State. The number of Chinese dissident writers currently living in exile in the West is a reminder that literature's subversive qualities must be taken seriously.[1] Far from the 'post-transgressive age' posited by Australian commentator Robert Manne, we live in a world where the power of literature to shock, threaten and provoke is alive and well.[2] This is made apparent when we consider the cases of Chinese writers such as Ma Jian or Gao Xingjian, who chose to leave China in the 1980s in order to be able to continue writing, or the more recent case of Liao Yiwu, forced to flee in 2011 without a word to either friends or family on the eve of the German publication of his prison memoir.

The history of English-language censorship makes it clear that anxiety about this potent aspect of literature has not been confined to non-democratic Asian states or totalitarian regimes. In *The Censor's Library*, for instance, Nicole Moore observes that Australia's anti-sedition laws have historically considered the use of language with the purpose of inciting rebellion as tantamount to acts of rebellion. The 1920 *Australian Crimes Act* specifically prohibited 'words or conduct deemed to incite discontent or rebellion against the authority of the state'.[3] Debates over an individual's right to freedom of speech, staunchly protected in the United States under First Amendment law, centre on the degree of correlation that can be drawn between words and actions. Arguments for the preservation of freedom of speech insist that a distinction must be maintained between words and acts, or as law professor Leslie Kendrick phrases it: 'A guilty mind alone is not sufficient to render speech unprotected.'[4] Counter-arguments commonly used to buttress anti-sedition laws contend that in certain cases a direct correspondence can be drawn between the two. In an essay on the nature of seditious harm, Sarah Sorial, a philosopher of law, concludes: 'If it can be shown that seditious speech "enacts permissibility conditions" that make harm legitimate in certain contexts, then it may be misguided to suggest that this type of speech should be protected.'[5] Words, and by extrapolation literature, have power because of their ability to incite or sanction harmful acts.

Despite legal acknowledgement of the potential power of words and literature, repeated truths continue to circulate about the crises of literature and the wider humanities, in the context of homogenizing globalization. Such worries are common to Chinese and Western audiences alike. News articles concerned about the decline of reading in younger generations periodically surface in *The China Daily*. For instance, a 2006 article, titled 'Survey: Fewer Readers, More Books', anxiously proclaimed: 'It appears to be a paradox that at a time when the book and publishing industry is booming, China's number of avid readers is falling.'[6] A more recent article, optimistically titled 'Books Get New Life', contained a pessimistic outlook on the fate of books and reading in China: 'As books become increasingly interactive and more like the Internet and video games, fewer and fewer people will actually read.'[7] Similarly to reporting in the West, these articles associate the value of culture and education with the act of reading books and fear that a decline of reading in younger generations signals a form of cultural degeneration.

On a global level, the humanities have adopted the defensive posture expected of a field under attack. In *The Value of the Humanities* (2013), Helen Small conducts a measured critique of the five main claims commonly made to justify research in the humanities. But she prefaces her volume by querying the reflex impulse underlying such claims: 'The humanities might ideally find justification simply in our doing them. The act of justification has seemed to many humanities scholars to beg more than one question: that the value of their subject area is in question, and that the value is capable of being expressed in the mode of justification.'[8] Small alights here upon the quandary of trying to quantify the value of the humanities, given that the commonly-used economic and capitalist-inflected discourses of value have little capacity to measure the work that the humanities does.

Globalized but not homogenized

Appraising the ways in which censorship interacts with the Internet as a global and globalizing phenomenon reveals the contradictory pressures of local and global at play in the new cultural-political horizon of the twenty-first century. On the one hand, the Internet instantiates a global space – a virtual world free from the bonds and limitations of geography. On the other hand, in this virtual realm the pervasiveness of cultural and national differences becomes unmistakeable. Different versions of 'the Internet' of course exist, depending on the language spoken, and the challenge of finding information within such a vast archive gives significant power to those who control the search engines.

The Chinese government uses a sophisticated combination of techniques to patrol and control online content. There is information-filtering technology capable of blocking overseas sites for users within China, referred to colloquially as the Great Firewall, and individual monitors are assigned to participate and steer conversation in chat rooms.[9] Dissimilar to the West, ISPs, ICPs and cybercafes are directly liable for the content that they distribute. They are legally co-opted into monitoring the content posted through their channels, being obliged to store user data, to remove any posts that contravene the government's guidelines for acceptable content, and to notify the government when this occurs. China's procedures for censorship have been so successful that those who find themselves on the banned list tend to disappear quietly, from a Chinese perspective, into a silent void. Rebecca Mackinnon, co-founder of the independent internet blog and news aggregator *Global Voices*, notes that 'China's Internet censorship is effective enough that most Chinese – even most Chinese Internet users – have not heard of the 48 [currently] jailed Internet writers'.[10] Gao Xingjian's Nobel Prize for Literature in 2000 was not considered a national victory within China because most citizens had never heard of Gao and his work, nor of why he had been in exile for over a decade.[11]

The Chinese government pursues individuals for writing or publishing material that flouts the censorship guidelines, such as in the cases of bloggers and human rights activists Hu Jia or Liu Di, in order to make public examples of them as a warning to others.[12] However, this is not the government's preferred strategy. In Gloria Davies' essay 'Affirming the Human in China', she explains: 'Rather, it is self-censorship that the government seeks to encourage, and this form of censorship is perhaps more insidious and damaging than overt censorship insofar as it fosters deceptive ways of speaking and writing that effectively corrupt the art of human expression itself'.[13] If self-censorship can be enforced, it offers numerous benefits over other forms, foremost of which is the way it avoids drawing attention to the very things which the government wishes to expurgate.

There can be a fine line between the silence or active erasure that censorship aims for, and the publicity or notoriety that state-sanctioned acts of prohibition can generate. Nobel Laureate J. M. Coetzee, who wrote during a time of oppressive censorship in apartheid South Africa, has observed the curious phenomenon that arises when the state exerts strong censorship over literary works: attempting to suppress literature has the unintended consequence of imbuing literature with far more significance and symbolic weight. Coetzee writes that:

> a logic seems to spring into operation that works to the state's disadvantage: the more draconically the state comes down on writing, the more seriously it is seen to be taking writing; the more seriously it is seen to be taking writing, the more attention is paid to writing; the more attention is paid to writing, the more its disseminative power increases. The book that is suppressed today gets twice as much attention tomorrow, precisely because it has been suppressed; the writer who is gagged today is famous tomorrow for having been gagged.[14]

This has certainly been the case for Chinese author Yan Lianke, who has had four of his novels banned over the past two decades. His debut novel, *Xia Riluo (Summer*

Sunset), a story about the ruination of two military heroes, was banned in 1994. In 2004, upon the publication of his political satire *Shou Huo* (*The Joy of Living/Enjoyment*, translated into English as *Lenin's Kisses*), Yan was asked to leave his non-combative position in the People's Liberation Army, even though *Shou Huo* was awarded one of China's top literary prizes, the Lao She. Then, in 2005, two more of Yan Lianke's novels were banned – *Wei Renmin Fuwu* (translated as *Serve the People*) and *Ding Zhuang Meng* (translated as *Dream of Ding Village*). The former is a satire set during the Cultural Revolution, featuring a couple who prove their love for each other (and attain sexual arousal) by destroying icons of Chairman Mao. The latter, a striking showcase for Yan's self-termed 'mythical-realist' style, depicts government corruption as a primary factor in expediting the AIDS epidemic for commercial blood donors in rural China.[15] Attempts by the mainland Chinese government to censor these last three novels prompted the media in Hong Kong and Taiwan to take up Yan Lianke's case, guaranteeing an audience and commercial viability for his work both inside and outside mainland China's borders. Yan's refusal to shy away from politically sensitive material in his fiction has played a large role in raising his international profile. It can be no coincidence that these three banned novels are currently the only ones to be translated into English; the fourth banned novel, *Si Shu* (*Four Books*), is banned in mainland China but was published in Hong Kong in 2010, and is due to be published in English translation too, in 2015.

Dream of Ding Village found publication in Hong Kong in 2006 and was translated into English in 2011. The novel is set in Yan's home province of Henan, one of the areas most affected by the AIDS epidemic, which spread in the 1990s through shoddy and unregulated blood collection practices. This is a disaster clearly close to Yan's heart, and the novel was written in order to publicize the plight of those caught up in the epidemic. Raising awareness about AIDS is important in a country where huge stigma still exists around what was formerly regarded as a 'foreigner's disease'. Yan has admitted consciously practising self-censorship in the hopes of circumventing the censors. In a 2006 interview with *The Guardian* he regretfully described curtailing his ambitions and eliminating references to an international blood trade where blood was pumped through underground pipelines from China to wealthy consumers in the United States. 'This is not the book I originally wanted to write,' he told his interviewer. 'I censored myself very rigourously. I didn't mention senior leaders. I reduced the scale. I thought my self-censorship was perfect.'[16] But the bowdlerized version still proved too controversial for the Chinese government, which refused its sale and distribution.

The novel's overseas success may explain a reversal in Yan Lianke's own opinion about the book. While in earlier interviews he lamented having practised self-censorship, considering it was banned anyway, by 2007 Yan was able to speak with pride about the novel's accomplishments. To interviewer Mary-Anne Toy, he declared: 'It is a genuine literal record of what happened in the early twenty-first century in China and through this work, the descendants of the Chinese nation can see what kind of disaster happened in China at that time.'[17] In the longer-run, the publicity generated by censorship helped Yan fulfil his initial aim of drawing attention to the AIDS epidemic in rural China. The publication of his banned novels in the Hong Kong and Taiwanese markets has kept these texts in circulation for Chinese readers and also made him one of China's most well-known authors, both inside and outside the country. In 2009, Yan Lianke came in at number 20 on the *Changjiang Times* 'China's Top 25 Most Highly Paid Author List', a clearly unintended result of the government's attempts to muzzle him.[18] After translation into English, *Dream of Ding Village* was shortlisted for the Man Asian Literary Prize in 2012, securing an international audience for its author.

Truth in fiction

In a highly-censored society such as China, suspicion naturally dogs narratives that purport to state the truth, for censorship's closest ally is propaganda. Where censorship omits the truth, propaganda manufactures narratives to disguise this omission and replace it. The difficulty in distinguishing truth from fiction in such an environment is illustrated by the 'Cardboard Bun Hoax' that occurred in Beijing in June 2007. An undercover news segment by Beijing TV reported street vendors selling steamed buns adulterated with cardboard and lye. Another news report the following month issued an apology, claiming that a freelance reporter had 'faked' the original story and been arrested. Expounding upon the 'fake news' category in Chinese investigative journalism, the editor of the *China Media Project*, David Bandurski, observes that the Chinese public was unsure which story to believe. Given the impending Olympics, people speculated that the authorities may have conducted an investigation to discredit a story that risked harming Beijing's reputation. Bandurski quotes from a 'well-known [but unnamed] newspaper columnist':

> Ten days ago the public thought the TV news story was real and the steamed buns were fake. Now authorities are saying the news report is a fake and the steamed buns are OK. But people are still totally at a loss. Which one is real and which one fake? Right now, what most frustrates the average person is that they don't have any way of penetrating the confusion.[19]

Thus, in an environment of strict censorship it becomes harder to tell the difference between what is true and what is not. Fictive and non-fictive modes of narrative therefore become less distinct. The veil of fiction can provide a means of conveying truths too dangerous to speak about explicitly, whereas those narrative forms that trade on their dedication to the truth (investigative journalism, interviews or memoir) may have their veracity thrown in doubt.

The relationship between literature and propaganda, truth and fiction, is particularly enmeshed in the Chinese case because, as in other socialist societies, for many years the production of literature was treated as an important ideological tool that came under State control. Of central importance was the Chinese Writers Association, which actively fostered a new generation of socialist writers by sponsoring literary prizes and organizing training sessions or seminars for younger writers. Professional writers were obliged to join the Writers Association for it enabled them to publish in literary journals, to take part in literary lectures and to apply for grants. Writers were organized in a hierarchical system of patronage – the most talented became salaried 'professional writers' within the association, others found paid positions either with the association or other cultural organizations. China only started dismantling the socialist system for the production of literature, with its focus on a planned arts economy, towards the end of the 1980s, moving gradually towards the more market-driven model that we are familiar with in the West. Despite the entrance of private businesses into the publishing industry, the production of Chinese literature – especially serious literature or what we would term 'literary' works – continues to be closely aligned with and controlled by the Communist Party. The inability to separate China's major writers from the Party was highlighted when Mo Yan was awarded the Nobel Prize for Literature in 2012. As vice-president of the Chinese Writers Association, Mo Yan came under heavy criticism for being a State writer who had successfully risen to great acclaim within the Party structure. His comments during a press conference in Stockholm that censorship was sometimes 'necessary' did little to dispel the notion that his refusal to speak out against the Communist Party was somehow a betrayal of his duty as a serious literary writer.[20]

Despite widespread condemnation, Mo Yan's caution might be well founded. The perils of casting off the mantle of fiction and engaging openly with the truth in Chinese literature are made clear by the case of Liao Yiwu, who spent four years in prison (1990–4) for writing 'Massacre', a poem about the Tiananmen Square protests. Before becoming politicized, Liao was as much a part of the socialist literary system as Mo Yan, holding a position as poet-in-residence at a municipal institute. He credits events at Tiananmen for awakening his sense of political and social responsibility as a writer, but in the longer term Liao's opposition to the government's strict censorship has been the driving force behind his work. Liao has expressed grave concern about the consequences of allowing the government to erase an event such as Tiananmen from Chinese cultural memory. Speaking in 2013, he says:

> The young people don't even know what happened in 1989. They first find out when they go abroad to Western countries. But, sometimes, then they don't even believe it. The Communist Party has tried to eliminate parts of history. That is bad for the younger generation. If they don't have this historical consciousness, they will just focus on getting material goods. We have to work on that, so everybody knows what happened.[21]

Liao here cautions against the way that newly imported capitalist values, with their disregard for the value of memory or history, may inadvertently support the government's campaign of propaganda.

After Liao's release from prison in 1994, the Chinese government attempted to keep him within their national borders – he was denied permission to leave 16 times.[22] He responded by collecting interviews with people from the margins of Chinese society. In 2001 a sanitized version of *Interviews with People from the Bottom Rung of Society* was published in China by the Yangzi Publishing House. It was an immediate bestseller and just as quickly banned by the Chinese government. But, providing an indication of the challenges that digital technology and the Internet pose to governments today, Liao and his work could not be contained. An unabridged collection of interviews was smuggled out of the country and published in Taiwan the following year (2002), with a selection published in English translation as *The Corpse Walker* in 2008. The 60 interviews Liao collected include personal stories from a people smuggler, a Buddhist monk denounced during the Great Leap Forward and the Cultural Revolution, a witness to the massacre at Tiananmen Square and a member of the Falun Gong. *Interviews with People* effectively gives voice to the underbelly of society, people who were not supposed to exist under the beneficence of Communism.

The presentation of these transcripts as verbatim reportage is in itself an act of defiance against censorship. As the 'Cardboard Bun Hoax' demonstrates, the present system of overt censorship and propaganda casts uncertainty over non-fiction narrative forms that purport to state the truth. Authors such as Mo Yan or Yan Lianke clearly signal to readers, and to the regime, that their works are fiction by exaggerating the fictive elements. In both cases any criticisms of the government or society are made under the cover of satire, and the exaggerated style of Mo Yan's magical realism or Yan Lianke's 'mythical realism' allows clear lines to be drawn between fictive and non-fictive forms of discourse, even if the distinction between truth and fiction within those discourses is less clear. Liao Yiwu's work refuses to play by these rules. By working in the non-fiction form of memoir and reportage, and insisting that his observations about society are 'true' even if they directly contradict the official version put forward by the Chinese government, Liao forces the reader to confront the fictions that pervade their everyday lives.

This is not to say that Liao's work is not literary. Liao's translator, Wen Huang, notes that there is an inherent literary dimension to Liao's work, since all the interviews are reconstructions rather than direct transcriptions.[23] Tienchi Martin-Liao, the president of the Independent Chinese PEN Centre, suggests that the danger of Liao's work lies in its honesty and lack of ambiguity: 'If it's just a novel or it's a fictive short story, it's OK. But he writes in a reportage style. And if people read it, they know it's the truth. It's not imagination.'[24] Liao himself has stated that the shift from poetry to memoir as his dominant mode of writing occurred as a direct response to his imprisonment and experiences thereafter. Describing the difficulty of writing poetry after what he saw in prison, he says:

> There is no way to talk about this violence using the language of an intellectual or a poet, and there is no way to convey the grief underneath the violence. You can't understand the malicious language in the prison, the kind of savagery that exists. It was the most dark and preposterous side of humanity. In order to adapt to that, whether you want to or not, you become a witness.[25]

The current leadership's preferred official narrative tells of a twenty-first-century China whose citizens have been newly liberated and given individual freedoms, far removed from the tightly regulated, State-controlled and oppressive environment of the Mao-era. Liao's work presents us with a powerful counter-narrative that disputes the extent of this transformation, suggesting instead that basic rights continue to be traded too easily for superficial freedoms.

As China embraces a socialist market economy and the rapid pace of change renders the Chinese landscape – both physical and social – unrecognizable, the silences imposed by censorship hold greater significance. Back in 1990, the astrophysicist Fang Lizhi outlined the insidiousness of the Communist Party's 'Technique of Forgetting History' in his famous 1990 essay, The Chinese Amnesia.[26] Fang observed that owing to an active policy of erasure and forgetting, Communist Chinese history followed a cycle whereby roughly once a decade there was agitation by students or intellectuals for greater freedom of speech and then violent retribution by the Party. Because these incidences were quickly expunged from the record, each generation of students continued to be surprised when their protests were met with brutality. Yan Lianke has suggested that, as a writer, the cycle of violence and forgetting is foremost on his mind:

> I used to assume history and memory would always triumph over temporary aberrations and return to their rightful place. It now appears the opposite is true. In today's China, amnesia trumps memory. Lies are surpassing the truth. Fabrications have become the logical link to fill historical gaps. Even memories of events that have only just taken place are being discarded at a dazzling pace, with barely intelligible fragments all that remain for people to hold on to.[27]

The very real dangers of cultural amnesia and the spectre of Tiananmen haunt those old enough to remember it. The truths recorded in literature, be it fiction or non-fiction, become an important means of anchoring the national culture to some recognizable sense of reality.

The value of literature

To the question 'What is this thing called literature?', the literary critics Andrew Bennett and Nicholas Royale reply: 'This is a question to which no one has yet provided an entirely satisfactory or convincing answer ... "[L]iterature" is a peculiarly elusive word. It has, in a sense, no essence.'[28] The examples of Chinese literature that I have discussed highlight this problem of defining literature exactly, for Liao Yiwu's work shows that literature is not merely fiction, and the cases of Yan Lianke or Mo Yan suggest that literature can be produced both in opposition to and in compliance with government-sanctioned regulations. I would suggest that it is this very intangible aspect of literature that qualifies it as such. Once this is acknowledged, it becomes easy to see why it makes governments nervous, for if the literary cannot be quantified, then it cannot be controlled. The translator and Chinese literary scholar Perry Link, blacklisted in China since 1996, has aptly noted that literature can be a double-edged sword for dictatorial governments:

> This power of literature was in part a result of its truth-telling function, which is observable in many other authoritarian states. Every regime that tells a public

story of itself grants a measure of power to people who tell other versions of the story; if those other versions are repressed, they naturally emerge less often, but have even greater power when they do.[29]

The truth-telling function of literature can be seen at work in the cases of Yan Lianke or Liao Yiwu, which leave no doubt that literature continues to have the power to inform, to inspire, to provoke and to incite action.

However, as China embraces a commercially-based system of literary production, it is not immune to the climate of anxiety gripping literature, the arts and humanities. A decade ago, in 2004, Richard Curt Kraus wrote about the relationship between politics and the arts in China: 'No longer does power simply treat art as its prettified voice, and no longer does the ruling Party embrace the arts at the centre of a grand scheme for rebuilding national identity and power. The privileged place of the arts is no longer unquestioned.'[30] The creeping of a sense of crisis into the humanities in China is revealing, for it suggests that the trepidation besetting the entire field may be more a response to capitalism, with its insistence on viewing monetary valuation as the only valid means of appraising value, than a reaction to any genuine decline in value.

Underlying debates about the marginalization of literature in the digital age, the decline of reading and readers, or the irrelevance of the humanities in any utilitarian sense, is the presumption that literature is a form of outmoded technology, soon to become obsolete. What seems to be forgotten in these debates is that the concept of obsolescence is in itself a technological term that has been normalized by the ever decreasing product cycles of the consumer-driven market. Literature, while it may be overtaken by other art forms in terms of mass popularity, remains an ideal medium for political agitation and subversion precisely because of the low-tech nature of literary production. This becomes evident when we look at Liao's struggle to write and publish his prison memoir. Liao wrote the manuscript of *For A Song and a Hundred Songs* three times. It was confiscated and destroyed the first two times (in the 1990s and then again in 2001). After writing it for a third time, Liao was able to smuggle a digital version of the text out of the country, where it was translated and prepared for publication in Germany.[31] Unlike newer media forms, literary production does not require expensive technology, nor does it necessarily involve assembling a group of people in one locale, such as to shoot a film or to stage a performance. The portability of a text-based manuscript in the digital age enabled Liao to write it in secret and then have it transported outside of China's geographic borders, beyond the reach of the censors.

Censorship is an ineluctable companion to power. Michael Holquist is frequently quoted as saying, 'To be for or against censorship is to assume a freedom no one has. Censorship *is*. One can only discriminate among its more and less repressive effects.'[32] To follow the censor's redactive pen is to reveal the vulnerabilities – perceived or real – in government's grasp of power on society. The repressive censorship exerted by China sits uneasily alongside the greater economic and personal freedoms enjoyed by its citizens today. It is yet to be seen whether relaxed controls in these areas of commerce and lifestyle will eventually translate into greater political freedom. While

242   Censorship and the Limits of the Literary

it is commonly assumed that the presence of Western companies will act as a liberating force, there is evidence that companies entering China could be co-opted into reinforcing the State's censorious grip on the populace instead.[33]

The official guidelines for censorship in China have never been overtly expressed, the way they were in the Soviet Union, which, in the longer run, has actually proven a more effective means of encouraging self-censorship.[34] In many ways, this is actually more alarming than overt censorship because it leaves no traces. A censored document contains the evidence that something has been removed – a palimpsest of the original remains. But if a writer censors him or herself, then no record of the original is ever made and, in time, it can be forgotten. On the eve of the twenty-fifth anniversary of the Tiananmen Square Massacre, Liao Yiwu was one of many people reflecting on the fate of the Tank Man, star of the most iconic image from that period, who was never heard of again. He was also thinking about the countless other people whose stance against the soldiers had not been recorded: 'Tank Man vanished into thin air … Twenty-five years have gone by, we have all grown old. But Tank Man in these pictures is still so young … A historical moment, a poetic moment. And on the other side of that moment, maybe three thousand lives were taken away, to be forgotten.'[35] An industry has grown up around Tiananmen – the numerous publications, the reproduction of images, the commemoration that occurs every year, worldwide, on 4 June. Taken cumulatively, in monetary terms, we might say there is value in the act of remembrance. But there is also another form of value in reflecting on that which we cannot remember. The images that we did not see, the people we will never know about, the silences that were inserted or orchestrated, whether on purpose or by chance. Isn't that why we turn to literature, after all? To try and capture, if only for a moment, that which eludes us.

Notes

1 Organizations in the West that monitor and report on the status of Chinese dissidents include the Congressional-Executive Commission on China (www.cecc.gov) and the IFEX network of organizations committed to defending and promoting free expression (www.ifex.org).
2 Robert Manne, 'Dead Disturbing. A Bloodthirsty Tale That Plays with the Fire of Anti-Semitism', review of *Dead Europe* by Christos Tsiolkas, *The Monthly*, 2 (June 2005).
3 Quoted in Nicole Moore, *The Censor's Library* (Brisbane: University of Queensland Press, 2012), p. 69.
4 Leslie Kendrick, 'Free Speech and Guilty Minds', *Columbia Law Review*, 114 (5) (2014), pp. 1295.
5 Sarah Sorial, 'Can Saying Something Make It So? The Nature of Seditious Harm', *Law and Philosophy*, 29 (3) (2010): 304.
6 Liu Weifeng, 'Survey: Fewer Readers, More Books', *China Daily* (2006), available at http://www.chinadaily.com.cn/cndy/2006-04/24/content_574499.htm [accessed 24 October 2014].

7 'Books Get New Life', *China Daily USA* (2012), http://usa.chinadaily.com.cn/ opinion/2012-04/23/content_15111261.htm [accessed 24October 2014].

8 Helen Small, *The Value of the Humanities* (Oxford: Oxford University Press, 2013), p. 1.

9 For a more in-depth description of the methods used by the Chinese government to censor material, please see Stephanie Wang and Robert Faris, 'Welcome to the Machine', *Index on Censorship*, 37 (2) (2008); Gudrun Wacker, 'The Internet and Censorship in China', in Christopher R. Hughes and Gudrun Wacker (eds), *China and the Internet: Politics and the Digital Leap Forward* (New York: Routledge, 2003), pp. 58–82; Richard Curt Kraus, *The Party and the Arty in China: The New Politics of Culture* (Lanham, MD: Rowman & Littlefield Publishers, 2004), ch. 4.; and Gloria Davies, 'Affirming the Human in China', *boundary 2*, 37 (1) (2010): 57–90.

10 Rebecca MacKinnon, 'Cyber Zone', *Index on Censorship*, 37 (2) (2008): 82–9.

11 For more on Gao Xingjian and the reception of his Nobel award in China, see Sylvia Li-Chun Lin, 'Between the Individual and the Collective: Gao Xingjian's Fiction', *World Literature Today*, 75 (1) (2001): 12–18; Gregory Lee and Noël Dutrait, 'Conversations with Gao Xingjian: The First "Chinese" Winner of the Nobel Prize for Literature', *The China Quarterly*, 167 (September 2001): 738–48.

12 Gloria Davies discusses Hu Jia in detail in Davies, 'Affirming the Human in China'. More on Liu Di can be found in Philip P. Pan, 'A Trip through China's Twilight Zone: One Woman's Quest for Truth in the Authoritarian Maze', *Washington Post Foreign Service*, 18 December 2004, A01.

13 Davies, 'Affirming the Human in China', p. 82.

14 J. M. Coetzee, 'Emerging from Censorship', *Salmagundi*, 100 (Fall, 1993): 45.

15 Yan discusses 'mythical-realism' in an interview with Chen Tao, 'Chronicles of Myth and Reality', *News China*, Dec. 2013, available at http://www.newschinamag.com/ magazine/chronicles-of-myth-and-reality [accessed 24 October 2014].

16 Jonathan Watts, 'Censor Sees through Writer's Guile in Tale of China's Blood-Selling Scandal: Champion of the Poor Yan Lianke Fears He Went Too Far in Toning Down His Latest Book', *The Guardian*, 9 October 2006.

17 Quoted in Mary-Anne Toy, 'A Pen for the People', *The Age*, 28 July 2007.

18 The list for the highest-paid Chinese authors in 2009 can be found translated into English by Martinsen, and in the original Chinese here: http://news.163. com/09/1130/05/5PBJB8J10001124J.html [accessed 24 October 2014].

19 David Bandurski, 'Garden of Falsehood', *Index on Censorship*, 37 (2) (2008): 53.

20 Mo Yan's defence of censorship was widely reported. See Louise Nordstrom, 'Mo Yan, Nobel Literature Prize Winner, Says Censorship Is Necessary', *The Huffington Post*, 12 June 2012. Criticisms voiced in public at the time included those of Salman Rushdie, who called Mo Yan a 'patsy for the regime', Herta Müller, who called it a 'catastrophe', and the artist Ai Weiwei, who said, 'Giving the award to a writer like this is an insult to humanity and to literature'. See Nick Clark and Clifford Coonan, 'Ai Weiwei Brands Nobel Prize for Literature Decision an "Insult to Humanity" as China's Mo Yan Named Winner', *The Independent*, 11 October 2012; Anna Molin, 'Nobel Literature Winner Skirts Support for Dissident', *The Wall Street Journal*, 6 Dec. 2012; Alison Flood, 'Mo Yan Accepts Nobel Prize, Defends 'Necessary' Censorship', *The Guardian* 11 December 2012. More on the Chinese Writers Association can be found in Perry Link, *The Uses of Literature: Life in the Socialist Chinese Literary System* (Princeton, NJ: Princeton University Press, 2000), pp. 118–22, and Shuyu Kong,

Consuming Literature: Best Sellers and the Commercialization of Literary Production in Contemporary China (Stanford, CA: Stanford University Press, 2005).

21 Yiwu Liao, Jeffrey Brown, and Tienchi Martin-Liao, 'Liao Yiwu Howls against the Chinese Government, Offers Memories of Prison,' *PBS News Hour,* 10 July 2013, available at http://www.pbs.org/newshour/bb/entertainment-july-dec13-poet_07-10/ [accessed 24 October 2014].

22 Yiwu Liao, 'Walking out on China', *The New York Times,* 14 September 2011.

23 Yiwu Liao, *The Corpse Walker* (Anchor Books, 2009), p. xii.

24 Liao, Brown, and Martin-Liao, 'Liao Yiwu Howls against the Chinese Government, Offers Memories of Prison'.

25 Tienchi Martin-Liao, '"If I'm Not Speaking That Means I'm Dead": An Interview with Liao Yiwu', *Sampsonia Way* (7 Jan. 2014), available at http://www.sampsoniaway.org/interviews/2014/01/07/if-i%E2%80%99m-not-speaking-that-means-im-dead-an-interview-with-liao-yiwu/ [accessed 24 October 2014].

26 Lizhi Fang, 'The Chinese Amnesia' (trans. Perry Link), *The New York Review of Books,* 27 Sept. 1990, available at http://www.nybooks.com/articles/archives/1990/sep/27/the-chinese-amnesia/ [accessed 24 October 2014].

27 Lianke Yan, 'On China's State-Sponsored Amnesia', *The New York Times,* 1 April 2013.

28 Andrew Bennett and Nicholas Royle, *This Thing Called Literature: Reading, Thinking, Writing* (Abingdon, Oxon: Routledge, 2015), p. 1.

29 Perry Link, *The Uses of Literature* (Princeton, NJ: Princeton University Press, 2000), p. 104.

30 Kraus, *The Party and the Arty in China,* p. 229.

31 Liao describes having written the first two versions in long-hand and the third version with a computer: 'With a computer, you can have a lot of back-ups. So my writing process took me from the age of da Vinci to the computer age.' Yiwu Liao and Jiayang Fan, 'Liao Yiwu: Four Years a Prisoner', *The Margins* (2014), available at http://aaww.org/liao-yiwu-four-years-a-prisoner/ [accessed 8 July 2014].

32 Michael Holquist, 'Corrupt Originals: The Paradox of Censorship', *PMLA,* 109, 1 (1994), p. 16.

33 See G. E. Dann and N. Haddow, ('Just Doing Business or Doing Just Business: Google, Microsoft, Yahoo! and the Business of Censoring China's Internet', *Journal of Business Ethics,* 79 (3) (2008): 219–34) for their assessment of the culpability of Microsoft, Google and Yahoo in assisting the Chinese government to violate its citizens' human rights.

34 Perry Link compares the Chinese and Soviet systems in *The Uses of Literature,* pp. 97–103.

35 Yiwu Liao, 'The Tanks and the People', *The New York Review of Books,* 3 June 2014, available at http://www.nybooks.com/blogs/nyrblog/2014/jun/03/tanks-people-tiananmen-square/ [accessed 24 October 2014].

References

Bandurski, D., 'Garden of Falsehood', *Index of Censorship* 37 (2) (2008): 45–54.

Bennett, A. and N. Royle, *This Thing Called Literature: Reading, Thinking, Writing,* Abingdon, Oxon: Routledge, 2015.

'Books Get New Life', *China Daily USA*, 23 April 2012, available at http://usa.chinadaily. com.cn/opinion/2012-04/23/content_15111261.htm [accessed 24 October 2014].

Chen, T., 'Chronicles of Myth and Reality', *News China*, Dec. 2013, available at http:// www.newschinamag.com/magazine/chronicles-of-myth-and-reality [accessed 24 October 2014].

Clark, N. and C. Coonan, 'Ai Weiwei Brands Nobel Prize for Literature Decision an "Insult to Humanity" as China's Mo Yan Named Winner', *The Independent*, 11 October 2012.

Coetzee, J. M., 'Emerging from Censorship', *Salmagundi*, 100 (1993): 36–50.

Dann, G. E. and N. Haddow, 'Just Doing Business or Doing Just Business: Google, Microsoft, Yahoo! and the Business of Censoring China's Internet', *Journal of Business Ethics* 79 (3) (2008): 219–34.

Davies, G., 'Affirming the Human in China', *boundary 2*, 37 (1) (2010): 57–90.

Fang, L., 'The Chinese Amnesia' (trans. P. Link), *The New York Review of Books* (27 Sept. 1990), available at http://www.nybooks.com/articles/archives/1990/sep/27/ the-chinese-amnesia/ [accessed 24 October 2014].

Flood, A., 'Mo Yan Accepts Nobel Prize, Defends "Necessary" Censorship', *The Guardian*, 11 December 2012.

Holquist, M., 'Corrupt Originals: The Paradox of Censorship', *PMLA*, 109 (1) (1994): 14–25.

Kendrick, L., 'Free Speech and Guilty Minds', *Columbia Law Review*, 114 (5) (2014): 1255–95.

Kong, S., *Consuming Literature: Best Sellers and the Commercialization of Literary Production in Contemporary China*, Stanford, CA: Stanford University Press, 2005.

Kraus, R. C., *The Party and the Arty in China: The New Politics of Culture*, Lanham, MD.: Rowman & Littlefield Publishers, 2004.

Lee, G. and N. Dutrait, 'Conversations with Gao Xingjian: The First "Chinese" Winner of the Nobel Prize for Literature', *The China Quarterly*, 167 (2001): 738–48.

Liao, Y., *The Corpse Walker* (trans. and intro. Wen Huang), New York: Anchor Books, 2009.

Liao, Y., 'Walking out on China', *The New York Times*, 14 September 2011.

Liao, Y., 'The Tanks and the People', *The New York Review of Books*, 3 June 2014, available at http://www.nybooks.com/blogs/nyrblog/2014/jun/03/tanks-people-tiananmen-square/ [accessed 24 October 2014].

Liao, Y., J. Brown, and T. Martin-Liao, 'Liao Yiwu Howls against the Chinese Government, Offers Memories of Prison', *PBS News Hour*, 10 July 2013, available at http://www.pbs.org/newshour/bb/entertainment-july-dec13-poet_07-10/ [accessed 24 October 2014].

Liao, Y. and J. Fan, 'Liao Yiwu: Four Years a Prisoner', *The Margins* (2014), available at http://aaww.org/liao-yiwu-four-years-a-prisoner/ [accessed 24 October 2014].

Lin, S. L.-C., 'Between the Individual and the Collective: Gao Xingjian's Fiction', *World Literature Today*, 75 (1) (2001): 12–18.

Link, P., *The Uses of Literature: Life in the Socialist Chinese Literary System*, Princeton, NJ: Princeton University Press, 2000.

MacKinnon, R., 'Cyber Zone', *Index on Censorship*, 37 (2) (2008): 82–9.

Manne, R., 'Dead Disturbing. A Bloodthirsty Tale That Plays with the Fire of Anti-Semitism', Review of *Dead Europe* by Christos Tsiolkas, *The Monthly*, 2 (2005).

Martin-Liao, T., '"If I'm Not Speaking That Means I'm Dead": An Interview with Liao Yiwu', *Sampsonia Way*, 7 Jan. 2014, available at http://www.sampsoniaway.org/

interviews/2014/01/07/if-i%E2%80%99m-not-speaking-that-means-im-dead-an-interview-with-liao-yiwu/ [accessed 24 October 2014].

Molin, A., 'Nobel Literature Winner Skirts Support for Dissident', *The Wall Street Journal*, 6. December 2012.

Moore, N., *The Censor's Library: Uncovering the Lost History of Australia's Banned Books*, St Lucia, Qld.: University of Queensland Press, 2012.

Nordstrom, L., 'Mo Yan, Nobel Literature Prize Winner, Says Censorship Is Necessary', *The Huffington Post*, 12 June 2012.

Pan, P. P., 'A Trip through China's Twilight Zone: One Woman's Quest for Truth in the Authoritarian Maze', *Washington Post Foreign Service*, 18 December 2004, A01.

Small, H., *The Value of the Humanities*, Oxford: Oxford University Press, 2013.

Sorial, S., 'Can Saying Something Make It So? The Nature of Seditious Harm', *Law and Philosophy*, 29 (3) (2010): 273–305.

Toy, M.-A., 'A Pen for the People', *The Age*, 28 July 2007.

Wacker, G., 'The Internet and Censorship in China', in Christopher R. Hughes and Gudrun Wacker (eds), *China and the Internet: Politics and the Digital Leap Forward*, New York: Routledge, 2003, pp. 58–82.

Wang, S. and R. Faris, 'Welcome to the Machine', *Index on Censorship*, 37 (2) (2008): 106–13.

Watts, J., 'Censor Sees through Writer's Guile in Tale of China's Blood-Selling Scandal: Champion of the Poor Yan Lianke Fears He Went Too Far in Toning Down His Latest Book', *The Guardian*, 9 October 2006.

Weifeng, L., 'Survey: Fewer Readers, More Books', *China Daily* 24 April, 2006, available at http://www.chinadaily.com.cn/cndy/2006-04/24/content_574499.htm [accessed 24 October 2014].

Yan, L., 'Darkness Visible', *Index on Censorship*, 37 (2) (2008): 40–4.

Yan, L., *Dream of Ding Village* (trans. C. Carter), New York: Grove Press, 2011.

Yan, L., 'On China's State-Sponsored Amnesia', *The New York Times*, 1 April 2013.

Contributors

Jumana Bayeh is an Early Career Fellow at Macquarie University in Sydney. She has held fellowships at the University of Edinburgh, the University of Copenhagen and the Lebanese American University in Beirut. She is the author of *The Literature of the Lebanese Diaspora: Representations of Place and Transnational Identity* (I. B. Tauris 2014).

Simon Burrows took up a Professorship in History at the University of Western Sydney in January 2013, moving from the School of History at the University of Leeds (UK). Best known for his ground-breaking digital project on 'The French Book Trade in Enlightenment Europe', he is also the author of *French Exile Journalism and European Politics, 1792–1814* (2000), *Blackmail, Scandal and Revolution: London's French Libellistes, 1758–1792* (2006) and *A King's Ransom: The Life of Charles Théveneau de Morande, Blackmailer, Scandalmonger and Master-Spy* (2010). He is currently working on a monograph entitled *Enlightenment Bestsellers*, scheduled for publication with Bloomsbury in 2015.

Karen Crawley is an early career researcher at the Griffith Law School. She holds Bachelors degrees from the University of Sydney in English Literature and in Law, and received her LL.M. and PhD from McGill University. She researches in the area of cultural legal studies, and has published on law's entanglements with theatre, photography and graphic novels. She is particularly interested in histories of moral regulation, criminal representations and the ironic effects of censorship.

Jeremy Fisher is Senior Lecturer in Writing at the University of New England, Australia, and researches publishing and writing practice. Before taking up his academic appointment, Dr Fisher worked in the Australian publishing industry for many years and was Executive Director of the Australian Society of Authors from 2004 to 2009. He is the author of *Perfect Timing, Music from Another Country* and *How to Tell your Father to Drop Dead*.

Sanaz Fotouhi is the author of *The Literature of the Iranian Diaspora: Meaning and Identity Since the Islamic Revolution* (I. B. Tauris 2015) and is co-producer of *Love Marriage in Kabul*, a Screen-Australia-funded documentary which was a finalist in the Sydney Film Festival documentary category in 2014. She has a PhD from the University of New South Wales, Australia.

Loren Glass is Professor of English and the Center for the Book at the University of Iowa. His publications include *Authors Inc.: Literary Celebrity in the Modern United States* (NYU Press 2004) and *Counterculture Colophon: Grove Press, the Evergreen Review, and the Incorporation of the Avant-Garde* (Stanford University Press 2013).

Geoffrey Little is Scholarly Communications Librarian and Librarian for History at Concordia University in Montreal. He also holds an appointment at McGill University where he teaches a graduate course on the history of books and printing. He has degrees in History and Information Studies from the University of Toronto.

Peter D. McDonald is Professor of English and Related Literatures at the University of Oxford and a Fellow of St Hugh's College. His research focuses on literature as a specific mode of thinking, and on literary institutions and the modern state since 1800. His most recent book, *The Literature Police: Apartheid Censorship and its Cultural Consequences,* appeared in 2009.

Nicole Moore is an Australian Research Council Future Fellow in English at the University of New South Wales, Canberra. She is author of *The Censor's Library: Uncovering the Lost History of Australia's Banned Books* (UQP 2012) and *Banned in Australia,* a bibliography (AustLit, 2008). Co-edited volumes include *The Literature of Australia* (W. W. Norton 2009) and a collection on Australian and New Zealand literature forthcoming in the MLA's Options for Teaching Series. Her latest book is *Reading through the Iron Curtain: Australian Literature in the German Democratic Republic,* co-edited with Christina Spittel (forthcoming Anthem 2015).

Lynda Ng is an Adjunct Fellow at the University of Western Sydney. From 2012–14 she was the Marie Curie Postdoctoral Fellow in English Literature at the University of Oxford. She works on transnational literature and has published essays on multi-culturalism in the post-9/11 era, Australian literature in a world literary context and contemporary Indigenous Australian literature. She is currently working on a study of Chinese diasporic literature.

Christina Spittel is a Lecturer in English at the University of New South Wales, Canberra. Her research interests include war and memory, especially in Australian fiction remembering the First World War, as well as book historical approaches to the literature of conflict. With Nicole Moore, she is co-editor of *Reading through the Iron Curtain: Australian Literature in the German Democratic Republic* (Anthem 2015).

Mary Spongberg is Dean of the Faculty of Arts and Social Sciences at the University of Technology Sydney. She is author of *Writing Women's History Since the Renaissance* and principal editor of the *Companion to Women's Historical Writing*. She is currently completing a monograph entitled *Empathetic Histories: Romantic Women Writers and the English Past.*

Tyne Daile Sumner is a teacher and researcher in the English and Theatre Studies Program at the University of Melbourne. Her research interests include post-war American poetry, publicity and American domesticity. Her current project, supported by the Macgeorge Bequest, is titled 'Distorted Confessions: Poetry, Performance, and Media during the Cold War'.

Paul Tickell teaches Indonesian at the Canberra campus of the University of New South Wales. He has previously held positions at Flinders University, the University of Western Australia and Monash University. His main research interests centre on the emergence of non-traditional literature in the Indonesian language, and in Indonesian cultural and literary history, in particular of the late colonial period. He is also actively involved in the translation of works of Indonesian literature into English with the Lontar Foundation in Jakarta.

Clara Tuite is Senior Lecturer in English at the University of Melbourne. She is the author of *Romantic Austen: Sexual Politics and the Literary Canon* (Cambridge University Press 2002) and *Lord Byron and Scandalous Celebrity* (Cambridge University Press 2015).

Ilona Urquhart teaches in Literary Studies at Deakin University, Geelong. She has recently been awarded her PhD with a doctoral dissertation titled *Diabolical Literature: Questioning the Morality of Modernism*. Her research explores modernist self-consciousness, religious concepts in secular contexts and the role of literature in modern societies.

Index

CPSIA information can be obtained at www.ICGtesting.com
Printed in the USA
LVOW07*2348191115

463354LV00008B/49/P